Congress and the Constitution

CONSTITUTIONAL CONFLICTS

A Series with the Institute of Bill of Rights Law

at the College of William & Mary

Series editors: Neal Devins and Mark Graber

Congress and the Constitution

NEAL DEVINS AND KEITH E. WHITTINGTON, EDITORS

Duke University Press   *Durham and London*   2005

© 2005 Duke University Press

All rights reserved

Printed in the United States of America on acid-free paper ∞

Designed by CH Westmoreland

Typeset in Monotype Sabon by Tseng Information Systems, Inc.

Library of Congress Cataloging-in-Publication Data appear on the last

printed page of this book.

Contents

෴

Acknowledgments

ᴄⱳᴏ

A great many people contributed to the completion of this book. First and foremost, we would like to thank the contributors, who worked with us as we tried to put together a book calling attention to the pivotal role that Congress plays in the shaping of constitutional values. We would also like to thank Valerie Millholland of Duke University Press. Based on a prospectus calling attention to the need for an interdisciplinary collection on this topic, Valerie signed onto this project. At approximately the same time, the editors of the *Duke Law Journal* agreed to publish a symposium held in 2001 on Congress and the Constitution. That symposium helped shape this project. Not only did some of the contributors to this book test their ideas in that symposium, but its success proved instrumental in propelling this project. Another symposium was equally instrumental. In 2002 the Institute of Bill of Rights Law at William & Mary hosted a conference at which the contributors to this book presented preliminary versions of their chapters. This conference both facilitated completion of the chapters and sharpened them. Thanks are owed to Dave Douglas, who then directed the institute, and Melody Nichols, the institute's administrative assistant, for their help and encouragement. Others at William & Mary helped support us in producing the manuscript. Felicia Burton of the Faculty Support Center worked with us and many of the contributors. Several research assistants tracked down citations, made sure that the notes conformed to Duke University Press guidelines, and helped prepare the index. Thanks, in particular, to Stacy Haney. Finally, thanks are owed to Miriam Angress and the production team at Duke University Press.

Congress and the Constitution

Introduction

⌇

NEAL DEVINS AND KEITH E. WHITTINGTON

Congress is the first branch of government established by the Constitution. Its priority within the constitutional text reflects the substantive importance that the Founders expected the legislature to have in the political system and its significance within their political theory. It was Congress, armed with the authority provided by popular election, that was expected to enjoy the greatest public support and to dominate national politics. It was Congress that would shoulder the task of making national policy and setting the national political agenda. It was Congress that carried the Founders' hopes for the success of the constitutional experiment, but it was also Congress and its frenetic ambitions that required the most careful attention at the constitutional convention in Philadelphia and the most detailed limitations in the constitutional text. Congress was at the center of the constitutional enterprise.

At the opening of the twenty-first century, Congress remains important and vibrant as a governmental body. While legislatures elsewhere have been reduced to mere sanctioning bodies for executives who do the real work of governance, Congress remains vital. Even so, Congress has not enjoyed great public esteem and is more likely to be seen as a threat to constitutional values than an embodiment of them. It is now, as one study of public opinion found, often regarded as a "public enemy." It routinely ranks a poor third in surveys of public confidence in the three branches.[1] Scholars and citizens alike perceive Congress as an arena of partisan conflict and electoral pandering, hardly as a bulwark of constitutional principles.

There has been little sustained attention to congressional treatment of the Constitution and constitutional issues. It has simply not been part of the research agenda of congressional scholars, who unsurprisingly have been preoccupied with other concerns that are perceived to be closer to the heart of legislative politics and more amenable to systematic study. Constitutional scholars have generally turned a blind eye to Congress as well. The study of the Constitution has largely been defined within the academy as the study of constitutional law as produced by the courts. From this perspective, Congress is a target of constitutional law, not a producer of it.

After long neglect, the time is ripe for more sustained study of Congress as a constitutional interpreter and responsible constitutional agent. Recent Supreme Court decisions have focused attention on the constitutional powers and responsibilities of Congress, and the sustained judicial inquiry into the relationship between Congress and the Constitution has encouraged a heightened awareness of Congress in constitutional scholars as well. At the same time, a somewhat independent scholarly turn to the "Constitution outside the courts" has opened up space for considering extrajudicial constitutional interpretation and the relationship between nonjudicial political actors and the Constitution. Now that constitutional scholars have begun to look beyond the courts, we believe a more careful examination of the Congress as an institution and a political entity will be needed in order to fully understand, appreciate, and evaluate congressional engagement with the Constitution.

CONGRESS AND THE SUPREME COURT

Judicial review was a political practice largely unknown before ratification of the U.S. Constitution. Indeed, the practice was so exotic that it did not even acquire a name until the beginning of the twentieth century. In its most paradigmatic form, judicial review involves the articulation and enforcement of constitutional constraints against Congress. This was, of course, the power discussed by Chief Justice John Marshall in *Marbury v. Madison*:

> The powers of the legislature are defined, and limited; and that those limits may not be mistaken, or forgotten, the constitution is written. To what purpose are powers limited, and to what purpose is that limitation committed to writing, if these limits may, at any time, be passed by those intended to be restrained?. . . . It is a proposition too plain to be contested, that the constitution controls any legislative act repugnant to it; or, that the legislature may alter the constitution by an ordinary act. . . . It is emphatically the province and duty of the judicial department to say what the law is. . . . [and if] the courts are to regard the constitution; and the constitution is su-

perior to any ordinary act of the legislature; the constitution, and not such ordinary act, must govern the case to which they both apply.[2]

By this logic Marshall sought the constitutional and political authority for the judiciary to set aside the work of a coordinate, and more electorally responsive, branch of government. Both Congress and the Court were agents of the Constitution established by the people, and the justices could not "close their eyes on the constitution, and see only the law."[3] Just over a decade after the Constitution was ratified, Marshall already sought to represent Congress as a troublesome constitutional agent, too much prone to forgetting the limits to its own powers. To rely upon Congress as a constitutional interpreter would give "to the legislature a practical and real omnipotence" and "subvert the very foundations of all written constitutions."[4] The seeds had been planted for regarding the legislature as a threat to, rather than a guardian of, the Constitution, and in turn for regarding the judiciary as the "ultimate interpreter" of the Constitution.[5]

If *Marbury* marks the paradigmatic case of judicial review, it also marks the relatively exceptional case. It is famously, if inaccurately, observed that after declaring a minor section of the Judiciary Act of 1789 unconstitutional in *Marbury*, the Court did not strike down another act of Congress for half a century, in the ill-fated *Dred Scott* case.[6] Though the Court has occasionally turned its constitutional fire on Congress, most notably during the standoff over the New Deal, it has far more often used the power of constitutional review against state and local governments. Over its history, the Court has struck down state and local statutory provisions in eight times as many cases as they have in cases involving federal statutory provisions, and many of the Court's most celebrated, and controversial, decisions have come in reviewing state laws. Although such decisions have often generated populist rhetoric about the antidemocratic nature of judicial review and sparked national political controversies, they do not stem from the constitutional principal-agent reasoning laid out by Marshall in *Marbury* but from the less contested logic of national supremacy.

Thus it was all the more striking when the Rehnquist Court embarked on its sustained assault on congressional power. Although the Rehnquist Court has not matched the Hughes Court that attacked the New Deal in intensity and significance, it has made up for that in endurance.[7] The Court struck down more acts of Congress in the 1990s than in any previous decade, including the 1930s. It has established doctrines that promise to continue to pinch Congress into the future. The justices have accompanied all this with strongly worded opinions denigrating the authority and capacity of Congress to interpret the Constitution.

The Rehnquist Court's offensive against Congress truly began in 1995. In that year the Court struck down federal statutes in four cases, the most since 1983. Of greater note was that in *United States v. Lopez*, the Court for the first time since the New Deal struck down an act of Congress as exceeding federal authority under the interstate commerce clause. Whereas the New Deal Court had established a pattern of deference to congressional judgments as to the extent of federal power relative to the states, *Lopez* suggested that the Court might now look more skeptically at such legislative judgments. That suggestion was given substance over the next several terms as the Court struck down numerous statutory provisions on a range of federalism grounds.

Consider, for example, the Court's decisions involving Section Five of the Fourteenth Amendment. Section Five gives Congress the "power to enforce, by appropriate legislation, the provisions" of the Fourteenth Amendment. In *City of Boerne v. Flores* (1997), the Court struck down the Religious Freedom Restoration Act (RFRA) as an inappropriate use of the Section Five power. With RFRA, Congress had sought to overturn the effects of the Court's decision in *Employment Division v. Smith* (1990), which changed the standard that the Court used to determine violations of religious free exercise. In *Boerne*, Justice Anthony Kennedy instructed, "[Congress] has been given the power 'to enforce,' not the power to determine what constitutes a constitutional violation. Were it not so, what Congress would be enforcing would no longer be, in any meaningful sense, the 'provisions of [the Fourteenth Amendment].' "[8] Indeed, returning to *Marbury*, Kennedy noted, "If Congress could define its own powers by altering the Fourteenth Amendment's meaning, no longer would the Constitution be 'superior paramount law, unchangeable by ordinary means.' It would be 'on a level with ordinary legislative acts.' "[9] Three years later, in a case involving both the commerce clause and Section Five, Chief Justice William Rehnquist emphasized, "No doubt the political branches have a role in interpreting and applying the Constitution, but ever since *Marbury* this Court has remained the ultimate expositor of the constitutional text."[10]

Unsurprisingly, this new judicial stringency has had the effect of concentrating the scholarly mind on the problem of congressional compliance with constitutional requirements. The new judicial doctrines have themselves met with substantial hostile fire from the law reviews,[11] but more importantly for present purposes, they have also encouraged constitutional scholars to look more closely at how Congress operates. For some, the main task is to determine why Congress has run afoul of constitutional limitations and how pervasive the legislative deficiency is. It may be possible to identify reforms by means of which Congress can adapt to the new judicial climate and make the consequences of the deficiency less severe. For others, the main task is to rehabilitate Congress, specifically in the eyes of the judges, and demonstrate how the legislature goes about the work of appropriately fulfilling its constitutional responsibilities. From either perspective, the Court's vigilance has prompted renewed examination of the relationship between Congress and the Constitution.

THE CONSTITUTION AND THE COURTS

The scholarly reaction to the federalism cases has reinforced a developing strand of research into the constitutional understandings and actions of political actors outside the judiciary. That literature takes up Rehnquist's off-handed recognition that "[n]o doubt the political branches have a role in interpreting and applying the Constitution." To the extent that this is true, then the *Marbury* logic as recently elaborated by the Court becomes problematic. If the political branches also interpret the Constitution, then it is not so obvious why the Court is necessarily the "ultimate expositor of the constitutional text." Certainly under those circumstances it is not so easy to identify congressional action with the "alteration" of the Constitution. More basically, the engagement of political actors with the constitutional text is largely terra incognita. Scholars have only begun to explore the nature, extent, and consequence of constitutional discourse beyond the courtroom.

The recent literature has important antecedents, produced by political scientists, which often did focus on Congress as a constitutional interpreter. Donald Morgan's *Congress and the Constitution: A Study of Responsibility* in 1966 was nearly unique in examining a wide range of cases that traced congressional responsibility for constitutional interpretation over the course of American history. Morgan was particularly distressed to find a decline in the acceptance of such congressional responsibility and the rise of "judicial monopolism" by which the "legislative function could receive definition solely in relation to policy" while the Constitution was understood to be "technical, and too abstruse for any but lawyers in the courtroom and judges on the bench to discuss with sense."[12] The consequence,

Morgan feared, would in the short term be an increasing judicial "activism, not only in its one remaining significant constitutional area—individual rights—but in all areas of interpretation," and in the long term that "the Constitution becomes not a way of political life in a democracy, but a rote-learned traffic code, to be evaded wherever expert opinion discovers loopholes."[13] Morgan's analysis included the results of a survey conducted in 1959 of congressmen about their attitudes toward the congressional role in interpreting the Constitution and proposals for institutional reform to improve congressional responsibility. Rather different has been the prolific output of Louis Fisher, a constitutional scholar at the Congressional Research Service. Fisher's work has often focused on the development of constitutional law in particular areas, but he has emphasized the participation of nonjudicial actors in shaping that law. Fisher has called attention to the interbranch "constitutional dialogues" and "constitutional conflicts" that have shaped law and practice over time.[14] In doing so, Fisher has been a particular advocate for the effectiveness, and even necessity, of "constitutional interpretation by members of Congress."[15] Also of note is Walter Murphy's article "Who Shall Interpret? The Quest for the Ultimate Constitutional Interpreter," which asserted the "fact of American political life that all public officials . . . often have to interpret the Constitution."[16] Reviewing the multiple possible answers that have been offered to the question of "who shall interpret the Constitution," Murphy argued for a "modified version of departmentalism," which denied that there was an "ultimate constitutional interpreter" and urged instead a shifting set of constitutional interpreters.[17] The article was important in its own right in again raising and defending the old Jeffersonian doctrine that held each branch of government to be independently responsible for constitutional interpretation and that had periodically risen to prominence ever since the early days of the republic.[18] It also reflected the preoccupations of a number of political scientists and lawyers loosely connected to Murphy and Princeton University, who would produce a number of works exploring "constitutional politics."[19]

More recent work on the Constitution outside the courts has given less particular attention to Congress as a constitutional interpreter, but it has effectively opened a vast new territory of research that should include more detailed examinations of the legislature. Early on, and most prominently, Bruce Ackerman's theory of unconventional constitutional amendments emphasized historical moments of constitutional politics that altered the inherited Constitution.[20] Ackerman has constructed an impressive normative and empirical argument for the claim that "we the people" have periodically empowered elected officials to transform the Constitution. Such moments of extraordinary constitutional deliberation on the part of elected officials eventually give way to a more normal politics of routine judicial interpretation and enforcement of the revised constitutional commitments. Congress plays an important role in that historical narrative, but the legislature is not Ackerman's particular focus. Stephen Griffin has likewise emphasized the Constitution as a "text-based institutional practice" that extends beyond the "legalized Constitution" interpreted and enforced by judges and recognizes the significance of the actions of other government officials in altering the effective constitution of the nation.[21] Keith Whittington has distinguished between the legalistic "interpretation" of constitutional meaning, primarily in the courts, and the political "construction" of constitutional meaning, primarily outside the courts, and has argued for the importance and distinctiveness of such constitutional constructions in shaping constitutional understandings and practices.[22] Larry Kramer has argued for a recovery of what he calls the early American practice of "popular constitutionalism," by which constitutional meaning is largely settled within the political arena, and Robert Post and Reva Siegel have called for "policentric interpretation of the Constitution by myriad political actors."[23] Mark Tushnet's "populist constitutional law" would dispense with judicial review entirely and emphasize the "thin constitution" of principles and values that are well recognized in the political arena.[24] Case studies have emerged examining how legislatures, including Congress, construe and extend constitutional meaning.[25]

The turn to examining the Constitution outside the courts has provided both normative theories suggesting its attractiveness and empirical investigations indicating its reality. Such scholarship has demonstrated the importance of nonjudicial actors in altering, preserving, interpreting, applying, and enforcing the Constitution. Existing studies have touched on the importance of ideas and institutions, constitutional entrepreneurs and average citizens, presidents and legislators, social movements, political parties, and interest groups, as well as courts and lawyers, in the American constitutional enterprise.

Among the tasks for the future is a detailed analysis of specific institutions and actors that engage the Constitution. Congress is a particularly important site for extrajudicial constitutional interpretation, and it is often crucial for both raising new constitutional controversies and settling old ones. The Rehnquist Court's challenge to the contemporary Congress gives immediate relevance to the question of whether Congress is best understood as a subordinate or a coordinate interpreter of the Constitution, and to the resources and constraints affecting constitutional deliberation in Congress. Making sense of Congress will clearly be central to our understanding of constitutional politics.

CONGRESS AND THE CONSTITUTION

This book assesses Congress's role in interpreting the Constitution and points the way forward to substantial research that still needs to be done in this area. By bringing together some of the leading law professors and political scientists who study Congress and the Constitution outside the Court, the thirteen chapters in this book highlight the ways in which Congress thinks about the Constitution, the relationship between Congress and the Supreme Court, the judiciary's role in checking Congress, and possible reforms to the current system.

The methodologies employed and conclusions reached vary significantly from one chapter to the next. Some chapters are historical accounts of how Congress has considered constitutional issues; others employ statistical models to assess Congress's interest in constitutional questions; still others look toward personal observation, the political science literature, or economic analysis to sort out the incentives that animate Congress. Moreover, there is an extraordinary range of opinion as to whether Congress takes the Constitution seriously and whether the system can be reformed to create greater incentives for lawmakers to pay closer attention to constitutional issues. Whatever the methodology or conclusion, all chapters underscore the pervasive role that Congress plays in shaping the Constitution's meaning. For example, a chapter on pre–Civil War interpretations of the Constitution reveals that nearly every constitutional question was debated in Congress. Likewise, a study of recent House and Senate committee consideration of constitutional questions reveals that nearly every congressional committee has held hearings which prominently featured constitutional issues.

The pervasiveness of constitutional issues in Congress helps explain the design of this book. Rather than organize the book around discrete policy issues (civil rights, federalism, budgetary policy) or subunits within Congress (individual committees, party leaders), the chapters almost always take a broader view of Congress as an institution. Several chapters are wide-ranging, largely positive accounts of the workings of Congress—law-makers' attitudes toward Congress's role as a constitutional interpreter, offices within Congress that help lawmakers learn about constitutional issues, Congress's willingness to use its confirmation power to shape constitutional decisions by both the executive and the courts, mechanisms by which lawmakers respond to Court rulings, the frequency with which committees consider constitutional questions, and the responsibilities of lawyers in Congress. Other chapters assess the deliberative quality of Congress, especially the quality of Congress's interpretation of the Constitution (and whether courts are likely to do a better job than Congress). Finally, some chapters examine relations between the Court and Congress, including the nexus between judicial and legislative action and how the courts should take the inner workings of Congress into account.

The book is loosely divided into three units, with many chapters touching on issues raised in more than one. The initial chapters take a broad view of Congress's interest in constitutional interpretation and the resources available to Congress. Chapters in this unit also consider how Congress makes use of hearings, its confirmation power, and committee lawyers to learn about constitutional questions and to shape constitutional values. The second part of the book considers relations between the Court and Congress. The initial chapters in this part are largely positive accounts of how lawmakers respond to Court decisions. Subsequent chapters are more normative, proposing ways for the courts to evaluate Congress's work product. The last part of the book, although grounded in concrete evidence, is more speculative. The quality of Congress's handling of constitutional questions and how the current system can be reformed are the subject of these chapters.

What follows is a thumbnail sketch of the book's chapters:

David Currie's "Prolegomena for a Sampler: Extrajudicial Interpretation of the Constitution, 1789–1861" underscores how, during the early republic, " 'the whole business of legislation [was] a practical construction of the Constitution.' "[26] Currie argues that judicial deference to congressional interpretations of the Constitution is inseparable from Congress's willingness to seriously consider the constitutionality of its handiwork. During the nation's early years, Congress's performance, while variable, was often first-rate. For example, a case study on Congress's consideration of the constitutionality of state secession in 1861 reveals that Congress sometimes does a better job of considering constitutional issues than the Supreme Court.

Lawmakers' attitudes about their responsibility to interpret the Constitution and the degree of deference that they owe to Supreme Court rulings are the subject of Bruce Peabody's "Congressional Attitudes toward Constitutional Interpretation." The heart of this chapter is a survey of members of the 106th Congress (1999–2001). Among other things, Peabody's survey suggests that today's lawmakers seem less interested in constitutional issues than members of earlier Congresses were and, correspondingly, that today's lawmakers are not especially upset with the Rehnquist Court's decisions striking down federal statutes. In reaching this conclusion, Peabody revisits Donald Morgan's similar study of the 1959–61 Congress (when the Warren Court's rulings on desegregation and other issues prompted an intense response from Congress, especially from Southerners). Specifically, Peabody finds that members of Congress who once thought that courts should defer to Congress now think that Congress and the courts should both interpret the Constitution, with neither branch necessarily deferring to the views of the other.

Lawmakers interested in asserting their institutional prerogatives often turn to congressional staff agencies for assistance. Lou Fisher, in "Constitutional Analysis by Congressional Staff Agencies," examines how the Government Accountability Office (formerly the General Accounting Office), the Congressional Research Service, the Congressional Budget Office, and House and Senate counsel help members of Congress come to grips with the constitutionality of their handiwork. Fisher makes use of numerous examples and mini–case studies to illustrate how these staff agencies can help members independently interpret the Constitution and, in so doing, protect their institutional prerogatives. At the same time, Fisher concludes that congressional staff agencies will be "largely marginalized" if members do not want to defend their institution.

Hearings are another way that lawmakers both sort out the constitutionality of legislation and signal their interest in constitutional questions. Keith Whittington's "Hearing about the Constitution in Congressional Committees" reviews and draws tentative conclusions from committee hearings in the 1990s. Whittington's study, although highlighting the predominant role played by the judiciary committees, reveals that constitutional issues played a prominent role in at least one hearing of every major House and Senate committee. More significantly, a committee is far more likely to hold hearings about a judicial decision that undermines its legislative agenda than a more far-reaching decision that does not. For example, the Republican-controlled Congress is not unhappy with the Rehnquist

Court's federalism revival and, as such, few hearings have been scheduled to assess (let alone assail) recent decisions striking down federal statutes.

The enormous power that committees wield in shaping constitutional values is also considered in Mike Gerhardt's "The Federal Appointments Process as Constitutional Interpretation." By reviewing ways that the Senate (typically acting through its committees) has exercised its confirmation power, Gerhardt highlights how it is that Congress seeks to impose its constitutional views on the courts, the presidency, and government agencies. The Senate Judiciary Committee, for example, has blocked the confirmation of judges who do not hold certain points of view that the committee deems critical. Also, the committee has secured promises from nominees to adhere to positions that the nominee would not otherwise support. Beyond judicial appointments, Gerhardt considers the nomination of executive branch officials, who help set the Court's agenda and whose interpretations of the Constitution are sometimes binding (when the issue is nonreviewable in the courts).

Courts too steer clear of some congressional interpretations of the Constitution (impeachment and congressional investigations, for example). Congress also interprets the Constitution in areas where the Court has yet to speak. These matters are the subject of John Yoo's "Lawyers in Congress." In sorting out how Congress exercises these responsibilities, Yoo calls attention to the contextual nature of congressional lawyering. In particular, congressional lawyers often put the brakes on overzealous congressional investigations and, in so doing, defend constitutional freedoms when courts will not. In sharp contrast, because Congress is not responsible for implementing the law, congressional lawyers are often willing to push the bounds of Supreme Court doctrine when engaging in the "creative role" of drafting legislation.

What then of instances where the Court strikes down federal legislation? Does Congress simply accept these defeats or does it revisit the issue through new legislation, including legislation challenging the Court's ruling? In "Congressional Responses to Judicial Review," Mitch Pickerill calls attention to the frequency with which lawmakers respond to the Court's exercises of judicial review. Pickerell also identifies the varied ways in which Congress responds to judicial invalidations, including the enactment of legislation and the approval of proposals to amend the Constitution. More strikingly, Pickerill's analysis suggests that Congress rarely challenges the correctness of Court rulings, but that nevertheless those rulings are rarely final in regard to the policies at issue in the litigation.

Congress often responds to the Court, but it does so primarily by modifying bills to accomplish legislative purposes while taking into account the Court's reasoning.

Congressional responses to Court decision making are also the subject of Mike Klarman's "Court, Congress, and Civil Rights." In examining the causal connection between *Brown v. Board of Education* and civil rights legislation of the mid-1960s, Klarman argues that the Court's decision played a profound but indirect role in motivating Congress. Specifically, rather than embrace civil rights reform because they thought *Brown* correctly decided, lawmakers acted reflectively—responding to the ugly and embarrassing southern backlash against the decision. Klarman also explains why it is that the Court is sometimes ahead of Congress on civil rights, while at other times Congress has taken the lead.

Relations between the Court and Congress are also examined in Bill Eskridge's and John Ferejohn's "Quasi-Constitutional Law: The Rise of Super-Statutes." The focus of their chapter is the power of Congress to enact legislation that is, like the Constitution, "fundamental and trumping." Pointing to the Sherman Act, the Civil Rights Act of 1964, and other "super-statutes," Eskridge and Ferejohn argue that Congress sometimes enacts legislation that penetrates "public normative and institutional culture." Moreover, because of the difficulties of amending the Constitution (and because fundamental law should connect with the people and popular needs), Eskridge and Ferejohn claim that courts should view these statutes as quasi-constitutional. By suggesting that Congress can shape fundamental law through the normal legislative process, "Super-Statutes" is a call for lawmakers and judges to see the legislative process as a mechanism for shaping the transcendent values that define our nation.

The question of whether Congress seriously studies issues that implicate constitutional norms is taken up in Neal Devins's "Congressional Fact Finding and the Scope of Judicial Review." In sorting out the judiciary's role in checking Congress, Devins compares the strengths and weaknesses of Congress and the courts. His examination suggests that courts should defer to Congress only when Congress has the institutional incentives to take fact finding seriously. Through case studies on federalism, separation of powers, and affirmative action, Devins argues that Congress's interest in getting the facts right is issue-specific. On separation of powers, Congress has the incentives to review its factual premises and correct errors; on federalism and affirmative action, Congress may be more interested in rewarding interest groups than in getting the facts right.

In "Institutional Design of a Thayerian Congress," Beth Garrett and Adrian Vermeule tackle the related issue of whether Congress's capacity to interpret the Constitution can be improved by making incremental changes to the lawmaking process. Arguing that legislators (while keenly interested in reelection) often act in the public interest, Garrett and Vermeule claim that the seriousness with which lawmakers think about constitutional issues may well be tied to the institutional design of the lawmaking process. For example, after showing how constitutional questions are shortchanged in "fire alarm" systems (in which affected interests monitor bills and tell lawmakers about perceived shortcomings), Garrett and Vermeule advance several reforms intended to facilitate lawmakers' consideration of constitutional questions. Their reforms include the raising of "constitutional points of order," the creation of an Office of Constitutional Issues, and mandatory committee findings on the constitutional implications of proposed legislation.

The seriousness with which Congress thinks about constitutional questions is also the subject of Mark Tushnet's "Evaluating Congressional Constitutional Interpretation: Some Criteria and Two Informal Case Studies." In part, Tushnet explains how judicial review distorts Congress's consideration of constitutional issues. For example, lawmakers may engage the Court in a constitutional dialogue, enacting legislation that is inconsistent with the Court's standards in order to push a change in doctrine. By contrast, when there is no possibility of judicial review, Congress is a freestanding interpreter. On war powers and impeachment, for example, Congress acts on its own, not in the shadow of judicial precedent. By looking at Congress's performance on these two issues, Tushnet argues that Congress seems to do as well as the courts, "at least when Congress acts free of the judicial overhang."

Barbara Sinclair likewise concludes that Congress is institutionally well equipped to interpret the Constitution. In "Can Congress Be Trusted with the Constitution? The Effects of Incentives and Procedures," Sinclair defends Congress's constitutional performance by looking to lawmakers' incentives and the inner workings of the legislative process. In particular, Sinclair explains why lawmakers seek to enact good public policy and how it is that the legislative process promotes fact finding and deliberation. And while constitutional issues may not be front and center in these legislative deliberations, Congress is still better positioned than the Court to set the national agenda on issues implicating federalism and the separation of powers. Sinclair therefore rejects one of the underlying premises of the Rehnquist Court's rulings limiting congressional power, namely the Court's skeptical view of lawmakers' incentives and work product.

By calling attention to the critical role that Congress can play and has played in shaping constitutional values, this book underscores the limits of Court-centered understandings of the Constitution. For one thing, lawmakers cannot lose sight of the Constitution. On some issues, the courts have not spoken and are not likely to speak. On other issues, the courts have spoken. But Congress can countermand the Court through legislation or use its confirmation power to shape the Court's direction. For identical reasons, the Court cannot lose sight of Congress. Not only can Congress check the Court, but the Court's willingness to defer to Congress is often tied to the Court's sense of the seriousness with which Congress approaches its constitutional responsibilities.

Doubts about the modern Congress have certainly fueled the Rehnquist Court's willingness to revive federalism and otherwise strike down federal statutes on First Amendment, separation of powers, and other grounds.[27] Moreover, justices who are ideologically predisposed to limit lawmakers' prerogatives are motivated to point the finger at Congress for overstepping its enumerated prerogatives. At the end of the Court's 2000 term, Justice Antonin Scalia (never hinting that the Court is sharply divided) complained that "Congress is increasingly abdicating its independent responsibility to be sure that it is being faithful to the Constitution."[28] Scalia also warned that the Court might increasingly strike down federal statutes "if Congress is going to take the attitude that it will do anything it can get away with and let the Supreme Court worry about the Constitution."[29]

In sorting out the veracity of Scalia's broadside, this book provides ample evidence of both the quality of Congress's constitutional handiwork and Congress's interest in the Constitution. Also, by highlighting how lawmakers' incentives and institutional design contribute to Congress's consideration of constitutional issues, this book calls attention to the risk of making overgeneralizations about Congress. Congress's performance may be tied to whether judicial review is available, whether lawmakers agree with the Court's decision, whether interest groups trigger necessary fire alarms, and several other variables.

More than anything, this book calls attention to the pivotal role that Congress plays in interpreting the Constitution and the need for additional research in this area. Reflecting that the study of Congress and the Constitution is still nascent, the book is more a wake-up call than a definitive statement. And while it raises more questions than it answers, we anticipate that subsequent studies will be more definitive. Increasing interest in both the Constitution outside the Court and the decisions of the Rehnquist Court limiting congressional prerogatives will undoubtedly result in more comprehensive research on the topics addressed here. This is as it should be, for Congress's role in shaping constitutional values may well be as important as the Supreme Court's.

NOTES

1 John R. Hibbing and Elizabeth Theiss-Morse, *Congress as Public Enemy* (New York: Cambridge University Press, 1995), 32.

2 Marbury v. Madison, 5 U.S. 137, 176–78 (1803).

3 *Id.* at 178.

4 *Id.*

5 Powell v. McCormack, 395 U.S. 486, 521 (1969), quoting Baker v. Carr, 369 U.S. 186, 211 (1962).

6 Mark Graber has demonstrated that the Supreme Court did in fact enforce constitutional constraints against Congress in a series of obscure land grant cases decided between *Marbury* and *Dred Scott*. Mark A. Graber, "Naked Land Transfers and American Constitutional Development," 53 *Vanderbilt Law Review* 73 (2000).

7 In this regard, the Rehnquist Court most closely resembles the early Burger Court, which also struck down a historically large number of federal laws over the course of several years.

8 City of Boerne v. Flores, 521 U.S. 507, 519 (1997).

9 *Id.* at 529.

10 United States v. Morrison, 529 U.S. 598, 616 n.7 (2000).

11 This hostile reaction may reflect the tendency of law professors to agree with the substantive objectives of the laws invalidated by the Court. See Barry Friedman, "The Cycles of Constitutional Theory," 67 *Law and Contemporary Problems* 149 (2004).

12 Donald G. Morgan, *Congress and the Constitution* (Cambridge: Harvard University Press, 1966), 334, 335.

13 *Id.* at 337, 338.

14 E.g., Louis Fisher, *Constitutional Dialogues* (Princeton: Princeton University Press, 1988); Louis Fisher, *Constitutional Conflicts between Congress and the President*, 4th ed. (Lawrence: University Press of Kansas, 1997); Neal

Devins and Louis Fisher, *The Democratic Constitution* (New York: Oxford University Press, 2004).

15   Louis Fisher, "Constitutional Interpretation by Members of Congress," 63 *North Carolina Law Review* 707 (1985).

16   Walter F. Murphy, "Who Shall Interpret? The Quest for the Ultimate Constitutional Interpreter," 48 *Review of Politics* 401 (1986). Twenty-five years earlier, Murphy chronicled the Supreme Court's sensitivity to Congress's disapproval of judicial decisions. Walter F. Murphy, *Congress and the Court* (Chicago: University of Chicago Press, 1962).

17   Murphy, "Who Shall Interpret?," 401, 417.

18   On the political circumstances for this periodic appearance of departmentalism, see Keith E. Whittington, "Presidential Challenges to Judicial Supremacy and the Politics of Constitutional Meaning," 33 *Polity* 365 (2001).

19   See Sotirios A. Barber and Robert P. George, *Constitutional Politics* (Princeton: Princeton University Press, 2001).

20   The argument was first presented in Bruce Ackerman, "The Storrs Lectures: Discovering the Constitution," 93 *Yale Law Journal* 1013 (1984). The fullest statement is Bruce Ackerman, *We the People* (Cambridge: Harvard University Press, 1991, 1998).

21   Stephen M. Griffin, *American Constitutionalism* (Princeton: Princeton University Press, 1996), 56.

22   Keith E. Whittington, *Constitutional Construction* (Cambridge: Harvard University Press, 1999).

23   Larry D. Kramer, *The People Themselves* (New York: Oxford University Press, 2004); Robert C. Post and Reva B. Siegel, "Legislative Constitutionalism and Section Five Power: Policentric Interpretation of the Family Medical Leave Act," 112 *Yale Law Journal* 1943 (2003).

24   Mark Tushnet, *Taking the Constitution Away from the Courts* (Princeton: Princeton University Press, 1999).

25   See, e.g., Susan R. Burgess, *Contest for Constitutional Authority* (Lawrence: University Press of Kansas, 1992); Neal Devins, *Shaping Constitutional Values* (Baltimore: Johns Hopkins University Press, 1996); John J. Dinan, *Keeping the People's Liberties* (Lawrence: University Press of Kansas, 1998); Michael Kent Curtis, *Free Speech, "The People's Darling Privilege"* (Durham: Duke University Press, 2000); Colton C. Campbell and John F. Stack Jr., eds., *Congress and the Politics of Emerging Rights* (Lanham, Md.: Rowman & Littlefield, 2002); Louis Fisher, *Religious Liberty in America* (Lawrence: University Press of Kansas, 2002).

26   David P. Currie, "Prolegomena for a Sampler," at 20 (quoting Representative Theodore Sedgwick of Massachusetts).

27   For a discussion of how increasing populist distrust of Congress has fueled the Rehnquist Court's federalism revival, see Christopher H. Schroeder,

"Causes of the Recent Turn in Constitutional Interpretation," 51 *Duke Law Journal* 307 (2001).

28 Stuart Taylor Jr., "The Tipping Point," 32 *National Journal* 1810, 1811 (2000).

29 *Id.*

Prolegomena for a Sampler

Extrajudicial Interpretation of the Constitution,

1789–1861

∽

DAVID P. CURRIE

The subject of this book is the role of Congress in constitutional interpretation. The chapters that follow discuss that subject from a variety of theoretical and institutional perspectives. How do members of Congress view their own constitutional responsibility to the Constitution? What resources are available within the legislative branch to assist Congress in resolving constitutional questions? How can executive agencies help to ensure that Congress has the necessary information to make informed decisions? Is Congress likely to take its constitutional responsibility more seriously in some kinds of cases than in others? To what extent are constitutional questions actually addressed in modern congressional hearings? How can congressional procedures be reformed to improve the conditions for sound constitutional decision making? To what extent can Congress be trusted with constitutional interpretation? How does Congress react to judicial decisions invalidating its handiwork? How does Congress affect constitutional interpretation indirectly through such processes as Senate approval of nominees for federal office, reorganization of agencies, and the prescription of qualifications for appointment? Do some "super-statutes" acquire a "quasi-constitutional" status that adds to the arsenal of fundamental norms against which, in the absence of explicit repeal, later legislation must be measured? Should the degree of deference that courts afford to congressional judgment be tailored to the degree of consideration that Congress actually gave to the constitutional question?

This chapter is designed as a prolegomenon for what follows. Its aim is to set the stage for the ensuing dissection of current problems by providing an overview of the role of extrajudicial actors in early constitutional interpretation, as illuminated by my study over the past ten years of eighteenth- and nineteenth-century materials.[1]

I begin with a brief discussion of the theoretical basis for extrajudicial interpretation and proceed to depict, in a general way, what one discovers on reading the early congressional and executive materials. In the modern spirit of verismo, I conclude this prologue with a slice of life, uno squarcio di vita—a brief case study designed to illustrate in somewhat greater detail the general conclusions put forward in this chapter.

WHO INTERPRETS THE CONSTITUTION?

Why the courts, of course—first and foremost the Supreme Court of the United States, but other courts as well. Witness the scads of judicial decisions, good and bad, that we all read and almost exclusively assign in courses on constitutional law; witness what is predominantly cited in briefs and oral argument in constitutional litigation; witness the stuff of standard law review articles and treatises on the Constitution.

Why? As Chief Justice Marshall told us in *Marbury v. Madison*,[2] the judges all swear to uphold the Constitution; they must not violate it by doing what the Constitution forbids, like trying criminal cases without juries, even if Congress has directed them to do so. But the judges are not alone in this regard. Others swear to uphold the Constitution as well: presidents, cabinet officers, members of Congress—indeed every federal, state, and local officer in the land.

When we study *Marbury v. Madison*, we learn that the oath argument is hollow: that an officer swears to do his constitutional duty does not tell us what that duty is. Another part of Marshall's opinion, moreover, seems to suggest that courts may have a special role to play in constitutional interpretation: As Hamilton had said in the *Federalist*, the courts are an important element in a system of checks and balances designed to keep other branches of government from exceeding constitutional limits on their powers. The Framers, the argument goes, could not have meant for Congress to be ultimate judge of the scope of its own authority; that would smack too much of appointing the rabbit to guard the cabbages.

Indeed in the early Congress occasional speakers suggested that questions as to the constitutionality of proposed legislation should be left to the courts, but they were quickly shouted down; from the first it was under-stood that legislative and executive officers had a parallel responsibility to determine in the first instance the extent of their own powers.[3] To para-phrase *Marbury*, it would indeed have been odd for the Constitution to place limitations on the authority of Congress and direct its members to ignore them, hoping that only the Court would defend them. As Presidents Jefferson and Jackson famously insisted, the Framers established multiple checks to ensure that their handiwork was respected.[4]

Thus it was not surprising that President Washington took the Con-stitution for his guide—keenly aware, as he was, that everything he did would establish a precedent and determined to cut square corners with the fundamental law. It was not surprising that Washington vetoed one bill on constitutional grounds and signed the bill creating the Bank of the United States only after soliciting formal opinions from four members of his Cabinet and convincing himself that the bill was constitutional. It was not surprising that when James Madison introduced the Bill of Rights in the House of Representatives in 1789 he said it would speak to the con-sciences of legislators as well as to their constituents and to the courts. It was not surprising that whenever a bill was introduced in Congress the threshold question was understood to be whether Congress had power to enact it. And thus it was not surprising that Representative Theodore Sedg-wick of Massachusetts could say during the First Congress, "the whole business of legislation is a practical construction of the Constitution."[5]

It is precisely because Congress too has a responsibility to address ques-tions of its own authority that when courts pass on the constitutionality of legislation they often defer to congressional judgment. It would make no sense for them to do so if Congress regularly left such questions to the courts. And it is for the same reason that congressional debates since the beginning have been filled with arguments over the meaning of vari-ous constitutional provisions—as are legislative committee reports, presi-dential messages, and opinions of the attorneys general. These voluminous and readily available materials accordingly provide a copious and fruitful source of information and ideas about the meaning of the Constitution—a source that until rather recently has been strangely neglected by lawyers, judges, and legal scholars.

HOW COMPREHENSIVE IS THE MATERIAL?

In the early Congress virtually everything became a constitutional question —from great controversies like those over the national bank and the president's removal power to ephemera of exquisite obscurity.[6] What information, for example, could be demanded in the census? (Only the number of free and unfree inhabitants in each state, which the Constitution made determinative for the apportionment of representatives and direct taxes? No, said Madison, anything that might be relevant to the exercise of any congressional function.) How should the president be addressed? (Someone suggested "His Highness, the President of the United States of America, and Protector of Their Liberties"; others objected that Article II's simple "President of the United States" was meant to be exclusive and that Article I forbade the government to confer titles of nobility.) Was the president at liberty to refuse his salary? (The consensus was no, since a president who impoverished himself would be at the mercy of Congress.) When a president died or was disabled, did the vice president become president or merely assume his powers and duties?[7] (Did it matter? Yes: for if he did assume the office, and the elected president recovered, there would be no way short of impeachment to get rid of him; if he did not assume the office, Congress could destroy his independence by reducing his salary.) [8] Whatever the constitutional conundrum, we are likely to find something about it in the legislative and executive record.

HOW SIGNIFICANT WAS EARLY EXTRAJUDICIAL INTERPRETATION?

In the nature of our court system, laws must be passed and executive actions at least imminently threatened before they can be judicially reviewed. It follows that in nearly every case I have considered, Congress and the executive determined the constitutionality of their own actions before the courts did. The legislative or executive decision was not necessarily final, since the judges could review and reverse it—provided that the issue arose in a concrete controversy neither unripe nor moot between adverse parties and was not itself deemed "political." Even if it did, it was generally outside the courts that constitutional issues of federal authority were initially defined and resolved.

Very few acts of Congress, moreover, were challenged before the courts during the early years, and nearly all of them were upheld. Indeed when the constitutionality of early legislative acts finally reached the courts—often many years after their enactment—the judges tended at best to repeat arguments previously made by executive officers or in Congress. In the case of the Bank of the United States, for instance, Fisher Ames in the House and Alexander Hamilton in the cabinet had anticipated Chief Justice Marshall's entire opinion, in addition to demonstrating what Marshall omitted and the modern observer might be inclined to think crucial: to which congressional powers the bank was necessary and proper and why.[9] Even when the courts ultimately did pass on the constitutionality of federal legislation, congressional and legislative arguments were often more thorough and persuasive.

Not only did the early Congress almost always interpret the Constitution before the courts did, and not only did it often do a better job; in many cases congressional debates provide our *only* official discussion of constitutional issues, for many crucial constitutional controversies have never been judicially resolved. Who, for example, has power to terminate a treaty? The Constitution prescribes how treaties are made; it is silent as to how, if at all, they are to be dissolved. Congress abrogated two treaties with France by statute in 1798, unfortunately without much reported argument.[10] (Both statutes and treaties, it would later be said, were the law of the land; and only Congress could repeal a law.) Some sixty years later, after considerable debate, the president and Senate canceled a commercial convention with Denmark.[11] (The authority of the president and Senate to make treaties, it was argued, implied authority to unmake them.) A century after that President Carter purported to annul a treaty with Taiwan without asking the Senate for approval. (The president, his supporters argued, had general authority over foreign affairs, and the requirement of Senate consent did not apply.) In its infinite wisdom, the Supreme Court declined to decide the case;[12] congressional debates remain our best official source on this basic constitutional question.

Consider also the perennial and much-mooted question of presidential authority to initiate hostilities abroad—one of the fundamental questions, as some saw it, of the Vietnam War. We know a great deal about this issue from legislative and executive sources: from firm pronouncements by Presidents Washington and Jefferson that they could act only in defense, from bitter congressional debates on President Madison's incursion into West Florida and President Polk's military expedition to the Rio Grande, and more recently from the discussion and adoption of the celebrated War Powers Resolution of 1973. The legislative and executive materials on this issue are extraordinarily rich, and I have exposed only the tip of the iceberg; we still have heard almost nothing about it from the courts.[13]

I think it fair to say that the original understanding of the Constitution was forged not in the courts but in Congress and the executive branch.

HOW RELEVANT ARE EARLY EXTRAJUDICIAL INTERPRETATIONS TODAY?

Constitutional questions tend to recur. It is striking how many recent controversies over the meaning of the Constitution were anticipated by legislative and executive discussions that took place a century and a half or two centuries ago. Who counts the electoral votes in a disputed presidential election? What are the standards for impeachment? May states set additional qualifications for members of Congress? May a member of Congress be an officer in the armed-forces reserves? May federal employees be required to surrender their political rights? Is the president subject to judicial process? May Congress impose affirmative duties on state officers?

All these questions and many more of current importance were raised and debated outside the courts during the early years.[14] Early extrajudicial materials remain an invaluable source of ideas and arguments on innumerable questions that continue to trouble us today. Even when the issue under discussion has no modern counterpart, moreover, the early materials afford valuable insights into the timeless and transcendent question of how one should approach the task of interpreting the Constitution; and it may not surprise you to learn that just about everyone was an originalist back then.

HOW GOOD WERE THE ARGUMENTS?

They were variable, of course, like those of the judges. Many members of Congress said nothing at all. Others said only things that were foolish, or pedestrian, or obvious.[15] Sometimes the debates are cloyingly repetitive. At other times important statutes were passed without any significant reported debate, or without any reported debate at all. Reporting was unofficial and spotty in the early days, and until 1795 the Senate worked behind closed doors. Sometimes, it appears, major constitutional questions were simply overlooked.

There was no reported debate, for example, when Congress in 1793 passed a statute to implement the extradition and fugitive-slave clauses of Article IV, § 2. It was not at all obvious, and many would later deny, that Congress had any such authority; for (in conspicuous contrast to the full faith and credit clause of Article IV, §1) neither clause said anything about legislative implementation. Little harm was done, however, for Congress had satisfactorily addressed the same question of implicit enforcement power in the context of the oath requirement of Article VI four years before.[16] In other cases, the failure of Congress to engage in debate or of journalists to record it could result in major embarrassment—as when opponents of federal spending for internal improvements devoted untold hours to attempting to prove that the constitutional basis for the government's takeover of lighthouses and other navigational aids in 1789 was not the commerce clause, as it most plausibly seemed to be.[17]

On other occasions, however, there was a great deal of first-rate argument. I do not say the debates were generally disinterested, or that the participants were commonly as detached as judges. Especially after the development of political parties in the 1790s, there was often a high degree of congruence between the constitutional views of the speaker and the political result he hoped to achieve; one suspects that in many a case it was the conclusion that compelled the argument, not the other way around.

But the same is at least equally true of advocates for parties before the courts, who nevertheless often produce arguments of the highest caliber. Political payoff, like a litigant's retainer, can provide a powerful incentive to good argument. The congressional and executive records sparkle with brilliant insights about the meaning of constitutional provisions. Even today it is often difficult to find constitutional arguments of substance that were not made a century or two ago by some executive officer or member of Congress. In the debates of 1798 over the Sedition Act, for example, George Nicholas and Albert Gallatin, with a remarkable economy of words, developed our whole modern theory of freedom of the press, to which nothing but the icing has been added in the ensuing two hundred years.[18]

WHAT SOURCES ARE AVAILABLE?

Unlike judicial opinions, legislative and executive materials are multiple and diffuse. (They are also incomplete, partly because the Senate initially sat only behind closed doors.) They range from the statutes themselves to congressional debates and committee reports, presidential messages, and opinions of the attorneys general.[19] Cabinet discussions are a harder nut to crack, but John Quincy Adams's memoirs and President Polk's diary afford revealing glimpses of the inner sanctum.[20] The letters and extracurricular speeches of the principal actors add fascinating details. One must turn to the diplomatic correspondence of Daniel Webster, for example, to discover that as secretary of state he definitively squelched belligerent schemes to intervene in actual or threatened armed conflicts in Haiti and Hawaii—on the now familiar ground that only Congress had the power to initiate hostilities.[21]

Newspapers of the time perform a similar service. Northern and southern editorials on secession, for instance, conveniently collected to facilitate access, reveal not only popular attitudes but also a wealth of arguments pertaining to the great constitutional question of the day.[22] Innumerable secondary sources help to put controversies in context and provide additional arguments as well. In addition to general histories of the relevant period, there are histories of individual states, biographies, and both monographs and articles about particular constitutional controversies—including, to mention only a few, whole books on such subjects of congressional consideration as the Burr conspiracy, the *Wheeling Bridge* controversy, and the Dorr Rebellion.[23]

Secondary sources help above all to ensure that we get our facts straight, which is of course fundamental. For it is crucial to understand the facts before we begin to analyze the constitutional questions. In my current work with nineteenth-century congressional sources I spend more time on the history than on the law. I have no illusion that I can improve on the work of historians, nor do I try. My model is Alexandre Dumas père: "Qu'est-ce que l'histoire? C'est un clou auquel j'accroche mes romans."[24] There is room here for lawyers as well as historians, and for others as well; specialization is as useful in scholarship as in the manufacture of pins.

FORGOTTEN CONTROVERSIES

Extrajudicial materials are not simply a repository of forgotten arguments; they are a treasure chest of forgotten incidents and issues as well. These materials may be familiar to historians, but they are largely unknown to legal scholars.

Did you know that Congress in 1813 authorized the appointment of a vaccine agent for the United States?[25] That President William Henry Harrison issued an executive order in 1841 anticipating the Hatch Act by forbidding federal officers and employees to take an active part in political campaigns?[26] That after the Senate had resoundingly rejected his treaty to annex Texas, President Tyler asked Congress to do so by joint resolution, and that Congress did?[27] That Congress proposed not one but two Thirteenth Amendments before the states finally ratified the one that put an end to slavery? The first, which fell one or two states shy of adoption (so far: remember the so-called Twenty-seventh Amendment) would have deprived little old ladies of their citizenship if they accepted gold watches from foreign governments.[28] The second, which would have forbidden any constitutional amendment giving Congress authority over slavery within the states[29] — a last-minute effort at compromise that was overtaken by the attack on Fort Sumter — raised a fascinating constitutional question of its own: Can those with power to amend the Constitution deprive themselves of that power?

One of the great rewards of reading the legislative and executive materials is tripping over the legal equivalent of a lost Mozart manuscript every couple of days.

PERSONALITIES

Another great bonus of research into extrajudicial sources is the fascinating people one gets to know in perusing these yellowing pages. Some of the greatest minds in public life applied their energies assiduously to constitutional questions outside the courts. In the House and later the Senate sat the great triumvirate of Henry Clay, Daniel Webster, and John C. Calhoun, who collectively dominated congressional debates for the better part of forty years. In the House were James Madison, Fisher Ames, Albert Gallatin, and John Quincy Adams — the last of whom had the patriotism as well as the humility to serve in Congress *after* his presidency. In the president's house, aside from the succession of midgets who served between Jackson and the Civil War, were Thomas Jefferson, Madison, the two Adamses, and Abraham Lincoln. In the cabinet sat such men as Alexander Hamilton, Jefferson, Gallatin, and Webster. These are the great figures we all heard about in grade school and beyond; to read what they said and wrote about constitutional issues provides them with flesh and blood.

The same is true of a larger number of significant statesmen of the second rank, such as Stephen A. Douglas, William H. Seward, Salmon P. Chase, and Charles Sumner—as well as those like Jefferson Davis and Alexander H. Stephens. Most gratifying of all, perhaps, is the great army of unsung bit players, since largely forgotten, who had their moment in the sun and contributed their often considerable mite to the constitutional mill: Ether Shepley of Maine, who most ably defended President Jackson's right to run his own administration;[30] John Vining of Delaware, who spoke up eloquently for the First Amendment rights of federal officers;[31] George Badger of North Carolina, who courageously conceded that Congress could outlaw slavery in the territories and lost his seat for his honesty;[32] Charles Pinckney of South Carolina and Jacob Collamer of Vermont, who on widely separated occasions warned their colleagues of the dangers of congressional selection of the president;[33] Thomas Jefferson Rusk of Texas, who in an otherwise highly partisan election contest insisted that Senate seats be filled even at the expense of his own party;[34] John Bouligny of Louisiana, who when informed that his state had seceded refused to leave the House (the people elected me, Bouligny argued, and the legislature cannot tell me to go home);[35] the seven now anonymous Jeffersonians who voted to acquit Justice Samuel Chase after a political impeachment and thus helped to preserve the independence of the courts.[36]

BREAKING THE BONDS: A CASE STUDY

I've promised you a brief case study to illuminate some of the general points I've been making. Here it is.

In December 1860 South Carolina purported to secede from the Union. Six other states followed suit before President Lincoln's inauguration; four more attempted to withdraw when he called up the militia after the attack on Fort Sumter.

It was 1869 before the Supreme Court, in *Texas v. White*, declared secession unconstitutional.[37] When it did, its reasoning was superficial at best. The Articles of Confederation, Chief Justice Chase wrote, had proclaimed the league they established "perpetual," and the Preamble to the Constitution announced that one of its purposes was to establish "a more perfect Union." Without the gloss of history, the text was not helpful: for all the Court told us, the imperfection of the Articles might have lain precisely in their perpetuity.[38]

Even President Buchanan, who thought secession unconstitutional but believed that Congress lacked the power to do anything about it, had done better than the Court: not only did he anticipate Chase's flimsy argument in his Annual Message to Congress in 1860, but he appended five others of his own.[39] Here they are in summary form, together with my own reflections on their persuasive force.

First. No clause of the Constitution, said Buchanan, provided for secession. So? It was plainly unnecessary to find affirmative authority for state action in the Constitution, since the states expressly retained all powers not delegated to the United States or prohibited by the Constitution.[40]

Second. Even the Articles were perpetual, said Buchanan, and the Constitution said it was more perfect than the Articles; it therefore was perpetual too. Defenders of the Union repeated this mantra like robots, and the Supreme Court was witless enough to rely on it in *Texas v. White*. I have already told you what I think of it: not much.

Third. That the Constitution gave Congress great powers and severely limited those of the states, as Buchanan emphasized, tells us nothing about the duration of the Union. It was understandable that the Framers would want the central government to be strong enough to serve its purposes so long as it existed; that is no reason to think they meant it to last forever.

Fourth. Buchanan also invoked the supremacy clause, as did a number of Unionists in Congress. This argument was not worth the sadly perishable paper on which it was printed. Yes, Article VI made the Constitution, federal statutes, and treaties the "law of the land" throughout the United States, but to say that forbade secession was to reason in a circle. For the question in issue was whether states that attempted to secede were still part of the "land" in which those laws were supreme; the Constitution gave them primacy nowhere else.[41]

Fifth. Neither advocates nor opponents of ratification, Buchanan said, had suggested that the Constitution permitted secession, although that would have been an excellent answer to those who thought that the document gave the United States too much authority. All right, but unless someone denied the right to secede, the failure to affirm it is not very probative; the question may not have been raised.

Sixth. Andrew Jackson had said during the nullification crisis that secession was "repugnant" to the "principles" and "object" of the Constitution;[42] Buchanan added that it would be "absurd" for a constitution to provide for its own destruction. These are bald conclusions, and they are not obvious. What principles? What object? Wherein lies the absurdity? Other associations can be dissolved unilaterally; some contracts of employment are at will; some laws (like the Sedition Act) are even programmed for self-destruction. Jefferson thought that the Constitution ought to be reexamined every generation. We don't; but how do we know the Framers meant their work to be permanent?

Seventh. There is no seventh. We have exhausted the president's arguments, and we have made no progress in disproving the right of secession. So far as anything in his message is concerned, it appears that under the Tenth Amendment the states may secede because there is nothing in the Constitution to prevent them from doing so.[43]

Let us look for guidance to the congressional debates.

There was no single, comprehensive discussion of secession in Congress; no one proposed a resolution declaring that states had or did not have the right to secede. The question came up incidentally in a variety of contexts: comments on the president's message, remarks relating to the establishment of select committees to deal with the crisis, arguments over proposed constitutional amendments and bills to augment the president's authority to employ military force. Much of the intermittent debate was pedestrian; I shall not burden you with all the details.

The first member of Congress to address the secession question seriously was Andrew Johnson, senator from Tennessee. Johnson had introduced his own package of constitutional revisions to save the Union, and in defending them he went out of his way to deny the legal right of a state to secede. In part he echoed Buchanan's half-baked arguments: the Constitution contained no provision authorizing secession; the Articles of Confederation declared themselves perpetual; and the new Constitution was meant to establish a more perfect Union. Like Buchanan, Johnson invoked Jackson, quoting extensively from his proclamation in response to nullification. He also added something of his own. The doctrine of secession, he said, was often attributed to the Virginia Resolutions of 1798–99. But James Madison, who wrote those resolutions, had gone to great lengths to deny that Virginia had meant to endorse a unilateral right of secession. Indeed, ten years earlier, when Hamilton had written that New York was considering reserving the right to withdraw from the Union in case no Bill of Rights was adopted, Madison had unequivocally replied that such a conditional ratification would be ineffective: "The Constitution requires an adoption *in toto* and *forever*." Moreover, the entire country had fought to secure Texas and paid to acquire Louisiana; no individual state could take them away.[44]

A few days later Judah Benjamin of Louisiana rose in the Senate to defend South Carolina's right to secede. He began with the right of self-government—enshrined, he argued, in the Declaration of Independence. As one legislature might repeal the acts of another, one convention might withdraw a ratification that its predecessor had given. The rights of third parties had always to be considered, but that was no obstacle to South Carolina's secession. For the Constitution was a compact, and "a bargain broken on one side is a bargain broken on all; and the compact is binding upon the generation of today only if the other parties to the compact have kept their faith." Madison had made that point explicitly in the federal convention in response to suggestions that the Articles, as they provided, could be modified only by unanimous consent: under the law of nations "a breach of any one article, by any party, leaves all the other parties at liberty to consider the whole convention as dissolved." "Acting on that principle," said Benjamin, "nine States of the Confederation seceded from the Confederation, and formed a new Government. They formed it on the express ground that some of the States had violated their compact." The Constitution having provided no tribunal to resolve disputes over "political matters," Benjamin continued, a state must determine for itself whether other parties had offended the new compact as well. And thus, he concluded, the right of secession was not a mere right of revolution but "results from the nature of the compact itself"; it was "one of those reserved powers which was not abandoned by it, and therefore grows out of the Constitution."[45]

Senator Edward D. Baker of Oregon, a close ally of Abraham Lincoln who had left his seat in the Illinois House to fight in the Mexican War, delivered a major address in response. Benjamin's entire argument, Baker said, was "based upon the assumption that the Constitution of the United States is a compact between sovereign States." That assumption was not new; it was what Calhoun had said in the nullification crisis. Webster, Madison, and Jackson had all denied it then, and they were right: the Constitution, Baker said, "declares itself to have been made by the people, and not by sovereign States, but by the people of the United States; not a compact, not a league, but it declares that the people of the United States do ordain and establish a Government." Thus in Baker's view Benjamin's argument fell of its own weight: since the Constitution was not a mere compact, the principle that breach of an agreement released other parties from their obligations did not apply.[46]

It was Senator James F. Simmons of Rhode Island, a few days later, who put meat on the bones of Baker's lean suggestion by quoting from the records of the Constitutional Convention. Mr. Simmons was no longer young, and he had first entered the Senate in 1841, yet I have had few occasions to refer to his constitutional views. His eyes had become so weak that he asked a colleague to read the relevant passages for him, and the later parts of his oration tended to wander. His quotation, however, was right on the money.

The question before the convention, Simmons reported, was Oliver Ellsworth's motion that the new Constitution be ratified by legislatures rather than by popular conventions in the several states, as had been proposed. Various speakers objected that state legislatures had no authority to surrender powers granted by state constitutions, that popular ratification would add democratic legitimacy to the new Constitution, that conventions would be more likely to approve the new order than legislatures invited to curtail their own authority. More to the point, George Mason of Virginia—the "distinguished ancestor," as Simmons acidly put it, of the present senatorial defender of secession[47]—had opposed Ellsworth's motion on the additional ground that "succeeding legislatures, having equal authority could undo the acts of their predecessors," leaving the "national Government" to "stand, in each State, on the weak and tottering foundation of an act of Assembly."

Mason's argument proved only that he wanted to prevent secession on the basis of simple legislation, not that he meant to forbid it altogether. Indeed one might extrapolate from his words to Benjamin's conclusion that a new *convention* might retract the ratification its predecessor had given, which is precisely what was attempted in South Carolina in 1860.[48] Ellsworth denied that a state could withdraw even a legislative ratification: "An act to which the States, by their Legislatures, make themselves parties, becomes a compact from which no one of the parties can recede of itself." But it was James Madison, heart and soul of the Philadelphia Convention, who had the last word, and he carried Mason's distinction to its logical conclusion:

Mr. Madison . . . considered the difference between a system founded on the Legislatures only and one founded on the people to be the true difference between a league or treaty and a constitution. The former, in point of moral obligation, might be as inviolable as the latter; in point of political operation, there were two important distinctions in favor of the latter: first, a law violating a treaty ratified by a preëxisting law might be respected by the judges as a law, though a perfidious one. A law violating a Constitution established by the people themselves would be considered by the judges as null and void. Secondly, the doctrine laid down by the law of nations in the case of treaties is, that a breach of any one article by any of the parties, frees the other parties from their engagements. In the case of a union of people under one constitution, the nature of the fact has always been understood to exclude such an interpretation.

And thus, Madison concluded, conventions rather than legislatures should be asked to ratify the new Constitution—in order, among other things, to prevent its being understood to be a mere interstate compact whose breach would justify the withdrawal of other parties.[49]

The Convention, as we know, followed Madison's advice; Article VII provided for ratification by convention, not legislation. Here is Senator Simmons's conclusion:

"[E]very Senator who has made an argument in favor of the right of a State to secede, has based it upon the argument, that the Constitution is a treaty, and not a Constitution. I agree that a treaty which is broken in one part is broken in all, and frees everybody. That was Mr. Madison's doctrine; but he said that a constitution formed by the people is not a compact, but a *pact* that excludes such an interpretation. Yet, everybody on the other side says it *is* a compact; and the distinguished Senator from Texas [Mr. Wigfall] says that the old men who made this Constitution, of all things in the world, knew nothing about it; that they were very good men for generals, and such like, but they knew nothing about the Constitution. Well, sir, they are good enough authority for me."[50]

They are good enough authority for me too. There is more to say about all this, and I shall say it in another place.[51] For present purposes let it suffice that this largely unknown discussion illustrates a number of the points I have attempted to make in this chapter. Both the president and members of Congress addressed themselves seriously to the merits of the constitutional question. They did so long before that question ever came up in court. The arguments were of high quality, and the best of them were made by people largely forgotten today. Finally, when the Supreme Court ultimately got around to resolving the question, it had far less to say about it than had already been said by Congress, or even the president. Indeed Senator Simmons's reminder of Madison's explanation why the Constitution should be ratified by popular conventions is worth more in resolving the secession debate than the whole tornado of airy persiflage poured forth by his congressional colleagues, by the president, or by the later Supreme Court.[52]

Extrajudicial actors have played a central part in shaping our understanding of the Constitution. It is not so much that Congress or the president definitively resolved the constitutional questions they confronted, though that was not infrequently the case. The spoor they have left behind rather contains myriad ideas and arguments on which to draw in applying the often open-ended terms of the Constitution to the kaleidoscopic variety of unforeseeable circumstances that only real life could engender; it is a source of insights that no constitutional interpreter can afford to ignore.

Those who moisten their toes in the sea of legislative and executive materials are in for a treat. They will learn fascinating things and meet fascinating people. They will also, as one of my colleagues recently pointed out, be able to tell the experts something they don't know about the Constitution.

Do nonjudicial officers continue to take as significant a part in constitutional interpretation as they did during the period I have so far studied? Ask me in ten years, when I have read further. I suspect they will have. For they have the same incentives as they had in the past. Not only do they continue to swear to uphold the Constitution, which it seems fair to assume most of them usually try to do; constitutional arguments continue to help them attain the political results they want in the legislative or judicial process—and even, in some cases at least, achieve reelection.

Does that mean the courts should defer to extrajudicial construction when called upon to interpret the Constitution? I think not. As *Marbury* reminds us, no one is likely to be a truly impartial judge of the extent of his own authority. Judicial deference to constitutional interpretations by other branches weakens the essential judicial brake on executive and legislative action. Nor is it only those constitutional provisions the Justices think most important that the courts ought to enforce;[53] I agree with Justice Black that they ought to enforce them all.[54]

That does not necessarily imply that Congress is free to ignore Supreme Court decisions limiting its power, as Abraham Lincoln seemed to suggest in his celebrated threat to seek reenactment of the Missouri Compromise ban on slavery in certain territories after the Supreme Court had struck it down. It is one thing for Congress or the president to reinforce the judicial check on unconstitutional legislation by providing supplementary checks of their own; it is quite another thing, though not necessarily an illegitimate thing in all cases, for Congress to challenge the Court to change its mind as to previously enunciated limits on legislative authority.[55]

As Mitchell Pickerill demonstrates elsewhere in this book, Congress on occasion has attempted to do more or less what Lincoln suggested. Two prominent recent examples include congressional efforts to reverse the decisions in *Employment Division v. Smith*[56] and *Miranda v. Arizona*.[57] In each case the Court struck down the resulting statute.[58] Whatever one may think of the constitutional controversies involved in those decisions, it seems to me the Court was quite right in considering itself not bound by Congress's determination: the argument that Congress must interpret the Constitution for itself demonstrates that the Court must do so too.

At the same time, however, even these recent incidents confirm that the courts are not the sole legitimate source of learning about the Constitution. Congress and the executive have an independent obligation to conform their conduct to constitutional demands, and in the exercise of that responsibility both have contributed amply to our understanding of the fundamental law.

This book is ample evidence that scholars increasingly recognize the significance of the role of Congress and executive officers in constitutional interpretation. We study the extrajudicial materials; we write about them; we increasingly work them into our courses; we analyze the role of Congress and the executive from points of view theoretical and practical, historical and political, legal and philosophical. It should be clear by now, if it was not clear before, that it is often impossible to discuss constitutional questions adequately without considering the legislative and executive materials.

NOTES

1   See David P. Currie, *The Constitution in Congress: The Federalist Period, 1789–1801* (Chicago: University of Chicago Press, 1997); *The Constitution in Congress: The Jeffersonians, 1801–1829* (Chicago: University of Chicago Press, 2001); *The Constitution in Congress: Democrats and Whigs, 1829–1845* (forthcoming); *The Constitution in Congress: Descent into the Maelstrom, 1845–1861* (forthcoming).

2 5 U.S. 137, 180 (1803).

3 See Currie, *The Federalist Period*, 120 n.27. Contrast the second President Roosevelt's untenable suggestion that in considering one of his proposed New Deal measures Congress should "not permit doubts as to constitutionality, however reasonable, to block the suggested legislation." Franklin D. Roosevelt to Rep. Samuel D. Hill, 6 July 1935, *The Public Papers and Addresses of Franklin D. Roosevelt*, ed. Samuel Irving Rosenman, vol. 4 (New York: Random House, 1938), 297-98.

4 See Jefferson's letter to Abigail Adams, 11 September 1804, *The Writings of Thomas Jefferson*, ed. Paul Leicester Ford, vol. 8 (New York: Putnam, 1897), 310-11 (explaining his pardon, on constitutional grounds, of persons convicted under the Sedition Act), and Jackson's veto message of 10 July 1832, in *A Compilation of Messages and Papers of the Presidents, 1789-1897*, ed. James D. Richardson, vol. 2 (Washington: U.S. Congress, 1900), 576, 582-83 (explaining his veto, largely on constitutional grounds, of a bill to extend the charter of the second Bank of the United States).

5 See Currie, *The Federalist Period*, ix, 4, 80, 116-22, 133.

6 These controversies are detailed in Currie, *The Federalist Period*.

7 Currie, *Democrats and Whigs*, chap. 2; see David P. Currie, "His Accidency," 5 *Green Bag* 2d 151 (2002).

8 This oversight in the Constitution was not corrected until the Twenty-fifth Amendment was adopted in 1967.

9 See McCulloch v. Maryland, 17 U.S. 316 (1819); Currie, *The Federalist Period*, 78-80.

10 See Currie, *The Federalist Period*, 250-53.

11 Currie, *Descent into the Maelstrom*, chap. 1; see George H. Haynes, *The Senate of the United States: Its History and Practice*, vol. 2 (New York: Russell & Russell, 1960), 670-71.

12 Goldwater v. Carter, 444 U.S. 996 (1979). The Court of Appeals had upheld the President's authority. 617 F.2d 697 (D.C. Cir. 1979).

13 See Currie, *The Federalist Period*, 84; Currie, *The Jeffersonians*, 123-30, 191-95; Currie, *Descent into the Maelstrom*, chap. 2. Other early examples are discussed in Currie, *The Jeffersonians*, chap. 7, and Currie, *Descent into the Maelstrom*, chap. 3.

14 See Currie, *The Federalist Period*, 288-91; Currie, *The Jeffersonians*, 23-38, 71-75, 77-82, 133-37; Currie, *Democrats and Whigs*, chaps. 6-9.

15 Cf. David P. Currie, "The Most Insignificant Justice: A Preliminary Inquiry," 50 *University of Chicago Law Review* 466 (1983).

16 See Currie, *The Federalist Period*, 13-15, 170-71.

17 See *id.* at 69-70; Currie, *Democrats and Whigs*, chap. 1.

18 See Currie, *The Federalist Period*, 260-62.

19 Comparable materials are available for the short-lived Confederate States of

America, and they afford a looking-glass view of the U.S. Constitution without northern ideas. For my examination of these materials see David P. Currie, "Through the Looking-Glass: The Confederate Constitution in Congress, 1861–1865," 90 *Virginia Law Review* 1257 (2004).

20   Charles Francis Adams, ed., *Memoirs of John Quincy Adams* (Philadelphia: Lippincott, 1874); Milo M. Quaife, ed., *The Diary of James K. Polk during His Presidency* (Chicago: McClurg, 1910).

21   Webster to Henry Lytton Bulwer, 5 July 1851, *The Papers of Daniel Webster*, series 3, Diplomatic Papers, ed. Kenneth E. Shewmaker (Hanover, N.H.: University Press of New England, 1987), 332; Webster to Luther Severance, 14 July 1851, *id.* at 277.

22   Dwight L. Dumond, *Southern Editorials on Secession* (New York: Century, 1931); Howard C. Perkins, ed., *Northern Editorials on Secession* (New York: Appleton, 1942).

23   Thomas P. Abernethy, *The Burr Conspiracy* (New York: Oxford University Press, 1954); Elizabeth B. Monroe, *The Wheeling Bridge Case: Its Significance in American Law and Technology* (Boston: Northeastern University Press, 1992); Arthur M. Mowry, *The Dorr War; or, The Constitutional Struggle in Rhode Island* (Providence, R.I.: Preston & Rounds, 1901).

24   "What is history? A nail on which to hang my novels."

25   See Currie, *The Jeffersonians*, 295–301.

26   Currie, *Democrats and Whigs*, chap. 6; see David P. Currie, "President Harrison and the Hatch Act," 6 *Green Bag* 2d 7 (2002).

27   Currie, *Descent into the Maelstrom*, chap. 2.

28   On the eve of the War of 1812, Congress approved a constitutional amendment removing citizenship from anyone who "shall accept, claim, receive, or retain any title of nobility or honour, or shall, without the consent of Congress, accept and retain any present, pension, office, or emolument of any kind whatever, from any emperor, king, prince or foreign power." See Currie, *The Jeffersonians*, 333–35.

29   Currie, *Descent into the Maelstrom*, chap. 7.

30   Currie, *Democrats and Whigs*, chap. 3.

31   See Currie, *The Federalist Period*, 62.

32   Currie, *Descent into the Maelstrom*, chap. 6.

33   Currie, *The Federalist Period*, 288–91; Currie, *Democrats and Whigs*, chap. 9.

34   *Id.*, chap. 8.

35   Currie, *Descent into the Maelstrom*, chap. 7.

36   Currie, *The Jeffersonians*, 37–38.

37   74 U.S. 700, 724–25.

38   As Jefferson Davis would later point out, the Framers might have thought the new Union "more perfect" in any number of ways, from the inclusion of

new legislative powers to the ability to enforce its own laws. The new Constitution, as Davis further observed, did not repeat the word "perpetual," which had not been understood to prevent "secession" of those states electing to ratify the new arrangement pursuant to Article VII. Jefferson Davis, *The Rise and Fall of the Confederate Government*, vol. 1 (1881; New York: Yoseloff, 1958), 119, 169, 194.

39 Buchanan's Annual Message to Congress, 5 December 1860, Richardson, *Papers of the Presidents*, vol. 5, 626, 631–34.

40 U.S. Const., Amend. x; see *Congressional Globe*, 36th Cong., 2d sess. (1861), 215 (Sen. Judah Benjamin of Louisiana); *id.* at 308 (Sen. Jefferson Davis of Mississippi).

41 See *id.* at 309, 487 (Sen. Davis). The same answer can be given to Representative Bingham's additional arguments (*Congressional Globe*, 36th Cong., 2d sess. (1861), appendix 82) that secession denied citizens of other states the privileges and immunities of citizens (Art. IV, § 2) and that Article I, § 10, denied to the states many of the powers that they would need for independence: Both provisions apply only so long as a state remains in the Union.

42 The reference is to Jackson's message to Congress, 16 January 1833, Richardson, *Papers of the Presidents*, vol. 2, 610, 617–18.

43 One early commentator thought it obvious that the drafters of that amendment were thinking "only of the powers of local government . . . and the civil rights of the citizens," not of disunion. John W. Burgess, *The Civil War and the Constitution*, vol. 1 (New York: Scribner's, 1901). He cited nothing in support of this view, and (apart from the distinct argument developed below) it seems less obvious to me.

44 *Congressional Globe*, 36th Cong., 2d sess. (1861), 118–19, 135–37.

45 *Id.* at 212–15, also quoting the Virginia and Kentucky Resolutions and concluding that they supported his case.

46 *Congressional Globe*, 36th Cong., 2d sess. (1861), 224–26. Benjamin had quoted from a speech of John Quincy Adams to show that even that high-church nationalist had acknowledged the right to secede, *id.* at 215, but Baker quoted additional passages to prove that Adams spoke only of the extralegal right to revolution. *Id.* at 225. Baker too conceded that right, but in an illuminating colloquy in which he chewed Benjamin into little pieces he demonstrated to the satisfaction of any modern observer that South Carolina had no such intolerable grievance as had justified previous revolutions, including our own. *Id.* at 227–29.

47 See *id.* at 464 (Sen. Mason, offering a resolution to suspend the operation of certain federal laws in seceding states and saying that he had no doubt of the right of a state to secede).

48 See *id.* at 212–13, 226.

49 These passages are found in Max Farrand, ed., *The Records of the Fed-*

eral Convention of 1787, rev. ed., vol. 2 (New Haven: Yale University Press, 1966); Simmons quoted them at *Congressional Globe*, 36th Cong., 2d sess. (1861), 404–5.

50   *Id.* at 405.

51   Currie, *Descent into the Maelstrom*, chap. 7.

52   As Jefferson Davis tells us, Daniel Webster in a moment of weakness in 1851 suggested that if the North failed to live up to the constitutional "compact," the South would be absolved from its duties. Davis, *The Rise and Fall of the Confederate Government*, vol. 1, 167, quoting Webster's Speech at Capon Springs, Va., 28 June 1851, reprinted in George T. Curtis, *Life of Daniel Webster*, 4th ed., vol. 2 (New York: Appleton, 1872), 512, 518–19. That was not what Webster had argued in 1832 (Currie, *Democrats and Whigs*, chap. 4); Webster himself promptly disclaimed any intention of espousing a constitutional (as contrasted with a revolutionary) right of secession (see his letter of 1 August 1851 to an unidentified citizen of North Carolina in Curtis, *Daniel Webster*, vol. 2, 520–21); and in any event what Madison said in the Convention in 1787 is more probative of the Framers' intentions than what Webster said more than half a century later.

53   United States v. Carolene Products Co., 304 U.S. 144, 152 n. 4 (1938).

54   See David P. Currie, "The New Deal Court in the 1940's: Its Constitutional Legacy," 1997 *Journal of Supreme Court History* 87.

55   See Lincoln's Speech at Chicago, 10 July 1858, *Created Equal? The Complete Lincoln-Douglas Debates of 1858*, ed. Paul M. Angle (Chicago: University of Chicago Press, 1958), 26, 36–37; the qualifications that he had stated in his earlier speech at Springfield, 26 June 1857, *The Collected Works of Abraham Lincoln*, ed. Roy P. Basler, vol. 2 (New Brunswick, N.J.: Rutgers University Press, 1953), 398, 400–402; and the thoughtful treatment by Herbert Wechsler in "The Courts and the Constitution," 65 *Columbia Law Review* 1001, 1008–9 (1965).

56   494 U.S. 872 (1990).

57   384 U.S. 436 (1966).

58   City of Boerne v. Flores, 521 U.S. 507 (1997); Dickerson v. United States, 530 U.S. 428 (2000). Compare the effort of the Senate in 1807 to override Chief Justice Marshall's narrow interpretation of the constitutional definition of treason, which the House scotched after arguments that Congress had no business prohibiting what the court had said it could not. See Currie, *The Jeffersonians*, 137–42.

Congressional Attitudes toward Constitutional Interpretation

∾

BRUCE G. PEABODY

For those interested in the relationship between Congress and the Constitution and, more specifically, the suitability and feasibility of greater legislative participation in constitutional lawmaking, current scholarship largely overlooks vital questions about lawmakers' subjective understanding of our supreme law. What exogenous and institutional factors are plausible influences on Congress's perception of both its responsibility and capacity to interpret the Constitution? Is Congress, for example, more inclined to engage constitutional issues when it is confronting particular policy areas or salient interbranch conflict? What background and political affiliations may incline individual legislators to surface and to press constitutional questions in committee and floor activity?

By examining attitudes in the 86th (1959–61) and 106th (1999–2001) Congresses, and the political contexts in which these views were formed, this chapter explores the nature and authority of specifically congressional constitutional analysis. Among other issues, it considers how members' conceptions of their role as interpreters are likely related to particular factors at the institutional and individual levels, such as Congress's evolving relationships with the other federal branches, the partisanship of a particular Congress or member, and the nature of the different public issues that lawmakers confront. In addition, this chapter reflects upon how various institutional resources and structures may shape the way members act upon their understandings of their constitutional responsibilities.

I begin this inquiry by constructing a theoretical typology of how members of Congress view congressional constitutional interpretation vis-à-vis the judiciary. I test the strength of this attitudinal model and the hypotheses to which it gives rise against two pieces of research—the first based on 203 questionnaires returned to the political scientist Donald Morgan from the 86th Congress in 1959,[1] and an original data set of survey responses (modeled on Morgan's research) from eighty legislators in the 106th Congress, obtained from 1999 to 2000. These two sets of surveys suggest that Congress expresses a persistent and surprising interest in asserting a distinctive constitutional voice, although it has somewhat conflicted and underdeveloped views about how to achieve this aspiration. While this chapter identifies significant political barriers to fostering a consistent and forceful congressional presence in constitutional affairs, it also suggests institutional organizations and strategies that may be promising bases for promoting this goal.

A preliminary caveat is in order. Statistically speaking, neither Morgan's nor my sample of congressional attitudes is necessarily representative of the overall population of Congress. For "small" populations, the appropriate sample size is approximately fifty percent of the overall population. Therefore, for the U.S. Congress ($n = 535$) a researcher would need responses from 224 members to produce a ± 5 margin of error at a ninety-five percent confidence rate. Technically, therefore, the survey research upon which this chapter is based does not lend itself to making confident statistical generalizations about the U.S. Congress. No superior, substitute data are available, however, and, while they are not strictly reliable as statistical measures, there are reasons to think that both Morgan's sample and the responses to my survey are somewhat representative of the overall population of Congress. In both projects, the professional, regional, and partisan backgrounds of the sampled respondents mirror those found in the Congresses as a whole, and at least in the contemporary survey, the backgrounds of nonrespondents did not significantly differ from those responding—alleviating one of the major sources of potential error in survey research.[2]

MAPPING CONGRESSIONAL ATTITUDES TOWARD CONSTITUTIONAL INTERPRETATION

As a prelude to advancing and then testing claims about what attitudes toward constitutional interpretation are likely to prevail in Congress, we might first map the conceivable range of stances that legislators can assume. I offer a continuum of views that lawmakers can hold toward both the enterprise of constitutional analysis and the authority of the courts, bounded by independent and deferential poles.

At one extreme we can identify an *independent* approach, not only rejecting judicial claims to supremacy over constitutional questions but even rejecting judicial review, the historic power of courts to invalidate what they view as unconstitutional political activity. More accommodating but still independent-minded legislators might support one of two basic versions of how to share with judges the authority to interpret the Constitution. Under a *coordinate* conception, Congress and the courts would have an equal and parallel responsibility to interpret the Constitution in the performance of their institutional duties, pursuant to their common commitment to upholding the Constitution as supreme law. In this view neither branch could insist upon the adherence of the other to its constitutional positions. Alternatively, a *separation-of-powers* approach holds that each branch has heightened interpretive authority corresponding to its distinctive constitutional prerogatives, governing responsibilities, and institutional capacities. Under this view, a branch of government owes greater deference to the others when interpreting the Constitution outside the areas of political life with which it is historically and institutionally affiliated.

Moving toward the more deferential end of the spectrum of potential legislative attitudes, we can delineate positions supporting a substantial interpretive role for members of Congress while still affirming the judiciary's authority to render ultimate constitutional judgment. Variants of this generally *subordinate* stance might hold that Congress can only engage constitutional questions when the courts invite supplementary interpretation, or when the judiciary reliably absents itself from particular areas of political life or policy—whether because of custom or announced practices such as the "political questions doctrine."[3] Finally, lawmakers might assume a *judicial exclusivity* position, holding that the judiciary alone has the power to apply the Constitution to politics. At best, these members of Congress would attempt to act for the courts, invoking past judicial decisions or trying to anticipate likely judicial resolutions of unfolding constitutional issues. On the whole, however, we can expect that most members supporting judicial exclusivity would eschew examining constitutional questions out of fear that they would encroach on what they perceive as a specifically judicial function.

While these categories help to establish a rough taxonomy of the attitudes that members of Congress could assume toward constitutional interpretation, what views will members actually express? To begin with, we might anticipate that modern legislators, generally speaking, would tend to adopt deferential views—recognizing the power of the judiciary to decide questions about constitutional meaning. In the context of what appears to be enduring, widespread, and diffuse popular support for the Supreme Court and the judiciary,[4] we should be somewhat surprised to find Congress adopting positions that might encroach upon judicial authority and even judicial supremacy, the doctrine that the federal courts possess ultimate authority over constitutional questions. Moreover, granting the courts' power over constitutional questions often serves legislative interests by allowing lawmakers to cede divisive, volatile political issues to another branch.[5] Given these observations, we might expect legislative support for judicial supremacy to be fairly commonplace, and open advocacy for the more independent approaches toward congressional interpretation to be rare. We should also expect overt resistance to judicial, and especially Supreme Court, rulings on constitutional matters to be relatively infrequent.

Notwithstanding these observations, we should not anticipate attitudinal uniformity in Congress. The diverse backgrounds, perspectives, and concerns of lawmakers suggest variation in legislative reactions to judicial review and judicial supremacy. Depending upon the ideological tilt of the judiciary's constitutional decisions, for example, we might expect a partisan dimension in congressional views about congressional interpretation. On the whole, when facing a conservative judiciary, Democrats should be more likely to express independent positions than Republicans, who would presumably be more deferential.

Among those legislators who did adopt more independent attitudes, we would also expect more innovative approaches to constitutional analysis, less dependent upon traditional court-centered modalities and categories, and exhibiting a greater willingness to confront unfavorable constitutional decisions handed down by judges. Independent constitutional thinkers in Congress should be more willing than others to look beyond strictly legal interpretive techniques and resources—among other reasons, to highlight what different concerns legislators bring to the interpretive process. We should also expect these independents to seek a wider array of institutional tools and advisors in developing their constitutional positions, and in considering whether and how to counter judicial decisions that they oppose.

Finally, we might speculate that members of Congress, whether generally favoring deferential or independent attitudes, would express the greatest interest in constitutional issues likely to affect their constituents' or their institutional interests directly, such as constitutional questions related to the scope of congressional authority or the balance of power between the legislative and executive branches. As a corollary to this observation, we should expect that when members of Congress did engage constitutional matters, they would turn to politically sensitive and "local" resources such as personal staff, committees, or colleagues. These resources "close to home" are more likely to assist legislators in securing their electoral and institutional interests than more legalistic and endogenous sources of assistance (such as private lawyers or legal experts in the executive branch).

CONSTITUTIONAL INTERPRETATION AND THE 86TH CONGRESS

How are these various suppositions vindicated or brought into question by what we actually find in Congress? In 1959 Donald Morgan submitted a questionnaire entitled "The Role of Congress in Constitutional Interpretation" to all members of the 86th Congress. In addition to asking biographical and background information, Morgan's questions sought information on three general topics. His questionnaires asked about (1) how legislators perceived their and judges' roles in confronting constitutional issues; (2) the factors that shaped members' approach to constitutional questions; and (3) the prominence of constitutional concerns in legislative activity. From 534 surveys that Morgan distributed, he received 203 replies, a 38 percent rate of return.

The results from the 86th Congress both support and challenge this chapter's initial hypotheses about the likely attitudes of legislators toward constitutional interpretation. Morgan's respondents were not especially inclined to defer to judicial constitutional analysis. Morgan reported that by a "two-to-one majority . . . members favored a positive role for Congress," refusing to defer to the courts on constitutional matters.[6] He concedes, however, that these views were varied, concealing a range of stronger and weaker attitudes about the extent to which Congress possessed independent authority to engage constitutional questions. Some of Morgan's legislators who expressed a taste for interpretive autonomy actually favored a fairly cautious role—with a number indicating support for congressional interpretation only when the constitutional issues were "clear," and others suggesting that judicial interpretation should generally be preferred to legislative constitutional analysis.

Still, the high rate of independent attitudes captured by Morgan is notable and somewhat contrary to initial expectations. Given the perhaps surprising proportion of respondents expressing interest in autonomous congressional interpretation, one might wonder whether Morgan oversampled legislators who held this view. But as noted earlier, Morgan's survey returns were otherwise quite representative of the Congress as a whole—his sample was "sufficiently large and well distributed to suggest typical [congressional] attitudes" toward constitutional interpretation.[7] In addition, it is not obvious why legislators skeptical about deferring to the courts would have a greater incentive to respond to Morgan's study than those defending judicial review and judicial supremacy.

Consistent with my earlier discussion, Morgan's research revealed diversity in the attitudes of members of Congress toward constitutional interpretation and judicial authority, in part reflecting their varied backgrounds. Overall, the survey revealed a clustering of responses pointing to two basic attitudes regarding Congress's appropriate role in constitutional interpretation. One group, consisting of what we might call "independent constitutionalists," apparently believed that Congress possessed its own institutional responsibility to surface, reflect upon, and address constitutional questions. These members endorsed the following constellation of views: (1) Congress should not pass constitutional questions along to the courts; (2) congressional examination of constitutional issues was conscientious and genuine (and not a cover for what Morgan identified as "political maneuvers"); and (3) discussions of the Constitution in Congress significantly affected committee and floor votes.

Morgan identified a second group of respondents who appeared to share particular attitudes about constitutional interpretation and the courts. These "deferential constitutionalists" possessed a much more jaundiced, skeptical view of congressional constitutional analysis. They were inclined to cede constitutional issues to the courts, were dubious about members' motives in discussing the Constitution, and expressed doubts about the influence of these debates on voting.

Morgan observed that these two congressional groups possessed distinct political, professional, and regional backgrounds. Senators and lawyers tended to fall into the independent constitutionalist camp, while deferential constitutionalists were typically House members and nonlawyers.

Midwesterners and Southerners supported propositions associated with independent constitutionalism, while members from the Middle Atlantic states generally advocated deferential attitudes toward the courts and their constitutional analysis.

The distinctive makeup of the 86th Congress and the political context surrounding it help us understand some of these results. During this period a number of legislators, especially Southerners and conservatives, famously opposed the Warren Court's early civil rights and civil liberties holdings—such as the *Brown* decisions of 1954 and 1955, *Cooper v. Aaron* (1958), and a raft of opinions affirming due process protections for communists and other so-called subversives (including four high-profile rulings handed down on "Red Monday" in June 1957). Indeed, the 86th Congress contained many of the same legislators who in the prior congressional term had introduced measures seeking, among other sanctions, to impeach Court justices, repeal judicial restrictions on Congress's investigation and contempt powers, and restrict the jurisdiction of the Court in controversial constitutional areas. This hostility to Warren Court decisions is captured by Morgan's survey: 94 percent of the southern respondents indicated their unwillingness to pass constitutional questions to the Supreme Court, and many of their responses included additional written comments expressing displeasure with trends in the Court's decision making.[8]

Morgan's research conformed with this chapter's initial expectations in suggesting that legislators were especially inclined to scrutinize certain categories of constitutional issues close to their core political concerns. Nearly 40 percent of those surveyed in 1959 identified "federal-state" relations as a constitutional topic to which Congress should pay special attention. This result likely reflected both members' general recognition of the importance of state issues to their constituents and, more specifically, the intensity of federalism concerns amid the redistricting and civil rights battles of the 1950s. Almost a third of the respondents also expressed keen interest in separation-of-powers disputes and individual rights. Relatively few survey responses pointed to foreign relations or "nonjusticiable" questions as worthy of special legislative scrutiny, no doubt reflecting, in part, constituents' lack of interest in these topics.

Finally, and again supporting my early speculation, Morgan's research revealed that legislators sought advice on constitutional issues from a variety of sources, demonstrating the greatest preference for advisors within Congress and therefore for those most likely to be sympathetic to lawmakers' particular interests and goals. Members identified committees, colleagues, and the Legislative Reference Service (renamed the Congressional Research Service, or CRS, in 1970), as the three most reliable sources of information on constitutional questions—entities and individuals likely to keep Congress's institutional and political concerns in mind.

CONTINUITY AND CHANGE IN CONGRESSIONAL INTERPRETATION

Because of numerous developments within and around the U.S. Congress since 1959, we might well anticipate that contemporary attitudes about congressional interpretation would differ substantially from those captured by Morgan's study. Congressional reforms in the 1970s (including, for example, efforts to shift power away from committee chairs and provide new mechanisms for confronting the "imperial presidency"), new electoral and institutional pressures (such as the rise of constituents' expectations and the emergence of the "permanent campaign"), and altered, often hostile, relations with the presidency, are all plausible influences on Congress's formation and enforcement of its constitutional understandings.[9] Obviously, just as with our assessment of Morgan's research on the 86th Congress, we also need to consider more proximate and perhaps Congress-specific factors that may affect how legislators from the 106th assess their role in constitutional interpretation.

I submitted an updated version of Morgan's study to the members of the 106th Congress, from the summer of 1999 through 2000. My resulting survey sample was based on returns from two groups of respondents. The first group consisted of those who responded after two mailings were sent to the entire membership of the 106th Congress. The second group of returns was obtained from a random sample of one hundred members of Congress whose offices received multiple mailings, telephone calls, and e-mail messages in an effort to obtain their responses. The second mailing was accompanied by a "Dear Colleague" letter asking for participation in the study and signed by Senators Arlen Specter (R-Pa.) and Carl Levin (D-Mich.). For this study, I decided to combine these two sample groups, both to increase my total number of respondents and to obtain a pool of respondents that appeared more representative of the 106th Congress as a whole (in terms of background and characteristics) than either of the disaggregated samples would have been. Despite my efforts to secure responses, a number of congressional offices indicated that it was their policy not to complete questionnaires of any kind, hardly a surprising result in light of the extensive contemporary demands on legislators' schedules.

What attitudes about constitutional interpretation and the courts should we expect from the 106th Congress specifically? Given the backdrop of the recently concluded impeachment process against President Bill Clinton and ongoing, combative relations between the Clinton White House and the Republican-controlled Congress, we might anticipate that constitutional issues would be fairly prominent in legislators' minds. In addition, important Court decisions in the 1990s invalidating federal initiatives and barring private legal action on federalism grounds provide a basis for thinking that constitutional questions about state and federal power and the role of the judiciary in constitutional interpretation would be of heightened legislative interest.

Table 1 summarizes the findings from the 1959 and 1999–2000 surveys. Comparing the two sets of survey returns reveals considerable consistency in members' attitudes over time. Just as in Morgan's prior survey, over 60 percent of contemporary respondents refused to cede constitutional questions to the courts, holding instead that Congress should "form its own considered judgment" on these issues. A southern senator's comment on one of the 1999–2000 surveys seems to reflect a widespread attitude among members of both the 86th and the 106th Congresses: "Members of Congress have a separate duty of fidelity to the Constitution and therefore should not defer all constitutional judgments to the courts" (Q73).

At the same time, a majority of respondents in both surveys thought that judges should give little deference to the constitutional views of members of Congress—indicating that the courts should give "no weight" or "limited weight" to legislative perspectives on constitutional issues. In keeping with Morgan's earlier findings, and my general expectations about the legislature, members of the 106th Congress also appeared most interested in constitutional issues related to federalism, separation of powers, individual rights, and more specific concerns of their constituents. Just as in the past, the constitutional implications of foreign affairs and nonjusticiable questions did not seem to hold lawmakers' attention.

Finally, and again like their predecessors, today's members claim to rely heavily on sources of advice within Congress itself, including colleagues, committees, and respected institutions like the CRS. On a number of measures, then, congressional attitudes toward constitutional interpretation and the courts look relatively stable over the past forty years.

But this continuity is only part of the story. In 1959 Congress could be

TABLE I *(all figures in percent)*

Category/variable	Morgan, 1959 (*n* = 203)	Combined survey, 1999–2000 (*n* = 80)
Question 1 (frequency with which constitutional questions occur?)		
Rarely/never	14	6.3
Occasionally	60	52.5
Frequently	26	40
Question 2 (should Congress defer to Court?)		
Yes	31	20
No	68	62.5
No Opinion		10.0
Both		1.3
Depends		5
Question 3 (constitutional questions raised in Congress are bona fide or political?)		
Bona fide	50	58.8
Political	28	27.5
No Opinion	7	8.8
Both	15	3.8
Question 4 (do constitutional discussions impact voting?)		
Yes	62	53.8
No	31	35.0
No Opinion		8.8
Both		1.3
Depends		1.3
Question 5 (how much should courts weigh congressional interpretation?)		
No weight	16	13.8
Limited weight	40	57.5
Controlling	40	13.8
Great deal	4	13.8

Category/variable	Morgan, 1959 (n = 203)	Combined survey, 1999–2000 (n = 80)
Question 6 (any questions to which Congress should pay special attention?)		
Foreign relations	10	2.5
Federal-state	38	28.8
Separation of powers	32	20
Individual rights	32	21.3
Nonjusticiable questions	8	2.5
All of the above		6.3
Other		18.8

Because of missing values, figures may not add to 100.

said to be composed of two groups: independent constitutionalists and deferential constitutionalists. Today we find a somewhat different distribution of attitudes (table 2). Members of Congress continue to express a variety of views regarding the roles of the courts and Congress in interpreting the Constitution, but the clustering of contemporary survey responses associated with "deferential constitutionalism" (a group favoring deference to the courts, and doubting the motivations behind congressional constitutional interpretation as well as its influence) has become more difficult to identify. Only 20 percent of those surveyed in 1999–2000 expressed a preference for deferring constitutional issues to the courts, and of these, a majority believed that Congress's efforts to wrestle with constitutional questions were bona fide (contrasting them with the earlier group who favored deference while asserting that congressional interpretation was largely political posturing).

In addition to this development, the relatively large, seemingly cohesive set of independent constitutionalists observable in 1959 appears to have been replaced with a slightly different group, representing about a third of the total contemporary sample. Just as in the past, a plurality of respondents today favors independent congressional analysis of constitutional questions while holding that Congress examines constitutional questions in a bona fide way. In contrast with previous attitudes, however, this group of contemporary legislators does not think that conscientious congressional interpretation should automatically be given special weight by judges. Instead, this new group of "joint constitutionalists" seems to hold the view that Congress and the courts should each interpret the Constitution conscientiously and independently, without necessarily deferring to the views of the other.

Other changes between the 1959 and contemporary surveys are more subtle. As noted, today's congressional survey respondents continue to give a small, and apparently decreasing, amount of their attention to constitutional questions in the area of foreign affairs, instead placing greater emphasis on federalism, individual rights, the separation of powers, and areas of special interest to their constituents (see table 1). However, a smaller percentage of those surveyed in 1999–2000 identified particular constitutional areas as requiring special congressional scrutiny, with the exception of constituent-specific concerns. Generic survey responses and individual written comments suggest that many respondents believed local and electorally salient matters such as "gun control," "federal-state-native American tribe relations," "civil rights," and the "sep[aration] of church and state" were the constitutional topics requiring the greatest legislative scrutiny.

Members of Congress today appear more inclined to seek help, especially "local" help, in wrestling with constitutional issues (see table 2). For example, the percentage of survey respondents who indicated that they looked to personal staff for constitutional advice doubled from 1959 to 1999–2000.

Contemporary lawmakers' generally decreased identification of constitutional areas of special interest may well reflect the more hectic pace of contemporary political life. The relentless demands of constituents, lobbyists, and campaigns are likely to crowd out or at least diminish the amount of time that lawmakers devote to reflecting on constitutional affairs. As one southwestern senator noted in responding to the contemporary survey, "Members of Congress have less time than judges to consider all [the constitutional] ramifications" of their work (Q43). The contemporary survey's failure to detect any obvious relationship between house affiliation and specific attitudes about congressional interpretation is a result that differs from Morgan's earlier research, but it is consistent with scholarship depicting an elision of differences between the House and Senate over the course of the twentieth century.[10]

A seemingly more curious observation generated by the 1999–2000 surveys is their inability to evince a clear relationship between partisanship

TABLE 2 *(all figures in percent)*

Category/variable	Morgan, 1959 (*n* = 203)	Combined survey, 1999–2000 (*n* = 80)	Combined survey, 1999–2000: respondents favoring deference (*n* = 16)	Combined survey, 1999–2000: respondents favoring independence (*n* = 49)
Question 7 (on whom do you rely for help with constitutional issues?)				
Other members	47	41.3	25	46.9
Own staff	33	66.3	50	71.4
Committee	52	55	56.3	53.1
Office of Legislative Counsel (respondent's chamber)	34	15	18.8	16.3
*House General Counsel		7.5	6.3	10.2
*Senate Legal Counsel		7.5	6.3	8.2
Legislative Research Service / Congressional Research Service	42	62.5	68.8	57.1
*Hearings		18.8	12.5	14.3
Department of Justice / Executive	19	16.3	12.5	14.3
Nongovernmental organization counsel	8	16.3	18.8	12.2
Private firm	7	11.3	6.3	12.2
*Law professor		31.3	18.8	34.7
Other		8.8	6.3	8.2

* Items added from original survey.
Because of multiple responses, figures may not add to 100.

and attitudes about constitutional interpretation. Republicans did not have obviously different attitudes from Democrats on congressional constitutional interpretation. Especially in the context of prominent, conservative criticisms of the judiciary in the 1980s and early 1990s, and executive-legislative disputes about the composition of the judiciary in an era of divided government, we might have expected to find evidence of a partisan dimension to the surveyed attitudes.

Similarly, comparing the 1959 and 1999–2000 surveys yields intriguing, somewhat unexpected results with respect to the connection between legal education and members' attitudes. Returns from Morgan's 1959 questionnaire suggested that lawyers in Congress tended to be committed to independent, congressional constitutional analysis and less willing to turn to the courts for assistance with constitutional questions. My survey, however, reflects few appreciable differences in the attitudes of lawyers and nonlawyers in this regard (see table 3).

In contrast, the contemporary study may point to distinctive views associated with members' participation on different committees. Legislators sitting on the Senate and House judiciary committees appeared more likely than others to believe that constitutional questions came up "rarely or never," and more inclined to indicate that these issues were surfaced strictly for "political" rather than "bona fide" reasons (table 3). Judiciary committee members also expressed greater skepticism than their colleagues about the impact of constitutional discussions on voting, although they were uniformly unwilling to defer to the courts on constitutional matters. While this combination of attitudes is somewhat difficult to account for (one might anticipate that those sitting on judiciary committees would exaggerate the salience of constitutional issues, for example), the contemporary survey may reflect judiciary members' sense of their particular responsibility to engage constitutional questions, as well as deep misgivings about Congress's general capacity to address these issues.[11]

ATTITUDINAL PUZZLES IN THE 106TH CONGRESS

Despite yielding a number of anticipated or at least explicable results, my survey of legislative attitudes also points to a number of puzzles that defy a ready explanation. To begin with, we need to revisit the question of why both legislative surveys reflect persistent and perhaps even growing support for autonomous congressional constitutional interpretation despite what seems to be general popular and political support for judicial authority to review constitutional questions. One possible explanation is simply that for both the 86th and 106th Congresses, specific high-profile issues (civil rights and civil liberties in the first case, and impeachment and separation-of-powers struggles in the other) heightened lawmakers'

TABLE 3 *(all figures in percent)*

Category/variable	Lawyers, 1999–2000 (n = 37)	Nonlawyers, 1999–2000 (n = 42)	Judiciary Committee Members, 1999–2000 (n = 6)	Non–Judiciary Committee Members, 1999–2000 (n = 48)
Question 1 (how frequently do constitutional questions occur?)				
Rarely or never	8.1	4.8	16.7	8.3
Occasionally	48.6	54.8	33	50
Frequently	40.5	40.5	50	39.6
Question 2 (should Congress defer to Court?)				
Yes	18.9	21.4	0	27.1
No	62.2	64.3	66.7	56.3
No Opinion	16.2	4.8	0	12.5
Both	2.7	0	0	4.2
Depends	0	7	16.7	0
Question 3 (constitutional questions bona fide or political?)				
Bona fide	66.7	52.4	50	50
Political	22.2	33.3	33.3	33.3
No Opinion	8.3	9.5	0	12.5
Both	2.8	4.8	16.7	4.2
Question 4 (do constitutional discussions impact voting?)				
Yes	51.4	54.8	50	43.8
No	37.8	33.3	50	39.6
No opinion	10.8	7.1	0	14.6
Both	0	2.4	0	2.1
Depends	0	2.4	0	0
Question 5 (how much should courts weigh congressional interpretation?)				
No weight	13.9	14.3	16.7	14.6
Limited weight	61.1	54.8	83.3	58.3
Controlling	13.9	14.3	0	14.6
Great deal	11.1	16.7	0	12.5

Because of missing values, figures may not add to 100.

awareness of their role in constitutional affairs. Clearly we need additional research to establish whether the attitudes described in this chapter are idiosyncratic in this way or held more generally.

We might also reconcile the respondents' support for independent constitutional interpretation with widespread popular and even legislative acceptance of the judiciary's interpretive authority by noting that congressional interpretation is compatible with adherence to judicial review and even judicial supremacy. Lawmakers who indicated that Congress should not defer constitutional questions to the courts were only logically prohibited from endorsing "judicial exclusivity," the doctrine that the courts alone have the power to interpret the Constitution. But legislators who seemed to support Congress's interpretive responsibilities did not necessarily challenge the judiciary's authority to decide constitutional questions, even in a hegemonic way. Some surveys likely reflected the position that while Congress was both capable of and authorized to interpret the Constitution, it remained ultimately subordinate to the judiciary's interpretive power. Indeed, as table 4 indicates, a large number of contemporary survey respondents expressed their belief in autonomous, conscientious congressional interpretation, while simultaneously allowing that judges were free to give "limited" or "no weight at all" to congressional construction of the Constitution.

But why would legislators insist upon Congress's role in constitutional affairs while simultaneously recognizing a (perhaps authoritative) judicial power to address constitutional questions? What perceived institutional and individual benefits might flow from adhering to this position?

To begin with, this perspective could reflect a cautious legislative strategy born of bipartisan ambivalence toward the policy record of the modern federal courts. For members somewhat wary of the courts' ideological trajectory, it is institutionally sensible to support the judiciary's general authority to resolve constitutional questions while still leaving Congress with a basis for resisting this power when judges' constitutional judgments venture too far outside legislators' preferences. Both conservatives and liberals in Congress have understandable reasons for supporting judicial review of constitutional issues even while "hedging their bets" by claiming to retain their own interpretive role. Conservatives, for example, would likely favor much of the Rehnquist Court's jurisprudence, while remaining cautious about generally deferring to an institution still associated with the Warren Court decisions of the 1960s. Conversely, liberal legislators might express interest in independent congressional interpretation as a way to

TABLE 4

Position	Deferential Constitutionalists (1959)	Independent Constitutionalists (1959)	Joint Constitutionalists (1999–2000)
Question 2 (deference to courts on constitutional matters?)	yes	no	no
Question 3 (congressional interpretation bona fide or political maneuvers?)	political maneuvers	bona fide	bona fide
Question 4 (floor/committee debates have influence on votes?)	no	yes	
Question 5 (how much weight should courts give to prior congressional interpretation?)	no or little weight	great weight	no or little weight

check the rightward drift of the courts, even while supporting judicial review and holding out hope that in the future the bench would be a force for progressive change.

In addition to this explanation, legislators might embrace congressional interpretation even while supporting judicial authority to interpret the Constitution as a form of what David Mayhew has called "position taking."[12] According to Mayhew, members of Congress frequently take stances on legislative issues without concern for achieving policy outcomes. Understood in this light, some legislators may simultaneously support independent congressional interpretation while not requiring any special judicial deference to this activity out of a sense that only Congress's capacity to speak out on constitutional issues should be preserved. One potential problem with this "position taking" account, however, is that most of the contemporary survey respondents who favored independent congressional and judicial constitutional interpretation also asserted that congressional interpretation was "bona fide" rather than politically motivated.

Finally, contemporary members' concurrent support for congressional and judicial interpretation may reflect their understanding that society will arrive at better political and legal outcomes with the participation of both Congress and the courts in constitutional decision making. A number of survey respondents, for example, indicated that Congress's interpretive power should be understood in the context of a system of checks and balances premised upon active interbranch conflict: just as judges could exercise the power of judicial review to scrutinize the actions of Congress, legislators retained the authority to monitor and even contest the judiciary's constitutional decisions. As one survey respondent offered, independent congressional interpretation is needed "to balance and check [judicial] power" (Q9). In the words of another, "each body should be looking at the Constitution with the reference of protecting its body from infringement by the other two" (Q22).

As a corollary to this point, a number of surveys argued that special benefits stemmed from distinctively congressional as opposed to judicial constitutional interpretation. "Each branch plays a different role, as it should," argued a Republican member of the House. "Congress taking into account public opinion gives an important perspective to the debate" (Q79). Overall, three-quarters of the 1999–2000 respondents indicated that the legislature approached constitutional questions differently from the courts, and 58 percent indicated that it should.

And how did members of the 106th Congress conceptualize the distinctiveness of their constitutional analysis? While numerous respondents simply indicated they brought "political considerations" to their consideration of constitutional questions, many elaborated upon this idea. A common understanding reflected in the survey returns was that while judges approached the Constitution as a legal document, interpreting it in light of traditional judicial norms such as *stare decisis*, members of Congress had a greater responsibility to apply and "assess the real world impact of [constitutional] questions," including policy consequences and likely public reaction. As one respondent argued, "[I]f a member believes a measure is clearly unconstitutional he should oppose it on that basis. [But whether] a measure is unconstitutional is often unclear. In those circumstances it is appropriate to consider whether the measure is good public policy" (Q45). Similarly, members explained that while the judiciary was supposed to be distanced from public opinion and free from electoral pressures, Congress had a responsibility to incorporate popular views in constructing the constitutional text. "[M]embers should reflect their views of the Constitution filtered by the views of their constituents. The courts should be independent of such considerations" (Q74). In emphasizing the explicitly political aspects of legislative constitutional analysis, some survey respondents also indicated their readiness to use constitutional interpretation as a tool for sweeping political change, in contrast to what they saw as judges' more precedent-bound and interstitial approach. According to one House member, the "[j]udge's scope tends to be more limited and members' scope is more political" and expansive. Finally, respondents claimed that while courts were slow to adapt to changing social conditions (given, among other factors, their relative insulation from the public and institutional reactiveness), Congress could be an agent of innovation, ensuring that the Constitution was applied to contemporary social concerns.

Even if one accepts one or several of these explanations for why lawmakers would support both judicial authority on constitutional questions and independent congressional constitutional interpretation, we are still left with a stubborn puzzle. If my readings of congressional attitudes are sound, why haven't we seen a greater incidence of contemporary constitutional debate in areas of political life in which the courts are relatively inactive? In other words, why doesn't the expression of legislative independence captured in the surveys translate into regular pronouncements by Congress of its own constitutional voice, especially where this activity doesn't seem to threaten the authority of the courts? Consider, as just one specific example of the apparent discrepancy between congressional attitudes and performance, the legislature's reaction to President Clinton's deployment of troops in Kosovo in 1999. Despite significant institutional and partisan incentives to act, and the absence of any obvious threat of encroaching upon the judiciary, Congress failed to provide a consistent, coherent constitutional challenge to the president's largely unilateral actions.[13]

While the question is obviously complex and demands more systematic analysis, we might offer two preliminary explanations for the apparent frequent disjuncture between congressional attitudes and observed behavior. First, congressional reticence to act on constitutional questions may reflect what Mark Tushnet has called the problem of the "judicial overhang," that is, the pervasive influence of judicial supremacy, even where the courts are not especially prominent.[14] Even when judges give wide leeway to elected officials—seemingly allowing them to construct their own views of constitutional powers and processes—judicial supremacy may still leave political actors unwilling to engage in constitutional interpretation. Second, and building upon arguments touched upon earlier, we might posit that while lawmakers perhaps want to assume a more forceful presence in constitutional affairs, this aspiration may simply be subordinated to more immediate, pressing political considerations—addressing constituents' needs, fundraising, campaigning, and the like. Again, this explanation would seemingly explain the absence of a significant relationship between specific traits of legislators and their constitutional views. Regardless of their background, most members are likely to feel stretched thin by their proximate electoral and institutional responsibilities. Actively developing congressional interpretation and confronting unfavorable court decisions may simply be forms of political "indulgence" that few members can afford.

Finally, the contemporary survey's failure to suggest a relationship between lawmakers' backgrounds and their attitudes toward constitutional interpretation points to two curious issues that need some explanation. First, as indicated, we might expect partisanship to be linked with attitudes toward congressional constitutional interpretation—with Democrats opposed to a fairly activist and conservative Rehnquist Court and Republicans, conversely, more inclined to defer. As noted, however, members of both parties may be guarded in their assessments of the Court's reliability as an ideological ally, especially given the close vote margins of many of its important decisions. Perhaps just as surprising is the contemporary survey's failure to reveal any obvious connection between lawmakers' legal training and their views about congressional interpretation. One might have thought that members of Congress with legal training would be more inclined to support independent congressional interpretation, a perspective consistent with some of Morgan's findings.[15] But the absence of findings in this regard may point instead to the complexity of the roles and responsibilities assumed by lawyers in Congress. As John Yoo has argued, lawyers in the legislature perceive that they have a "dual" role in both advocating for the institution and its goals while providing restraints on "unwise assertions of constitutional power."[16] Stated somewhat differently, the imprecision of my survey inquiries may subsume nuances in the views of lawmakers, including those with a legal background. Lawyers in Congress may hold the perspective that the legislature's authority and responsibility to engage constitutional questions "modulates in response to the nature of congressional activity."[17] In investigations or oversight of the executive branch, for example, lawyers in Congress are likely to exhibit greater independence and assertiveness on constitutional questions than when considering whether a particular piece of legislation will pass the scrutiny of the courts. These subtleties are unlikely to be captured by the survey questions I employed.

CONGRESSIONAL INTERPRETATION IN THE TWENTY-FIRST CENTURY

A theme recurring in this book, at least implicitly, is that the U.S. Congress can and should cultivate a greater role in constitutional affairs. Assuming that this proposition is normatively defensible, what does this chapter tell us about the prospects of this project in the twenty-first century?

To begin with, it suggests that invigorating congressional interpretation of the Constitution may be more attainable than one might initially think. A majority of congressional respondents in both surveys insisted on their independent responsibilities to assess constitutional questions, and further indicated that members treated these questions conscientiously and with some frequency. While these results obviously need to be absorbed with considerable caution,[18] they suggest at the very least that a significant number of contemporary legislators are open to expanding Congress's role in constitutional interpretation.

At the same time, this chapter implicates a number of significant barriers to achieving this goal. Legislators' varied and sometimes confusing attitudes toward congressional interpretation and the courts, and their reticence to engage constitutional questions in areas where we would expect their involvement are but two reasons to believe that lawmakers are somewhat conflicted and uncertain about how to participate in constitutional decision making.

That said, this chapter provides some clues for how one might foster in Congress greater confidence in its ability to engage in constitutional interpretation. We might begin by noting that the survey data reaffirm the importance of the "electoral connection," even in the context of constitutional matters. Lawmakers appear most likely to heed constitutional issues in political areas closest to their constituents' concerns, including federalism, individual rights, and state- or district-specific matters (table 1). Clearly, Congress's capacities as an independent constitutional interpreter are importantly shaped by public attitudes. To the extent that judicial supremacy, and its potential demerits, become more widely debated in the mainstream of American politics, legislators might begin to articulate and assert their constitutional voices with greater clarity and strength, and with improved prospects for a receptive audience among other political élites as well as the electorate.

A finding closely related to these observations is that members of Congress need to develop a clearer sense of what individual and institutional roles they wish to play in constitutional matters, and the political implications of committing themselves, whether actively or tacitly, to different interpretive positions. Although my research indicates that members are open to contributing to constitutional analysis, they need to have a more vivid sense of what doing so entails, including the political stakes of assuming this responsibility. Lawmakers should also be more fluent with what kinds of political (in)action might reinforce rather than challenge the judiciary's claims to supremacy. Among other implications, these points suggest that scholars and other legislative experts might assist lawmakers in developing their views about both constitutional interpretation and the circumstances in which they would be prepared to advance their constitutional positions even when they are at odds with those of the courts. At a minimum, those interested in energizing Congress's role as a constitutional interpreter might consider preparing guidelines specifying when Congress could expect to engage in constitutional construction without running afoul of the courts, although this tack might implicitly reinforce the judiciary's claim to interpretive supremacy in other circumstances.[19]

This chapter further indicates what existing resources could assist the legislature in developing its interpretive capacities, and gives some hints about whether additional entities or structures may be needed. The surveys suggest that increasing demands on legislators' time over the past four decades have caused them to turn to a greater number and variety of sources in addressing constitutional issues. At the same time, members continue to prefer interpretive experts "close to home" as opposed to those in exogenous organizations such as private law firms or the Department of Justice. Thus, personal staff and committee experts are likely to be especially helpful to lawmakers in forming a clearer sense of when and how Congress can engage constitutional questions, and for all legislators the American Law Division of the Congressional Research Service could be an especially influential guide. Proponents of congressional interpretation might also consider developing additional nonpartisan and Congress-wide (rather than office-based) institutions to help form a more unified, forceful legislative voice, especially in contentious constitutional areas. These unifying efforts would admittedly be difficult in the contemporary congressional environment in which individual electoral pressures sometimes crowd out institutional perspectives.

Finally, this chapter points to the need for congressional leaders to provide guidance and incentives in promoting Congress's profile in constitutional affairs. The diversity of members' attitudes, their reliance on somewhat "local" interpretive resources, and their apparent predilection for constitutional matters of concern to constituents are all factors that hinder the legislature from asserting cogent, consistent constitutional positions over time. New legislative rules and structures—such as committees or subcommittees specifically charged with coordinating and articulating the constitutional views of the legislature—might help to reduce these centrifugal forces.[20]

There is no shortage of prominent recent events that invite a widespread discussion about the appropriate place of constitutional values and constraints in our public life. Many of these controversies, including the conflict with Iraq, the Bush administration's response to the September 11 terrorism attacks, ongoing disputes with the White House about executive privilege and other presidential powers, and the impeachment trial of Bill Clinton, illustrate the centrality of Congress in constitutional affairs. But while the 1959 and 1999–2000 surveys indicate that individual legislators periodically wrestle with the constitutional implications of their work, this chapter further suggests that Congress, researchers, and the citizenry will be well served by thinking more self-consciously and methodically about each governing branch's responsibilities to interpret and apply our preeminent political and legal text.

NOTES

Portions of this research were published in Bruce Peabody, "Congressional Constitutional Interpretation and the Courts: A Preliminary Inquiry into Legislative Attitudes, 1959–2001," *Law and Social Inquiry*. Many thanks to Keith Whittington, Neal Devins, Elana Kagan, David Currie, Bruce Larson, Adam Rappaport, Scott Gant, Mark Miller, and Michael Solimine for their comments on drafts of this chapter, and to Louis Fisher, Marc Hetherington, John Isaacs, Gordon Kerr, Suzy Kerr, Senator Carl Levin, and Senator Arlen Specter for lending support to this project.

1   See Donald G. Morgan, "Project on the Role of Congress in Constitutional Interpretation," unpublished manuscript on file at the Harvard Law School Depository (Cambridge, 1959); Donald G. Morgan, *Congress and the Constitution: A Study in Responsibility* (Cambridge: Belknap Press of Harvard University Press, 1966).

2   See Kenneth Goldstein, "Getting in the Door: Sampling and Completing Elite Interviews," 35 PS: *Political Science and Politics* 669, 670 (December 2002).

3   For a classic expression of this doctrine see Baker v. Carr, 369 U.S. 186 (1962).

4   See, e.g., Herbert M. Kritzer, "Into the Electoral Waters: The Impact of Bush v. Gore on Public Perceptions and Knowledge of the Supreme Court," 85 *Judicature* 32 (2001); Scott E. Gant, "Judicial Supremacy and Nonjudicial Interpretation of the Constitution," 24 *Hastings Constitutional Law Quarterly* 359 (winter 1997); Neal Devins, *Shaping Constitutional Values* (Baltimore: Johns Hopkins University Press, 1996), 10.

5   See Mark Graber, "The Non-Majoritarian Problem: Legislative Deference to the Judiciary," 7 *Studies in American Political Development* 35 (1993).

6   Morgan, *Congress and the Constitution*, 369.

7   *Id.* at 8, see also 366. Unfortunately Morgan does not provide information comparing the respondents and nonrespondents in his survey.

8   *Id.* at 336.

9   See generally Richard L. Hall, *Participation in Congress* (New Haven: Yale University Press, 1996), 21–24; Barbara Sinclair, *Legislators, Leaders, and Lawmaking: The U.S. House of Representatives in the Postreform Era* (Baltimore: Johns Hopkins University Press, 1995); David W. Rohde, *Parties and Leaders in the Postreform House* (Chicago: University of Chicago Press, 1991).

10 See, e.g., Sinclair, *Legislators, Leaders, and Lawmaking*.

11 See, e.g., John C. Yoo, "Lawyers in Congress," in this volume; Mark C. Miller, "Congress and the Constitution: A Tale of Two Committees," 3 *Seton Hall Constitutional Law Journal* 317 (1993).

12 David Mayhew, *Congress: The Electoral Connection* (New Haven: Yale University Press, 1974).

13 See Ryan C. Hendrickson, "War Powers, Bosnia, and the 104th Congress," 113 *Political Science Quarterly* 241 (1998).

14 Mark Tushnet, *Taking the Constitution Away from the Courts* (Princeton: Princeton University Press, 1999), 57–66.

15 Morgan, *Congress and the Constitution*, 361.

16 Yoo, "Lawyers in Congress," 136. While Yoo's focus is on lawyers who work in Congress but are not legislators, many of his arguments would certainly apply to lawmakers with a legal background.

17   *Id*. at 146.

18   In addition to the methodological difficulties already discussed, one should note that members of Congress may express bolder positions in academic surveys than when facing actual opportunities to assert their status as independent constitutional interpreters.

19   Such guidelines might roughly parallel those released in 1995 and updated in 1998 by the former secretary of education Richard Riley, discussing what kinds of religious practices in educational settings were consistent with the Court's First Amendment jurisprudence.

20   Cf. Elizabeth Garrett and Adrian Vermeule, "Institutional Design of a Thayerian Congress," in this volume.

Constitutional Analysis by Congressional Staff Agencies

∽

LOUIS FISHER

Members of Congress have ample resources to help them understand and decide constitutional issues. Many lawmakers come to Congress after acquiring extensive experience on legal matters, and deepen that knowledge with years of committee work. Their personal and committee staff develop expertise on both technical and political levels, while lawmakers have access to experts from the private sector. Interest groups monitor constitutional issues and weigh in with their analyses, all of which are available on Capitol Hill. As for the general capability of Congress to interpret the Constitution, I have debated this publicly with Abner J. Mikva.[1]

In this chapter I focus on the assistance that comes from congressional staff agencies: the Government Accountability Office (formerly General Accounting Office; GAO), Congressional Research Service (CRS), Congressional Budget Office (CBO), Senate Legal Counsel, and House General Counsel. All these agencies have learned how to deal with highly political, partisan issues in a manner that meets the needs of the two rival political parties. The assistance ranges from day-to-day contacts with personal and committee staff to briefings, short and long reports, and testimony before congressional committees.

Federal judges want to know how well Congress considers the constitutionality of legislation. Unfortunately, I must limit my discussion of specific assistance to what congressional staff agencies do *on the record*. Often, as a result of objections that we raise in private meetings or in confidential memos, some legislative ideas do not reach the draft stage, or bills in draft form are not introduced. Other bills are changed substantially because of input from congressional staff. The congressional public record may therefore look barren even though the constitutional issue has been fully explored.

GOVERNMENT ACCOUNTABILITY OFFICE

Congress created the GAO in 1921 to strengthen legislative control over executive agencies. The enabling statute directed the comptroller general, as head of the GAO, to investigate "all matters relating to the receipt, disbursement, and application of public funds," and gave GAO investigators "the right to examine any books, documents, papers, or records" of executive agencies.[2] Lawmakers rely on the GAO to conduct general oversight over the agencies, placing it in close touch with disputes ranging from statutory interpretation to constitutional analysis.

The GAO is by far the largest of the legislative support agencies. After reaching a staffing level of 5,300 by the early 1990s, it was severely cut and lost more than a third of its staff and budget. The current staffing level of about 3,200 includes a very large, experienced group of professionals able to analyze legal and constitutional disputes. This capability exists throughout the GAO, but I will focus primarily on the Office of General Counsel, which has a staff of about 130 lawyers.

Some of the GAO's legal analysis centers on its responsibility for overseeing the Federal Vacancies Reform Act of 1998. Congress has long been frustrated by the practice of the executive branch to circumvent the Senate's confirmation role by temporarily placing people who need to be confirmed in "vacant" executive branch positions. At issue are positions that require presidential appointment and Senate confirmation. By statute, Congress first limited those vacancy assignments to thirty days. When that limit was regularly ignored, Congress increased it to 120 days. Compliance was so poor that Congress in 1998 raised the limit again, to 210 days (although under some circumstances, the employee can remain in the position for somewhat longer).

The statute is sufficiently vague that there is ongoing tension whenever the Justice Department announces new interpretations of what it means. The GAO regularly finds that agencies do not promptly report all vacancies and acting officials to Congress and the GAO. Although the information is required to be reported immediately, delays of four weeks or so are not unusual. Also, acting officials sometimes remain in their positions beyond the 210-day limit.[3] The GAO's effort to oversee the act is time consuming, but without close and ongoing congressional review the statute would soon be a nullity.

Related to these temporary appointments are presidential recess appointments. The Constitution provides that the president "shall have Power to fill up all Vacancies that may happen during the Recess of the Senate, by granting Commissions which shall expire at the End of their next Session." Attorneys general have interpreted "may happen" broadly, encompassing vacancies that "happen to exist" at the time of the recess, including those that occur while the Senate is in session and available to give advice and consent. The word "recess" means more than the final adjournment at the end of a session or a Congress, but generous Justice Department interpretations can open the door to recess appointments during short recesses. To minimize the opportunities for abuse by the executive branch, the GAO monitors this area with great care.

During the mid-1980s, the GAO completed a number of studies on what would soon emerge as the Iran-contra affair. In December 1986 it found that disbursements of economic support funds to Honduras did not violate the International Security and Development Cooperation Act. In a report that same month, however, it identified problems in controlling funds for the Nicaraguan Democratic Resistance (the contras). Congress had made $27 million available for humanitarian assistance to the contras, but a GAO audit disclosed irregularities with false receipts, and also disclosed that some of the funds were used to purchase ammunition and grenades. After the Iran-contra affair became public the next year, the GAO completed a study in June 1988 on the legality of certain U.S. military training exercises in Central America. Although it found that financing some of the exercises with appropriated funds was questionable, it concluded that the use did not constitute a violation of law. In August 1989 the GAO commented on the refusal of the Justice Department to allow the GAO to review compliance by the executive branch with congressional requests for documents related to Iran-contra.[4]

The GAO protects the legislative power of the purse by analyzing the legality of expenditures. Over the years, it has devoted much of its attention to the proper use of the Impoundment Control Act and the reprogramming of funds within appropriations accounts. GAO officials have testified a number of times on the advisability of transferring to the president some form of an "item veto." Proposals in this area range from constitutional amendments to bills on "expedited rescission" and "enhanced rescission."

Whatever the form, the recommendations contemplate a change in the relationship between Congress and the president. Testifying in 1992, the assistant comptroller general Harry S. Havens cautioned that a change in the rescission process "cannot be expected to be a major tool in reducing the deficit." He explained that the rescission proposal at that time would have applied only to discretionary spending in the annual and supplemental appropriations bills, which represented about 37 percent of the year's budget. Factors that "are actually driving the deficit—notably, debt service and health care—involve mandatory spending that cannot be proposed for rescission." Beyond this analysis of the technical impact on the budget, Havens noted that the item veto proposal would represent "a major shift of power from Congress to the President in an area that was reserved to Congress by the Constitution and which has historically been one of clear legislative primacy."[5]

Another proposal that would alter the balance between the executive and legislative branches is a biennial budget, which would require Congress to pass a two-year appropriations bill one year and concentrate on oversight the following year. Many of the states historically adopted biennial budgeting because their legislatures only met every other year. Congress, beginning in 1789, has met every year. Moreover, Susan J. Irving, associate director of budget issues for the GAO, testified in 1997 about the difference between executive-legislative relations at the state level and at the federal level: "By and large, the States give their governors a great deal more power on fiscal matters than the Constitution or the Congress gives the President of the United States."[6]

During the presidency of George W. Bush, the GAO sought documents from the energy task force chaired by Vice President Dick Cheney. The administration claimed that the GAO tried to interfere with the "deliberative process" needed for executive operations, while the GAO insisted that it only wanted "facts" about the "development" and "formulation" of energy policy. The dispute began on 19 April 2001, when Representatives John Dingell and Henry Waxman wrote to Comptroller General David Walker, asking him to determine who served on the task force. Initially the two lawmakers wanted minutes, drafts, notes, logs, diaries, e-mails, voice mails, computer tapes, and other documents, but in subsequent months the GAO backed away from its broad definition of "records" and scaled down the request. Unable to obtain the information, the GAO took the matter to district court, which held that the comptroller general lacked standing to bring the suit. The GAO decided not to appeal. It also announced that in the future it would seek support from at least one full committee with jurisdiction over a records dispute before resorting to litigation.

CONGRESSIONAL RESEARCH SERVICE

The CRS provides analytical support for members of Congress and legislative committees. Whatever disputes develop in Congress, or between Congress and the executive branch, or between Congress and the judiciary, are fair game for CRS analysts. When I came to the CRS in 1970, it had a staff of about 300, but the Legislative Reorganization Act of that year projected a threefold increase to deepen the analytical capacity of CRS. After reaching a level of about 850, in recent years we have stayed around 700. The great bulk of CRS staff are professionals who do their own work with little direct help from a support staff. By this I mean that CRS is a relatively flat organization with few of the hierarchical trappings of other organizations. Staff members collect their own materials and write their own reports. Our studies generally have one name on them, which maximizes accountability, motivation, and clarity. Of course there is a clearance process within a division and at the front office, to assure objectivity and balance, but by placing responsibility on a single analyst we don't have to absorb and reconcile the multiple views involved with a group product.

Most of the constitutional analysis is done by the American Law Division, which has about fifty attorneys and a support staff of twelve. Other CRS divisions, however, are also involved in constitutional disputes. The two principal ones are Government and Finance (my division) and the Foreign Affairs, Defense, and Trade Division. Over my thirty-three years with CRS, I have probably testified more than other CRS analysts on constitutional issues, covering such issues as war powers, executive spending discretion, presidential reorganization authority, the legislative veto, the item veto, Gramm-Rudman-Hollings, executive privilege, executive lobbying, CIA whistle blowing, covert spending, the pocket veto, recess appointments, the balanced budget amendment, and biennial budgeting.

Two of the most prominent members of the American Law Division, with regard to constitutional analysis, are Johnny Killian and Mort Rosenberg. Killian joined CRS in 1963 and Rosenberg arrived in 1972. On any major constitutional collision between Congress and the president, they are likely to be involved. Much of their work is of a confidential nature:

preparing legal memos for congressional offices and legislative committees. Often, however, their memos become part of the public record by being printed in the *Congressional Record*, committee hearings, or committee reports.

Rosenberg's lengthy tenure at the CRS has allowed him to develop an expertise and institutional memory with regard to many executive-legislative disputes, particularly involving congressional oversight, investigative prerogatives, temporary and recess appointment powers, and conflicts about the structure and order of the administrative bureaucracy. His involvement with the Vacancies Act, restructuring of the Department of Energy, and access to Justice Department documents illustrates the breadth of his work. In April 1997 Rosenberg was contacted by a Senate office that was concerned about the Justice Department practice of making temporary appointments to advice and consent positions. The department argued that any agency whose enabling legislation vested functions and authorities in the agency head, and allowed that officer to delegate functions to subordinates, need not follow the limitations placed in the Vacancies Act. His memos, detailing the legislative and administrative history of the statute, concluded that it was still the exclusive vehicle for temporarily filling advice and consent positions at Justice and other executive departments. On the basis of those memos, the senator wrote to Attorney General Janet Reno and objected that her temporary appointments were contrary to law. She rejected the legal position.

Rosenberg worked with several Senators to draft remedial legislation and testified before House and Senate committees.[7] Working with a CRS colleague, Roger Garcia, he demonstrated that nearly 25 percent of advice and consent positions in the executive branch were vacant and were being occupied by acting officials, most of them in noncompliance with the Vacancies Act. When the Senate Governmental Affairs Committee reported out legislation, the committee report made reference to Rosenberg's testimony and writings on the Vacancies Act.[8] The remedial bill became law as part of the Omnibus Consolidated and Emergency Supplemental Appropriations Act (P.L. 105-277).

In 1999 Congress was concerned about the capability of the Department of Energy (DOE) to ensure the security of its nuclear weapons laboratories. The goal was to restructure DOE by establishing a new, semiautonomous agency (the National Nuclear Security Agency, or NNSA) and assigning to a new undersecretary the responsibility for the operations of all department programs related to national security functions. A Senate conferee asked

Rosenberg to review the restructuring proposal to see if it raised any constitutional issues. His memo, concluding that certain officers could only be appointed by the president or the head of the department, prompted changes in the legislation to assure its constitutionality.

A second Senate bill, also designed to establish a separate agency within DOE to administer nuclear security and production activities, required five CRS specialists (including Rosenberg) to analyze the competing proposals.[9] When President Clinton signed the bill, he objected to the semiautonomous nature of the NNSA officers and directed the secretary of energy to assume the duties of the newly created undersecretary. Clinton also indicated that he might not submit a nominee for undersecretary until Congress remedied what he considered legal and constitutional deficiencies.

Responding to a request by the House Armed Services Committee, Rosenberg concluded that Clinton's failure to submit a nomination for undersecretary and to allow a temporary assignee to fill the position for an indefinite period raised serious constitutional questions, and he explained how the concept of dual office holding for an indefinite period deviated from statutory requirements. A special panel of the committee issued a report, citing Rosenberg's memo and concluding that the secretary was not complying with either the letter or spirit of the law. Rosenberg testified at oversight hearings.[10] After several confrontations, the secretary finally retreated from his position on dual office holding and a nominee for undersecretary was submitted and confirmed. To nail down the understanding, Rosenberg worked with Congress to secure the undersecretary's independence by creating a three-year term, a prohibition of dual office holding, for-cause removal protection, and a prohibition of the secretary's use of reorganization authority for NNSA (P.L. 106-398).

Rosenberg has been involved in dozens of disputes concerning congressional access to information in the executive branch. As a recent example, in 2001 the House Committee on Government Reform requested documents related to law enforcement corruption dating back thirty years in the FBI's Boston office. Several people were convicted of murder on the false testimony of informers whom the government wanted to protect as part of undercover operations into organized crime. On 12 December 2001 President Bush asserted a claim of executive privilege over this information. Rosenberg, asked to testify on 6 February 2002,[11] laid out the historical record of congressional access to predecisional, deliberative prosecutorial memoranda, as well as the testimony of trial attorneys, FBI field agents, and other subordinate agency employees regarding the conduct of open and closed cases. After he and other witnesses found the president's claim of executive privilege to be unprecedented, the Justice Department agreed to provide the committee with all relevant Boston FBI documents. This capitulation, Rosenberg concluded, probably had more to do with a recognition of the political realities (unanimous, bipartisan support on the committee) than the force and insight of the historical and legal precedents arrayed against the White House. Also, the president's claim was a public relations disaster because of the scope and egregiousness of the FBI improprieties.[12]

I will describe two of my experiences with constitutional disputes. In 1985 various drafts of the Gramm-Rudman-Hollings bill would have required congressional agencies (either the CBO or the GAO) to carry out what seemed to me to be clearly executive duties. In one of the bills, the directors of the Office of Management and Budget (OMB) and the CBO were jointly charged with estimating total revenues and budget outlays for each fiscal year to determine whether the deficit would exceed the maximum deficit amount assigned for that year, and specifying the percentages by which certain expenditures should be reduced to eliminate the excesses. Upon receipt of their report, the president would issue a "sequestration" order to eliminate the amount of the deficit excess.

The Senate conducted no hearings on the constitutionality of Gramm-Rudman. However, the House Committee on Government Operations held a hearing on 17 October 1985, inviting four people to testify. I joined the comptroller general, Charles Bowsher, the director of OMB, Jim Miller, and the director of the CBO, Rudolph Penner, to discuss the bill, but I was the only one who addressed the constitutional issue. I testified that CBO, because it was part of the legislative branch, could not be given "substantive enforcement responsibilities, as would be the case under Gramm-Rudman."[13] I concluded that *Buckley v. Valeo* (1976) prohibited Congress from imposing substantive and enforcement responsibilities on legislative officers.

That I was the only one to testify on constitutional issues prompted Representative Mike Synar (D-Okla.) to remark to me: "You sit there as the only person whom I can find in this city or anywhere in this country who has done the type of constitutional scrutiny and analysis which is necessary to give any of us assurances that we are not going down a path that may be dangerous."[14] By the time the bill emerged from conference committee, it was decided to authorize the comptroller general to certify the results submitted by CBO and OMB. A three-judge court held that the delegation of certain executive powers to the comptroller general, who functioned as a legislative agent, was unconstitutional, and that ruling was affirmed by the Supreme Court.[15]

A more recent experience involves the CIA whistle-blowing bill. In 1996 the Justice Department issued an eight-page memo objecting to two proposed statutes that might have empowered federal employees to provide information to either House of Congress or to a committee. The Justice memo claimed that a congressional enactment "would be unconstitutional if it were interpreted 'to divest the President of his control over national security information in the Executive Branch by vesting lower-ranking personnel in that Branch with a 'right' to furnish such information to a Member of Congress without receiving official authorization to do so.' "[16] At the request of the Senate Intelligence Committee, I evaluated Justice's position in a ten-page memo.[17] The committee then held two days of hearings in 1998. Professor Peter Raven-Hansen of the George Washington University law school and I appeared on the first day to rebut the department's position that the president has ultimate and unimpeded authority over the collection, retention, and dissemination of national security information. On the second day I testified alongside Randolph Moss, deputy head of the Office of Legal Counsel. Committee members heard our opening remarks and asked questions to crystallize the legal issues. Unlike some congressional hearings, the committee was not divided along partisan lines. Instead, the questions focused on the institutional interests of Congress to obtain information needed from the executive branch. Later that afternoon, the bill that the Justice Department characterized as an unconstitutional invasion of presidential prerogatives was reported out, nineteen to zero.[18] The Senate report said that the administration's "intransigence on this issue compelled the Committee to act."[19] The bill passed the Senate by a vote of ninety-three to one.[20]

The House Select Committee on Intelligence also rejected the administration's claim that the president exercised exclusive control over national security information. I testified before the House committee as well.[21] Like the Senate, the House committee dismissed the assertion that the president, as commander in chief, had "ultimate and unimpeded constitutional authority over national security, or classified, information. Rather, national security is a constitutional responsibility shared by the executive and legislative branches that proceeds according to the principles of practices of comity."[22] The two committees reported and enacted legislation with this language: "national security is a shared responsibility, requiring joint

efforts and mutual respect by Congress and the President." The statute fur-
·ther provides that Congress, "as a co-equal branch of Government, is empowered by the Constitution to serve as a check on the executive branch; in
that capacity, it has 'a need to know' of allegations of wrongdoing within
the executive branch, including allegations of wrongdoing in the Intelligence Community."[23]

CONGRESSIONAL BUDGET OFFICE

The CBO was created in 1974, as part of the Congressional Budget and Impoundment Control Act. With a staff of about 220, the CBO devotes most
of its time to making estimates of the cost of bills, revenue estimates, economic forecasts, budget projections, and the policy analysis done by program divisions. However, CBO directors and analysts in the area of budget process often tackle issues that concern the balance between Congress
and the president. They realize that the CBO was established as part of a
broad-gauge effort by Congress to shore up its capabilities in exercising
the constitutional power of the purse.

One of the struggles between the executive and legislative branches has
been over whether to grant to the president some kind of item-veto authority. Like the GAO, the CBO has had a long involvement with this issue.
In hearings in 1992 the CBO director Robert D. Reischauer punctured the
notion that the item veto could offer substantial relief for the string of deficits that had begun in the early 1980s. He testified that the item veto was
"likely to have little effect, either on total spending or on the deficit."[24]
He explained that the item veto would only apply (at that time) to discretionary spending, not to the part of the budget that is growing much more
rapidly (mandatory spending, or entitlements).[25] Moreover, for those who
automatically associated Congress with wasteful, pork-barrel spending, he
noted that in recent history presidents "are not necessarily penurious and
Congress is not necessarily profligate."[26] In eleven of the sixteen years preceding his testimony, he said that Congress had appropriated less in discretionary spending than the president had requested.[27] Testifying in Senate hearings in 1995, Reischauer again counseled against the belief that the
item veto "would be a powerful tool of spending and the deficit. I urge you
to be very skeptical about such claims."[28] Evidence from the states, he said,
suggested that the item veto "has not been used primarily to hold down
overall State spending, but rather it has been used by Governors to substi-

tute their priorities for those of the legislatures."[29] In this way, Reischauer used very straightforward language to warn lawmakers that the result of an item veto would not be primarily less spending in total, but rather more spending where presidents decided money should go.

Another executive-legislative dispute in the budget process area is the proposal for biennial budgeting: voting for two-year appropriations and concentrating on legislative oversight in the off year. In 2000 the CBO director Dan L. Crippen cautioned that a biennial budget cycle "would not come without costs. Members would need to weigh the potential gains from more time for oversight and a more efficient appropriations process against the potential drawback of weakened Congressional control of the budget, less accountable federal agencies, and a budget process that might be less responsive to changing conditions."[30] This position appears in his written statement. During the question period, however, Crippen suggested that the executive branch might lose some leverage from a two-year cycle. The White House had been quite successful in the "budget summits" that were arranged at the end of the year to deal with budget crises: "The executive branch would lose a modicum of power if you made appropriations bills less recurrent, more combined, and only once every two years do you have these end-of-the-year sessions or negotiations."[31]

A third budget reform proposal also implicated the balance between Congress and the president. In 1992 Reischauer testified on the "ramifications of a balanced budget amendment to the Constitution." While conceding that the general goal of a balanced budget was desirable and that economic benefits would flow from greatly reduced deficits, he warned that a strict balanced budget rule would neutralize the automatic stabilizers that help dampen business cycles.[32] He also expressed concern that adherence to a balanced budget from year to year could risk granting to the president extraordinary power over spending levels.[33] Testifying later on the same issue, Reischauer said that a "stand-alone" constitutional amendment for a balanced budget risked "transferring substantial authority over the budget to the executive branch and the judiciary." Presidents might end up with enhanced power to impound appropriated funds, and the courts could become "heavily involved in budgeting if processes and definitions were subject to dispute."[34] When Representative Frank J. Guarini stated his concern that the separation of powers would change so that Congress "would be the lesser of three bodies," Reischauer agreed that this would be "a real danger."[35]

SENATE LEGAL COUNSEL

In the 1960s Congress began to debate the need for in-house counsel to represent the institutional interests of Congress in court. That need was heightened by the decision of the Justice Department, at times, to withdraw its defense of congressional interests being litigated. Finally, as part of the Ethics in Government Act of 1978, Congress created the Senate Legal Counsel. The statute authorized the president pro tempore to appoint the counsel and deputy counsel from among recommendations submitted by the Senate majority and minority leaders. The practice has been for the majority leader to select the counsel and the minority leader the deputy counsel. To the great good fortune of the Senate, the first counsel, Michael Davidson, served in that post over a distinguished career that lasted from 1979 to 1995. When he was replaced in 1995 by Thomas Griffith, Davidson agreed to stay on to the end of year as special counsel to help with the transition. The current Senate legal counsel is Patricia Bryan. The deputy Senate counsel is Morgan Frankel, who joined the office in 1981.

With its small staff, the Office of Senate Legal Counsel has been extraordinarily active in analyzing constitutional issues. It does so in a Senate that operates on a more bipartisan basis than the House and with greater sensitivity to the rights of the minority party. On the floor the Senate acts primarily by unanimous consent motions, which require the majority leader to touch base with colleagues from both parties before reaching a final agreement on how to proceed with a pending bill. Litigation by the Senate legal counsel requires approval from both parties. In striving to provide courts with a sense of the history of Congress, its practices, and its powers, the Senate legal counsel is ably assisted by the Senate historian's office, the Senate Library, and other institutions on Capitol Hill.

Davidson's first appearance as Senate legal counsel before the Supreme Court was in *INS v. Chadha* (1983), in which he defended the constitutionality of the legislative veto. In preparing for oral argument, he asked me to set up a meeting where he could question CRS experts about the various types of legislative vetoes. I brought together a group that could discuss in a sophisticated manner legislative vetoes that covered such areas as trade, immigration, arms sales, war powers, impoundment (deferrals), executive reorganization, and agency regulations. I doubt if anywhere in the country Davidson could have met with specialists who knew their subjects from every possible angle: history, politics, statutes, administrative practice, and case law. An 802-page CRS study on the origin, growth, and functioning of the legislative veto also helped Davidson to write his briefs and prepare for oral argument.[36]

A year after the Court's decision in *Chadha*, Davidson and his staff wrestled with another constitutional issue, this time involving the claim by the Reagan administration that a provision in the Competition in Contracting Act (CICA) of 1984 was unconstitutional and would not be obeyed by executive officials. In effect, the president decided to exercise an item veto. According to the theory developed by the Justice Department, the president was at liberty to implement not the whole of a law but only portions of it. At that point, Representative Jack Brooks intervened by threatening to delete all funds for the Office of Attorney General.[37] That gentle message was not lost on Attorney General Edwin Meese, who ordered agencies to comply with the disputed provision. But the matter headed into court, where the administration suffered a number of defeats at the district and appellate levels.[38] In each case the Senate legal counsel weighed in to defend the statute against the administration's position.

Later in the 1980s the Senate legal counsel was back in court defending such statutes as Gramm-Rudman-Hollings and the independent counsel law.[39] Both of those cases went to the Supreme Court, as did the Line Item Veto Act of 1996, which the Senate legal counsel also defended.[40] Other constitutional issues argued by the Senate legal counsel have included the pocket veto and the Senate's procedure for impeachment.[41] In the pocket veto dispute, Morgan Frankel argued the case before the Supreme Court. When the Senate conducted impeachment trials of District Judges Harry E. Claiborne (1986), Walter L. Nixon Jr. (1989), and Alcee L. Hastings (1989), the Senate legal counsel provided legal assistance to the Impeachment Trial Committee.[42] The Senate became directly involved when Judge Hastings brought a lawsuit against the Senate, requiring the Senate legal counsel to participate to defend the Senate's institutional interests.[43] When the Senate held its impeachment trial for President Bill Clinton, Griffith and Frankel provided legal counsel.

In some cases, the Department of Justice chooses not to defend a challenged statute. Either house of Congress may then decide to participate. For example, Frankel filed an amicus brief to help successfully defend the *qui tam* provisions of the False Claims Act. A company claimed that the provisions giving litigative discretion to private plaintiffs encroached upon the constitutional powers of the executive branch. Interestingly, Justice decided not to participate in this case. A district court held that the provisions did not violate the separation of powers doctrine, did not violate the appointments clause, and did not abrogate the case or controversy limitation of Article III.[44]

Recent cases in which Senate legal counsel have participated include a constitutional challenge to the practice of excluding the District of Columbia from the apportionment of congressional districts. Griffith joined with others in opposing the plaintiffs. A three-judge court held that the District could not be treated as a "state" for purposes of the apportionment of congressional representatives.[45] Patricia Bryan joined with other colleagues from the Senate Legal Counsel office to argue against a claim by Representative Bob Schaffer that the Cost of Living Adjustment (COLA) in a federal statute violated the Twenty-seventh Amendment. The Tenth Circuit held that he lacked standing to bring the suit.[46]

HOUSE GENERAL COUNSEL

Like the Senate, the House of Representatives recognized the need to have in-house counsel to defend the prerogatives of the House in court. Unlike the Senate, however, the House did not rely on a statute to create the office. Instead, Speaker Thomas P. O'Neill in 1979 selected Stanley M. Brand to be the first House general counsel. Officially Brand functioned as counsel to the clerk of the House, but with the speaker's backing he gained an independent status in representing the House's institutional interests in court. By 1983 reporters noted that he had turned "what was once a sleepy office with almost no capacity to litigate into a group of three lawyers who are among the most frequent litigators before the federal courts here."[47] In a case that helped shape the speech or debate clause, Brand argued before the Supreme Court to represent the position of Speaker O'Neill as amicus curiae.[48] Brand was in the thick of the fight over access to documents in the Environmental Protection Agency, leading to a vote by the House holding the administrator of the EPA, Anne Gorsuch Burford, in contempt.[49] Assisting in these cases and others was Brand's deputy counsel, Steven R. Ross.

The House general counsel functions in an institution that is far more partisan than the Senate. House rules make it easier for the majority party to govern. There are no opportunities for members of the minority party to engage in filibusters or defeat unanimous consent motions. Stalling tactics are possible, such as making dilatory motions. However, what the majority party wants to do in the House it does. Some House committees and subcommittees have a tradition of bipartisan cooperation, but floor procedures are dictated by the majority party.

Most of the work of the House General Counsel is bipartisan, with the office dedicated to protecting the institutional interests of the House. Occasionally there are collisions between the two parties. In the early 1980s Republicans objected that the apportionment system used by the Democrats to assign lawmakers to committees provided Republicans with fewer committee seats than they were entitled to receive on the basis of the number of seats they held in the House. The system, they said, violated the Fifth Amendment right to due process, equal protection, and the First Amendment rights of association and free speech. Brand, providing legal counsel for Speaker O'Neill, eventually prevailed in court.[50]

Brand left in October 1983 and was succeeded by Ross, who remained in that position for the next decade. Charles Tiefer, having served as assistant Senate legal counsel from 1979 to 1984, moved to House general counsel and filled the positions of deputy general counsel and solicitor from 1984 to 1995. Brand, Ross, and Tiefer were all active in appearing in court to defend the interests of the House. In *Chadha*, Eugene Gressman was hired to argue the House case before the Supreme Court, with Brand joining him on the briefs. In all the CICA cases (*Lear Siegler* and *Ameron*), the House general counsel participated along with Senate legal counsel. Ross handled oral argument in the Gramm-Rudman case. In *Morrison*, although Davidson participated in oral argument before the Court, the House only filed an amicus brief. The House submitted a brief in the pocket veto case, *Burke v. Barnes*, but did not participate in oral argument.

Both the Senate legal counsel and the House general counsel submitted amicus briefs in defending the Flag Protection Act of 1989.[51] The Department of Justice, following the terms of the statute, wanted to expedite the case so that the Court would decide it before the end of the term. The House general counsel filed a brief requesting additional time. The Republicans objected that the brief was "wholly inconsistent" with statutory language and legislative intent.[52] The brief stated that the two Republican leaders had "declined" to join the Democratic leaders in the brief. However, the House Republican leader, Bob Michel, and the Republican whip, Newt Gingrich, said they had not been informed about the filing of the brief.[53] Michel was successful in having a resolution adopted that required the House general counsel to withdraw the brief. An amended brief recommended no timetable for Court action.[54] Brand, Ross, and Tiefer frequently testified before congressional committees and prepared legal briefs that were made available to the public.[55] The Senate legal counsel office also prepares legal memos, but primarily for internal use, not public consumption. An unusual exception is a Senate legal counsel memo originally intended as a brief in a recess appointment case. Because of Republican opposition to the filing of the brief, the draft memo was printed in the *Congressional Record.*[56]

By the early 1990s the politics of the House had become increasingly bitter, with some Republicans viewing Ross "as another partisan fixture controlling the political and constitutional fortunes of the House as a whole."[57] After Ross left in 1993, Tiefer became the acting House general counsel. On 4 April 1994, Speaker Thomas Foley appointed Thomas J. Spulak House general counsel, and he remained in that position until the end of the year. Tiefer stayed with the office until the spring of 1995. When the Republicans took over the House in 1995, Speaker Newt Gingrich made his own appointments to the House general counsel office. First he turned to Cheryl Lau, a former secretary of state of Nevada who had run unsuccessfully for governor in 1994. She did not have the Capitol Hill experience of Brand, Ross, and Tiefer.[58] After a stint, Lau was replaced by Geraldine R. Gennet, who remains House general counsel today. Kerry Kircher serves as deputy general counsel.

During Gennet's tenure, the House general counsel office has been active across a broad front of constitutional issues. Some of the cases have named the clerk of the House of Representatives as a defendant, including those challenging the constitutionality of COLAs for members of Congress[59] and of a House rule that required a three-fifths majority for legislation increasing federal income taxes.[60] Both cases failed for lack of standing by the members who brought the action. In other cases, the House general counsel office successfully defended the qualified immunity of congressional staff in the course of their committee investigations,[61] the use of the speech or debate clause to protect against the compulsory disclosure of congressional investigative reports,[62] and the First Amendment right of members of Congress to express their views on public policies.[63] House general counsel participated with Senate legal counsel in defeating the lawsuits that challenged the constitutionality of excluding the District of Columbia from representation in Congress.[64]

In a case involving a subpoena served on the House Committee on Energy and Commerce, a district judge granted the motion to quash the subpoena on the grounds stated in the Memorandum of Points and Authorities filed by the House general counsel.[65] This case grew out of the financial collapse of Enron and the effort by the Arthur Andersen firm to subpoena the committee for certain staff notes, memoranda, and other internal work product related to its investigation of Enron, particularly the committee's interview of David B. Duncan, a former Andersen partner. House General Counsel argued that the subpoena had to be quashed because it violated the speech or debate clause.

A recent constitutional issue handled by the House General Counsel is the "Seven Member Rule." In 2001 seventeen Democrats and one Independent in the House invoked a statute, first enacted in 1928, that requires executive agencies to furnish information if requested by seven members of the House Committee on Government Reform or five members of the Senate Committee on Governmental Affairs.[66] The lawmakers wanted census data from the Department of Commerce. After the administration challenged the constitutionality of this statutory provision (§ 2954), a federal district court ruled in favor of the lawmakers.[67] In the appeal to the Ninth Circuit, the House submitted two amicus briefs: one by the Office of General Counsel, the other by the House Democratic leadership. The Office of General Counsel circulated its brief to the leadership of both parties, but the two Democratic leaders decided not to join. The brief argued that executive-legislative struggles over access to information should be left to the political process, not the courts. After warning that a broad reading of § 2954 would conflict with House rules designed to maintain institutional control over the House's investigatory authority, the brief affirmed the right of Congress to obtain executive documents needed for legislative and oversight functions, objected that the Commerce Department construed § 2954 too narrowly, and concluded that executive agencies have an obligation to respond in good faith to legislative requests under the 1928 statute. The two Democratic leaders filed a separate brief, supporting the district court ruling that § 2954 mandates disclosure of the census data to the plaintiffs. This brief also argued that the procedure for holding someone in contempt (requiring action by the full House or Senate) is distinct from statutes that mandate release of executive branch information to Congress. The brief placed § 2954 in the "tradition of statutes mandating the public release of unprivileged Executive information, without resort to contempt powers or processes," and described § 2954—like the Freedom of Information Act—"as a sensible mandatory disclosure statute for documents not subject to executive privilege."

CONCLUSIONS

No one providing constitutional analysis to Congress should have any illusions. We in the congressional staff agencies understand that our voice is one of many, that many minds have been made up and are unlikely to change, and that congressional decisions often turn more on matters of politics, partisanship, and personality than legal analysis. Still, we have the advantage of being well positioned to see that constitutional values are fully and fairly advanced, and of forming contacts with lawmakers and their staff that develop over the years to build bonds of trust and understanding.

Research by congressional staff agencies makes a difference on controversies of great importance to the country. Our efforts, individually and collectively, are part of a process that makes representative democracy work as best it can. Congress is not the easiest branch to defend. It is probably the hardest. Yet without an effective and independent Congress, it would be impossible to talk meaningfully about the rule of law, checks and balances, and constitutional government. The key issue is whether lawmakers are interested in protecting their institutional prerogatives. If they are, congressional staff agencies will make significant contributions. If members do not understand their institution, or do not want to protect it, congressional staff agencies will be largely marginalized.

NOTES

I appreciate suggestions and assistance from Aldo Benejam (GAO general counsel office), Sandy Davis (CBO), Michael Davidson (former Senate legal counsel), deputy Senate legal counsel Morgan Frankel, House general counsel Geraldine Gennet, Gary Kepplinger (deputy comptroller general), CBO general counsel (and former GAO general counsel) Robert Murphy, Michael Stern (senior counsel, House general counsel office), and Charles Tiefer, formerly with Senate legal counsel and House general counsel. The views expressed here, of course, are mine.

1   Abner J. Mikva, "How Well Does Congress Support and Defend the Constitution?," 61 *North Carolina Law Review* 587 (1983); Louis Fisher, "Constitutional Interpretation by Members of Congress," 63 *North Carolina Law Review* 707 (1985).

2   42 Stat. 25, § 312(a), and 26, § 313 (1921); 31 U.S.C. § 712 (2002).

3   General Accounting Office, letter from General Counsel Anthony H. Gamboa to Senator Tom Harkin, Chairman, Committee on Agriculture, Nutrition, and Forestry, Subject: Violation of the 210-Day Limit Imposed by the Vacancies Reform Act, 18 March 2002, B-289367; General Accounting Office, *Presidential Appointments: Agencies' Compliance With Provisions of the Federal Vacancies Reform Act of 1998*, May 2001, GAO-01-701.

4   This paragraph is based on summaries in GAO's database: No. 131994 (2 December 1986, study on disbursements of economic support funds to Honduras); No. 131728 (5 December 1986, study on controlling funds to the Nicaraguan Democratic Resistance); No. 542492 (17 June 1988, study on U.S. military activities in Central America); and No. 139293 (9 August 1989, study on GAO authority to review executive branch compliance with congressional requests for documents related to the Iran-contra affair).

5   House Committee on Rules, *Legislative Line-Item Veto Proposals: Hearings before the House Committee on Rules*, 102d Cong., 2d sess., 15 September 1992, 274.

6   Senate Committee on Government Affairs, *S. 261: Biennial Budgeting and Appropriations Act: Hearing before the Senate Committee on Governmental Affairs*, 105th Cong., 1st sess., 23 April 1997, 28.

7   Subcommittee on the Constitution, House Committee on the Judiciary, *Oversight of Civil Rights Division of the U.S. Department of Justice: Hearing before the Subcommittee on the Constitution, House Committee on the Judiciary*, 105th Cong., 2d sess., 25 February 1998, 46–55; Senate Committee on Governmental Affairs, *Oversight of the Implementation of the Vacancies Act: Hearing before the Senate Committee on Governmental Affairs*, 105th Cong., 2d sess., 18 March 1998, 40–44, 62–115, 170–79.

8   Senate Committee on Governmental Affairs, *Federal Vacancies Act of 1998*, 105th Cong., 2d sess., 23 Feb. 1998, S. Rept. 105-250, 9–10.

9   The CRS memo was quoted extensively during Senate debate on the conference report; *Cong. Rec.*, 106th Cong., 1st sess., daily ed. 21 September 1999, 145, nos. 122–123, S11113–15; *Cong. Rec.*, 106th Cong., 1st sess., daily ed. 22 September 1999, 145, no. 124, S11190–91.

10 Special Oversight Panel on the Department of Energy Reorganization, House Committee on Armed Services, *National Nuclear Security Administration: Hearing before the Special Oversight Panel on the Department of Energy Reorganization, House Committee on Armed Services*, 106th Cong., 2d sess., 2 March 2000, 16 March 2000, 6–10, 50–75, 173–76, 213–14.

11 House Committee on Government Reform, *Investigation into Allegations of Justice Department Misconduct in New England*, vol. 1, *Hearings before the House Committee on Government Reform*, 107th Cong., 1st and 2d sess., 6 February 2002, 562–604.

12 Vanessa Blum, "White House Caves on Privilege Claim: DOJ Turns Over Prosecutorial Memos to House Committee," *Legal Times*, 18 March 2002, 1; Fox Butterfield, "FBI Covered Up for Boston Mobsters, Lawsuits Assert," *New York Times*, 31 May 2002, § A, p. 15; Fox Butterfield, "Ex-FBI Agent Sentenced for Helping Mob Leaders," *New York Times*, 17 September 2002, 18.

13 House Committee on Government Operations, *Balanced Budget and Emergency Deficit Control Act of 1985: Hearing before the House Committee on Government Operations*, 99th Cong., 1st sess., 17 October 1985, 200, see also 198–200, 207–12.

14 *Id.* at 221.

15 Bowsher v. Synar, 478 U.S. 714 (1986).

16 Memorandum for Michael J. O'Neil, general counsel, Central Intelligence Agency, from Christopher H. Schroeder, acting assistant attorney general, Office of Legal Counsel, 26 November 1996, 2–3, quoting language in a Justice brief in *American Foreign Serv. Assoc. v. Garfinkel*.

17 Most of that memo is reproduced in my prepared statement, printed in Senate Select Committee on Intelligence, *Disclosure of Classified Information to Congress: Hearings before the Senate Select Committee on Intelligence*, 105th Cong., 2d sess., 4 February 1998, 5–13.

18 Senate Select Committee on Intelligence, *Disclosure to Congress Act of 1998*, 105th Cong., 2d sess., 23 February 1998, S. Rept. 105-165, 2.

19 *Id.* at 5.

20 *Cong. Rec.*, 105th Cong., 2d sess., daily ed. 9 March 1998, 144, no. 23, S1561–64 (daily ed. 9 March 1998).

21 House Permanent Select Committee on Intelligence, *Record of Proceedings on H.R. 3829, the Intelligence Community Whistleblower Protection Act: Hearings before the House Permanent Select Committee on Intelligence*, 106th Cong., 1st sess., 20 May 1998, 32–53.

22 House Select Committee on Intelligence, *Intelligence Community Whistleblower Protection Act of 1998*, 105th Cong., 2d sess., 1998, H. Rept. 105-747, part 1, 15.

23 112 Stat. 2413, § 701 (b) (1998); see House Select Committee on Intelligence, *Intelligence Authorization Act for FY99*, 105th Cong., 2d sess., 1998, H. Rept. 105-780, 19; Thomas Newcomb, "In From the Cold: The Intelligence Community Whistleblower Protection Act of 1998," 53 *Administrative Law Review* 1235 (2001).

24 House Committee on Rules, *Legislative Line-Item Veto Proposals: Hearings*

before the House Committee on Rules, 102d Cong., 2d sess., 25 September 1992, 257.

25 *Id.* at 258.

26 *Id.*

27 *Id.*

28 House Committee on Government Reform and Oversight and Senate Committee on Governmental Affairs, *Line-Item Veto: Joint Hearing before the House Committee on Government Reform and Oversight and the Senate Committee on Governmental Affairs*, 104th Cong., 1st sess., 12 January 1995, 62.

29 *Id.*

30 House Committee on Rules, *Biennial Budgeting: Hearing before the House Committee on Rules*, 106th Cong., 2d sess., 10 March 2000, 147.

31 *Id.* at 152.

32 House Committee on the Budget, *The Balanced Budget Amendment*, vol. 1, *Hearings before the House Committee on the Budget*, 102d Cong., 2d sess., 6 May 1992, 151.

33 *Id.* at 167–68.

34 House Committee on the Budget, *The Balanced Budget Amendment*, vol. 2, *Hearings before the House Committee on the Budget*, 102d Cong., 2d sess., 3 June 1992, 481.

35 *Id.* at 490.

36 "Studies on the Legislative Veto," prepared by the Congressional Research Service for the House Committee on Rules, 96th Cong., 2d sess. (Comm. Print, February 1980).

37 Subsection "Funds Cutoff Threatened" in "11 Legal Services Board Nominees Win Approval of Senate Committee," *Washington Post*, 9 May 1985, § A, p. 17.

38 Lear Siegler, Inc., Energy Products Div. v. Lehman, 842 F.2d 1102 (9th Cir. 1988); Ameron, Inc. v. United States Army Corps of Engineers, 809 F.2d 979 (3d Cir. 1986); Ameron, Inc. v. U.S. Army Corps of Engineers, 787 F.2d 875 (3d Cir. 1986); Ameron, Inc. v. U.S. Army Corps of Engineers, 610 F.Supp. 750 (D. N.J. 1985); Ameron, Inc. v. U.S. Army Corps of Engineers, 607 F.Supp. 962 (D. N.J. 1985).

39 Bowsher v. Synar, 478 U.S. 714 (1986); Morrison v. Olson, 487 U.S. 654 (1988).

40 Raines v. Byrd, 521 U.S. 811 (1997). The Senate legal counsel and the House general counsel filed a joint amicus brief. Michael Davidson, as a private citizen, joined a brief with Charles J. Cooper, Lloyd Cutler, and Alan Morrison in defending the position of Senator Robert C. Byrd.

41 Burke v. Barnes, 479 U.S. 361 (1987); Nixon v. United States, 506 U.S. 224 (1993). In *Nixon*, Senate legal counsel joined with the government's brief in defending the Senate's impeachment procedure. See Charles Tiefer, "The

Senate and House Counsel Offices: Dilemmas of Representing in Court the Institutional Congressional Client," 61 *Law & Contemporary Problems* 47, 53–55 (spring 1998).

42 Rebecca Mae Salokar, "Legal Counsel for Congress: Protecting Institutional Interests," 20 *Congress and the Presidency* 131, 143–44 (1993).

43 Hastings v. U.S. Senate, 887 F.2d 332 (D.C. Cir. 1989); Hastings v. U.S. Senate, Impeachment Trial Com., 716 F.Supp. 38 (D.D.C. 1989).

44 United States ex rel. Stillwell v. Hughes Helicopters, Inc., 714 F.Supp. 1084 (D. Cal. 1989).

45 Adams v. Clinton, 90 F.Supp.2d 35 (D.D.C. 2000) (three-judge court), aff'd, 531 U.S. 941 (2000). In a separate case, a district judge held that residents of the District of Columbia lacked standing to bring an action against Senate officers for denying their right to vote for representation in the Senate; Adams v. Clinton, 90 F.Supp.2d 27 (D.D.C. 2000).

46 Schaffer v. Clinton, 240 F.3d 878 (10th Cir. 2001).

47 David Lauter, "As Chief Lawyer for the House, Stanley Brand Is Making His Mark," *National Law Journal*, 16 May 1983, 44.

48 United States v. Helstoski, 442 U.S. 477 (1979). Brand also argued before the Court in Helstoski v. Meanor, 442 U.S. 500 (1979).

49 United States v. House of Representatives of United States, 556 F.Supp. 150 (D.D.C. 1983).

50 Vander Jagt v. O'Neill, 699 F.2d 1166 (D.C. 1983).

51 United States v. Eichman, 496 U.S. 310 (1990).

52 *Cong. Rec.*, 101st Cong., 2d sess., 22 March 1990, 136, pt. 4:4998.

53 *Id.*

54 *Cong. Rec.*, 101st Cong., 2d sess., 22 March 1990, 136, pt. 4:5005–6; *C.Q. Weekly Report*, 24 March 1990, 923.

55 E.g., memo from Ross and Tiefer to the House Committee on Asian and Pacific Affairs, 11 December 1985, on whether compliance with a ruling of the subcommittee chairman is "voluntary." *Cong. Rec.*, 99th Cong., 1st sess., 27 February 1986, 132, pt. 3:3038.

56 *Cong. Rec.*, 103d Cong., 1st sess., 1 July 1993, 139, pt. 11:15267–74.

57 Terence Moran, "House Counsel Feels the Heat," *Legal Times*, 9 June 1992, 1.

58 Daniel Klaidman, "From Hill Outsider to House In-Houser," *Legal Times*, 16 January 1995, 1.

59 Schaffer v. Clinton, 240 F.3d 878 (10th Cir. 2001).

60 Skaggs v. Carle, 110 F.3d 831 (D.C. Cir. 1997).

61 Popovic v. United States, 997 F.Supp. 672 (D. Md. 1998).

62 Pentagen Technologies v. Comm. on Appropriations, 20 F.Supp.2d 41 (D.D.C. 1998).

63 X-Men Sec., Inc. v. Pataki, 196 F.3d 56 (2d Cir. 1999).

64 Adams v. Clinton, 90 F.Supp.2d 35 (D.D.C. 2000) (three-judge court), aff'd, 531 U.S. 941 (2000); Adams v. Clinton, 90 F.Supp.2d 27 (D.D.C. 2000).

65 United States v. Arthur Andersen, Crim. No. H-02-121 (MH) (D. Tex. 2002).

66 45 Stat. 996, § 2 (1928), codified at 5 U.S.C. § 2954 (2000).

67 Waxman v. Evans, CV 01-4530 LGB (AJWx) (D. Cal. 2002).

Hearing about the Constitution in Congressional Committees

KEITH E. WHITTINGTON

Much of the important work of Congress is done in committees. It has always been this way. Although many issues in the early Congress were debated on the chamber floor in the "committee of the whole," ad hoc select committees were appointed to work out the details of legislation. Standing committees with stable membership and jurisdiction over routine legislative subjects were soon established and multiplied, though the Senate was initially more resistant to the growth of the committee system than was the larger House of Representatives. By the early twentieth century, the House had nearly sixty standing committees and the Senate even more, though many of these committees lacked substantial business. Though the number of committees was soon pared back, their importance only increased. The observation of a young Woodrow Wilson remains largely true today: "The House sits, not for serious discussion, but to sanction the conclusions of its Committees as rapidly as possible. It legislates in its committee-rooms; . . . so that it is not far from the truth to say that Congress in session is Congress on public exhibition, whilst Congress in its committee-rooms is Congress at work." Congress "both deliberates and legislates" in committee.[1]

Congressional committees are nonetheless largely uncharted territory for constitutional scholars. The new scholarly interest in extrajudicial constitutional interpretation has been more likely to focus on floor debates or committee activities of extraordinary interest, such as the hearings of the Senate Judiciary Committee on the nomination of Robert Bork to the Supreme Court, than on the congressional committee system generally and its routine work. If committees are the primary sites in which Congress both deliberates and legislates, however, an adequate picture of congressional efforts to interpret and implement the Constitution will have to take into account the normal work of the committees.

This chapter lays the groundwork for such further exploration. In particular, it examines congressional committees through the lens of their public hearings. There is no claim that the primary work of committees is done in formal hearings, however. Committee members and staff do much of their work out of the public eye. Hearings do not provide direct access to the investigation and negotiation that ultimately produce legislative action. Hearings are more the product of committee work than the work itself.

Committee hearings are staged events for public consumption, but as such they provide useful information. They are an important platform for members of Congress to take "action in the public sphere."[2] As David Mayhew has recently emphasized, legislators do not only write laws and cast votes. They also strive to win public notice, and in doing so to help shape public opinion and advance favored causes. Senator Joseph McCarthy's interrogation of witnesses before the Senate Permanent Investigation Subcommittee, Representative Barbara Jordan's speech to the House Judiciary Committee on Watergate and presidential impeachment, and the spectacle of tobacco company executives denying that nicotine is addictive before Representative Henry Waxman's House Subcommittee on Health and the Environment were all significant political events, though they did not produce new information. Committee hearings are also an important vehicle by which legislators seek to create a public record. Through hearings, committee members communicate with legislative colleagues, officials in the executive branch, interested activists, and the general public. Moreover, both lobbyists and legislators regard hearings as second in importance only to direct personal communication among interested parties.[3] In hearings, legislators put political relationships and concerns on display and establish the warrants of authority for legislative action. It is not only that hearings are accessible in a way that the informal contacts between legislators and lobbyists are not; they are also part of the public face of Congress and as such are of intrinsic interest. As John Mark Hansen noted, "hearings are often less a forum for gathering information than a ritual for legitimizing decisions."[4] It is precisely within those rituals of legitimization that we may expect the Constitution to be invoked.

This chapter maps congressional encounters with the Constitution in committee hearings in the 1990s. It seeks to identify how often and in what form constitutional issues arise in a significant way in committee hearings, and by implication in Congress. An examination of congressional hearings will help to illuminate the quantity and nature of legislative deliberation on the Constitution. By sampling committee hearings that address constitutional issues, the chapter considers both the extraordinary and the ordinary, placing such prominent episodes of congressional constitutional politics in the 1990s as the impeachment of President Bill Clinton within the context of the more routine legislative business that often escapes scholarly notice. As these hearings indicate, congressional committees, like courts, regularly encounter the Constitution in the course of carrying out their normal responsibilities.

This chapter sheds light on a number of features of constitutional deliberation in Congress. Drawing on a sample of committee hearings from the 1990s in which constitutional issues were discussed, it asks when such hearings were held, by whom, and in which issue areas, and the extent to which they were driven by the action of the other branches of government. The timing of these hearings indicates the importance of elections in driving constitutional discussion in Congress. Though the Judiciary Committees are clearly an important site for constitutional deliberation in Congress, they do not monopolize it. Congress considers a wide range of constitutional topics, giving as much attention to structural matters as to issues of individual rights. The courts may not be as important in spurring Congress into such discussions as is generally thought, while the actions of the executive branch may be more important than is generally thought.

CONGRESSIONAL COMMITTEE HEARINGS

That committee hearings are public makes them a relatively accessible source of information about Congress. That they are largely stage-managed raises questions about how that information can be leveraged so as to gain a useful perspective on the reality of congressional deliberation and lawmaking. Recognizing their importance, political scientists have long studied congressional committees, investigating such issues as who serves on them, how they are organized, and what they do. In recent years, congressional scholars have been particularly interested in the composition of legislative committees, a subject which might allow us to draw inferences about whose interests those committees actually serve.

Various arguments have been put forward in favor of viewing different committees as primarily serving the interests of the committee members themselves, the majority party, or the chamber as a whole. "Constituency" committees, such as Agriculture and Armed Services, may be especially oriented toward distributing goods, such as federal funds, to a set of interests closely tied to them and their members. Certain key "prestige" committees, such as Rules and Appropriations, may be tightly controlled by party leaders to insure that they serve the goals of the majority party. Other "policy" committees, such as Foreign Affairs and Banking, may be more oriented toward developing technical policy expertise that would be broadly useful to the legislature as a whole.[5]

To those who adopt this focus on committee power and interest, public hearings are a sideshow of little relevance that as a consequence have received relatively little attention. Even in this context, however, hearings may provide evidence of systematic differences in attitudes adopted by different committees in pursuing their work. The members of the Judiciary Committees, for example, appear to take a far more deferential and legal-professional approach to the decisions of the federal courts than do the members of other congressional committees, who may be more apt to view the courts as just another competing policymaker.[6] The mere presence or absence of hearings on a given subject can also provide useful information on change in the public agenda and jurisdictional control over issues.[7]

If hearings can tell us little about whether committees primarily serve informational or distributional purposes, they can inform us of other aspects of congressional politics. They have been most often used to provide insight into the relationship between Congress and interest groups. Hansen's study of the farm lobby in the twentieth century made pioneering use of hearings, for "lawmakers are on display in congressional hearings, and their reactions to witnesses yield important clues about their relationships with those witnesses."[8] The inclusion and reception of interest groups in hearings reflect, in public, the measure of access to legislators that these groups enjoy in private. Many scholars examining hearings as a means for understanding interest group activity have focused on the types and number of groups represented as witnesses. The witness lists for public congressional hearings have provided evidence of the enduring importance of organized interests since the end of the nineteenth century.[9] The dynamics of group participation in committee hearings provide evidence on the effects of institutional change within Congress, such as the decentralizing reforms of the early 1970s, as well as partisan turnover, such as the Republican takeover of the House in 1995.[10] The ideological and organizational characteristics of the groups invited to testify can provide information on interest and legislative organization.[11] One finding of particular interest to constitutional scholars is that according to a systematic study of judicial confirmation hearings, organized interests have long played an important role in confirmation politics, but the type of groups prominent in confirmation hearings has shifted over time and been increasingly concentrated in the cases of controversial nominations.[12] Moreover, there is evidence that interest mobilization matters to the voting behavior of senators in judicial confirmations.[13]

The content of the discussions at legislative hearings has also been mined for insight into legislative politics. The methodologies for exploiting the content of hearings have been more diverse than those for examining the participation at hearings. In keeping with Hansen's interest in the degree of legislative access enjoyed by different interest groups, he focused on the quality of the congressional questioning posed to different witnesses, observing that "excluded groups confront hostile questions; irrelevant groups receive no questions; favored groups field softball questions" and that the behavior of legislators in hearings ranges "from contentiousness to attentiveness to solicitousness."[14] Similarly, Paul Peterson and Jay Greene found "the degree of conflict displayed in the questioning of executive branch witnesses testifying before congressional committees and subcommittees" to be a more useful "indicator of interbranch conflict" than legislative voting behavior.[15] Rhetorical analysis of patterns of questioning in hearings has been used to shed light on the relative lack of power of women in the legislative process.[16] Scholars have also analyzed the arguments marshaled by participants in legislative hearings to lay bare the process by which authority is claimed and support is built for particular policy proposals.[17] The examination of confirmation hearings of the Senate Judiciary Committee suggests that senators have used the questioning of nominees to try to influence the future direction of constitutional interpretation by the Supreme Court.[18] Hearings can provide a wealth of information about which issues and people Congress takes seriously.

THE CONSTITUTION IN CONGRESS IN THE 1990S

The 1990s are an especially propitious period for examining congressional engagement with the Constitution. The period includes the impeachment of President Bill Clinton and the associated discussion of the constitutional power of impeachment, as well as the numerous more routine examples of constitutional discourse. In the midterm elections of 1994, the Republican Party captured control of Congress. At the start of the 104th Congress in 1995, the Republicans had been out of power in the House of Representatives for four decades and in the Senate for eight years, and it might be expected that new constitutional issues would rise to the congressional agenda with the change in party control. Moreover, in the 1990s the U.S. Supreme Court began a period of unprecedented constitutional activism, striking down more acts of Congress over the latter part of the decade than any prior Court over a comparable period. This judicial shock to the legislative routine might also be expected to generate a congressional response in the form of increased constitutional discussion.

The data for this chapter are drawn from committee hearings in the U.S. House of Representatives and the U.S. Senate from 1991 to 2001. The Congressional Information Service (CIS) publishes an abstract and witness list for public hearings held by the committees and subcommittees of Congress. CIS also assigns multiple topic keywords to each hearing. Using an online version of the CIS database accessible through Lexis Nexis, I searched for every congressional hearing between 1991 and 2001 containing a variation on the word "constitutional" anywhere in the CIS entry, including the abstract, keywords, hearing title, and witness identifiers. I then examined each entry to exclude those that did not make substantive reference to the U.S. Constitution, such as hearings discussing the constitution of Russia or including constitutional law professors testifying on the assets of Holocaust victims. This left a dataset of 406 congressional hearings.

The dataset is undoubtedly underinclusive of the entire set of hearings that raised constitutional issues during the 1990s. Hearing abstracts and keywords only capture issues that formed a substantial part of the witness testimony. The search procedure would have left out hearings that included relatively brief mentions of constitutional issues. This procedure also depends on CIS coding of hearings, and it is possible that some types of constitutional issues and discussions are not reflected in the CIS entries. Moreover, the CIS employs a large number of keywords that are relevant to constitutionalism. Although the search procedure employed would have picked up a central CIS keyword (such as "constitutional law"), it would not necessarily have picked up others (such as "civil liberties"). Nonetheless, there is substantial overlap in the CIS coding (hearings with the keyword "civil liberties" are often also given the keyword "constitutional law"), and many additional hearings were included based not on the keyword but on terms elsewhere in the CIS entry. In sum, these 406 hearings are a sample of the total universe of hearings raising constitutional issues during the period, but it is a sample that is likely to capture a large proportion of the relevant universe and that is broadly representative of the types of constitutional issues that come before Congress. The discussion in the remainder of this chapter will draw on this dataset.

Timing

Of the 406 hearings, 232 were held in the House, 168 were held in the Senate, and six were held by joint committees. The median number of hearings held per year was thirty-nine, with a high of sixty in 1995 and a low of twenty-three in 2000 and 2001. The number of hearings held in the House exceeds the number held in the Senate in every year except 1994.

There are several notable features to the distribution of these hearings over time. The most obvious is the large number of hearings in 1995, immediately after the Republican takeover of Congress. The number of hearings touching on constitutional issues held in 1995 is more than 60 percent larger than the decade average and over a quarter larger than the next-closest year. Moreover, the majority of those hearings were held in the first quarter of 1995, tailing off over the course of the year. The committee activity over the later months of 1995 is about average for the period as a whole. The House was driving most of the extraordinary activity, while the Senate was merely operating at the top of its normal range. This spike in constitutionally oriented committee hearings clearly reflects the heyday of the "Gingrich revolution." Newt Gingrich's assumption of the speakership was accompanied by a burst of activity, as Republican-controlled committees drew public attention to a number of constitutional issues of general interest to the Republican members and specifically attached to the "Contract with America." The Senate, led by Robert Dole, followed behind. The change of party control did not, however, create a new equilibrium of heightened interest in constitutional issues. In the 1990s the Republican Congress as a whole was no more interested in constitutional issues than the Democratic Congress had been.

Quarterly data also reveal a spike of activity in the late spring of 1992, again mostly driven by the House. Congress held twenty-three hearings on constitutional matters in the second quarter of 1992, only two fewer than were held in the first quarter of 1995. Explanations for this surge of activity are more elusive, however. Whereas the committee activity of 1995

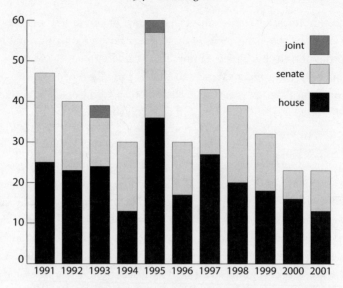

FIGURE I: Congressional Hearings with Constitutional
Discussions, 1991–2001

was clearly the result of a newly empowered majority taking action on its agenda, the activity of 1992 appears to have been designed by the Democratic majority to lay the groundwork for the presidential and congressional elections that year. This hypothesis would be in keeping with the finding that the incidence of presidential vetoes, and presumably of legislation designed to elicit vetoes, increases in presidential election years under divided government, including 1992 when George Bush lost his bid for re-election.[19] Although the hearings late that spring covered a wide ground, they included a number of items that were of particular interest to election-year Democrats, such as hate crimes, access to abortion clinics, statehood for the District of Columbia, and the proposed Balanced Budget Amendment. Having apparently been front-loaded into the late spring and early summer of 1992, hearings on constitutional issues disappeared from the congressional agenda in the late fall and winter. Constitutional discussions in congressional committees appear to reflect not only the positive legislative agenda of new political majorities but also the prospective electoral calculations of incumbent majorities.

The other timing issue of note is the lack of correlation between the aggregate number of congressional hearings and the level of judicial scrutiny of federal statutes. Historically, the Supreme Court has been quite deferential to Congress. Unlike the policies of state and local governments, which over the course of the twentieth century were struck down at a rate of ten per year, the policies of the federal government are rarely struck down on constitutional grounds: just over once per year during the twentieth century. Given this expectation of deference, it would be unsurprising if Congress took the constitutional scruples of the courts seriously into account when considering legislation. Constitutional law has rarely been an active obstacle to federal lawmaking. This situation suddenly changed in the late 1990s. The Supreme Court struck down four federal statutes in 1995 and maintained that pace through the rest of the decade. In the late 1990s the Rehnquist Court launched the most significant and sustained assault on congressional powers since the early New Deal, and in fact it quickly outpaced the record of invalidations of federal statutes set by the Hughes Court in the mid-1930s. These rulings had little aggregate effect on congressional hearings at which constitutional issues were discussed, however. Excluding the hearings in early 1995 brought about by the Gingrich revolution and largely contemporaneous with the Court's new activity, Congress actually held fewer hearings discussing constitutional issues after the Court announced its increased scrutiny of federal legislation than before. Tightening the judicially enforced constitutional constraints on Congress does not appear to have led to more constitutional deliberation in congressional committees.

Activity across Committees

As might be expected, there is substantial variation in which congressional committees encounter the Constitution in the course of their deliberations. Perhaps more surprisingly, constitutional discourse in Congress is not the monopoly of the Judiciary Committees. Without question the judiciary committees generate the bulk of constitutional discussion in Congress, but constitutional issues make an appearance in a wide range of committees and contexts.[20]

The location of hearings on constitutional subjects matters. Constitutional issues, though raised, may receive less attention or attention of a lower quality if heard in committees with little interest or expertise in constitutional issues. More importantly, constitutional issues are likely to be treated differently depending on the interests and attitudes of the committee hearing them. As Frank Baumgartner and Bryan Jones have elaborated, Congress is a "jurisdictional battlefield" with committees competing to claim various issues as their own. The political agenda is constituted in part by which committees dominate an issue. "Policy changes in Congress often come about a result of jurisdictional battles rather than changes of heart by individual legislators," as "advocates of change" find ways to "bypass their opponents."[21] It makes a substantial difference, for example, whether pesticides or tobacco is being discussed in an agriculture committee or a health and environment committee. Similarly, it is possible that a rather different political dynamic would have emerged if congressional hearings on policies concerning homosexuality in the armed forces had been held before the Judiciary Committees rather than the Armed Services Committees. Similarly, just as it would matter if health and environment committees never heard about pesticides, it would matter if committees other than the Judiciary Committees never heard about the Constitution in the course of their deliberations. To the extent that the Constitution is broadly relevant to American governance, it might be hoped that the Constitution would make an appearance before a variety of committees with a variety of policy concerns.

The Judiciary Committee in the House and the Senate each provide a forum for far more constitutional discussion than any other committee does. In the House, hearings held by the Judiciary Committee account for nearly half of all the hearings in the sample. In the Senate, the Judiciary Committee accounts for nearly 60 percent of total activity. In neither chamber does a second committee rival the Judiciary Committee as a central location for constitutional deliberation. Instead, such deliberation is spread across nearly every other committee in each chamber. For many committees, encounters with constitutional issues are quite rare. Over the entire decade, the Senate Intelligence Committee and the House committees on the Merchant Marine; Armed Services; Hunger; and Children, Youth and Families each make only a single appearance in the sample. Others are regularly, though modestly, active in the area. In the Senate, both the Governmental Affairs and Indian Affairs committees held ten or more hearings addressing constitutional matters in the 1990s. In the House, three committees (Resources; Government Reform; and Energy and Commerce) were in the double digits. The median number of hearings held by a House committee in the sample was three, with a median of five hearings in the Senate.

Although the Judiciary Committees can be expected to build up more general expertise in constitutional issues and are clearly more specifically interested in such issues, other committees have issue-specific expertise

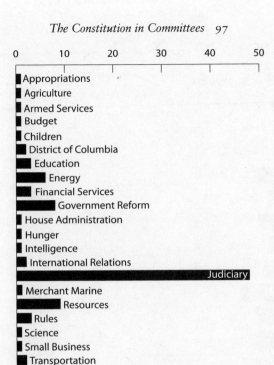

FIGURE 2: Percentage distribution by Committee of Hearings in the House Raising Constitutional Issues, 1991–2001

and subject-area jurisdiction that are surely relevant to serious discussion of some constitutional issues. Even so, the relatively active committees tended to face a range of distinct constitutional issues rather than repeatedly holding hearings raising the same concern. Both the hearings held by the House Administration Committee addressed campaign finance reform, as did three of the five hearings of the Senate Rules and Administration Committee. But those committees are the exceptions. As a consequence of the Supreme Court's decision in *Employment Division v. Smith* (1990), the Senate Indian Affairs Committee was quite busy during the period surveyed, with hearings relating to religious liberty concerns, but even so, religious liberty was raised in only three of the committee's ten hearings in the sample. The House Government Reform Committee, which has nineteen hearings included in the sample, addressed a different constitutional and policy issue in nearly every hearing, discussing everything from free speech in the reauthorization of the National Endowment of the Arts to

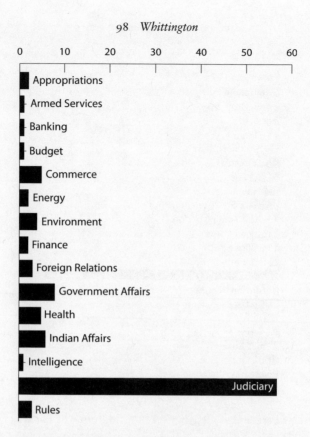

FIGURE 3: Distribution by Committee of Hearings in the Senate
Raising Constitutional Issues, 1991–2001

the separation-of-powers dimension of the first Bush administration's restriction of public access to presidential papers.

The mere fact that constitutional issues are raised in a congressional
committee hearing does not mean that they are raised in a substantial fashion. Constitutional issues may receive minimal consideration in a hearing
oriented toward more direct policy or political concerns. Glancing references to the Constitution are largely excluded from the dataset, as such
references are unlikely to appear in the CIS abstract or keyword coding
of a hearing. Given that baseline, there may still be substantial variation in how centrally focused committee hearings are on constitutional
issues. It seems particularly likely that constitutional considerations raised
outside the confines of the Judiciary Committees would get short shrift.
Ultimately, testing that supposition adequately would require a specific

analysis of the interaction between legislators and witnesses who raise constitutional issues.

An initial cut on the problem can be had by examining how much space at committee hearings is given to witnesses who discuss constitutional matters. The treatment of the subject matter, organization of the panels, and number of relevant witnesses were examined to distinguish between hearings that were centrally concerned with constitutional issues and those that addressed but were not significantly focused on them. A proposal to create a line-item presidential veto, for example, raises intrinsic constitutional issues relating to the separation of powers, but any given hearing on the topic may focus less on the constitutional dimension of such a reform than on its implementation and fiscal consequences, and the testimony may be from governors and budget officials rather than constitutional law professors or scholars from the Congressional Research Service.

Overall, 60 percent of the hearings held in the House and 68 percent of the hearings held in the Senate were centrally concerned with constitutional issues. When constitutional issues are raised in committee hearings, they appear often to occupy a significant place in those hearings. If we focus on this subsample of committee hearings that were centrally concerned with constitutional issues, then the distribution of hearings across committees becomes more concentrated in the Judiciary Committees. The House Judiciary Committee's share of these hearings rises to 63 percent in the subsample, compared to 48 percent in the dataset as a whole. The Senate Judiciary Committee's gain is more modest, rising to 63 percent from the already high 57 percent.

Even so, focused constitutional deliberation occurs in a variety of committees. In the House, twenty-three committees were represented in the dataset as a whole. Of these, seven were above the House average in their proportion of hearings centrally focused on constitutional issues, and together they account for 80 percent of such hearings. Six of the twenty-three House committees drop out of the subsample entirely, having held no hearings that meet this heightened standard of constitutional deliberation. In the Senate, nine of the original fifteen committees were above the chamber average in holding hearings centrally focused on constitutional issues. Committees that held relatively few constitutionally oriented hearings were marginally more likely to minimize constitutional issues in the hearings that they did hold, especially in the House. At the same time, some relatively active committees in the larger sample were substantially less prominent in the subsample, as a significant number of their hearings did not meet the heightened standard of constitutional focus. The House Committees on Resources and on Energy and Commerce together accounted for 15 percent of the larger sample, but fell to half that proportion of the subsample of more constitutionally intensive hearings.

Activity across Subject Matter

These committee hearings addressed a wide range of specific constitutional issues. We might imagine a variety of mechanisms that would tend to draw congressional attention to particular constitutional subjects. Congress and the judiciary might be driven by similar forces to address the same set of constitutional issues (though they might not agree on the same set of outcomes), or the congressional agenda for constitutional deliberation might be largely set by the Court. On the other hand, Congress and the Court might have distinct constitutional agendas, as the two institutions might be driven by different pressures or feel competent to address different issues.

Supreme Court cases typically address a single constitutional issue, since appellate litigation is organized around individual legal questions. By contrast, committee hearings tend to be organized around substantive political problems, and as a consequence they often touch on more than one constitutional issue in a single hearing (though a hearing will rarely give serious treatment to more than two issues). Accordingly, hearings in the sample were coded for up to two distinct constitutional issues. A second subject code was assigned to 31 percent of the hearings. As can be seen in table 1, a significant proportion of constitutional deliberation in Congress comes in a context that is effectively unique to the legislative branch: constitutional amendments. Of the congressional hearings in the sample, 11 percent involved discussions of proposed constitutional amendments. Considering that no amendments were sent to the states for ratification during this period, it is particularly striking that so much of the congressional time spent on constitutional issues was dedicated to changing the Constitution. Amendment proposals were often legislative perennials and the subject of multiple hearings in a session and repeated hearings over time. Particularly prominent proposals during this period included a balanced budget amendment, a flag desecration amendment, and a crime victim's rights amendment, though numerous others received attention, in-

TABLE 1 Distribution of Constitutional Issue Areas in
Congressional Hearings *(all figures in percent)*

Amendment	11
Federalism	13
Separation of powers	11
Structural	19
Rights and liberties	45
Confirmations	2

cluding amendments to alter the Electoral College, impose congressional term limits, and facilitate statehood for the District of Columbia.

Judicial confirmation hearings are another form of constitutional deliberation unique to the legislature. Confirmation hearings are also distinctive in that they range over many issues, in keeping with the broad constitutional jurisdiction of most of the federal courts. Although relatively high-profile and undoubtedly important, they occupy a relatively small share of the sample.

In terms of more specific substance, Congress spent substantial time considering both structural features of the Constitution and various rights and liberties. Federalism issues are largely self-explanatory. Hearings coded as "separation of powers" implicated the relationship of the branches of government to one another or the relative power of the branches of government. These included hearings concerned with the line-item veto, "judicial taxation" (the authority of the federal courts to order remedies that require governments to levy taxes), and the power of the Congressional Review Board to veto the decisions of the Metropolitan Washington Airports Authority. Hearings coded as "structural" addressed other matters relating to constitutional structure and the exercise of government power. These included hearings concerned with the territorial status of the District of Columbia and Puerto Rico, the design and implementation of the census, the extension of the terms of specific patents, and the proposed balanced budget amendment.

"Rights and liberties" is the largest category of subjects considered in committee hearings, and table 2 provides a more detailed breakdown. Free speech received substantial attention in contexts ranging from campaign finance reform to the regulation of pornography to hate crimes to tobacco

TABLE 2 Distribution of Issue Areas within
"Rights and Liberties" *(all figures in percent)*

Civil rights	12
Due process	20
Free speech	26
Liberties	17
Property rights	11
Religious liberty	10
Voting rights	3

advertising. Matters of criminal and civil due process were also extensively considered in both legislative and oversight hearings. Civil rights encompassed the rights associated with membership in disadvantaged groups. Property rights and religious liberty are coded separately, given the political issues that were being raised during the period. The category of "liberties" is a residual for civil liberties issues not otherwise coded: in practice it primarily covered what might be regarded as modern substantive due process, most notably in the realm of privacy.

There are few clear patterns to the distribution of these issue areas across Congress. There were no significant differences in the subjects discussed in the two chambers, with the exception of the Senate's exclusive participation in confirmation hearings. The Judiciary Committees were prominent in every area. The only committee with comparable breadth across subjects was the House Ways and Means Committee, though it was substantially less active. The only areas in which another committee rivaled the Judiciary Committees were property rights and religious liberty. Property rights were the least discussed issue considered by the House Judiciary Committee, and the Resources Committee held a larger proportion of the hearings discussing that issue in the House (at 40 percent of the total) than the Judiciary Committee did. In the Senate, the Indian Affairs Committee held a relatively large share of the hearings addressing religious liberty and property rights—half as many as the Judiciary Committee. Some issues attracted the attention of nearly every committee. Structural issues were the most widely discussed, followed by the separation of powers and (especially in the House) federalism. Matters of rights and liberties tended to be somewhat more concentrated in the Judiciary Committees.

Most issues received fairly steady attention from Congress across time.

Perhaps surprisingly in this regard, there was no appreciable increase during the period surveyed in congressional deliberations over federalism. Though the Rehnquist Court's federalism revival beginning in 1998 may have caused some additional consideration of federalism constraints by Congress, that effect was swamped by the more general attention that Congress gave to the issue throughout the 1990s. Congress clearly was in a dialogue with the Court in the area of religious liberty, which remained a persistent concern throughout the period. Some issues did receive greater attention during particular sessions of Congress. Due process was of greater interest to the 102d Congress (at the beginning of the period) than to later Congresses, though the 102d was relatively uninterested in separation-of-powers questions. The 104th Congress, which followed the 1994 elections, had the most distinctive profile. It gave particular attention to constitutional amendments and civil rights, and continued the momentum from the previous session in the area of property rights.[22] Hearings in all three areas fell off again during the 105th Congress.

Responding to Coordinate Institutions

Do congressional committees voluntarily engage in constitutional deliberation? James Madison recognized the "enterprising ambition" of the legislature, "everywhere extending the sphere of its activity and drawing all power into its impetuous vortex."[23] Though legislatures are enterprising, they are also fundamentally reactive. They are designed to be responsive, especially to constituents. At the same time, however, political entrepreneurs are always looking for opportunities to gain political advantage. That includes legislators, who may be looking for the issue or policy that will win them new electoral support or thrust them into the national spotlight. It would be extraordinarily difficult to establish the causes for congressional hearings of any sort, including those discussing constitutional issues, or to distinguish between hearings that are responding to external actors and events and those that reflect the personal interests of legislators.

It might still be possible, however, to distinguish between committee hearings that are directly responding to the actions of others and those that are not. In evaluating how responsible Congress is as a constitutional interpreter, we may well want to know whether Congress engages in constitutional deliberation on its own initiative or rather is pushed to do so. Likewise, in considering the importance of extrajudicial constitutional interpretation, it would be useful to know whether Congress helps

TABLE 3 Hearings in Response to Actions of
Coordinate Branches *(all figures in percent)*

	House	Senate	Total
Judiciary	13	14	13
Executive	9	7	8

set the constitutional agenda or "merely" acts on the agenda established by others.

Depending on the question of interest, we might define what constitutes a congressional reaction in a variety of ways. As a starting point, the extent to which congressional issues arise in congressional hearings in response to the actions of others is here defined narrowly. In particular, hearings were coded for whether they were explicitly and directly responding to the actions of a coordinate branch of the federal government, either the executive or the courts. Committee hearings were often quite explicit on this point, simply stating that the subject of the hearing was this or that judicial or executive action. Thus in 1997 the Senate Judiciary Committee held hearings on "Congress' Role in Protecting Religious Liberty," evaluating the effects of that year's Supreme Court decision in *Boerne v. Flores*, which overturned the Religious Freedom Restoration Act, and the House Committee on Government Reform held hearings on the Internal Revenue Service's decision that year to suspend portions of its affirmative action program in response to a district court ruling that the program was unconstitutional. Hearings were coded as not being held in response to the actions of other branches if they merely dealt with issues raised by earlier court decisions or with the legal and policy environment created by the judicial doctrine, as was true of hearings on the Unborn Victims of Violence Act and on campaign finance reform.

If congressional constitutional deliberation mostly responds to actions of others, then the judiciary is potentially a natural instigator. We often think of the courts as the primary constitutional interpreter in the American system, and Congress might only hear about the Constitution when the courts force a dialogue, for example by imposing constitutional restrictions on congressional power. The president is a prominent, if more occasional, constitutional interpreter as well, and may initiate constitutional discussions in Congress. Somewhat differently, presidential actions may motivate Congress to turn to the Constitution in order to do battle over institutional prerogatives.

One-fifth of the congressional hearings are accounted for by direct responses to the actions of the coordinate branches. Responses to judicial decisions constituted a larger proportion of those, at 13 percent of all the hearings in the sample, than did responses to executive action, at 8 percent. There was no significant difference between the responses of the two chambers. Hearings in this category were held in a variety of committees, and some committees were particularly unlikely to give serious attention to constitutional issues without outside prodding. Most notably, the Armed Services Committees only considered constitutional issues as the result of executive action, namely President Clinton's executive order on homosexuals in the military and President George W. Bush's executive order on the use of military tribunals to try terrorists. Constitutional issues were especially likely to be central in such hearings, however: this was so for 71 percent of the hearings responding to executive action and 79 percent of the hearings responding to judicial decisions. There was a sharp spike in hearings held in response to executive action in both 1999 and 2001, but little variation over time in committees' response to judicial decisions, despite the increasing activism of the Rehnquist Court in the late 1990s.

ROUTINE CONSTITUTIONAL DISCOURSE

An overview of congressional deliberation on constitutional issues in committee hearings suggests that such deliberation is fairly routine. The issues arise in the normal course of the committee's work in legislation and oversight and are regularly given some consideration, and they are often the central focus of committee hearings. At the same time, elections seem to have the potential to encourage even greater discussion of constitutional matters, either because they have brought to power new legislative majorities with a new agenda to discuss or because incumbent legislators turn to constitutional issues in their quest to gain advantage in an upcoming electoral contest. Though the courts play into congressional constitutional deliberations, they do not appear to be an especially important driving force behind such deliberations, and judicial actions are only somewhat more important in raising constitutional issues in congressional hearings than are the actions of the executive branch. The Judiciary Committees are clearly the dominant locations for constitutional discussions in Congress, but they are hardly alone in giving attention to constitutional issues and appear to be somewhat more important in discussions of civil rights and civil liberties than in considering structural aspects of the Constitution. A notable portion of congressional discussion of the Constitution occurs in the context of proposed constitutional amendments, and Congress gives roughly equal attention to questions of constitutional structure and of constitutional rights.

There is substantial skepticism of congressional constitutional interpretation. Not least, the Supreme Court itself seems to doubt that Congress takes its constitutional responsibilities seriously or spends much time deliberating on constitutional meaning. Even some scholars who give credence to the possibility of congressional engagement with the Constitution tend to relegate such activity to extraordinary moments outside of normal politics.[24] Congress appears to hear about the Constitution more often than these skeptics might expect, and it seems to do so for its own reasons, whether to win the approval of favored constituents, to protect its institutional prerogatives and legislative handiwork, or simply to adhere to valued normative commitments. The quality of committee deliberations on constitutional meaning has yet to be examined, but this chapter gives some initial reason to take seriously the possibility of congressional constitutional interpretation.

This chapter also suggests that while careful attention should be given to the constitutional discussions that occur in the Judiciary Committees, other congressional committees should not be ignored, for they often engage constitutional issues as well. Other committees become particularly important once we focus our attention on matters of constitutional structure that receive less attention from scholars and judges than individual rights claims do but receive substantial attention from legislators.

Given the unprecedented activism of the Rehnquist Court against Congress in the 1990s, it is striking that its decisions do not leave more of a mark on the record of congressional hearings during this period. Some Supreme Court decisions clearly do generate hearing activity. Notably, the Court's doctrinal shift on religious free exercise in the Oregon peyote case, *Employment Division v. Smith*, set off an explosion of hearings concerned with limiting the effects of the decision that continued through the entire period. Similarly, a 1994 Supreme Court decision invalidating a local ordinance that regulated the flow of solid waste as unconstitutionally restricting interstate commerce generated a number of hearings investigating the usefulness of congressional intervention. This sort of activity suggests that when Congress is dissatisfied with judicial decisions, it will often engage them. The relative lack of attention by congressional committees to the federalism revival in the Court in the late 1990s may reinforce the view that the Republican-controlled Congress was simply not unhappy with the Court's work.[25] Interest groups upset by those decisions appear to have been less successful in winning a congressional audience for their complaints than were churches troubled by the *Smith* decision or municipalities concerned about waste disposal. The routine attention that Congress gives to federalism in its committee hearings may also indicate that the Court's recent focus on the commerce clause and state sovereign immunity is not central to legislative concerns or necessary to create legislative interest in the general subject.

Those interested in the "Constitution outside the courts" should look to committee hearings to gain an understanding of how the Constitution is used in legislative and electoral politics. It now seems clear that the Constitution often makes an appearance in congressional deliberations. It remains to be determined how legislators respond to constitutional arguments and approach constitutional considerations, or the extent to which legislators replicate judicial analysis or entertain unconventional constitutional claims, or from whom legislators hear constitutional concerns expressed. There is a great deal of empirical ground still to be explored.

NOTES

1   Woodrow Wilson, *Congressional Government* (New York: Meridian, 1956), 69, 62.

2   David R. Mayhew, *America's Congress* (New Haven: Yale University Press, 2000).

3   Kay Schlozman and John Tierney, *Organized Interests and American Democracy* (New York: Harper and Row, 1986); Joel Aberbach, *Keeping a Watchful Eye* (Washington: Brookings Institution, 1990), 135.

4   John Mark Hansen, *Gaining Access* (Chicago: University of Chicago Press, 1991), 23.

5   See generally Steven S. Smith and Christopher J. Deering, *Committees in Congress*, 3d ed. (Washington: CQ Press, 1997); Keith Krehbiel, *Information and Legislative Organization* (Ann Arbor: University of Michigan Press, 1992); Barry R. Weingast and William Marshall, "The Industrial Organization of Congress," 96 *Journal of Political Economy* 132 (1988); Gary W. Cox

and Mathew D. McCubbins, *Legislative Leviathan* (Berkeley: University of California Press, 1993).

6 Mark C. Miller, "Congress and the Constitution: A Tale of Two Committees," 3 *Seton Hall Constitutional Law Journal* 317 (1993); Mark C. Miller, "Congressional Committees and the Federal Courts: A Neo-Institutional Perspective," 45 *Western Political Quarterly* 949 (1992).

7 Frank R. Baumgartner and Bryan D. Jones, *Agendas and Instability in American Politics* (Chicago: University of Chicago Press, 1993).

8 Hansen, *Gaining Access*, 24.

9 *Id.*; Daniel J. Tichenor and Richard A. Harris, "Organized Interests and American Political Development," 117 *Political Science Quarterly* 587 (2002).

10 Valerie Heitschusen, "Interest Group Lobbying and U.S. House Decentralization: Linking Informational Focus to Committee Hearing Appearances," 53 *Political Research Quarterly* 151 (2000); William T. Gormley Jr., "Witnesses for the Revolution," 26 *American Politics Quarterly* 174 (1998).

11 Kevin M. Leyden, "Interest Group Resources and Testimony at Congressional Hearings," 20 *Legislative Studies Quarterly* 431 (1995); Ken Kollman, "Inviting Friends to Lobby: Interest Groups, Ideological Bias, and Congressional Committees," 41 *American Journal of Political Science* 519 (1997).

12 Roy B. Flemming, Michael C. MacLeod, and Jeffrey Talbert, "Witnesses at the Confirmations? The Appearance of Organized Interests at Senate Hearings of Federal Judicial Appointments, 1945–1992," 51 *Political Research Quarterly* 617 (1998).

13 Gregory A. Caldeira and John R. Wright, "Lobbying for Justice: Organized Interests, Supreme Court Nominations, and the United States Senate," 42 *American Journal of Political Science* 499 (1998); Gregory A. Caldeira, Marie Hojnacki, and John R. Wright, "The Lobbying Activities of Organized Interests in Federal Judicial Nominations," 62 *Journal of Politics* 51 (2000).

14 Hansen, *Gaining Access*, 24.

15 Paul E. Peterson and Jay P. Greene, "Why Executive-Legislative Conflict in the United States Is Dwindling," 24 *British Journal of Political Science* 38 (1993).

16 Lyn Kathlene, "Power and Influence in State Legislative Policymaking: The Interaction of Gender and Position in Committee Hearing Debates," 88 *American Political Science Review* 560 (1994); Laura R. Winsky Mattei, "Gender and Power in American Legislative Discourse," 60 *Journal of Politics* 440 (1998).

17 Diane Elizabeth Johnson, "Transactions in Symbolic Resources: A Resource Dependence Model of Congressional Deliberation," 38 *Social Perspectives* 151 (1995); Fay Lomax Cook, Jason Barabas, and Benjamin I. Page,

"Invoking Public Opinion: Policy Elites and Social Security," 66 *Public Opinion Quarterly* 235 (2002).

18 Stephen J. Wermiel, "Confirming the Constitution: The Role of the Senate Judiciary Committee," 56 *Law and Contemporary Problems* 121 (1993).

19 Tim Groseclose and Nolan McCarty, "The Politics of Blame: Bargaining Before an Audience," 45 *American Journal of Political Science* 100 (2001).

20 Hearings held by subcommittees were categorized by the parent committee. Committees are referred to by their current name.

21 Baumgartner and Jones, *Agendas and Instability*, 201, 202.

22 The heightened interest in civil rights in the 104th Congress may seem incongruous, but that session included hearings on such topics as English-only proposals, children born to illegal immigrants, and especially racial preferences.

23 *The Federalist* 48 (James Madison).

24 E.g., Bruce Ackerman, *We the People*, vol. 1 (Cambridge: Harvard University Press, 1991).

25 See also Keith E. Whittington, "Taking What They Give Us: Explaining the Court's Federalism Offensive," 51 *Duke Law Journal* 477 (2001); Barry Friedman and Anna L. Harvey, "Electing the Supreme Court," 78 *Indiana Law Journal* 123 (2003).

The Federal Appointments Process as Constitutional Interpretation

MICHAEL J. GERHARDT

Woodrow Wilson seems to have spoken for every president when he once complained, "The matter of patronage is a thorny patch which daily makes me wish I had never been born."[1] Yet one is hard pressed to find members of Congress, particularly senators, expressing similar discontent. Senators have particularly relished their involvement in the federal appointments process. They have perennially considered the authority vested in them to give "Advice and Consent" to presidential nominations of "Officers of the United States" as instrumental to their achievement of many objectives, including rewarding friends and allies, punishing political foes, and most importantly, implementing their preferred constitutional visions. Senators are as interested as presidents in shaping constitutional interpretation.

That members of Congress use the federal appointments process to influence constitutional interpretation hardly means that they have invariably done so. The appointments clause sets up a dynamic in which it is difficult for a single authority invariably to dominate the appointments process or to shape constitutional meaning as it likes. This dynamic flows from the constitutional framework that formally pits the president and the Senate against each other. The Framers expected that conflicts would ensue from this design, as each branch tried to aggrandize its powers at the expense of the other. They hoped that the ensuing friction would prevent one branch from becoming tyrannical. In practice, the ensuing friction has also obscured the precise principles vindicated in confirmation contests. To the extent that conflicts do get resolved, presidents are more likely than not to have them resolved to their advantage. By fixing the power to nominate in a single person, the appointments clause gives presidents an edge over the diffuse Senate in maximizing their net influence over appointments, since it is very difficult for a critical mass of senators to remain united repeatedly in opposition to a president's nominees. On appointments matters, the Senate thus primarily occupies a defensive posture in which it is confined to exercising a veto. Moreover, much of the critical action on appointments occurs in settings in which the critical decisions are made by one or a few senators whose actions cannot be attributed to the Senate as a whole. Even when the Senate as an institution takes formal stands on nominations, the significance of its final actions is unclear. Senators have many reasons for their votes on nominees, of which only one involves implementing their preferred constitutional visions.

These problems call for a special perspective in assessing the significance of congressional activity in the federal appointments process. In this chapter, the perspective I adopt is institutional: I focus primarily on the historical patterns and practices of the Congress, particularly the Senate, on appointments matters that have shaped constitutional meaning. I sketch five ways in which the Congress or the Senate as an institution has affected constitutional interpretation. I hope that this sketch will guide future research on the effects on constitutional meaning of congressional or senatorial actions within the appointments process. These operations include formulating the procedures to govern the nomination and confirmation phases of the appointments process; enacting statutes dictating the qualifications for certain offices, allocating power among different offices, or directing the manner in which some appointments are made; and undertaking committee action and Senate votes on presidential nominations. Through these and other activities, the Congress or the Senate seeks to impress its preferred constitutional views upon other institutions, including the presidency, the Supreme Court, lower federal courts, cabinet departments, agencies, and future Congresses and Senates. Moreover, the Congress or the Senate uses its authority within the appointments process to keep some constitutional debates open, settle others, and check presidential efforts to minimize congressional or senatorial influence over appointments by finding ways to transform its posture on appointments matters from a defensive to an offensive one. These efforts also reflect a significant way in which popular constitutionalism might operate—that is, how the Congress or the Senate responds to, or incorporates, popular opinion and social developments in its implementation of constitutional values.

PATTERNS

In this first part, I examine the aggregate influences of the Senate on federal appointments. These effects may be inferred from the Senate's rejection of various nominations. The rates of rejection are highest for nominations to the Supreme Court[2] and successively lower for nominations to other courts, to cabinet offices, and to subcabinet offices. The varying rates of rejection reflect not only different levels of deference given by the Senate to different kinds of nominations but also senators' efforts to shape the composition of the federal judiciary, constitutional doctrine, and presidents' choices of nominees.

Twenty-seven Supreme Court nominees have failed to be confirmed by the Senate—a rate of rejection of almost 29 percent—and the Senate has approved at least fourteen others only after close votes or intense, contentious confirmation proceedings.[3] Of the twenty-seven failed nominations, at least ten failed primarily because of the nominee's constitutional or political views, which the opposition viewed as signaling how the nominee would likely have performed in office if confirmed;[4] and of the other fourteen closely contested nominations, the nominee's political or constitutional views were the most commonly cited basis for opposition.[5] The majority of the most contentious Supreme Court nominations occurred when the opposition party controlled the Senate. In particular, the opposition party controlled the Senate for fifteen of the twenty-seven rejected Supreme Court nominations.[6] By contrast, the president's party controlled the Senate in all but one closely contested Supreme Court nomination.[7] As reflected in these statistics and the Senate debates on contested nominations, it appears as if concerns about Supreme Court nominees' views generally tend to transcend rigid party loyalty. Presidents have had limited success in counting on members of their own party to fall into line in support of their Supreme Court nominations. Senators tend to treat Supreme Court nominees with less deference than other nominees because once confirmed they wield unique power to decide questions of constitutional and statutory meaning, and because their life tenure makes them immune to political retaliation.

A similar pattern, with some significant differences, appears to hold for nominees to lower courts. The latter rank second behind Supreme Court nominees in terms of the percentage rejected or forced to be withdrawn by the Senate. In the last century, one critical difference between Supreme

Court and lower-court selection has been that the sheer number of lower court vacancies has compelled senators to carefully pick their battles over judicial nominations. Senators cannot stop or even closely inspect all judicial nominations. To check presidential dominance of judicial selection, they have developed procedures—discussed more fully below—that allow much of the Senate's critical decision making on judicial nominations to be made by the Judiciary Committee rather than by the Senate as a whole. Consequently, most of the obstruction of judicial nominations has been carried out by a small (and not necessarily representative) number of senators.

The Senate defers still more to cabinet nominations than to lower court nominations. The Senate has formally rejected only nine cabinet nominations,[8] all but one during periods of divided government. In addition, the Senate forced the withdrawals of nine other cabinet nominations (all but one with the president's party in control of the Senate, thus reflecting the limited extent to which presidents can count on party fidelity to carry such nominees successfully through the process), confirmed over nine hundred cabinet officers, and on relatively few occasions confirmed cabinet officers after close votes or contentious hearings.[9] For instance, in 2001 the Senate confirmed John Ashcroft by the closest vote ever for a successful nominee to be attorney general.[10] These statistics reflect widespread recognition among senators of several aspects of cabinet selection: a president is entitled to have his own team to facilitate the discharge of his constitutional responsibilities; the close working relationship that cabinet officials will have with the president will keep them in line (and make it easier both for the president to hold them accountable for their mistakes and for the president to be held accountable for their mistakes); and senators will have the means to make these officials (unlike federal judges) accountable through congressional oversight. The statistics on senatorial deference to cabinet nominations also reflect a practice of effectively treating cabinet nominees with a presumption of confirmation, which may be overcome only by some serious questions about the cabinet nominee's conflicts of interest (such as Charles Warren's close professional associations with the industry he was expected to monitor through enforcement of the antitrust laws as President Coolidge's attorney general), ethics or integrity (Zoë Baird's violation of tax laws that she was expected to enforce as President Clinton's attorney general), failure to abide by certain standards of behavior (John Tower's engaging in personal misconduct that military personnel under his supervision as President George H. W. Bush's defense secretary would have been discharged for committing), or commitment to especially problematic political or constitutional views (Roger Taney's actions to dismantle the National Bank as President Jackson's acting treasury secretary and Henry Stanberry's support for President Johnson's Reconstruction policies and impeachment defense).[11]

Finally, the Senate has deferred to presidents' subcabinet nominees (and agency appointments) to a greater extent than to their other nominations. One survey indicates that the Senate as a whole or in committee has formally rejected or forced the withdrawals of fewer than two hundred of the more than two million executive nominations made since 1932.[12] The large number of such nominations ensures that every president can expect the Senate to confirm the vast majority of them. It also ensures that every president will have at least a few (if not more) subcabinet nominees rejected, forced to be withdrawn, or confronted with some substantial opposition in the Senate.[13] A common basis for opposing nominees is problems with their political and constitutional views, or doubts about their ability or inclination to enforce policies supported by most or a few influential senators. Senators evidently care about these problems because they expect the officials to function with little daily supervision (and almost never by the presidents who nominated them) and to work closely with members of Congress and their staffs in monitoring the effectiveness of the laws in their fields. Indeed, senators will likely oppose nominees whom they cannot trust to enforce certain policies or to work well with Congress.

Beyond demonstrating different levels of deference to different kinds of nominees, the Senate's votes on presidential nominations have been instrumental in shaping the Supreme Court's agenda. On the one hand, rejections and forced withdrawals have fortified some of the Court's constitutional decisions.[14] In the last century, senators have used the judicial confirmation process to bolster the scope of the national government's power over American territories, the constitutional foundations of the New Deal and Great Society, the imposition of the death penalty, and such landmark decisions as *Brown v. Board of Education*, *Griswold v. Connecticut*, and *Roe v. Wade*. For instance, the Democratically controlled Senate's confirmations of all of Presidents Franklin D. Roosevelt's and Harry Truman's thirteen appointees to the Supreme Court from 1937 through 1949 undoubtedly helped to end economic due process *and* to fortify the New Deal's constitutional foundations. Similarly, the Senate's rejection of Robert Bork prevented the appointment of a justice who appeared determined to vote to overrule *Roe*, while the Senate fortified *Roe* by confirming

Ruth Bader Ginsburg, who had signaled some support for it, to replace Justice White, who had repeatedly voted to overrule it. On the other hand, Senate confirmation votes have either weakened some constitutional decisions or precluded judicial closure on some constitutionally sensitive questions. Salient examples in the last century have arguably included takings, criminal procedure, and separation of church and state. A test for determining which senatorial actions fortify or undermine constitutional precedents is to consider whether a nominee with views similar to those of a rejected nominee is confirmable (at least within the same or a similarly constituted Senate). For instance, it appears unlikely that the Senate would confirm a nominee who, like Bork, was openly opposed to many landmark precedents with which a critical mass of senators seemed to agree.

The effect on the appointments process of Senate actions (including the Senate's attempts to block certain appointments) has not only been negative: Senate pressure has also dictated or made a significant difference to the choices of people nominated to certain offices. For example, the Senate has dictated the choices of at least three Supreme Court nominees—Samuel Miller (1862), Edwin Stanton (1869), and Benjamin Cardozo (1932).[15] This has also been frequently true for cabinet and other offices. The choices for these offices have often been dictated by individual members of Congress whose advice the presidents have felt obliged, for one reason or another, to follow. To be sure, the notion that senators have influenced the ideological composition of the federal courts has been challenged in important empirical work by the political scientist Nancy Scherer. She suggests that even in periods of divided government, presidents primarily determine the ideological composition of federal district and appellate courts.[16] There are, however, three problems with her analysis. First, she fails to acknowledge that senators have helped to shape the pool of nominees. Through a variety of means (particularly senatorial courtesy and committees), senators filter out prospective nominees to whom they object. Second, Scherer discounts the fact that by confirming nominees with well-known constitutional views, the Senate has ratified those views. By confirming various officials, the Senate assumes responsibility for authorizing them to occupy offices in which they will have opportunities to act upon and implement their constitutional views. Third, in response to Senate pressure or in an effort to avoid messy confirmation contests, presidents have changed their criteria for nominations. After Bork's rejection, presidents tended to pick judicial nominees, most famously David Souter, without the extensive paper trails that might have made them easy targets as staunch ideologues. Even though Democrats controlled the Senate in 1993 and 1994, President Clinton wanted to preserve his political capital for other legislative priorities, particularly national health care, and therefore wanted to avoid time-consuming, politically costly Senate contests over his choices to replace the retiring Justices Harry Blackmun and Byron White. He thus abandoned the preference he had stated earlier as a candidate and as president to nominate as justices people with substantial experience as political leaders. He modified his selection criteria and opted for the relatively safe choices of Ruth Bader Ginsburg and Stephen Breyer, circuit judges who Senate leaders from both parties had signaled would be easily confirmed.

PROMISES

I now identify two important ways in which senators have used confirmation proceedings to influence nominees' constitutional interpretation. The first is by pressuring nominees to make explicit promises or concessions. For instance, in 2002 two of President George W. Bush's nominees to the federal court of appeals—Michael McConnell and Miguel Estrada— each conceded in confirmation hearings that *Roe v. Wade* was settled law. Neither had committed himself to such a view before his hearings, so there is good reason to suppose each made the concession to curry favor with Democrats, then in the majority on the Senate Judiciary Committee. (Nevertheless, most Democrats remained skeptical, and precluded any final actions on either nomination pending the outcome of the 2002 midterm elections.) While it is reasonable for Estrada and McConnell to expect that any decisions they would have to make as appellate judges on abortion rights must at least pay lip service to relevant Supreme Court precedent, their statements under oath are likely to become significant if either is ever nominated to the Supreme Court. (It is conceivable that the concessions might decrease either's chances for being nominated to the Court by a president committed to dismantling *Roe*.) One can imagine Estrada or McConnell being asked to repeat his views on *Roe* as settled law in a Supreme Court confirmation hearing. Assuming that each did so, it would be difficult for either to rule against *Roe* if confirmed, without appearing to have lied under oath not once but twice in confirmation hearings. What were once thought to be safe votes against *Roe* now seem to have become reluctant votes to reaffirm it.

There are many other examples of significant promises made in confirmation proceedings. These are by no means confined to judicial nominees. For instance, in 2001 several nominees to high-ranking positions in the executive branch, such as John Ashcroft (attorney general), Ted Olson (solicitor general), Gale Norton (interior secretary), and other nominees to offices with responsibility for environmental protection, promised in their confirmation hearings to vigorously enforce federal laws with which they had previously expressed disagreement.[17] The Senate confirmed these officials, all of whom have taken great pains to keep their word by enforcing laws with which they disagreed.

The second way the Senate wields its confirmation authority to influence nominees' constitutional judgments is by affecting their attitudes. Even if they are not required to make explicit promises, many nominees are sensitized in their confirmation proceedings to how the Senate will likely react if they take certain positions. This knowledge can affect their performances in the offices to which they have been confirmed. Some ambitious lower court judges, executive officials, or agency heads may therefore moderate their actions or take certain positions for strategic reasons, including preserving their viability for other appointments. Even Supreme Court justices may be sensitive to future confirmation politics. For instance, one can imagine that while deciding whether to reaffirm *Roe v. Wade*, Justices O'Connor, Kennedy, and Souter each understood the importance to Democratic senators of the stability of *Roe* as a precedent, especially after the latter two had been grilled about their attitudes toward *Roe* in their confirmation proceedings. Had these justices cast the pivotal votes to overturn *Roe*, they could reasonably have foreseen that their votes would have a profound effect on judicial confirmations.[18] They all may have figured (to varying degrees) that by casting pivotal votes to reaffirm *Roe* they helped to take the issue off the table in future judicial confirmation hearings and thereby make it easier for conservatives to get confirmed to the lower courts and particularly to the Supreme Court, as long as they acknowledged that *Roe* was settled law. They may also have expected that if they voted to overrule *Roe* they would make most Democratic senators and some Republicans more intensely interested in barring nominees to the Court with unacceptable views about *Roe*, or perhaps more skeptical of judicial nominees' pledges of fidelity to *Roe* as settled law. This expectation may have played an important role in both the Supreme Court's reconsideration of *Roe* and its subsequent decision to grant certiorari in only one abortion rights case in the past decade.[19] The vigilance of some senators, particularly Democrats, in blocking the nominations of people committed to undoing *Roe* seems to have coincided with the case's being taken off the Court's agenda.

PRACTICES

In deliberating and acting upon various nominations, the Senate develops procedures and practices that shape constitutional meaning in three significant ways. First, the Senate's practices and procedures themselves reflect a significant way in which the Constitution is constructed outside the courts. They reflect the Senate's final, nonreviewable judgments about the scope of its authority within the federal appointments process. How the Senate handles such matters, including informal arrangements both within it and reached between senators and presidents,[20] defines significant phases of the constitutional path—the crucible—through which presidential nominees have to maneuver to be confirmed. No one seriously believes that a judicial challenge to the Senate's final or procedural judgments on appointments is possible, even its practice of empowering one or only a few senators to make effectively final decisions about the fate of nominees.

Second, the Senate's practices and procedures for handling judicial nominations reflect both recognition and vindication of the constitutional principle of judicial independence. The Constitution largely leaves this principle to the federal appointments process for safeguarding. Within the Senate, the questioning of judicial nominees and debates over them frequently (but not always) reflect remarkable sensitivity to the preservation of this principle. For instance, senators are often careful not to ask judicial nominees, including those to the Supreme Court, how they would rule in particular cases; and the Senate has yet to reject any judicial nominees because of their refusal to answer questions about how they would perform as judges or justices.[21]

Third, the Senate offers a significant means for popular input on the grounds for opposing or supporting constitutional ideologies as espoused by various nominees. In various ways senators, like presidents, are receptive to popular opinion or pressure, which can be and often is mounted for and against different constitutional views. Indeed the Senate, which has a diverse membership of one hundred, can be said to enjoy an institutional advantage over the president, who is only one individual, in its ability to mediate public attitudes or social norms—informal understandings among the populace about proper interpersonal interaction and behavior[22]—and to incorporate these attitudes and norms into its decisions on appointments matters.

When the Senate checks presidential nominations, it sometimes assesses how well they have accorded with social norms. There have been more than a few dramatic contests over Supreme Court appointments in which senators have responded to and tried to track or implement social norms. Such seems to have been the case with the Senate's rejection of John Parker, in which Progressive Republicans and Democrats joined labor and civil rights organizations in opposing Parker's nomination based on his apparently racial and anti-labor bias. In rejecting Parker's nomination, the Senate seems to have both responded to and perhaps reinforced social norms on the importance of not discriminating against African Americans because of their race.[23] Similarly, in rejecting Robert Bork, the Senate may have been acting in part against his perceived hostility to an emerging social norm according to which the state should not force women into motherhood against their will.[24] The Senate thus sometimes checks presidents' readings of public attitudes or social norms on constitutional values.

QUALIFICATIONS

Another significant way in which the Congress has used the federal appointments process to influence constitutional meaning is by enacting statutes defining qualifications for offices. It is a well-settled practice for the Congress to enact such statutory restrictions for inferior offices and for offices requiring presidential nomination and senatorial confirmation.[25] Indeed, the First Congress did so in the Judiciary Act of 1789, which provided for an attorney general who would render advice to the president and represent the United States before the Supreme Court, and for district attorneys who would represent the United States elsewhere, and also required that each of these officials be "a meet person learned in the law."[26] As David Currie has observed, "Nobody seems to have suggested [at the time] that in [restricting the president's discretion in nominating these officials] Congress offended the appointment provisions of Article II."[27] In his classic study on presidential powers, Edward Corwin expressed a similar judgment that

> [b]y far the most important limitation on presidential autonomy [in the nominating process] is . . . that which results from the fact that, in creating an office, Congress may stipulate the qualifications of appointees thereto. First and last, legislation of this sort has laid down a vast variety of qualifications, depending on citizenship, residence, professional attainments, occupational experience, age, . . . sound habits, political, industrial, or regional affiliations, and so on and so forth. It has even confined the President's selection to a small number of persons to be named by others. Indeed, it has contrived at times, by particularity of description, to designate a definite eligible, thereby, to all intents and purposes, usurping the appointing authority. . . . For the proposition is universally conceded that some choice, however small, must be left the appointing authority.[28]

A modern example of such requirements is the many independent and quasi-independent commissions, such as the Federal Trade Commission and the Federal Election Commission, whose members must be nominated by the president, subject to confirmation by the Senate, and are statutorily required to be diverse along specific guidelines in terms of party affiliation. Another recent example is the Lobbying Disclosure Act of 1995, which disqualifies anyone who had worked as a foreign lobbyist or as a lobbyist for any foreign government from becoming the U.S. trade representative or deputy trade representative, both offices requiring nomination by the president and confirmation by the Senate. Also, through the Federal Vacancies Reform Act of 1998 (FVRA),[29] Congress required the executive branch to fully disclose to Congress and the comptroller general information related to vacancies, and make special arrangements for vacancies occurring during presidential transitions.

The FVRA is merely one of numerous statutes in which members of Congress have defined limits to a president's nominating authority. The fate of such statutes has largely been left for the Congress and presidents to work out between them. The congressional debates do not reflect consensus on any bright line marking precisely where the imposition by Congress of qualifications for certain offices violates presidential nominating authority. Instead, congressional debates reflect perennial concern among members of Congress over the appropriate balance to strike between on the one hand exercising their authority to create offices and set forth qualifications for their occupants and on the other avoiding possible encroachments on the independence, prerogatives, and authority of the other branches. In addition, Congress and the president have frequently agreed to waivers allowing some members of Congress to be appointed to offices whose salaries they had voted to increase, in spite of the ineligibility clause's apparent prohibition against such appointments.[30] To date, the federal courts have never interfered with, or second-guessed, Congress's judgments about the significance and applicability of this prohibition. These judgments, like others on statutory qualifications for certain offices, are final.

COMMITTEES

I now examine the impact of senatorial committees on constitutional interpretation. Over the past century, senators' activities on pending nominations have increasingly occurred in committees. The Senate delegates to its committees the responsibility to hold hearings and make recommendations regarding presidential nominations to offices in the areas for which the committees are responsible. Just about every Senate committee has some responsibility over federal appointments. These committees and their chairs wield enormous influence over the fate of nominees. The chairs are responsible for scheduling hearings and votes on pending nominations, while the committees vote on recommending nominations for the full Senate to consider, and sometimes even vote on whether to forward to the full Senate a nomination that it has previously voted not to recommend. By means of the authority they each wield, committees and their chairs are frequently the final words on subcabinet and lower court nominations.

The complaints about the Judiciary Committee often tend to be among the fiercest, particularly because of the numerous instances in which the committee or its chair has used procedural tactics to block judicial nominations. The criticisms of the Judiciary Committee are also fierce because of the nature of the committee and the stakes involved. The Judiciary Committee is generally regarded as not being representative of the Senate as a whole, in that its Democratic members are perceived as more liberal and its Republicans more conservative than their counterparts in the Senate as a whole. The lack of representativeness of the Judiciary Committee is especially frustrating under circumstances when the committee or its chair has terminated a judicial nomination even though the full Senate would have approved it had it been given the chance to vote on the nomination.

From mid-2001 until the fall of 2002, Republicans frequently experienced such frustration, because they believed that the committee and its chair—Patrick Leahy of Vermont—blocked several nominations even though the nominees would probably have been confirmed by the whole Senate.

The Judiciary Committee's actions are constitutionally significant for three reasons. First, all senators accept the Senate's authority to make the arrangements by which it has delegated authority to the Judiciary Committee and accept the committee's authority as a gatekeeper. They appreciate that they may each benefit from this authority over time, so they are willing to endure the derailing of nominations that they supported because they know that eventually they can return the favor. Second, once one accepts that committees may take final actions on nominees, it follows that nominees are not constitutionally entitled to have a full Senate vote on their nominations. Both President Clinton's and the first President Bush's pleas for the Senate to render final votes on every judicial nomination ultimately failed, because they could not find a way around the long-standing acceptance of the Senate's reliance on committees to facilitate the exercise of its authority over federal appointments (along with the exercise of all its other authorities).[31] Third, committee actions can have a negative impact on constitutional interpretation. Through its gatekeeping function the Judiciary Committee can keep away from the courts certain points of view, not just once in a while but in the long term. It is rare for a committee to forward a nomination to the full Senate with a negative recommendation or for the Senate to overturn a committee's recommendations against confirmation.[32] The committee's negative judgments on judicial nominees are thus almost always final. The Senate's rules and traditions provide exceptions for Supreme Court and cabinet nominees, however, whose nominations can be forwarded to the full Senate in spite of their having been reported unfavorably by relevant committees.

Moreover, the committee's composition is important not just for blocking nominations but also for signaling preferred criteria for presidents to follow in making judicial nominations. A president may be inclined or pressured to make different kinds of judicial nominations depending on the composition of the Senate Judiciary Committee. It was therefore not surprising that immediately after Republicans retook control of the Senate and the Judiciary Committee in January 2003, President George W. Bush renominated several people whose circuit court nominations had been rejected or left in limbo just a few months before by the Judiciary Committee under the Democrats. The Judiciary Committee wasted no time in approving, along straight party-line votes, two judges—Charles Pickering and Priscilla Owen—whose circuit court nominations had been previously rejected by the Democratically controlled committee.

The full Senate rarely overturns a committee's positive recommendation on a nominee, but there are no guarantees. It is unusual, but not unheard of, for the full Senate to reject a nomination recommended by a committee. In addition, senators have sometimes successfully filibustered nominations, including President Johnson's nomination of Abe Fortas as chief justice of the United States and President Clinton's nominations of Henry Foster as surgeon general and Walter Dellinger as solicitor general. More recently, the Judiciary Committee forwarded Miguel Estrada's nomination to the U.S. Court of Appeals for the District of Columbia with a positive recommendation, but Democrats subsequently filibustered the nomination. With only forty-one votes needed to preclude cloture and most of the Senate's forty-eight Democrats and the Senate's lone independent solidly behind the filibuster, the filibuster became the final word on Estrada's renomination. The same coalition filibustered five other circuit court nominations by President Bush. While it plainly blocks a majority of the Senate from doing what it wants, the filibuster is one of many mechanisms available to senators interested in exercising their gatekeeping function of barring the confirmation of nominees whose constitutional views they do not know or trust. These mechanisms have included, inter alia, allowing a lone member of the Judiciary Committee to veto the scheduling of a committee vote on any nominee. Senator Hatch terminated this practice when he was the chairman of the Senate Judiciary Committee. The fallout from his decision remains to be seen.

REORGANIZATION

The final part of this chapter considers how Congress uses the federal appointments process to shape constitutional meaning through laws creating, abolishing, and restructuring offices. The effect of these statutes has been to influence (1) which authorities will make certain appointments and when they will make them, (2) how judges or justices might react, and (3) which officials will exercise which powers. The first effect is evident with numerous statutes. Every statute that creates or abolishes an office directs who shall make certain appointments and when the designated officials shall make them. These statutes demonstrate the Congress's efforts to stretch its influence over the timing and manner of exercise of different powers and to delineate the outer boundaries of its other powers.

Some notorious instances from the late eighteenth and nineteenth centuries include statutes creating new executive departments to aid the president in carrying out his duties with respect to war, finance, and foreign affairs; the National Bank; the Freedmen's Bureau (enacted pursuant to Congress's authority under section 5 of the Fourteenth Amendment); the office of attorney general and subsequently the Department of Justice; and the Interstate Commerce Commission. In the twentieth century and the early twenty-first, Congress became even more active, creating some offices (including new cabinet departments—most recently the Department of Homeland Security—agencies and commissions, and the Office of the Independent Counsel) and eliminating others (including the Office of the Independent Counsel shortly after the end of President Clinton's impeachment trial in the Senate).

The Congress has also used its power to create or abolish offices to influence judicial appointments. It has altered the number of seats on the Supreme Court seven times, the last of which was in 1869.[33] And it has routinely used its power to create "inferior courts" to create or abolish judgeships, depending on its support for the president in office at the time of enactment. For instance, the Congress created a substantial number of new judgeships for Presidents Carter, Reagan, and George H. W. Bush to fill at the outset of their administrations. It did not do the same for Bill Clinton until 1999, at which time he had less than two years left in office. Even then, the number of new judgeships created was fewer than a dozen.[34]

The enactment of statutes creating or abolishing offices has sent two sets of signals. The first, directed toward the executive branch, has been intended to streamline or circumscribe its power to make certain appointments and the circumstances in which it may make them. The second set of signals has been directed at judges or justices: the most famous example is offered by President Franklin D. Roosevelt's Court-packing plan.[35] A popular conception of the plan is that it pressured Chief Justice Charles Evans Hughes and Justice Owen Roberts to change their approaches to construing the commerce clause, thus obviating the plan, though this interpretation has been hotly contested by legal scholars, historians, and political scientists.[36] Another way that the Congress's creation and abolition of federal offices has had an effect on constitutional interpretation has been through its reallocation of power. Congress might redefine the duties of an office, lengthen or shorten the tenure of particular officers,[37] or reapportion responsibilities by removing some power from one official and vesting it in another over whom it might have greater influence. In doing so Congress often attempts to tinker with the line separating "inferior officers" who may be appointed by department heads without Senate confirmation from "officers of the United States" who must be nominated by the president and confirmed by the Senate.[38] The huge majority of statutes of this sort have either survived or not been subjected to judicial review; the choices reflected in them as to which officials should wield which powers have largely been determined through negotiations between the Congress and the president.

The recent debates over the proposed Department of Homeland Security further illustrate the Congress's role in allocating power among different offices. Shortly after September 11, 2001, President Bush issued an executive order creating an Office of Homeland Security (OHS) in the White House. He named Governor Tom Ridge of Pennsylvania as the director of OHS and designated him as a member of the White House staff. As such, Ridge was not subject to Senate confirmation and served at the president's pleasure. Ridge initially refused to testify before the House or Senate about his actions, plans, or counsel as the director of OHS, based on his claims that as a White House staff member much of what he did was insulated from congressional review by executive privilege and that requesting him to appear before Congress encroached upon presidential operations and prerogatives. In response, many members of Congress proposed to transform Ridge's position into a new department, whose leader would have to be confirmed by the Senate and therefore make himself accountable in confirmation hearings. The president responded by making his own ambitious proposal to reorganize the federal government as a whole, a proposal that included establishing a new Department of Homeland Security. Some Democrats resisted the proposal because it provided that virtually every employee of the new department would serve at the pleasure of the president and thus be largely insulated from congressional pressure or retaliation. Shortly after the Republicans retook control of the Senate in the midterm elections of 2002, Congress approved the president's plan, which became the most extensive reorganization of the federal government since the creation of the Defense Department.

CONCLUSION

My purpose has been to highlight some significant ways in which the Congress has used its authority over federal appointments to effect constitutional interpretation. Through formal actions, the Congress has impressed its constitutional views upon other institutions, including presidents, federal courts, and future Congresses. The other branches have also accepted practices and outcomes that have secured a significant role for the Congress, particularly the Senate, in influencing and directing the nominees chosen and the criteria by which they are chosen. In this role the Congress, particularly the Senate, has shaped the balance of power on appointments matters if not the general balance of power between itself and the other branches, fortified constitutional principles, kept some constitutional debates alive, supported the implementation of some constitutional views, and blocked the implementation of other constitutional views. No wonder members of Congress, particularly senators, relish the federal appointments process.

NOTES

1   For both Wilson's and other presidents' complaints about the pressures of the federal appointments process, see Joseph Harris, *The Advice and Consent of the Senate: A Study of the Confirmation of Appointments by the United States Senate* (Berkeley: University of California Press, 1953), 36–37 (Washington), 47 (Thomas Jefferson), 70 (Polk), 93 (Taft); Michael J. Gerhardt, *The Federal Appointments Process: A Constitutional and Historical Analysis* (Durham: Duke University Press, 2000), xiii (Wilson), 336 (Cleveland).

2   See generally Henry J. Abraham, *Justices, Presidents, and Senators: A History of the U.S. Supreme Court Appointments from Washington to Clinton*, rev. ed. (Lanham, Md.: Rowman and Littlefield, 1999).

3   I treat as closely contested nominations those in which at least a third of the Senate opposed the nominees. Examples include Clarence Thomas (1991), William Rehnquist for chief justice of the United States (1986), Sherman Minton (1949), Charles Evans Hughes for chief justice of the United States (1930), Louis Brandeis (1916), Mahlon Pitney (1912), Melville Fuller for chief justice of the United States (1888), Lucius Lamar (1888), Stanley Matthews (1881), Nathan Clifford (1858), John Catron (1837), Philip Barbour (1836), and Roger Taney for chief justice of the United States (1836).

4 The ten Supreme Court nominees whom the Senate rejected because of their constitutional or political views were John Rutledge, Alexander Wolcott, George Woodward, Ebenezer Hoar, Caleb Cushing, John Parker, Abe Fortas, Clement Haynsworth, Harrold Carswell, and Robert Bork.

5 See Calvin R. Massey, "Getting There: A Brief History of the Politics of Supreme Court Appointments," 19 *Hastings Constitutional Law Quarterly* 1, 5–7 (1992).

6 The twelve Supreme Court nominees who failed to be confirmed by the Senate when it was controlled by the president's party were John Rutledge (1795), Alexander Wolcott (1811), Roger Taney as associate justice (1835), George Woodward (1845), Ebenezer Hoar (1869), George Williams (1873), Caleb Cushing (1874), William Hornblower (1893), Wheeler Peckham (1894), John Parker (1930), Abe Fortas as chief justice (1968), and Homer Thornberry (1968).

7 The one exception was Stanley Matthews, whom the Senate confirmed by a single vote when he was renominated for the Court by President Garfield.

8 The nine cabinet nominees whom the Senate rejected are, in chronological order, Roger Taney as President Jackson's treasury secretary, Caleb Cushing as President Tyler's treasury secretary, David Henshaw as President Tyler's navy secretary, James Green as President Tyler's treasury secretary, James Porter as President Tyler's secretary of war, Henry Stanberry as President Andrew Johnson's attorney general, Charles Warren as President Coolidge's attorney general, Lewis Strauss as President Eisenhower's commerce secretary, and John Tower as President George H.W. Bush's defense secretary. See Michael J. Gerhardt, "Norm Theory and the Future of the Federal Appointments Process," 50 *Duke Law Journal* 1687, 1690 (2001). A handful of cabinet nominees have withdrawn their nominations before Senate confirmation proceedings or final votes. These have recently included Zoë Baird (who withdrew her nomination as President Clinton's attorney general because of fallout from her decision not to pay Social Security taxes for a nanny who was an illegal immigrant) and Linda Chavez (who withdrew her nomination as President George W. Bush's secretary of labor because of her controversial opinions regarding certain labor issues).

9 See generally William Ross, "The Senate's Constitutional Role in Confirming Cabinet Nominees and Other Executive Officers," 48 *Syracuse Law Review* 1123 (1998).

10 Gerhardt, "Norm Theory and the Future of the Federal Appointments Process," 1692 n.15.

11 For detailed discussions of failed cabinet-level nominations, see Harris, *The Advice and Consent of the Senate*, 66–68 (Tyler), 59–64 (Jackson), 119–24 (Coolidge); Ross, "The Senate's Constitutional Role in Confirming Cabinet

Nominees and Other Executive Officers," 1135–36 (Andrew Johnson); Gerhardt, *The Federal Appointments Process*, 164–65 (Eisenhower and George H. W. Bush).

12 See Gerhardt, "Norm Theory and the Future of the Federal Appointments Process," 1692 n.17.

13 See Ross, "The Senate's Constitutional Role in Confirming Cabinet Nominees and Other Executive Officers," 1137–43.

14 See generally David Yalof, *Pursuit of Justices* (Chicago: University of Chicago Press, 2000).

15 See generally Gerhardt, *The Federal Appointments Process*, 46–48, 49,173–74.

16 See, e.g., Nancy Scherer, "Who Drives the Ideological Makeup of the Lower Federal Courts in a Divided Government?," 35 *Law and Society Review* 191 (2001).

17 See, e.g., Douglas Jehl, "The 43rd President: Interior Choice Sends Signal on Land Policy," *New York Times*, 30 December 2000, § A, p. 1; Katherine Q. Seelye, "Bush Is Choosing Industry Insiders to Fill Several Environmental Positions," *New York Times*, 12 May 2001, § A, p. 10.

18 Some judges' or justices' opinions reflect their sensitivity to how their opinions will affect the confirmation process. See, e.g., Harris v. Alabama, 513 U.S. 504, 519–20 (1995); Planned Parenthood v. Casey, 505 U.S. 833, 995–96 (1992) (Scalia, J., dissenting); Compassion in Dying v. State of Washington, 85 F.3d 1440, 1449 (1996).

19 Stenberg v. Carhart, 530 U.S. 914 (2000).

20 These arrangements include, among other things, institutional norms, which refer to the behavioral regularities of presidents and senators regarding appointments matters that persist in the absence of formal rules and that trigger sanctions when breached.

21 Democratic senators' opposition to George W. Bush's appellate court nominee Miguel Estrada was based in part on the administration's refusal to release to the Judiciary Committee Estrada's work product from his tenure as a Justice Department official. Democrats first made the request in 2001 at a time when they ran the Judiciary Committee because of the decision in midterm by Senator James Jeffords of Vermont to leave the Republican Party and become an independent, thereby tipping the balance of control in the Senate back in favor of the Democrats. The Judiciary Committee subsequently voted, strictly along party lines, not to recommend Estrada's confirmation to the full Senate. The vote effectively killed Estrada's nomination. When Republicans regained control of the Senate after the midterm elections of 2002, Democrats became the minority party. Because President Bush had renominated Estrada earlier in the year, the Judiciary Committee again had a chance to vote on his nomination. But this time the committee,

with a Republican majority, voted strictly along party lines to recommend the nomination to the full Senate. Democrats blocked a floor vote by filibustering the nomination. By the end of Bush's first term, Democrats had blocked floor votes on nine other judicial nominations by filibustering.

The Democrats' filibusters provoked angry reactions from most Republicans. They denounced the filibusters as illegitimate obstructionism. They also began to consider ways to eliminate such filibusters.

The maneuvering within the Senate regarding the filibuster was not over by the time this book went to press. In the meantime, for two commentaries on the constitutionality of the filibuster, see Michael J. Gerhardt, "The Constitutionality of the Filibuster," *Constitutional Commentary* (forthcoming) (defending the constitutionality of the filibuster and questioning the propriety of efforts to eliminate it); and John O. McGinniss and Michael B. Rappaport, "The Constitutionality of Legislative Supermajority Requirements: A Defense," 105 *Yale Law Journal* 483, 496 (1995) (agreeing on the constitutionality of the filibuster but defending efforts to eliminate it).

22   William N. Eskridge Jr. and John Ferejohn, "Quasi-Constitutional Law: The Rise of Super-Statutes," in this volume.

23   See generally Kenneth W. Goings, *The NAACP Comes of Age: The Defeat of John J. Parker* (Bloomington: Indiana University Press, 1990).

24   See generally Mark Silverstein, *Judicious Choices: The New Politics of Supreme Court Confirmations* (New York: W. W. Norton, 1994); Paul Simon, *Advice and Consent: Clarence Thomas, Robert Bork, and the Intriguing History of the Supreme Court's Nomination Battles* (Bethesda, Md.: National Press Books, 1992); Ethan Bronner, *Battle for Justice: How the Bork Nomination Shook America* (New York: W. W. Norton, 1989).

25   The Supreme Court apparently agrees at least with respect to inferior offices. See United States v. Perkins, 116 U.S. 483, 485 (1886) (unanimously holding that the Congress has complete authority to impose qualifications on inferior officers).

26   1 Stat. 73, 92–93, § 35 (24 September 1789).

27   David P. Currie, *The Constitution in Congress: The Federalist Period, 1789–1801* (Chicago: University of Chicago Press, 1997), 43.

28   Edward S. Corwin, *The President: Office and Powers, 1787–1984*, 5th rev. ed. (New York: New York University Press, 1984) (citation omitted).

29   5 U.S.C. §§ 3345–49d (Supp. V 1999).

30   See generally Michael Stokes Paulsen, "Is Lloyd Bentsen Unconstitutional?," 44 *Stanford Law Review* 1 (1994).

31   The Senate's frequent failure to hold final votes on pending nominations parallels the Senate's failure in other contexts to take final action. For instance, the committee system operates as a gatekeeper on legislation; there is no obligation on the Senate to vote on every bill, and many bills fail to

make it out of committee. Similarly, presidents have negotiated treaties on whose ratification the full Senate has not voted. Again, no one seriously argues that the Senate has a constitutional obligation to vote on a treaty that a committee has refused to forward to the floor.

32   One study indicates that since 1945 the Senate has confirmed only seven nominations that had not received a favorable committee report. See Robert C. Byrd, *The Senate 1789-1989*, vol. 4, *Historical Statistics, 1789-1992* (Washington: Government Printing Office, 1988), table 7-2 at 687.

33   See generally Jamie L. Carson and Benjamin A. Kleinerman, "Political Institutions and American Development: Evolution in the Size of the Supreme Court," at http://www.msu.edu/pipc/carsonkleinerman2001.pdf (last visited 3 October 2002).

34   See Gerhardt, *The Federal Appointments Process*, 385 n.38.

35   See W. E. Leuchtenburg, *Franklin D. Roosevelt and the New Deal, 1932-1940* (New York: Harper and Row, 1963).

36   The plan's failure might have had a different effect altogether. It might have crystallized critical popular support for maintaining the Court's size at nine and against efforts, like those undertaken until right after the Civil War, to modify the Court's size to reward or punish certain presidents.

37   See generally *In re* Investment Bankers, Inc., 4 F.3d 1556, 1562 (10th Cir. 1993) (noting that the argument that an extension of the tenure of an office raises problems under the appointments clause "has been rejected by every court that has ever considered it"), cert. denied, 114 S. Ct. 1061 (1994).

38   On some occasions the Supreme Court has reviewed the constitutionality of congressional efforts to reallocate authority, see Edmond v. United States, 520 U.S. 651 (1997); Weiss v. United States, 510 U.S. 163 (1994); Freytag v. Commissioner, 501 U.S. 868 (1991); Morrison v. Olsen, 487 U.S. 654 (1988); Young v. United States *ex rel.* Vuitton, 481 U.S. 787 (1987); Buckley v. Valeo, 424 U.S. 1 (1976); Humphrey's Executor v. United States, 295 U.S. 602 (1935); *Ex Parte* Seibold, 100 U.S. 371 (1879); United States v. Germaine, 99 U.S. 508 (1879); United States v. Hartwell, 73 U.S. (6 Wall.) 385 (1868).

Lawyers in Congress

◦∿◦

JOHN C. YOO

When academics examine the role of the government lawyer, they tend to focus on the conflicting duties of members of the executive branch. Some question whether prosecutors are using the power of the state in a fair manner. Others write about the competing loyalties and incentives of the lawyers who work for the federal agencies that regulate private industry. Still others write about the tension between the partisan goals and professional responsibilities of lawyers who serve in the high-profile political positions in the executive branch, such as those who work in the White House counsel's office, the Office of Legal Counsel of the Justice Department, or, most famously, the solicitor general's office.

Curiously, these academics commonly ignore what the Framers considered the most dangerous branch of government: Congress. This neglect may occur for several reasons. Congress is a notoriously difficult subject for legal scholars to grapple with. When Congress passes a statute, it does not issue documents like judicial opinions that provide relatively clear decisions, explain the authority of the decision-making body, and set out the reasons for the decision. Unlike the executive branch, Congress does not leave behind a trail of memoranda, briefs, or records of meetings that allows the legal scholar to reconstruct decision paths and thought processes. Congress is home to a cacophony of people, issues, arguments, reports, hearings, speeches, and events, in which it is often difficult for an outsider to determine what has happened, why it has happened, and sometimes when it happened. A legal scholar researching Congress sometimes must feel as the head of the KGB once did while gathering intelligence on the United States: when the subject under study makes so much noise, it is difficult to tell what is important and what is not.

Legislative lawyers also may receive little attention because of the image of Congress in legal academia. Public choice scholars, for example, view Congress as a great auction house, in which legislation is sold to those narrowly focused, rent-seeking interest groups that channel the most money into legislators' campaign coffers. Under this approach, lawyers serving in Congress would play the role of glorified sales clerks or, if they have risen to higher levels as congressional aides, personal shoppers. Others view Congress as a willful, unpredictable, and even arbitrary institution that lacks the procedural protections and decision-making neutrality possessed by the executive or judicial branches. While one might expect some discussion of the role that congressional lawyers can play in structuring the legislative process to enhance deliberation, little attention has been given to this topic, perhaps because the legislators and even their aides are seen as the willful, self-interested actors that the legislative processes must control.[1] Even in positive political theory literature, which seeks to model the strategic interactions of goal-oriented legislators, congressional lawyers continue to receive scant attention.

Whatever the reason, scholarly neglect of attorneys in Congress is unfortunate. The role of congressional lawyers is richer and more complex than the standard story about the executive branch lawyer's internal tug of war between politics and public service. Because of the unique institutional function of Congress in our political system, the functions and duties of the lawyers who serve in the legislature also are unique. To illustrate these features of the congressional lawyer's role, I will discuss different events that occurred in Congress during my service as general counsel of the Senate Judiciary Committee from 1995 to 1996. My work in the Senate began just as the "Contract with America" was sweeping through the House and was meeting with resistance in the Senate, and it ended just after Senator Bob Dole resigned as majority leader and President Clinton appeared to be on his way to reelection. During that period, Senator Orrin G. Hatch of Utah was chairman of a committee of ten Republicans and eight Democrats—some freshman senators elected in 1994, others veterans who had been in the Senate for several decades. While I served as general counsel, the Judiciary Committee handled the Partial-Birth Abortion Bill, the Property Rights Bill, the habeas corpus reforms of the Anti-Terrorism Act, the investigations into Whitewater and what was later called "Filegate," and the criticism of President Clinton's nominees to the federal judiciary.

My experiences may provide some concrete examples about the interaction between Congress and the Constitution that is the subject of this book. By examining the role of lawyers, who are the congressional staff most fully aware of constitutional issues, scholars can get a better sense of how constitutional concerns affect the regular, everyday operations of Congress. My view is that the Constitution does not pull on Congress in any one way. Rather, the impact of constitutional issues modulates depending on the nature of the congressional activity. Thus, Congress may experience more freedom vis-à-vis the Constitution when it is engaging in the creative role of enacting new legislation, but it may prove more conscious and careful of constitutional rules when performing its investigative function.

THE LAWYER AS CONSTITUTIONAL ADVISOR

A significant part of the congressional attorney's job is to be a constitutional advisor to a member, a committee, or both. The unique institutional function of Congress in our republican system defines the contours of its lawyers' duties in the same manner that the function of the executive branch shapes the contours of its lawyers' duties. The latter experience a struggle between their loyalty to their president's political agenda, their allegiance to their agency or institution, and their duty to uphold the law, as passed by Congress, as interpreted by the judiciary, or as established by the Constitution. A related question arises concerning the breadth of executive branch interpretations of the law. Since the beginnings of the Republic, presidents such as Thomas Jefferson, Andrew Jackson, and Abraham Lincoln have argued that the executive branch has an independent, coordinate power to interpret the Constitution. Such a power is rooted in the president's oath to defend and uphold the Constitution, and his constitutional duty to "take Care that the Laws be faithfully executed."

The view that the executive branch has independent authority to interpret and enforce the Constitution is shared by many scholars,[2] but recently the view has gained ground that the Supreme Court's power to "say what the law is" requires that judicial precedent bind the executive branch.[3] Basically, the Supreme Court articulated the same argument in *Cooper v. Aaron*;[4] it holds that the Supreme Court interprets the Constitution, that its decisions are law, and that therefore its decisions are entitled to supremacy and to enforcement by the executive branch. Others have argued recently that the other branches should obey the Supreme Court because it performs the function of settling contested issues,[5] although this view seems to ignore the purpose of the separation of powers in guaranteeing that no one branch of government holds such final, authoritative power.

While congressional lawyers may undergo the same internal conflict as those in the executive branch, the Court's claims for judicial supremacy may have less force as applied against them. Congress's function as the lawmaking, rather than law-enforcing, branch requires attorneys in Congress to think more creatively about law. As is often the case, Congress must interpret the Constitution in areas that the Supreme Court has never reached and may never reach in the course of deciding cases or controversies.[6] Fulfilling its constitutional duty as the voice of the people inevitably forces Congress to test the outer limits imposed on its powers by the Constitution in order to solve current problems.

Attempting to remain faithful to the will of the people, Congress at times will articulate a vision of the Constitution that is at odds with that held by the Supreme Court. Perhaps the most notable example was the New Deal Congress's efforts to pass sweeping economic regulations in the face of hostile judicial precedent concerning the scope of the commerce clause. To be sure, the Supreme Court can and does strike down congressional efforts to reverse judicial decisions of constitutional law.[7] Nonetheless, the same rationale that compelled Presidents Jefferson, Jackson, and Lincoln to challenge judicial supremacy applies with at least equal force to Congress: Congress is an equal coordinate branch and is entitled to interpret the Constitution in the course of fulfilling its own constitutional duty of legislating. Although Congress may not force the judiciary to follow its theory of constitutional law, the Supreme Court cannot compel Congress to adopt the Court's positions, nor can it necessarily prohibit Congress from using the other powers at its disposal to achieve the ends it believes to be constitutional.

In assisting Congress in the performance of these functions, lawyers in Congress play an important role in advising members of the Senate and House. At a formalist level, because Congress does not bear the responsibility of executing the laws, congressional lawyers may not bear the same obligation to support judicial interpretation of the Constitution as that imposed on members of the other branches. Thus, any claim that Supreme Court decisions must be enforced because they are "law" might not apply to Congress with the same force as it does to the executive branch. Unlike the solicitor general, congressional lawyers do not hold any special relationship with another branch, such as the Supreme Court, that might override their loyalty to the members or institution of Congress. Even if one believed that congressional lawyers possess the same obligation to support the Constitution as that imposed on lawyers in the other branches of government, lawyers in Congress may still enjoy greater freedom to interpret the Constitution than their executive or judicial peers. If we view the committee counsel or legislative aide as the attorney, and the member of the House, the senator, or the committee as the client, then the proper job of the counsel or aide when confronted with a constitutional question is to explain the different approaches and arguments available. The client retains the ultimate authority to choose which actions to pursue and which legal arguments to adopt, and he or she cannot make that decision without being presented with the full range of constitutional arguments and options. Of course, this role is little different from that played by executive branch or private attorneys. Similarities to other lawyers, however, may end when it comes to the scope of arguments that congressional lawyers may make, because their clients have different constitutional duties. As mentioned above, Congress has less of a law-enforcing function and more of a creative, lawmaking role. To the extent that congressional lawyers have a duty under state bar rules of professional responsibility not to advance arguments contrary to fairly clear judicial precedent, it seems that the duty to enable the member of Congress to perform his or her creative lawmaking function must trump that obligation.[8] Furthermore, unlike with lawyers outside the legislative branch, there is less need for quality control with congressional lawyers, because any frivolous legal arguments they might make do not reach any court; they are instead filtered through Congress.

Under either view of the constitutional obligations of the congressional lawyer, it is the role of the lawyer to provide the Congress and its members with the full range of constitutional arguments and options. The lawyer plays a tempering role as well, however. At least in my experience, senators take seriously the prospect that the Supreme Court may invalidate legislation that they support. Aside from their desire to avoid having their legislation struck down, they also want to avoid Supreme Court invalidation because of both the negative public attention that it would draw and the delay that it would create for legislative efforts to solve national problems. A congressional lawyer can advise a senator to vote against a bill because it is flatly unconstitutional or, even more usefully, to modify or oppose a bill because it will be invalidated by the Supreme Court. To render accurate predictions about the future actions of a coordinate branch of government, the congressional lawyer necessarily draws on his technical knowledge of the legal and judicial system, as well as his political acumen.

The substantial political costs associated with Supreme Court intervention allow the lawyer to restrain unwise assertions of constitutional power, or at least to persuade members of Congress to consider carefully certain courses of action. Of course, the lawyer must also balance this cautionary role with the lawyer's job to enable the client, who has the independent right to interpret the Constitution, to achieve his or her goals.

These dual aspects of the lawyer's role were evident during the Senate Judiciary Committee's consideration of several significant constitutional questions from 1995 to 1996. One example involved the proposed Partial-Birth Abortion Ban Act of 1995.[9] In that bill, opponents of abortion (including Chairman Hatch) proposed legislation that would ban certain types of late-term abortions throughout the country. Two questions were immediately raised: whether such a ban would violate a pregnant woman's right to an abortion and whether Congress enjoyed the enumerated power to pass a nationwide ban.[10] The Office of Legal Counsel of the Justice Department (OLC) quickly circulated an opinion letter maintaining that the bill would violate a woman's right to an abortion as recognized in *Roe v. Wade*[11] and affirmed in *Planned Parenthood v. Casey*.[12] According to the OLC, the violation rested on the bill's failure to provide an explicit exception for abortions performed to save the life or health of the mother and its inclusion of criminal penalties, which would have a chilling effect on physicians who perform abortions.[13] Other opponents argued that in light of *United States v. Lopez*,[14] the nationwide regulation of abortion lies outside Congress's commerce clause powers.[15]

In advising Chairman Hatch and the Judiciary Committee on the constitutionality of this legislation, committee lawyers undertook two tasks. First, they provided dual justifications for the legislation, one that might pass muster before the Supreme Court and the other relying as an original matter on constitutional text, history, and tradition without reference to recent Supreme Court doctrine. For the first justification, committee lawyers noted that the undue burden test adopted by the plurality in *Casey* failed to specify clearly whether an exception for the life or health of the mother was required in all cases. As the bill lacked such an exception, they recommended that to be safe the Senate could amend the bill to add one, but they also stated that it was unclear if the ban, without the exception, would fail constitutional muster.

In the second, alternative justification for the proposed statute—the one outside the context of the Supreme Court's opinions—committee lawyers noted that Congress could reach its own interpretation of the Constitution and could decide, if it wished, to enforce it rather than the doctrines of the Supreme Court. Following the reasoning of the dissent in *Casey*, Congress could maintain that abortion rights could be regulated by government free from the restrictions of the Fourteenth Amendment, based on a reading of the text of the Fourteenth Amendment and its original understanding. Such an aggressive use of Congress's authority to interpret the Constitution was unnecessary, however, because Congress could argue merely that in this gray area, in which the Court's own precedents were unclear—phrases like "undue burden" or "the health of the mother" leave a lot of room to maneuver—the legislature could interject its own interpretation without challenging the whole structure of abortion rights. Given the unsettled nature of this area of the law, Congress might have a special duty to use its lawmaking powers to either clarify this situation by legislation or force the Court to reconsider its own precedents in a politically controversial area.[16]

The congressional lawyer's role also might include providing senators with strategic advice about the benefits and costs of relying upon different constitutional bases for action. It seemed unwise for pro-life senators to pursue a more aggressive effort to challenge the Supreme Court, given that the justices of the *Casey* plurality (Justices O'Connor, Kennedy, and Souter) were still on the Court and that President Clinton's two appointments (Justices Ginsburg and Breyer) clearly were pro-choice. Further, the Court's general approach to abortion rights was in harmony with the opinion of the majority of Americans (as indicated by polling data). As a result, it was very likely that any veiled effort to reverse *Roe v. Wade* would fail, and the negative political fallout from such an attempt would be correspondingly severe. On the other hand, polling data also showed that public opinion supported the narrower ban on what the bill defined as partial-birth abortions. As such, Congress could enjoy a political upside and potential judicial success if it chose to operate within the Court's constitutional framework. This meant either amending the statute to include an exception for the life or health of the mother, or producing convincing evidence that the life and health of the mother were implicated in a statistically insignificant number of cases in which the procedure at issue was used.

While strategic judgments of this sort cannot restrict Congress's power to interpret the Constitution, they can influence how individual senators choose to use that power. As an advisor, the lawyer in Congress performs a dual role in both recognizing the independent force of Congress's interpretive powers and tempering it. Congressional lawyers can moderate this power not by urging deference to the Supreme Court's opinions but by demonstrating to members of Congress the political benefits of operating within the Court's jurisprudence. Lawyers are able to do this, of course, because of the substantial prestige and respect that the Court has gained among the American public. However, as the Court expands the scope of its review further into areas of social regulation over which the nation is deeply divided, it may weaken the congressional lawyer's ability to recommend cooperation by Congress and may provoke more congressional challenges to the Court.

Members of Congress listen to constitutional advice not just because it may make good strategic sense, however. Staff lawyers advising their members do more than just chart out methods for legislators to sail their laws past the judiciary. This is so because members of Congress take an oath to uphold and defend the Constitution, and they take that job seriously.

THE LAWYER AS DEAL MAKER

A second, more common role of the congressional lawyer is in developing legislation. Because many important members of congressional staffs have law degrees, congressional lawyers often supervise the legislative process: the meetings with interest groups, the hearings, the committee markups, the deals between legislators, the floor debates, the public and press relations, and the votes. To be sure, the staff lawyer's role usually does not extend in a significant way to setting legislative and political priorities and initiating legislation, which are within the domain of the members of Congress, the executive branch, and nongovernmental interest groups. Nonetheless, the lawyer's role in operating the procedures through which these proposals must pass raises interesting issues concerning the nature of the legislative process and the lawyer's role in it.

For example, some students of the legislative process believe that Congress primarily acts as a forum for the making of deals between interest groups.[17] In this model, legislators are motivated by the desire for reelection; to be reelected, officeholders need to raise money and political support to fund their campaigns. Interest groups promote legislation by guiding political support and funneling campaign contributions to these candidates; in return, legislators enact laws that benefit these groups. Interest groups will usually form when a small class of interested individuals or entities can receive high rents from some narrow piece of legislation. Of course, interest groups will also form to stop legislation that harms them; the more concentrated the harm inflicted by a bill, the more likely an interest group will form to stop it. Legislation will pass, this model predicts, when the rents received by an interest group surpass the cost in campaign contributions of making it pass, and when the costs imposed on others by the legislation are spread diffusely. Although some public choice scholars are dubious that legislative process advances the "public interest," pluralists view interest group politics as desirable because the process facilitates stability, moderation, and broad satisfaction with the political system.[18]

Of course, the model described here is an extreme simplification of the public choice theory of legislation. Nonetheless, if the interest group–driven theory of politics is correct, it will influence the nature of the lawyer's role in lawmaking. A congressional staff lawyer in this system might perform duties similar to that of a corporate transaction attorney. For example, staff lawyers might want to use their skills to help different groups find common ground to reach mutually advantageous deals and provide ways for the actors to be sure that the others will keep their promises. They might want to make sure that members of Congress received support from the interest groups in exchange for legislative support of the groups' goals. They might counsel their members and even the interest groups on different ways to structure a legislative deal so as to maximize benefits, on the likely strategies of opponents who want to stop the deal, and on how to reduce legislative transaction costs.

Other models of the legislative process might alter a lawyer's duties accordingly. Consider, for example, a new body of political theory known as the new institutionalism or positive political theory. This approach holds that political outcomes depend on the interaction of multiple decision makers and the manner in which they anticipate the positions and responses of each other.[19] Institutions and rules play important roles in this model because they regulate the manner in which the players interact. A congressional lawyer who believed positive political theory to be correct might expend considerable energy ensuring that the different players in the system communicated to one another accurately and that the procedural rules that determined their role in the legislative process were followed. A different reaction to public choice theory, neorepublicanism—which can trace its roots back to the legal process school—holds that the legislative process should be designed to promote deliberation and reason in order to use government power to promote the common good.[20] If such theories were correct, Congress would seek to follow legislative procedures that led to well-informed, deliberate, efficient decisions.

The potential conflict between these different roles makes itself apparent in the advancement of legislation through Congress. For example, if the lawyer views the legislative process solely as an arena for interest group bargains, then the lawyer's duty may be to ensure the passage of legislation regardless of the method. The most effective approach might be to slip the desired legislation directly into a bill that must be passed at all costs, such as a continuing resolution or an emergency spending measure. The lawyer could tuck the provision into the larger bill by amendment directly on the floor of the House or Senate, preferably by voice vote, without a hearing or committee markup. This method reduces the chances that opposing interest groups, the press, or the public will discover the legislation and seek to stop it. Acting stealthily also undercuts the significant power of the majority leadership to set the legislative agenda by controlling floor consideration of bills. One might expect such behavior to occur when important financial and business interests are seeking a narrow change in a regulatory law that would impose significant, but diffuse, costs on the public, such as when an industry wants its treatment under the antitrust laws relaxed so that it can engage in activity that might raise consumer prices. Legislative history, if any, could be produced by the interest group itself, and legislators and their staff would rely on the interest group to mobilize support among other members of Congress, track the progress of the legislation, and generate and distribute information about the proposal.

Such maneuvers are not limited to bills of interest to financial or business groups. The attachment of riders to appropriations bill or continuing resolutions is a time-honored tactic that can be used for legislation more public-spirited in nature. In 1996, for example, the Senate Judiciary Committee considered the Prison Litigation Reform Act, which placed substantive limits on the authority of federal courts to manage prisons.[21] While the bill received a hearing, it never received an executive markup or approval by the Senate Judiciary Committee for floor consideration. Proponents of the bill, who included members of the committee, succeeded in attaching the legislation to a funding vehicle whose passage was imperative. While opponents of the legislation knew of the riders and had some opportunity to debate them on the merits, this process was certainly not as open and robust as that afforded by a usual up-or-down vote on a stand-alone bill.

All legislation does not follow this path, however. For example, during the 104th Congress, I helped manage the Judiciary Committee's consideration of a bill offered as the Omnibus Property Rights Act of 1995.[22] The bill sought to codify recent Supreme Court decisions in the area of takings[23] and to create bright-line rules to govern when federal agencies had to pay just compensation for imposing regulations on private property.[24] Unlike narrower special interest legislation, this bill went through the regular process of legislative decision making. It was introduced as a free-standing bill by Senator Dole and thirty-one cosponsors. The Judiciary Committee held three hearings, which included witnesses such as property owners, senators, Justice Department officials, the chief judge of the U.S. Court of Claims, law professors, lawyers, and the counselor to the secretary of the interior department.[25] Several days of committee meetings were held, during which senators engaged in vigorous debate over the constitutionality and effectiveness of the bill. In the end, the committee passed the bill 10–7 and issued a report in which no outside interest group had any hand. Although successfully reported out of committee, the bill never came to the floor for a vote because of the likely success of a threatened filibuster.

If the simplistic version of the public choice model of legislation held complete sway, these stages of congressional decision making might have been superfluous. A senator's individual wishes or a party's agenda on legislation would have been bought and paid for by an interest group, and therefore a more effective tactic might have been to hold minimal hearings, if any, then bypass a committee vote and seek to attach the bill as a floor amendment to an omnibus spending bill or a continuing resolution. Instead, in this case the Judiciary Committee tried to ensure that Congress received a wide range of information and that it carefully and fully deliberated on policy decisions. As a result, the committee used the full legislative process, which gave all interested parties—property owners and environmentalists alike—an opportunity to present their opinions, recommend changes, and observe committee actions. If we were bestowing narrow benefits on rent-seeking interest groups, such as property owners, I was not aware of it. During the process of moving the bill forward and drafting the committee report, neither property rights groups nor environmental groups played a significant role, although I was always open to the compelling arguments of my academic colleagues in the executive branch. More importantly for purposes of the distributional approach to legislation, these groups generally were not funded, did not seem to make large campaign contributions, and did not determine legislative priorities. To be sure, the staff had not placed the property rights bill on the congressional agenda; no doubt outside interest groups influenced that decision. Once the legislative process began, however, the influence of interest groups waned in favor of control by the congressional staffs.

A political scientist might observe that the committee's procedures operated to gather, generate, and disseminate information: Congress is organized, some scholars have maintained, so that policymakers can collect information to address uncertainty concerning the effect of decisions.[26] However, this was a by-product of the legislative process, not its main focus. For example, the committee did not use hearings or other devices in any meaningful way to gather information about the impact that different takings provisions would have on property rights and environmental regulations. Such information is more readily available and digestible in the form of written studies and case reports. Instead, hearings were an opportunity for committee members to test-fly different arguments and ideas to justify the bill. Hearings provided not only an opportunity to present victims' stories to the other members of Congress and the press but also a forum for legislators to explain why they were supporting or attacking the bill. Committee reports and markups served the same purpose. One senator spoke for almost three straight days in markup about why he was voting against the property rights bill. He did so less to win senators to his position—the votes were all accounted for before the markup even began, or there would have been no markup—than to float criticisms of the bill to see which ones gained the most "traction." Such discussions in committee allowed the testing of arguments to see which ones would gain favor among the press, interest groups, and ultimately the public. Although it would be a gross overstatement to say that hearings or markups acted as glorified press conferences, they did serve to test arguments—running the traps or bulletproofing, as it were—and create a "record" upon which debate over the legislation could occur.

Throughout this process, the congressional lawyer seeks to achieve certain procedural goals. The goals are not simply to distribute information favorable to the lawyer's side but rather to see that certain elements of what might be called legislative procedural due process are followed: (1) all hearings allow both the majority and minority to call witnesses; (2) witnesses receive the opportunity to make full statements for the record and to supplement the record with additional materials after the hearing; (3) senators of both parties receive equal time to ask questions and present their observations; (4) the executive branch enjoys the right to testify on any issue; (5) both sides may include statements of virtually any length in the committee reports; and (6) senators may speak for an almost unlimited time during markup. These procedures, which are developed and observed by committee lawyers, ensure that the majority and minority have an equal opportunity to make their arguments known. Committee lawyers might have even more affinity for procedural fidelity, given their training and experience in the law.

Disseminating information by itself, however, serves little purpose. I would suggest that lawyers in Congress work to guarantee the free flow of information because doing so leads to greater deliberation about the merits of policy decisions. Presenting arguments in hearings and markups forces the other side to respond to them. Contrary to the more pessimistic theories of legislation, no senator likes to vote yes or no simply because he or she was told to do so by an interest group. During my tenure working for the Senate, no senator in the Judiciary Committee rose and came out for or against the property rights bill simply on the orders of the Sierra Club or the Defenders of Property Rights. Not surprisingly, a legislator—regardless of motivation for voting on a bill—wants an argument, a rationale, and a justification for his or her vote, and the testing of these reasons leads to greater deliberation before the public on issues of policy.

To be sure, the existence of procedures does not lead inevitably to the conclusion that Congress and its staff are working toward greater deliberation in policymaking. One could argue that legislative due process and the institutions that operate by it, such as committees, arose to ease problems that a public choice model of legislation might face. For example, if the legislature amounted to a bazaar with few, if any, procedures (other than the rule of the highest bidder), then the legislative process might devolve quickly into a political state of nature. Legislators might engage in extreme tactics—such as loading up every appropriations bill at the last minute with all manner of riders—because of a prisoner's dilemma problem. Procedures such as limiting the number of riders, or requiring bills to undergo the open process of hearing and committee markup, might arise after a series of tit-for-tat interactions by legislators. Rules could create the context necessary to allow interest groups to purchase laws—by providing mechanisms for measuring political support, for guaranteeing that legislators will keep their promises, and for facilitating bargaining—that avoid a sort of tragedy of the legislative commons.[27]

It might be thought that in pursuing either set of goals—greater deliberation or interest group politics—the congressional lawyer is not giving full loyalty to the client (the senator or committee that hired him or her), the majority leader that heads the Senate, or the political party that forms the network for the majority and sets its agenda. In regard to deliberation, it can be argued that individual members, committees, and party caucuses are best served when Congress acts in an open, considered manner rather than in a haphazard, ad hoc one. Not only may better public policy result, as neorepublicans like to think, but a deliberative process promotes the image of Congress in the public mind, thereby bolstering the legislature's power to impose its preferences upon the other branches. For a congressional lawyer, this goal is also in the best interests of the party, the leadership, and the senator or committee; strengthening the political reputation of Congress enhances the means by which these various clients will seek to promote their agendas. With regard to public choice or institutionalist theories, the lawyer allows the process to function smoothly by making sure that rules are clear and are obeyed. Without these rules, the resulting uncertainty would undermine the bargaining or strategic interaction necessary for the passage of legislation.

It might also be thought that the congressional lawyer is playing a role that is in tension with democratic government. If the people want a policy, and they elect representatives to implement that policy, then lawyers delay and slow down progress toward that goal by imposing legislative due process procedures. Visiting the United States in the early nineteenth century, Alexis de Tocqueville observed that lawyers love order and formalities, which were "naturally strongly opposed to the revolutionary spirit and to the ill-considered passions of democracy."[28] As a result, American lawyers, like the European nobility, "conceive a great distaste for the behavior of the multitude and secretly scorn the government of the people."[29] The lawyer's procedural, formalist way of thinking buttresses the existing procedural hurdles for legislation, such as the Senate, the filibuster, the presidential veto, and judicial review, which themselves are countermajoritarian. Although the congressional lawyer may not knowingly play this role, what the lawyer does further enhances the mechanisms established by the framers to tame the legislature, which they feared "is every where extending the sphere of its activity, and drawing all power into its impetuous vortex."[30] In this respect, the congressional lawyer acts as an unknowing agent of the separation of powers.

THE LAWYER AS INVESTIGATOR

Congressional lawyers' role as a check on the power of the institution they serve comes to the fore when Congress employs its powers of investigation and oversight. Congress's power to conduct such inquiries inheres in its power to study and pass legislation, and it has used this power since the very beginning of the Republic to investigate maladministration in the executive branch, to determine whether social conditions require new legislation, and to review the success of existing laws. Congress's constitutional power to conduct investigations and its auxiliary power to force witnesses to appear before it and produce evidence go formally unchecked. Congress may conduct investigations into any subject, so long as it does so in furtherance of a valid legislative purpose.[31] It may call any witness, seek any evidence related to its investigation, and hire an army of lawyers and staff to conduct the investigation. To force recalcitrant witnesses to testify, Congress may use its own power to impose civil contempt sanctions, pursuant to which the House or Senate can issue and execute an arrest warrant and imprison the witness. While Congress must observe the procedural guarantees of the Bill of Rights in conducting its investigations, it may be under no legal obligation to obey other protections not rooted in the Constitution.[32] Since 1857, however, Congress has limited its own investigatory powers by passing a criminal contempt law that requires it to vote on whether to adopt a contempt resolution, and which then requires a contempt citation to be referred to a U.S. attorney for prosecution.[33] Because this procedure enables the president to order the U.S. attorney not to pursue a prosecution or even to pardon a witness convicted of contempt, it allows for some separation-of-powers check on Congress's investigatory powers.

Despite its untrammeled powers of investigation, Congress generally recognizes several unwritten rules of restraint. In 1996, for example, the Judiciary Committee led the investigation into the Clinton administration's alleged improper collection and handling of the FBI security files of members of previous Republican administrations. Before the committee's hearings, staff lawyers sent letters to the White House and the Justice Department that were framed very much like discovery requests in federal civil litigation. Claims of privilege were accepted if a proper explanation was provided, documents were delivered in boxes at the last minute,

Bates stamps and document indices were used. Committee staff conducted depositions at which the witness was permitted to bring counsel, invoke privileges, and refuse to answer questions. Staff lawyers recognized claims of attorney-client privilege, and they avoided areas involving the personal privacy of individuals (such as hiring records), even though Congress is under no obligation to observe discovery protections that are not rooted in the Constitution. Committee staff even recognized claims of executive privilege, despite Congress's independent authority, as suggested earlier, to interpret the Constitution. Staff did not force witnesses taking the Fifth Amendment to do so on television.

In following these unwritten rules, the congressional lawyer's restraining role is placed in the sharpest relief. Here lawyers are acting to control perhaps Congress's most unrestrained power, which can operate free from any substantial check by the executive or judicial branches. As with the committee's adoption of the federal discovery rules, these norms of behavior serve the purpose of supplying an off-the-shelf, widely understood system that allows attorneys to impose order upon the investigatory process. Lawyers need these rules, furthermore, precisely because the investigatory process itself has no inherent rules and, as such, is most vulnerable to abuse by Congress in the service of personal or wholly partisan agendas.[34] As the only barrier between the individual and the broad power of Congress to conduct investigations, congressional lawyers are acting at their bravest; they cannot rely on Supreme Court decisions or other institutions to support their efforts to regulate congressional power.

One thing to note about these experiences is the manner in which the role of the congressional lawyer modulates in response to the nature of congressional activity. In offering constitutional advice, lawyers appear to take more of a technician's role in charting out different paths of argument for the member of Congress to justify certain decisions. In investigations, however, lawyers play perhaps their most independent, public-spirited role in restraining the unchecked power of Congress. Lawyers' activities in the field of legislation seem to fall somewhere in between, with their role fluctuating between facilitating interest group deals and being agents of deliberation and open government.

Perhaps one way to explain these changing roles is that when Congress acts in a less public-spirited, more partisan, or more self-interested manner, lawyers respond by expanding their roles in restraining Congress.

When Congress itself is promoting deliberation, or using fair procedures, or exercising its independent right to interpret the Constitution, then the lawyer's role is less pronounced because it is less necessary. This function underscores the lawyers' role as a tempering, even civilizing force in politics. While Congress is not a free-for-all, it does exercise its enormous constitutional powers in a more ad hoc, immediate, and unrestrained manner than the other branches do. Congress does not have an Office of Legal Counsel to advise against passing bills that are unconstitutional; it does not have a cabinet or a National Security Council to deliberate policy and weigh options; there are no higher bodies of review, no precedents, no doctrines that it must obey.[35] The Framers designed Congress to be the most reactive and sensitive branch of government to the wants and desires of the people; it cannot be as hidebound as the other branches in expressing the popular will.

Lawyers serve as an important check on such unleashed power by informally restraining and channeling Congress's political will. By training, lawyers understand the importance of neutral principles, of fair processes, and of rational arguments, and when working for Congress they inject these values into an institution that by its nature is designed to "exercise will instead of judgment."[36] On a smaller scale, lawyers in Congress perform the same function that Alexis de Tocqueville saw them play in American society as a whole, the function of restraining ill-considered democracy.[37] While they work to execute the will of Congress, congressional lawyers also act to temper that will, to ensure that it results from judgment as much as from passion.

The role of lawyers may help in analyzing the relationship between Congress and the Constitution, the subject of this book. Different scholars will have different attitudes concerning the approach that Congress takes toward the Constitution, both as a source of its powers and as a limit on them. An important consideration in judging the persuasiveness of these theories is to examine whether it is likely that individual members and their staffs, acting through committees as well as through the Congress as a whole, are likely to be motivated to act in the manner proposed. Here I have sought to provide some examples from my experience as a staff lawyer in Congress that may provide some context to explain how Congress handles its relationship with the Constitution.

NOTES

A slightly different version of this essay appears in 61 *Law and Contemporary Problems* 133 (spring 1998).

1 See Elizabeth Garrett and Adrian Vermeule, "Institutional Design of a Thayerian Congress," in this volume.
2 See Michael S. Paulsen, "The Most Dangerous Branch: Executive Power to Say What the Law Is," 83 *Georgetown Law Journal* 217 (1994). See also Alexander M. Bickel, *The Least Dangerous Branch: The Supreme Court at the Bar of Politics* (Indianapolis: Bobbs-Merrill, 1962), 263–64; Edward S. Corwin, *Court over Constitution: A Study of Judicial Review as an Instrument of Popular Government* (Princeton: Princeton University Press, 1938), 15–17; Edwin Meese III, "The Law of the Constitution," 61 *Tulane Law Review* 979 (1987).
3 See, e.g., Dan T. Coenen, "The Constitutional Case against Intracircuit Nonacquiescence," 75 *Minnesota Law Review* 1339 (1991); see generally Symposium, "Executive Branch Interpretation of the Law," 15 *Cardozo Law Review* 21 (1993); Symposium, "Elected Branch Influences in Constitutional Decisionmaking," 56 *Law and Contemporary Problems* 1 (autumn 1993).
4 358 U.S. 1, 18–19 (1958).
5 See Larry Alexander and Frederick Schauer, "On Extrajudicial Constitutional Interpretation," 110 *Harvard Law Review* 1359 (1997).
6 See generally Gerhard Casper, *Separating Power: Essays on the Founding Period* (Cambridge: Harvard University Press, 1997); David P. Currie, *The Constitution in Congress: The Federalist Period, 1789–1801* (Chicago: University of Chicago Press, 1997); Stanley Elkins and Eric McKitrick, *The Age of Federalism: The Early American Republic, 1788–1800* (New York: Oxford University Press, 1993); Keith E. Whittington, *Constitutional Construction: Divided Powers and Constitutional Meaning* (Cambridge: Harvard University Press, 1999).
7 See City of Boerne v. Flores, 117 S. Ct. 2157 (1997) (striking down the Religious Freedom Restoration Act); United States v. Eichman, 496 U.S. 310 (1990) (striking down the Flag Protection Act of 1989).
8 Just as states are not permitted to use their taxing powers to interfere with the effective operation of federal instrumentalities, see McCulloch v. Maryland, 17 U.S. (4 Wheat.) 316 (1819), so too they may not be allowed, through their authority over state bar organizations, to interfere with the proper conduct of members of the legislative branch. Relying on the supremacy clause, Attorneys General Richard Thornburgh and Janet Reno took a similar posi-

tion in 1989, when they concluded that federal prosecutors should not be held liable to state bar ethics rules when contacting parties without first alerting their attorneys.

9 House Committee on the Judiciary, *Partial-Birth Abortion Ban Act of 1995*, 104th Cong., 1st sess., 27 September 1995, H.R. 1833.

10 See Senate Committee on the Judiciary, *The Partial-Birth Abortion Ban Act of 1995: Hearing before the Senate Comm. on the Judiciary*, 104th Cong., 1st sess., 22 November 1995, 104-260 [hereinafter *Partial-Birth Abortion Ban Hearings*].

11 410 U.S. 113 (1973).

12 505 U.S. 833 (1992).

13 The Clinton administration's position was recapitulated in the written testimony by the assistant attorney general for the Office of Legal Counsel of the Justice Department in a Senate hearing on the bill. See *Partial-Birth Abortion Ban Hearings*, 300-305 (testimony of Walter Dellinger).

14 514 U.S. 549 (1995) (holding that congressional action must have a substantial effect on interstate commerce).

15 See *Partial-Birth Abortion Ban Hearings*, 193 (testimony of Louis Seidman).

16 For other examples, see *Religious Freedom Restoration Act*, 42 U.S.C. §§ 2000bb-2000bb-4 (1994), and the *Omnibus Property Rights Act of 1995*, 104th Cong., 1st sess., S. 605 (1995).

17 See, e.g., James Buchanan and Gordon Tullock, *The Calculus of Consent* (Ann Arbor: University of Michigan Press, 1962); Mancur Olson, *The Logic of Collective Action* (New York: Schocken, 1968); William Riker, *Liberalism against Populism* (Prospect Heights, Ill: Waveland, 1982).

18 See William N. Eskridge Jr. and Philip P. Frickey, *Cases and Materials on Legislation: Statutes and the Creation of Public Policy* (St. Paul: West, 1994), 50; Theodore Lowi, *The End of Liberalism*, 2d ed. (New York: W. W. Norton, 1979).

19 See, e.g., Peter Ordeshook, *A Political Theory Primer* (New York: Routledge, 1992).

20 See, e.g., "Symposium: The Republican Civic Tradition," 97 *Yale Law Journal* 1493 (1988).

21 See John Choon Yoo, "Who Measures the Chancellor's Foot: The Inherent Remedial Authority of the Federal Courts," 84 *California Law Review* 1121, 1174-77 (1996).

22 *Omnibus Property Rights Act of 1995*, 104th Cong., 1st sess., S. 605.

23 See, e.g., Dolan v. City of Tigard, 512 U.S. 374 (1994); Lucas v. South Carolina Coastal Council, 505 U.S. 1003 (1992); Nollan v. California Coastal Commission, 483 U.S. 825 (1987).

24 See *Omnibus Property Rights Act of 1995*, 104th Cong., 1st sess., S. 605 § 204(a)-(f) (1995); see also Senate Committee on Judiciary, *S. 605: The*

Omnibus Property Rights Act of 1995, 104th Cong., 2d sess., 1 March 1996, S. Rept. 104-239, 20–26.

25 Senate Committee on Judiciary, *S. 605: The Omnibus Property Rights Act of 1995*, 104th Cong., 2d sess., 1 March 1996, S. Rept. 104-239, 12–13.

26 See, e.g., Keith Krehbiel, *Information and Legislative Organization* (Ann Arbor: University of Michigan Press, 1991); William N. Eskridge, "Overriding Supreme Court Statutory Interpretation Decisions," 101 *Yale Law Journal* 331, 356–57 (1991).

27 A cynic might argue that the rules also conceal interest group deals being struck. Even if it were true that legislation is the product of interest group demands, members of Congress could not afford to admit that this was the true state of affairs. Procedures would give the appearance that deliberation in the public interest was going on. But once these procedures are established, they would begin to have a normative force of their own and later actors in the legislative game might follow them simply because they exist.

28 Alexis de Tocqueville, *Democracy in America*, vol. 1, ed. J. P. Mayer and Max Lerner, trans. George Lawrence (New York: Harper and Row, 1996), 264.

29 *Id.*

30 *The Federalist* 48 (James Madison).

31 See Watkins v. United States, 354 U.S. 178, 198 (1957); see also McGrain v. Daugherty, 273 U.S. 135, 172 (1927); Kilbourn v. Thompson, 103 U.S. 168, 190 (1880).

32 See Special Committee to Investigate Whitewater Development Corporation and Related Matters, Senate Committee on Banking, Housing and Urban Affairs, *Refusal of William H. Kennedy III to Produce Notes Subpoenaed by the Special Committee to Investigate Whitewater Development Corporation and Related Matters*, 104th Cong., 1st sess., 19 December 1995, S. Rpt. 104-191, 11–12.

33 See 2 U.S.C. § 192 (1994).

34 It might be argued that Congress as an institution also needs these investigatory rules. Procedural rules protecting witnesses reduce the chances that the proceedings will be dismissed as a raw exercise of power. They are also so widely accepted on normative grounds as to be a cheap way to establish that the investigations will be perceived as fair.

35 Of course, Congress has a committee structure and procedural rules that enhance deliberation. See Charles Tiefer, "The Flag-Burning Controversy of 1989–1990: Congress' Valid Role in Constitutional Dialogue," 29 *Harvard Journal on Legislation* 357 (1992). Congress adopts these processes at its own pleasure, however, and it often bypasses their use.

36 *The Federalist* 78 (Alexander Hamilton).

37 See de Tocqueville, *Democracy in America*, vol. 1, 262–70.

Congressional Responses to Judicial Review

∾

J. MITCHELL PICKERILL

Referring to the Supreme Court's exercise of judicial review, Justice Antonin Scalia recently remarked, "We don't strike laws down. We just ignore them."[1] What exactly is the status of legislation that has been rendered constitutionally invalid by the Court? Traditional notions of judicial review suggest that the only way to revive an unconstitutional statute is to amend the Constitution to overcome the Supreme Court decision. However, in recent years an increasing number of scholars have questioned the "finality" of the Court's exercise of judicial review, arguing that Congress can and should challenge the Court's constitutional decisions through normal legislative means. The question is thus raised: Has Congress in fact responded to the Supreme Court's exercise of judicial review? And if so, how?

This chapter will show that Congress does respond to judicial review in a variety of ways. Judicial nullification of federal statutes does not necessarily, or even usually, signify that judicial review is the final action on a statute. However, congressional responses to judicial review may not always amount to challenges to the Court's constitutional holdings either. After the Court has invalidated legislation, Congress may do nothing, amend the Constitution or pass new legislation to override the Court, pass legislation to circumvent the Court, pass legislation to comply with the Court, or repeal the legislation to comply with the Court. The evidence in this chapter will show that by far the most common congressional response to judicial review is for Congress to modify legislation in a manner that complies with the Court's constitutional holding but preserves statutory policy in some form. Careful examination of congressional responses will demonstrate that revised legislation rarely challenges or overrides the Court's constitutional interpretations. Consequently, judicial review should not be viewed as an obstacle to legislation: instead it frequently forces revisions of legislation that reflect and incorporate the Court's constitutional views.

CONGRESSIONAL RESPONSES
AND COORDINATE CONSTRUCTION

Although it is common to view the Supreme Court's exercise of judicial review as the final nail in the coffin for legislation, scholars who advocate "coordinate construction" of the Constitution outside the Court have argued forcefully that as a coequal branch of government, Congress may challenge or ignore the Court's interpretation. Coordinate construction advocates have provided anecdotal evidence and detailed case studies showing that Congress does challenge Court decisions by passing responsive legislation. One well-known example involves *INS v. Chadha* (1983) and the legislative veto.[2] In that case, the Court invalidated portions of the Immigration and Nationality Act that granted Congress a one-house legislative veto over decisions by the Immigration and Naturalization Service (INS) regarding the deportation of aliens. The Court held that the legislative veto violated separation-of-powers provisions, specifically constitutional requirements of bicameralism and presentment. As Louis Fisher and others have shown, however, Congress has largely ignored the Court's holding and continues to use legislative vetoes.[3] As I will discuss in more detail later in this chapter, Congress eventually amended the Immigration and Nationality Act to recodify legislative vetoes over INS decisions, and as Fisher illustrates, Congress continues to use legislative vetoes in other policy areas and over other administrative agencies. Hence, coordinate constructionists presume that Congress substituted its own constitutional interpretation for that of the Court, thus overriding the Court's holding in *Chadha*.

In addition to the anecdotal or case study evidence provided by coordinate construction scholars, others have applied rational choice theory and more systematic quantitative methods to congressional responses to Supreme Court decisions. Rational choice and separation-of-powers models have analyzed how the Court and Congress each have the opportunity to influence the meaning of a statute, and how the members of each branch will consider the other during the decision-making process. A number of studies have analyzed how and why Congress "overrides" statutory construction decisions of the Court by passing legislation to undo the judicial interpretation.[4] The approach taken in these studies assumes that justices on the Supreme Court compete with members of Congress over a priori policy preferences, and thus members of Congress will pass legislation to override a Court decision if a majority of the members disagree with the Court decision.

While much of the empirical scholarship on "congressional overrides" has focused on court decisions involving statutory construction, at least one study has extended that conceptual framework to congressional responses to judicial review. Citing coordinate construction scholars and theories, James Meernik and Joseph Ignagni conclude that Congress engages in coordinate construction when it amends legislation that addresses the Court's judicial review decisions.[5] They find that members of Congress often modify legislation in response to the Court's judicial review decisions, and they conclude that Congress overrides the Court's constitutional decisions, thus exercising coordinate construction with frequency.

The analytical picture painted by these studies is helpful for understanding how the Court and Congress interact over matters of judicial review and constitutional interpretation, but there are some limitations. Case studies such as the legislative veto example provide great detail to affirm that Congress does sometimes deliberately defy the Court and reject judicial supremacy by passing legislation to override or challenge the Court's constitutional interpretations. However, those studies do not provide systematic evidence as to when and how often we should expect Congress to do so. Rational choice theories and the study by Meernik and Ignagni provide more theoretical rigor and systematic evidence on the matter, but they lack detail and context regarding the substantive nature of congressional responses. Moreover, both approaches only consider one category of congressional response and assume that a congressional response amounts to an override, independent constitutional interpretation, or challenge to the Court's constitutional interpretations. I suggest here that these studies overestimate the frequency with which Congress overrides or challenges the Court's constitutional interpretations, and they fail to account for important variations in the nature of congressional responses to judicial review.

An analogy to the presidential veto can help illustrate how the exercise of judicial review, like the president's exercise of the veto, may not always stop Congress from pursuing legislation even if Congress is unable to "override" the other institution. Members of Congress may prefer modified legislation to no legislation. Consider welfare reform legislation considered and passed in Congress during 1995–96. After gaining a majority of both houses in Congress in 1994, the Republicans were determined to pass welfare reform legislation. In 1995 they passed two welfare reform statutes, largely along party lines. President Bill Clinton vetoed both bills, claiming they went too far in cutting funds and other measures. The Republican majority did not throw in the towel, however. After Clinton's state of the union address in 1996, in which he signaled his willingness to sign a bipartisan and less extreme welfare reform bill, Republicans worked with congressional Democrats to pass a third version of welfare reform. On 22 August 1996 President Clinton signed the welfare reform bill into law as Public Law 104-193. While the Republicans had to modify many of the provisions of the bill, they were able to accommodate the president's preferences and still pass far-reaching, landmark legislation that accomplished many of their original political and policy goals. Thus the presidential veto was not the final word on welfare reform, but it had a significant influence on how the final legislation was drafted by forcing Congress to address and incorporate into the bill the president's preferences.

The battle over the welfare reform bill is one example of what Charles Cameron refers to as "veto bargaining." According to Cameron, "the president may use actual vetoes not only to block legislation, but to shape it."[6] After the president has vetoed a bill, the two branches may end up "haggling" over the content of legislation, which may kill the legislation or may lead Congress to make concessions to the president so that a modified version of the bill can get passed and signed. Cameron concludes, "In most cases Congress and the president find their way to an agreement that reflects the preferences of both parties."[7]

Likewise, legislation may be modified after judicial review to accommodate the Court and reflect the preferences of both institutions. That is, when the Court strikes down a law as unconstitutional, Congress may choose to make concessions to the Court by modifying the law to comply with the Court's constitutional interpretation while maintaining the basic statutory policy. Veto-like bargaining between Congress and the Court will surely be different from that between Congress and presidents. Congress and presidents can negotiate directly, face to face. Communication between the Court and Congress is indirect at best, and as Robert Katzmann has shown, Congress is oftentimes "oblivious" to courts and unaware of judicial decisions.[8] Thus, members of Congress must be aware of the Court's decisions, and the Court's written opinions must be a source of information and communication to Congress regarding the Court's preferences. Another difference between veto bargaining and judicial review bargaining is a temporal element—vetoes are exercised shortly after legislation is passed and before it is implemented, whereas judicial review is often exercised many years after legislation has gone into effect. Thus, the political and policy climate in Congress is likely to have changed more after judicial review than it would have done after a presidential veto.

Although these differences exist, it is plausible that members of Congress do make concessions to the Court's *constitutional interpretations* in furtherance of *political and policy goals* in Congress. From classic studies by David Mayhew and Richard Fenno to more recent studies by Douglass Arnold and others, theories and observations of legislative behavior suggest that members of Congress act primarily to satisfy their various constituencies for the sake of winning reelection and making good public policy. According to these congressional scholars, "the electoral connection" explains most congressional behavior, in addition to the desire to make good public policy, congressional leadership, party positions, committee structures, institutional procedures, and potential presidential vetoes. Members of Congress are largely interested in being able to "claim credit" for popular legislation and policies and for being on the "right side" of issues in the eyes of their constituencies.

Based on these views of Congress, it is unlikely that the first reaction of members of Congress to a judicial review decision is always to ask, "Do we like the Court's constitutional interpretation?" Rather, it is probably something more along the lines of, "Do we (or does an important constituency) care about the statute and the public policy that was being implemented under the statute?" If the answer to the latter question is yes, *then* members of Congress confront the question, "What do we have to do to revive the statute?" Hence, members of the Court and of Congress may sometimes operate on different policy dimensions—the Court on a *constitutional policy* dimension, and Congress on a *public policy* dimension.[9] Congressional responses to judicial review are perhaps not appropriately conceptualized solely as battles over a priori and unidimensional policy preferences in which either judicial supremacy reigns and the Court wins, or Congress overrides or challenges Court decisions in an exercise of coordinate construction and Congress wins.[10] We should often expect legislative responses to judicial review to be designed and drafted in an attempt to satisfy the Court's constitutional tests, while retaining or other-

wise focusing on the core public policy elements of the original statute—
thus reflecting the preferences of both institutions. Much will depend upon
the nature of the Court decision and what information the written opin-
ion(s) conveys to Congress. How Congress defies, challenges, accommo-
dates, or complies with the Court is an empirical question that has not
been adequately explored by scholars.

HOW DOES CONGRESS RESPOND TO JUDICIAL REVIEW?

To evaluate congressional responses to Court decisions, I analyzed data
based on Court decisions that struck down federal legislation for violating the Constitution. I selected and listed the Supreme Court cases from
the 1953–54 through 1996–97 terms in which federal statutes were struck
down as unconstitutional from Congressional Quarterly's *Guide to the
Supreme Court* (2d ed., 1990) and annual *Supreme Court Yearbook* (1991
through 1997 editions), and from the United States Supreme Court Database. I also compiled a separate list of the relevant legislation and citations
from those sources, resulting in seventy-four observations.[11] The unit of
analysis is a combination of the Court decision and the federal statute that
was struck down.[12]

I looked up each statute in the *U.S. Code Service* and *U.S. Code Annotated*. Using the annotations provided therein, I recorded full citations and
dates of all legislation passed by Congress that established, amended, or
repealed the provisions of the statute reviewed by the Court from the original passage of the legislation through December 2000. I then read every
legislative action cited in the annotations as having taken place after the
relevant Supreme Court decision and determined whether the action represented a response to the Court. I coded for five categories, based on the
annotations: (1) no response, (2) the statute or relevant provision is repealed and nothing is passed to replace it, (3) the statute or relevant provision is repealed and a new law is passed, (4) the statute is amended to address the constitutional issue at hand, and (5) the Constitution is amended.

"No response" was recorded if the annotations do not indicate that the
statutory provision struck down by the Court was repealed, amended, or
modified. In other words, neither the *U.S. Code Service* nor the *U.S. Code
Annotated* reported that Congress passed any public laws affecting the invalidated statute. "Repealed" was recorded if the annotations explicitly

reported "repealed" and the part of the statute struck down by the Court was repealed by public law but not modified or replaced by a new statute. "Repealed and passed new law" was recorded if the annotations indicated that the law was repealed or moved. In this situation Congress repealed the invalidated statute but passed a new public law, usually codified in a new part of the U.S Code, that clearly addressed the same policy as the old legislation, but in a new statutory scheme. "Amended statute to address issue" was recorded if Congress passed legislation that modified the specific language or provisions of a statute explicitly addressed in the Court opinion striking it down as unconstitutional. Lastly, "Amended Constitution" was recorded if the annotation indicated that Congress passed and the states ratified a constitutional amendment addressing the subject matter of the unconstitutional statute.

If Congress acted and amended or modified the law, or replaced it entirely, I compared the new version with the old and identified the differences. I only recorded Congress's action as a response if it clearly adverted to the specific provision and language addressed in the Court's opinion. Some of these responses complied with the Court's holdings, while others rejected or challenged the Court's position, creating a distinction among these congressional responses that begs for further interpretive analysis that will be discussed in more detail in the next section of this chapter. To further establish that congressional action was in response to the Court decision, I reviewed committee reports and other pieces of legislative history where it existed. References to Court decisions in the legislative histories helped to affirm that the legislative action was in response to the Court decision and aided in determining the degree of deference shown by Congress to the Court's constitutional holdings.

These data measure whether Congress responds to a judicial review decision by modifying the specific legislation invalidated by the Court or taking other action. Thus, while "congressional responses" to Supreme Court decisions might be conceptualized more broadly to include, for example, more general "court curbing" efforts, the analyses here will be limited to congressional action on judicially nullified legislation. Table 1 lists some examples of statutes that were invalidated by the Supreme Court according to the category of congressional response. Table 2 shows that Congress has only formally overridden the Court by amending the Constitution once, but it has modified the unconstitutional legislation by amending it or passing new legislation to address the constitutional infirmity thirty-five times. The first three categories collectively make up congres-

TABLE I Examples of Congressional Responses and Invalidated Statutes

No Response	Repealed	Amended Statute	Repealed, Passed New Law	Amended Constitution
Brady Bill	Subversive Activities Control Act	Gun Free School Zones	FECA (campaign finance provision)	National Voting Age
Cable TV Consumer Protection Act	Aliens and Nationality Code (citizenship revocation)	Gramm-Rudman-Hollings (deficit reduction)	Narcotic Drugs Import-Export Act	
Flag Protection Act	Marijuana Tax Act	Social Security (survivors' benefits)	Immigration and Nationality Act (legislative veto)	

sional responses in which Congress revived and saved the statutory policy —Congress has acted to save unconstitutional statutes 48 percent of the time. In only 14 percent of the cases did Congress repeal, and thus abandon, the statute. Congress has failed to respond 38 percent of the time. In Table 3 congressional responses are reported based on who the chief justice was at the time of the Court decision. Half of the cases in which Congress has not formally responded (fourteen of twenty-eight) are from the Rehnquist Court. For both the Warren and Burger Courts, Congress formally responded much more often. Table 3 establishes that over time, Congress has frequently responded to judicial review by amending the old legislation or passing new legislation to replace it, and this pattern is particularly true for the statutes struck down by the Warren and Burger Courts.

The time involved in this sequence might help to explain why Congress has not responded to the Rehnquist Court decisions as often as it did to the Warren and Burger Court decisions. The amount of time between the enactment of a statute by Congress and its invalidation by the Court varies.

TABLE 2 Congressional Responses to Judicial Review,
1954–1997 (*n* = 74)

Congressional Response	Frequency
Amend Constitution	1 (1%)
Amend Legislation	27 (36%)
Repeal, pass new legislation	8 (11%)
Repeal legislation	10 (14%)
No response	28 (38%)

Occasionally, federal laws have been reviewed and declared unconstitutional within about a year. On the other hand, it took the Court sixty years to strike down a law prohibiting the inclusion of alcohol content on malt beverage labels.[13] Overall, there is a mean of 144.4 months (about twelve years) and median of 116 months (less than ten years) between passage of a federal statute and its invalidation by the Supreme Court. In addition to the time from enactment to Court decision, the time from a judicial review decision by the Court until a congressional response can vary. Overall, Congress has responded to unconstitutional statutes forty-six times (including repeals of unconstitutional statutes). The mean response time between a Court decision and a congressional response is 80.5 months (6.7 years), and the median is 44 months (3.7 years).

This analysis shows that Congress has responded to the Court's exercise of judicial review fairly often and that it is common for years to pass from the original passage of legislation to Court decision to congressional response. Thus, the data suggest that Congress may eventually respond to many of the more recent decisions from the Rehnquist Court even though it has not done so yet.[14] However, these descriptive statistics and data are limited in terms of what they teach us about the nature of congressional responses; that is, given that Congress appears likely to respond to a majority of judicial review decisions, it is necessary to ask if congressional responses to judicial review challenge or circumvent the Court's constitutional interpretations, or rather defer to or comply with the Court's constitutional interpretations. To understand the nature of congressional responses in more depth, it is necessary to examine the language and substance of those responses.

TABLE 3   Congressional Response under Selected Chief Justices

Congressional Response	Warren Court, 1953–1969 (n = 22)	Burger Court, 1969–1986 (n = 34)	Rehnquist Court, 1986–1998 (n = 18)
No response	5 (22.7%)	9 (26.5%)	14 (77.8%)
Repealed	8 (36.3%)	2 (5.9%)	0 (0.0%)
Amended to address issue	7 (31.8%)	17 (50.0%)	3 (16.7%)
Repealed, passed new law	2 (9.1%)	5 (14.7%)	1 (5.6%)
Amended Constitution	0 (0.0%)	1 (2.9%)	0 (0.0%)

A DEEPER LOOK

In this section, I explore some examples of congressional responses to judicial review to illustrate their variable nature. While some congressional responses may challenge or circumvent the Court's constitutional interpretations, many others incorporate the interpretations into new versions of the law, and still others comply with the Court in other ways.

Amending the Constitution

The clearest, strongest, and most formal method of reversing the Court's constitutional doctrine is to amend the Constitution. However, Congress has only amended the Constitution in response to the Court decisions analyzed in this chapter once, less than 1 percent of the time. That decision was *Oregon v. Mitchell* (1970), in which the Court struck down the Voting Rights Act of 1970, which established a national voting age for state and local elections.[15] Shortly thereafter, in 1971, Congress passed and the states quickly ratified the Twenty-sixth Amendment to the Constitution, establishing a national voting age of eighteen years.

Repealing Legislation

In contrast to a constitutional amendment, which is the strongest challenge to judicial review, Congress can show total deference to the Court by repealing the legislation altogether. Congress repealed legislation in response to ten, or 13.5%, of the seventy-four cases examined here. For example, in 1950 Congress passed the Subversive Activities Control Act (SACA), requiring members of the Communist Party to register with the Subversive Activities Control Board. That provision was eventually challenged, and in *Albertson v. Subversive Activities Control Board* (1965) the Supreme Court struck it down on its face for violating individuals' rights against self-incrimination guaranteed by the Fifth Amendment, because the "mere association with the communist party present[ed] a sufficient threat of prosecution."[16] Three years after *Albertson*, Congress voted to repeal the statute and in essence give up on the public policy that it represented.[17] Congress may have done so for numerous reasons. The Court's decision was clearly an important factor, as the legislative history of the repealing legislation makes explicit reference to *Albertson*.[18] Also, the statute faced opposition from special-interest groups during the litigation, with two amicus briefs filed against the statute, and none in support. Most likely, SACA is an example of a statute that had outlived its usefulness. By 1965 it had little political support, and being on record as voting for its repeal may have been perceived politically as the "right side" of the issue, allowing members of Congress to engage in "position taking" of the sort identified by Mayhew.

Modifying or Passing New Legislation

The most likely congressional response to judicial review is some sort of modified or new legislation. Scholars often assume that legislation passed in response to judicial review is designed to overcome the Court's constitutional interpretation. Undoubtedly, Congress does sometimes challenge or override the Court's constitutional holdings. For instance, after *INS v. Chadha* (1983) Congress repealed the old Immigration and Nationality Act, which included the legislative veto provisions, and passed new legislation, which included another legislative veto provision. In the new statute, Congress claimed authority as "an exercise of the rulemaking power of the Senate," under Article I, Section 5, of the Constitution.[19] Studies have shown how Congress has defied the Court by continuing to use legislative vetoes in various policy areas.[20] While Congress may challenge the Court in this way, for it to do so is in fact rare. Instead, congressional responses that amend or modify laws are usually more deferential to the Court's constitutional interpretation. The legislative veto is the only one of the congressional responses considered in this chapter that in my estimation can be characterized as a clear and direct attempt to override the Court decision (other than the Twenty-sixth Amendment passed in response to *Oregon v. Mitchell*).[21]

It is much more common for Congress to amend legislation in a manner that makes clear concessions to the Court's decision. Sometimes, Congress simply narrows the scope of the statute. For example, in *United States v. Lopez* (1995) the Supreme Court invalidated the Gun Free School Zones Act of 1990 (GFSZA) for violating Congress's commerce power.[22] Congress initially passed the GFSZA in 1990 to prohibit guns in and around schools. Interestingly, some in Congress were paying attention to the *Lopez* litigation even before the Supreme Court handed down its decision. In 1994—before the Supreme Court decision but after the Court of Appeals found the statute unconstitutional—the lawmakers in Congress who had initially drafted the GFSZA amended the statute, to state explicitly that Congress was acting pursuant to its commerce power and to provide findings of fact that guns in schools were a national problem with ties to the national economy.[23] The majority opinion in the Supreme Court decision noted the findings of fact, but it did not consider whether they might save the statute.

In his analysis for the five-member majority, Chief Justice Rehnquist wrote that one flaw of the GFSZA was the absence of a "jurisdictional element which would ensure, through case-by-case inquiry, that the firearm possession in question affects interstate commerce."[24] Congress responded by further amending the statute in hopes of satisfying the Court. Passed in 1996, these amendments explicitly modify the crime; under the new GFSZA, "it shall be unlawful for any individual knowingly to possess a firearm *that has moved in or otherwise affects interstate or foreign commerce* at a place the individual knows or has reason to know is a school zone" (emphasis added).[25] In essence, the amendment created a jurisdictional element: for the federal government to have jurisdiction, the gun would have to be shown to have traveled in interstate commerce—a direct response to the *Lopez* decision.

The amendment to the GFSZA cannot properly be characterized as an "override" of the Court's constitutional decision, nor can members of Congress or other relevant lawmakers be described as engaging in serious or independent construction of the Constitution. Instead, lawmakers in Congress drafted the language of the amendments to the GFSZA in an effort to satisfy but subtly circumvent the Court. The response to *Lopez* is not an outright challenge to the Court, as was the response to *Oregon v. Mitchell* or even the response to *INS v. Chadha*. The GFSZA amendment showed a small degree of deference by narrowing the scope of the regulation in a manner that might satisfy at least some members of the *Lopez* majority. The statute was modified in a fairly minor and some might say technical way that was tailored to accommodate the majority of the Court. The GFSZA is a statute through which members of Congress could "claim credit" for addressing the public policy problem of guns in schools, and the "right side" of the public policy issue was clear. Moreover, the "technical" alteration of the statute facilitated those goals. And when the bill's sponsor, Senator Herb Kohl (D-Wis.), ran for reelection in 2000, his television ads touted his authorship and sponsorship of the bill without mentioning the constitutional issue at all. Thus, members of Congress managed to circumvent the Court's *Lopez* decision with a technical fix to achieve political and policy goals, with only minor attention to the underlying constitutional issue.

Often Congress is even more deferential to the Court's constitutional doctrine. A good example of a congressional response to a Supreme Court decision that showed much more deference — or outright compliance — involves the Federal Election Campaign Act (FECA) and *Buckley v. Valeo* (1976).[26] In FECA, originally passed by Congress in 1971, Congress attempted to curb campaign abuses in federal elections. Among the many provisions of FECA, the statute created the Federal Election Commission (FEC) to implement and enforce the statute, and it regulated campaign contributions and expenditures. In *Buckley* the Court invalidated two provisions of FECA. First, it held that some of the provisions of FECA regulating expenditures made by candidates for political office, and by others on behalf of candidates, were unconstitutional because they violated the freedoms of speech and association protected by the First Amendment. Second, the Court invalidated provisions of FECA that called for some members of the FEC to be appointed by the president pro tempore of the Senate and the speaker of the House of Representatives. The Court ruled that members of the FEC were Article II "Officers of the United States" and, as such, must be appointed by the president with the "advice and consent of the Senate."

Within a year, Congress amended FECA by repealing the "unconstitutional" provisions and replacing them with new ones.[27] First, Congress repealed the provisions that limited expenditures on behalf of candidates for federal office, and it passed new provisions that nearly codified the Court's First Amendment holding in *Buckley*. The new provisions did not place limits on the types of expenditures that the Court declared were protected under the First Amendment, and it only regulated those campaign activities that the Court said could be regulated under the First Amendment. Similarly, by specifying that the president will appoint all members of the FEC, Congress complied with the Court on the issue of composition of the FEC. In modifying FECA, Congress showed a large degree of deference to the Court. The Court did not prevent Congress from pursuing the public policy of campaign reform entirely, but the constitutional decision in *Buckley v. Valeo* had a clear impact on the means that Congress was able to use to pursue the policy. In any event, it is clear that the congressional responses to *Buckley* did not challenge the Court's interpretations of the First Amendment or separation of powers and instead made significant concessions to the Court.

The congressional responses to *Lopez* and *Buckley* were swift, in large part because the members of Congress and staff who originally drafted the GFSZA and FECA were still in Congress and committed to the public policies embodied in those statutes. However, just as the nature and amount of deference shown to the Court by Congress can vary, so can the time frame for congressional responses to judicial review. Even after longer periods have passed, Congress frequently modifies legislation in response to judicial review. For instance, in *Railroad Retirement Board v. Kalina* (1977), the Court summarily affirmed a lower court ruling that the Railroad Retirement Act of 1937 unconstitutionally discriminated on the basis of gender. Under the statutory scheme, widows were assumed to be dependents entitled to Railroad Retirement Annuity benefits; by contrast, widowers had the burden of proving that at least half of their support had come from their wives. Six years later, Congress responded to the Court decision by amending the statute to delete the gender references and require all survivors, regardless of gender, to show that they had depended upon their deceased spouse for at least half of their support.[28]

Another example involves *Richardson v. Davis* (1972), in which the Court struck down provisions of the Social Security Act that made illegitimate children ineligible for survivor's benefits. As in *Kalina*, the Court declared that the scheme violated the equal protection component of the Fifth Amendment. In 1977 Congress passed a law that amended the survivors' benefits provision so that illegitimate children would be eligible.[29] The majority in Congress was (and still is) committed to the underlying policies of social security. The Court's decision thus spurred Congress to alter the way the law was implemented. By the 1970s it was inconceivable that a majority in Congress would repeal major provisions of the act.

Moreover, a simple modification of the eligibility requirements was all that was needed to satisfy the Court's equal protection doctrine. In these cases, Congress paid close attention to the language from the written opinions in the Court decision, and crafted a revision that appeared to satisfy the demands of the Court.

No Response

While I have shown how the content of congressional responses can vary in important ways, it is worth considering decisions for which there have not been congressional responses. On the one hand, it is difficult to conclude that Congress will never respond to a Court decision simply because it has not responded yet, especially given the length of time that can pass in the lawmaking process before congressional responses are made. So there may be decisions in the "no response" category that will eventually result in a congressional response. On the other hand, there may be explanations for why Congress does not respond, either quickly or at all. It may be that the Court struck the statute down "as applied" rather than "on its face"— a distinction overlooked in most studies of the interaction between Court and Congress. When the Court invalidates legislation as applied, Congress does not need to modify the legislation to make it constitutional; instead, those who implement the law—usually executive branch or other administrative officials—must alter the manner in which they do so. By contrast, when the Court invalidates legislation on its face, the Court is declaring that the legislation as drafted can never be applied constitutionally.

An example of an "as applied" decision is *Marshall v. Barlow's, Inc.* (1978). That case involved a provision of the Occupational Safety and Health Act (OSHA), passed in 1949.[30] The relevant provisions allow for general workplace inspections by officials of the Occupational Safety and Health Administration (OSHA) to ensure that employers meet OSHA safety and health regulations; the provisions do not make reference to search warrants. The litigation involved an inspection in which OSHA officials did not first obtain a warrant but claimed authority under the act to conduct the inspection. The Court held that under the Fourth Amendment administrative agencies needed to obtain a warrant for general administrative searches, but that once a warrant was obtained administrative searches of this type were permissible. The Court further established a fairly broad definition of probable cause needed for general administrative search warrants. Congress has not modified these provisions of OSHA. The reason ap-

TABLE 4 Congressional Responses and
As Applied–On Face Disposition

Congressional Response	As Applied ($n = 23$)	On Face ($n = 51$)
Amended Constitution	0 (0.0%)	1 (2.0%)
Amended statute	3 (13.0%)	24 (47.1%)
Repealed, passed new law	3 (13.0%)	5 (9.8%)
Repealed	1 (4.3%)	9 (17.6%)
No Response	16 (69.9%)	12 (23.5%)

pears clear: the Court stated that if OSHA officials first obtained a warrant in a manner consistent with the Court's opinion, the law could be applied constitutionally. Hence, Congress does not need to modify the law for it to continue to be applied; rather, it is OSHA's responsibility to apply it in a manner consistent with the Court's opinion.

Table 4 presents the frequencies of congressional responses to court decisions struck down as applied and on their face. Of the seventy-four cases examined here, twenty-three (31 percent) were struck down as applied while fifty-one (69 percent) were struck down on their face. Including repeals, Congress has only responded to seven of the twenty-three (30 percent) as applied decisions; in contrast, it has responded to thirty-nine of the fifty-one (77 percent) on face decisions. Thus, Congress is substantially more likely to respond to the Supreme Court decisions when there is a clear necessity for congressional action just to keep the statutory policy alive.[31] When legislation is struck down as applied, there is no need to amend legislation to maintain the basic public policy. This distinction suggests that the Court's written opinions do serve a communicative and informational function. Members of Congress appear to be well informed on the need for congressional, as opposed to administrative, action if a statute is to be revived after judicial review.

There may be other reasons why a Congress does not respond to judicial review, even when legislation is invalidated on its face. As an example, consider the Brady Handgun Violence Prevention Act ("Brady Bill"), portions of which were struck down in *Printz v. United States* (1997). For our purposes here, what is important is that the Brady Bill established a national waiting period for gun purchases, during which time the statute mandated local law enforcement officials to conduct background checks of prospective gun owners. The Supreme Court ruled that under the Tenth Amendment the federal government could not mandate state and local officials to conduct federal policy, and relevant provisions of the Brady Bill were struck down. Although Congress has not yet responded to the *Printz* decision, there is an explanation for the lack of response. Under the statute, the federal government was supposed to have developed a national computerized system for an "instant check" of prospective gun buyers, and the waiting period and mandatory background checks were to be phased out after five years under a sunset clause in the statute. The statute was originally passed in 1993, and *Printz* was handed down in 1997. Thus, by the time Congress passed a response to the Court decision, the relevant statutory provisions would have expired anyway. Hence, the lack of a congressional response may not always indicate that Congress has given up on the relevant public policy.

WHAT TO MAKE OF IT ALL?

The common occurrence of congressional responses to the Supreme Court would appear to support a claim of frequent coordinate construction in Congress. However, a mere count of the number of times Congress responds to judicial review does not shed much light on the nature of the responses. As the examples cited above illustrate, Congress's responses to judicial review are often compliant with or deferential to the Court. In fact, in my estimation the only congressional responses to judicial review that amount to challenges of the Court's constitutional holding were the responses to *Oregon v. Mitchell* and *INS v. Chadha*. Sometimes congressional responses are "technical" fixes intended to circumvent the Court decisions, as with the congressional response to *United States v. Lopez*. More often, however, congressional responses are compliant with the Court's constitutional interpretation. Congress often abandons legislation and repeals legislation. And when Congress responds to judicial review, it usually defers to the Court's constitutional policy, and adapts the statute at issue so that it might conform to the Court's constitutional interpretation in order that the underlying policy can survive, in one form or another.

In drafting responses to judicial review, members of Congress appear to pay close attention to the Court's opinions in determining the nature of concessions that are necessary to save legislation. This attention suggests a dynamic relationship between the Court and Congress, in which congressional action on public policy issues affects the Court's constitutional law, and the Court's constitutional interpretations affect the form and substance of statutes. This relationship often takes the form of a Court that establishes constitutional parameters while Congress works within those parameters to pursue public policy. In many ways, then, the exercise of judicial review brings about bargaining between Congress and the Court, much the same as the exercise of the presidential veto brings about bargaining between Congress and presidents. For example, consider the statutory provisions involving various government benefits struck down by the Court for violating equal protection principles discussed earlier. In those statutes and in other similar ones, Congress established a public policy rationale for providing government benefits to needy children, the elderly, the retired, the poor, and other disadvantaged groups. Congress made public policy judgments about the best means for delivering those benefits. The Court then evaluated the public policy means used in those statutes in light of the constitutional values expressed in the text of the Constitution, and it demanded that the statutes incorporate a certain understanding of equality in the implementation of the public policy. In response, Congress conceded to the Court on this view of equality but maintained the basic public policy rationale for these types of government benefits.

This chapter has shown that congressional responses to judicial review are highly variable, with Congress often making concessions to the Court. Over time, members of Congress show an impressive commitment to statutory policy, often bargaining or haggling with the Court to satisfy both the Court's constitutional preferences and Congress's public policy preferences. Members of Congress do not appear to routinely or frequently challenge the Court's constitutional interpretations. This acquiescence raises a number of considerations and implications for debates over coordinate construction and the Constitution outside the Court, as well as for empirical research on the interaction between Court and Congress.

If Congress frequently, indeed usually, complies with the Court's constitutional interpretations, what are the implications for normative theories of judicial supremacy and the Constitution outside the Court? On the one hand, the Court's judicial review decisions are not usually "final," as most of the legislation struck down by the Court lives on. On the other hand, the types of congressional responses described above do not indicate that members of Congress engage in serious constitutional deliberation with respect to judicially nullified legislation. Rather, congressional responses usually incorporate the Court's constitutional interpretations into modified or new legislation. It would seem that the normative preferences of neither judicial supremacy nor coordinate construction theories are fully realized, although judicial supremacists may take solace from the infrequency with which the Court's constitutional interpretations are overridden.

This chapter has focused on how Congress responds when the Court exercises judicial review to strike down federal legislation. However, there are at least two other types of Court cases that might result in yet different types of congressional responses to judicial review. First, Congress might use a Court decision that *upholds*, as opposed to nullifies, the constitutionality of legislation to expand on a policy.[32] Second, Congress might respond to the Court's invalidation of state laws in various ways. Future consideration of congressional responses to judicial review might explore and account for variations among congressional responses under these circumstances and conditions.

There are further implications as well for empirical studies of the interaction between Court and Congress. The analyses in this chapter have been largely descriptive. Accurate description is a necessary precursor for explanation, but an important goal of empirical political science is to explain political phenomena. The variations in congressional responses described here warrant further examination with an eye toward explanation. Finally, simple counts of legislation passed in response to Court decisions do not indicate the extent to which Congress challenges or complies with the Court. My examination of congressional responses to judicial review illustrates the importance of combining the systematic study of congressional responses to the Court with interpretive analyses of the actual Court decisions and statutes in question.

Finally, the evidence in this chapter should be considered alongside Bruce Peabody's findings and arguments in this volume. According to Peabody's survey results, many members of Congress express the view that they share responsibility with the justices for interpreting the Constitution; however, it is not at all clear that these general views are likely to translate into frequent specific instances of serious constitutional deliberation or challenges to the Court's constitutional doctrines. Peabody is surely correct that constitutional deliberation in Congress will be "constrained by public attitudes." Peabody's study thus highlights the importance of understanding the relations between Court and Congress over constitutional matters as involving multiple dimensions of political, policy, and legal attitudes. Scholars should recognize that when drafting, debating, and taking positions on statutes, members of Congress are most likely to operate primarily along the political and public policy dimensions, and that the constitutional dimensions of legislation will often be of secondary importance in the legislative process. Consequently, we should only expect Congress to challenge or override the Court's constitutional decisions when those decisions also create political or policy problems for members of Congress.

NOTES

1   Antonin Scalia, "Constitutional Interpretation," *Sherman L. Bellwood Lecture at the University of Idaho College of Law* (Moscow, Idaho, 2000).

2   462 U.S. 919.

3   Louis Fisher, "The Legislative Veto: Invalidated, It Survives," 56 *Law and Contemporary Problems* 273 (1993); Louis Fisher, "Separation of Powers: Interpretation Outside the Courts," 18 *Pepperdine Law Review* 57 (1990).

4   E.g., William N. Eskridge Jr., "Overriding Supreme Court Statutory Interpretation Decisions," 101 *Yale Law Journal* 331 (1991).

5   James Meernik and Joseph Ignagni, "Judicial Review and Coordinate Construction of the Constitution," 1997 *American Journal of Political Science* 447. See also Rafael Gely and Pablo T. Spiller, "The Political Economy of Supreme Court Constitutional Decisions: The Case of Roosevelt's Court-Packing Plan," 12 *International Review of Law and Economics* 45 (1992).

6   Charles M. Cameron, *Veto Bargaining: Presidents and the Politics of Negative Power* (Cambridge: Cambridge University Press, 2000).

7   *Id.* at 176.

8   Robert A. Katzmann, *Courts and Congress* (Washington: Brookings Institution Press / Governance Institute, 1997).

9   Donald G. Morgan, *Congress and the Constitution: A Study of Responsibility* (Cambridge: Belknap Press of Harvard University Press, 1966).

10 By contrast, leading studies of Supreme Court decision making measure the policy preferences of justices along a single dimension and thus fail to account for the difference between the constitutional and public policy dimensions of Court decisions. E.g, Jeffrey A. Segal and Harold J. Spaeth, *The Supreme Court and the Attitudinal Model* (Cambridge: Cambridge University Press, 1993).

11 Harold Spaeth, *United States Supreme Court Judicial Database* (Ann Arbor: Inter-University Consortium for Political and Social Research, 1997).

12 Three Supreme Court cases, *Leary v. U.S.*, 395 U.S. 6 (1969), *Frontiero v. Richardson*, 411 U.S. 677 (1973), and *Buckley v. Valeo*, 424 U.S. 1 (1976), were coded as two observations each because each struck down two separate and distinct statutory provisions for separate and distinct reasons.

13 Rubin v. Coors Brewing Company, 514 U.S. 476 (1995).

14 There are also reasons to suspect that the current Congress is unlikely to respond to at least some of the Rehnquist Court's judicial review decisions. See generally Neal Devins, "Congress as Culprit: How Lawmakers Spurred on the Court's Anti-Congress Crusade," 51 *Duke Law Journal* 435 (2001); Keith Whittington, "Taking What They Give Us: Explaining the Court's Federalism Offensive," 51 *Duke Law Journal* 477 (2001).

15 400 U.S. 112; 42 U.S.C. 1973bb.

16 382 U.S. 70, 77.

17 P.L. 90-237, 5 Stat. 766 (1968).

18 See, e.g., House Committee on Un-American Activities, *H.R. 12601*, 90th Cong., 2d sess., 1967, H. Rept. 733; Senate Judiciary Committee, S. 2171, 90th Cong., 2d sess., 1967, Conf. Rept. 1038.

19 P.L. 101-649, Title III Sect. 302(h), 104 Stat. 5053, 29 November 1990. In this statute and in others, Congress has claimed authority to use legislative vetoes as part of its rulemaking powers, found in Article I, Section 5, of the U.S. Constitution: "Each House may determine the Rules for its Proceedings."

20 Fisher, "The Legislative Veto"; Fisher, "Separation of Powers."

21 Of course the cases examined here do not include congressional challenges to Supreme Court decisions that strike down state laws. For example, the passage of the Religious Freedom Restoration Act was a clear attempt by Congress to override the Court's decision in *Employment Division v. Smith* (1990), which involved a state law and is not included in this dataset.

22 514 U.S. 549; 18 U.S.C.S. 922(q)(1)(A) (1990).

23 P.L. 103-322, 108 Stat. 1996 et seq. (13 September 1994).

24 Lopez, 514 U.S. at 561.

25 P.L. 104-208, Div. A, Title I, 101(f), Title IV, 657, 658(b), 110 Stat. 3009-362, 3009-372.

26 424 U.S. 1; 2 U.S.C. 437(c) (1972, as amended 1974).

27 The old provisions were repealed in P.L. 94-283, Title II, Section 201(a), 90 Stat. 496, and the new regulations in P.L. 94-283, Title I, Section 112(a), 90 Stat. 487 (11 May 1976).

28 P.L. 98-76, Title I, Sections 104(a),(b), 106 (a)–(g), Title IV 409 (a), 413 (a), 414 (a), 415; 97 Stat. 415, 417, 418, 435, 436 (1983).

29 P.L. 95-216, Title II, Sections 202, 204(e), 91 Stat. 1524 (1977).

30 29 U.S.C. 657(a), P.L. 91-596, S 8(a).

31 I also used a multinomial logit to predict whether Congress would repeal

legislation or act to save it (through constitutional amendment, modified legislation, or new legislation), using no response as a baseline category and controlling for the level of consensus for the decision, whether a lower court was reversed, the age of the statute, and the involvement of interest groups in the case. The coefficients for legislation struck down on its face were positive, large, and statistically significant for repealed legislation (2.81; $p = .02$) and saved legislation (1.91; $p = .002$).

32   See, e.g., Kevin den Dulk and J. Mitchell Pickerill, "Bridging the Lawmaking Process: Organized Interests, Court-Congress Interaction, and Church-State Relations," 35 *Polity* 419 (2003).

Court, Congress, and Civil Rights

MICHAEL J. KLARMAN

In his book *Stride toward Freedom* (1958), Martin Luther King Jr. noted that "[i]f the executive and legislative branches were as concerned about the protection of the citizenship rights of all people as the federal courts have been, the transition from a segregated to an integrated society would be much further along than it is today." This chapter addresses two questions concerning the relationship between judicial and legislative action on civil rights. First, why was one branch sometimes in front of the others on civil rights issues? Second, what was the causal connection between *Brown v. Board of Education* and the landmark civil rights legislation of the mid-1960s?[1]

WHO'S OUT FRONT AND WHY?

In 1870–71 Congress, responding to vigilante atrocities committed by southern whites against blacks, passed legislation that was aimed at suppressing such violence. Because the Fourteenth and Fifteenth Amendments contain explicit "state action" requirements, the legislation tested constitutional limits. In 1875 Congress passed a statute forbidding race discrimination in (privately owned) places of public accommodation, which raised similar "state action" issues. In 1883 the Supreme Court reversed a federal conviction of whites who lynched a black man, ruling that Congress could not constitutionally reach vigilante violence against blacks and invalidating the relevant provision of the 1871 act. That same year, and for the same reason, the justices struck down the public accommodations provision of the Civil Rights Act of 1875. In the period immediately following the Civil

War, Congress reached more progressive results on civil rights than did the Court. Why?[2]

First, the timing of the actions of the two branches matters. Congress passed the 1870–71 legislation during the peak of Reconstruction and the Civil Rights Act of 1875 as that era drew to a close. Judicial invalidation of the legislation came several years later. National opinion on race had changed dramatically in the interim. By 1883 many northern whites had tired of national intervention to protect the political and civil rights of southern blacks, and some had concluded that the Fifteenth Amendment was a mistake. Whether the justices would have resolved these cases differently had they arisen ten years earlier is impossible to know. But lower courts that adjudicated similar issues in the early 1870s reached more racially progressive results. The justices' constitutional interpretations generally reflect the social and political context of their times. That a Court adjudicating civil rights issues several years after the demise of Reconstruction would reach results different from a Congress that enacted legislation during the peak of civil rights ardor is hardly surprising.

Second, congressmen who voted for civil rights legislation possibly had greater incentives to support it, and thus to believe that it was constitutional, than did the justices who adjudicated its constitutionality. The 1870–71 legislation focused on protecting the voting rights of southern blacks. The Republican Party did not exist in the South before the Civil War, and its only significant chance of establishing a southern base afterward was to enfranchise blacks, who were 40 percent or more of the population in eight southern states and could be counted upon to overwhelmingly support the party of emancipation. The public accommodations provision of the Civil Rights Act of 1875 requires a different explanation: A lame-duck Republican Congress possibly conceived of the measure partly as a reward to loyal black voters, who felt strongly about the issue. Supreme Court justices, by contrast, are not directly accountable to voters. This is not to say that the justices are unmindful of public opinion, only that Republican justices, who still dominated the Court in 1883, might not have felt the same exigency as Republican congressmen did about protecting blacks' voting rights and responding to black voters' interests.

Finally, the justices may have felt more constrained by legal concepts than congressional representatives did. "State action" has always been a constitutional keystone. Constitutional constraints apply, for the most part, to state actors, not to private parties. Imagining a constitutional system without a concept such as "state action" is nearly impossible. Congressional representatives, by contrast, are probably less concerned about creating an internally coherent body of legal doctrine and more concerned about solving concrete problems. Congress is under no obligation to explain why it has adopted a particular view of state action in one context and another elsewhere. Judges operate according to professional norms that impose precisely such an obligation. Thus, Congress in 1875 had a much easier time forbidding race discrimination in privately owned places of public accommodation, despite the state action requirement of the Fourteenth Amendment, than the justices had in 1883 reconciling that statute with the Constitution.

From roughly 1890 to 1910, neither Congress nor the Court displayed any significant sympathy for civil rights. The justices rejected constitutional challenges to segregation and black disfranchisement, upheld a scheme for separate and *un*equal black public education, and adopted rules that made it virtually impossible for black criminal defendants to prove race discrimination in jury selection. Simultaneously, Congress sanctioned racial segregation in institutions of higher learning, repealed most of the Reconstruction-era legislation that protected black voting rights, and made no effort to enforce Section 2 of the Fourteenth Amendment, which seemed to *require* Congress to reduce the congressional representation of southern states as a remedy for black disfranchisement.[3]

This era reveals that both Congress and the Court are broadly reflective of popular opinion. By the turn of the century, most white Americans had lost interest in protecting the rights of southern blacks and supported southern "home rule" on the race issue. Given free rein, southern whites began to formalize Jim Crow and to nullify the Fifteenth Amendment. At a time of escalating white-on-black violence and strong white support for "racial purity," segregation appeared to be progressive racial policy, and the Court easily sustained it in *Plessy v. Ferguson* (1896). Likewise, black disfranchisement seemed preferable to having whites kill black voters, as they did in Wilmington, North Carolina, in 1898 and Atlanta in 1906. In addition, most justices of the era likely agreed with most white Americans that the Fifteenth Amendment had been a mistake.

Court decisions that sustained segregation and disfranchisement were not based on absurd constitutional interpretations. Conventional legal sources such as text, original intent, and precedent did not plainly bar segregation. Nor did the Fifteenth Amendment, which explicitly forbids disfranchisement based on race, clearly prohibit literacy tests or poll taxes, even if racially motivated. Congress's failure to enforce Section 2 of the

Fourteenth Amendment, which uses obligatory language, seems a clearer instance of nullification than do the Court's decisions that failed to invalidate disfranchisement measures. But by 1900, with their party securely in control of the national government, most Republicans were unenthusiastic about penalizing southern states for disfranchising blacks.

A disjuncture between the civil rights policies of Congress and those of the Supreme Court began to appear in the second decade of the twentieth century. In four sets of rulings the justices invalidated local ordinances that segregated the races residentially, struck down the grandfather clause (an electoral device that made black disfranchisement politically feasible by insulating illiterate whites from its effects), invalidated a state law that authorized railroads to provide first-class accommodations to whites only, and barred two legal devices that southern states used to coerce black agricultural labor. This was the same decade in which the first presidential administration openly sympathetic to the South since the Civil War held office. While the administration of Woodrow Wilson introduced segregation to the federal civil service, southern congressmen took advantage of the racial climate to introduce bills to nationalize southern racial policies, including proposals to repeal the Fifteenth Amendment, bar interracial marriage, and segregate transportation in the District of Columbia. What explains the Court's pro–civil rights rulings in a political and social environment that was hostile to progressive racial reform?[4]

The best explanation may be that the justices invalidated policies if they approached formal nullification of the Constitution. As the *Washington Post* observed, the grandfather clause—which immunized from literacy tests those who could vote, or whose ancestors could, before the adoption of the Fifteenth Amendment—was "so obvious an evasion that the Supreme Court could not have failed to declare it unconstitutional." The peonage law invalidated in *Bailey v. Alabama* (1911)—which criminalized entering into a labor agreement that provided advance wages with the fraudulent intent to subsequently breach and created a statutory presumption of fraudulent intent from the fact of the breach—was nearly as obvious a contravention of the Thirteenth Amendment's prohibition on slavery and involuntary servitude, given the dominant contemporary understanding that the amendment forbade the criminalization of ordinary contractual breaches. Moreover, the rulings did not ameliorate black disfranchisement or peonage. These decisions suggest that the justices may abide by clear constitutional norms even in an unreceptive social and political climate, especially if the rulings are inconsequential. By contrast, Congress is less inclined to contravene dominant public opinion even in the face of clear constitutional commands, such as Section 2 of the Fourteenth Amendment.[5]

The Court continued to be more progressive on civil rights than Congress was in the period between the world wars. On three occasions, the Senate failed to pass anti-lynching bills that carried the House, while the justices decided several landmark criminal cases that condemned aspects of southern lynch law. Yet on other race issues, the Court was no more progressive than Congress was; the justices continued to validate school segregation and the exclusion of blacks from Democratic Party primaries.[6]

The interwar period reveals that the Court is sometimes more representative of national opinion than Congress is. All of this era's race rulings were consonant with dominant public opinion. In the 1920s and 1930s most white Americans still supported school segregation and black disfranchisement, but they did not countenance farcical trials in which possibly innocent black defendants were sentenced to death on the basis of tortured confessions while lacking adequate legal representation. Most northern whites were appalled by Alabama's efforts to execute the Scottsboro Boys—nine black teenagers who were wrongly convicted of raping two white women on a freight train in northern Alabama in 1931 and sentenced to death. The Court's two decisions reversing their convictions—first because of inadequate legal representation, and second because of the exclusion of blacks from the juries that indicted and convicted them—almost certainly commanded majority support in the nation. So did anti-lynching legislation, according to Gallup polls, but Congress could not pass it because of Senate filibusters by southern Democrats.[7]

The gap between the civil rights positions of Congress and the Court became greatest during and after the Second World War, which proved to be a watershed in American civil rights history. African American soldiers returned from the war determined to experience some of the democracy for which they had been fighting. The war's democratic, anti-fascist ideology was conducive to progressive racial change, and the ensuing cold war gave Americans powerful incentives to improve domestic racial practices in an effort to win the allegiance of non-caucasian third world nations. The war also disrupted traditional patterns of racial subordination, opening new political and economic opportunities for African Americans and accelerating their migration from the South to the North, with attendant consequences for national racial policy.[8]

The Second World War's impact on the civil rights rulings of the Court was dramatic. In 1944 *Smith v. Allwright* invalidated the Texas Democratic Party's exclusion of blacks, overruling by an 8–1 vote a unanimous decision from just nine years earlier—an unprecedented turnabout in American constitutional history. In 1948 *Shelley v. Kraemer* barred judicial enforcement of racially restrictive covenants, rejecting dicta from a unanimous Court ruling of 1926 and the result reached by nearly twenty state supreme courts. Most famously, in 1954 *Brown v. Board of Education* invalidated public school segregation, rejecting nearly three-quarters of a century's worth of precedent and departing from the original understanding of the Fourteenth Amendment. Meanwhile, Congress remained unable to pass a single civil rights bill. Every two years in the 1940s, the House passed bills to eliminate poll taxes in federal elections, which failed in the Senate. In 1950 fair employment practices legislation also failed to survive a Senate filibuster. In the 1950s Congress neither endorsed *Brown* nor passed proposed enforcement measures, such as empowering the attorney general to bring school desegregation suits or cutting off federal education funds to institutions that practiced racial segregation. Finally, in 1957 Congress passed its first civil rights law in eighty-two years, but it was limited to voting rights and failed to adequately protect even them.

Drafters of the Fourteenth Amendment had anticipated that Congress, not the Court, would be its primary enforcer. This assumption was vindicated in the 1870s and 1880s, but belied during and after the Second World War. What accounts for the postwar Court's being so much more racially progressive than Congress?

Antimajoritarian features of the Senate are the most powerful explanation. The House almost certainly reflected majority national opinion when it passed anti–poll tax bills in the 1940s. Likewise, opinion polls suggest that a slender national majority endorsed *Brown* from the beginning. But the Senate is not majoritarian. Under procedural rules then in force, a two-thirds vote was necessary to cut off a filibuster. Moreover, committee chairs exercised inordinate power over legislation. When Democrats controlled Congress, as they usually did during this period, Southerners tended to control committee chairmanships by virtue of their greater seniority. Senator James Eastland of Mississippi bragged of having a special suit designed, with extra pockets to be stuffed with civil rights bills. The possibility that the Court's progressive race rulings reflected national opinion better than did Congress's refusal to enact civil rights legislation is bolstered by President Harry S Truman's enthusiasm for civil rights. In 1946 Truman appointed a civil rights committee that advocated path-breaking racial reforms, and in 1948 he issued executive orders that desegregated the military and the federal civil service. The Truman administration also filed briefs urging the justices to invalidate the judicial enforcement of racially restrictive covenants and public school segregation. Presidents infrequently take positions on domestic policy issues that are dramatically inconsistent with dominant public opinion. Congress, not the Court or the president, was the outlier on civil rights.[9]

The Court's relative progressivity on civil rights may have another explanation as well. Though the constitutional interpretations of the justices generally reflect the cultural and historical moments that they occupy, they are members of an élite subculture, which is characterized by greater education and higher economic status. Justices are very well educated; they have attended college and law school, and often the most élite ones. In general, they are also relatively wealthy. On many policy issues that become constitutional disputes, opinion correlates strongly with socioeconomic status, with élites holding more liberal views on social and cultural issues (though not on economic ones). Early in the twenty-first century, such issues include gay rights, abortion, and school prayer. In 1954 racial segregation was such an issue: 73 percent of college graduates approved of *Brown*, but only 45 percent of high school dropouts did. Racial attitudes and practices were changing dramatically in postwar America. As members of the cultural élite, the justices were among the first to be influenced. Their culturally élite status increased the chances of their invalidating segregation before national opinion had solidified against it. Yet the potential attitude gap between the justices and the public is limited, as they live in the same culture and time period. As little as ten years before *Brown*, racial attitudes had probably not changed enough for even a culturally élite institution such as the Court to have condemned school segregation.[10]

Presumably, congressional representatives are also members of the cultural élite, yet they lagged far behind the justices in achieving progressive racial results. Why? First, representatives have to respond to constituents to be reelected, while the justices enjoy lifetime tenure. Of course, the justices are not completely removed from public influence, but their relative insulation affords them some leeway in responding to their own culturally élite values, whereas representatives have to respond more directly to popular opinion or risk early retirement. Second, as we have seen, the U.S. Congress—especially the Senate—is far from majoritarian. Not only did southern senators exercise disproportionate power, but they represented only the perspectives of southern whites. Just 20 percent of southern blacks were registered to vote in the early 1950s, as a result of disfranchising measures such as literacy tests and poll taxes, the discriminatory administration of voting requirements, and the threat and reality of physical violence.

Though Congress's anti-majoritarian features and the justices' culturally élite attitudes help to explain why the Court was more progressive on race than Congress in the 1940s and 1950s, fortuity was also important. The justices generally reflect élite opinion, but there are obvious exceptions. Correlations exist between high socioeconomic status and liberal positions on certain cultural issues, but they are not perfect. On the Court early in the twenty-first century, Justices Antonin Scalia and Clarence Thomas are members of the cultural élite who certainly do not share its liberal political propensities. Constitutional rulings always reflect some element of fortuity in the composition of the Court. Justice Stanley Reed, who was from Kentucky, was not an eager supporter of *Brown*; he planned to dissent until virtually the last minute and suppressed his opinion only for the good of the Court. Had there been five Justice Reeds, *Brown* almost certainly would not have been decided as it was. Nor was the presence of five Reeds inconceivable in 1954, given that Presidents Franklin D. Roosevelt and Harry S Truman had been virtually indifferent to the racial attitudes of appointees when they reconstituted the Court in the late 1930s and 1940s.

In the 1960s both the Court and Congress blazed new trails on civil rights. The justices carved out important new constitutional protections for the NAACP, reversed dozens of convictions of sit-in protestors, accelerated the school desegregation process, revolutionized federal courts doctrine (and many other legal areas as well) in ways that facilitated civil rights advances, invalidated poll taxes, and expanded "state action" in novel and creative ways. Meanwhile, Congress was passing three landmark pieces of civil rights legislation. The Civil Rights Act of 1964 forbade race discrimination in public accommodations and private employment, authorized cut-offs of federal funds to institutions that engaged in race discrimination, and authorized the attorney general to bring school desegregation suits. The Voting Rights Act of 1965, by threatening to appoint federal voter registrars in the most recalcitrant counties of the Deep South, finally enabled southern blacks to meaningfully participate in politics. The Fair Housing Act of 1968 forbade race discrimination in the sale and rental of housing.

Both the Court and Congress were responding to the direct-action phase of the civil rights movement, which commenced in 1960 and quickly captivated the nation. By contrast, in the late 1950s the justices had backed off from the implementation of *Brown*, even to the point of signaling their approval of tokenist compliance measures. They had also rejected constitutional challenges to literacy tests, despite the important role that they played in disfranchising blacks. The justices reentered the school desegregation fray in the same month that street demonstrations in Birmingham transformed national opinion on race. Most of the Court's important civil rights decisions came after, not before, the development of direct-action protest in 1960.[11]

Congress's adoption of path-breaking civil rights legislation in the mid-1960s was directly attributable to the civil rights movement. Congress had passed civil rights bills in 1957 and 1960, but they were limited to voting rights and failed to provide effective enforcement mechanisms. The 1964 and 1965 laws were true landmarks. The former vastly accelerated school desegregation, and the latter enfranchised blacks virtually overnight in the most retrograde parts of the Deep South. Both laws emerged directly from civil rights protest—the first from Birmingham and the second from Selma.

Court decisions of the 1960s reveal how important social and political context are to constitutional interpretation. The justices created new constitutional doctrines, repudiated ancient maxims of law, and engaged in extraordinary legal gymnastics in their defense of the civil rights movement. *New York Times v. Sullivan* (1964), which created novel First Amendment protection for newspapers against libel suits, was a case about protecting the civil rights movement from being bankrupted by southern segregationists who were alleging defamation. The Warren Court's criminal procedure revolution was also rooted in the justices' concerns about racial injustice (and poverty). In civil rights cases the justices began to look at legislative motive, which for more than a hundred years they had generally treated as irrelevant to a statute's constitutionality. They also began to repudiate traditional rules requiring deference by federal courts to state court decision making. The Court reversed sit-in demonstrators' convictions on contrived rationales because the justices sympathized with the civil rights cause.[12]

This brief canvass of civil rights history reveals that the constitutional interpretations of both Congress and the Supreme Court broadly reflect popular opinion. Most people expect Congress, as a political institution, to reflect majority sentiment. Some hold onto a romantic image of the Court as capable of rescuing from oppression the "helpless, weak, . . .

or . . . non-conforming victims of prejudice." But the justices reflect dominant public opinion too much to protect truly oppressed groups. Not only did the Court fail to intervene against slavery before the Civil War, but it extended positive constitutional protection to the institution. The justices validated the internment of Japanese-Americans during the Second World War and the persecution of political leftists during the McCarthy era. And, as we have seen, during the heyday of Jim Crow, they sustained segregation and disfranchisement.[13]

Constitutional law generally has sufficient flexibility to accommodate dominant public opinion, which the justices have little inclination, and limited power, to resist. For example, conventional sources of constitutional law did not plainly bar segregation, which in 1896 seemed like progressive racial policy, given escalating white-on-black violence and most whites' strong commitment to preserving "racial purity." Accordingly, courts are likely to protect only those minorities that are favorably regarded by majority opinion. Ironically, when a minority group is most in need of judicial protection, because of severe oppression, it is least likely to receive it. Groups must command significant social, political, and economic power before they become attractive candidates for judicial solicitude. The justices would not have dreamed of protecting women or gays under the equal protection clause before the women's and gay rights movements. Similarly, segregation and disfranchisement began to seem objectionable to the justices only as blacks became a vital New Deal constituency and achieved middle-class status and professional success, earning federal judgeships, military generalships, prestigious clerkships with Supreme Court justices, and, in the case of Ralph Bunche, the Nobel Peace Prize.

BROWN AND THE CIVIL RIGHTS MOVEMENT

How much did *Brown* influence congressional action on civil rights? The connection was real but more complicated than is generally appreciated. Members of Congress plainly did not feel compelled by *Brown* to adopt legislation to enforce the decision. Throughout the 1950s Congress failed even to enact symbolic statements affirming that *Brown* was the law of the land. Congress did pass tepid civil rights legislation in 1957, but it covered only voting rights and even that ineffectively so. A section empowering the attorney general to bring desegregation suits was eliminated from the final bill. In the 1950s Congress declined even to offer financial support to desegregating school districts.

Congress passed landmark civil rights legislation in the mid-1960s not because of *Brown* but because of the civil rights movement. Televised scenes of southern law enforcement officers brutalizing peaceful civil rights demonstrators in Birmingham and Selma, Alabama, dramatically altered northern opinion on race and enabled passage of the Civil Rights Act of 1964 and the Voting Rights Act of 1965. How did *Brown* contribute to the enactment of that legislation?

Brown had many consequences. It increased the salience of the segregation issue, encouraged blacks to believe that racial change was possible, and motivated blacks to litigate against segregation. I have explored these consequences elsewhere and wish here to focus on another ramification of *Brown*, which is less well appreciated yet possibly more important: *Brown* crystallized southern whites' resistance to racial change, radicalized southern politics, and increased the likelihood that direct-action protest, once it developed, would incite a violent response. Civil rights demonstrators of the early 1960s often sought racial reforms that were less controversial than school desegregation—voting rights for blacks, desegregated lunch counters, and more jobs for blacks. If not for the fanaticism that *Brown* produced in southern politics, such demands might have been received sympathetically or at least without unrestrained violence. *Brown* ensured that when street demonstrations came, politicians such as Bull Connor, Jim Clark, Ross Barnett, and George Wallace were there to meet them.[14]

One barometer of the impact of *Brown* on southern whites was the resurgence of the Ku Klux Klan, which had earlier seemed set to "disappear permanently from the American scene." After *Brown*, the Klan reappeared in force in states such as South Carolina, Florida, and Alabama. The legal assault of southern states on the NAACP was another instance of post-*Brown* racial retrogression. Before *Brown*, most white southerners thought the NAACP "at worst was a bunch of Republicans." But after the decision, the association "became an object of consuming hatred." The NAACP's southern membership, which had steadily risen since the Second World War, plummeted after *Brown*, as affiliation became too dangerous. With a lurking threat of school desegregation, whites in the Deep South suddenly found black voting intolerable. Impressive postwar expansions in black suffrage in Mississippi, Alabama, and Louisiana were halted and then reversed. *Brown* also retarded progress in desegregating southern universities, which had been fairly steady since *Sweatt v. Painter* (1950). The post-*Brown* backlash also reversed progress in desegregating sports. Integration of minor league baseball teams and collegiate sporting competitions was sharply curtailed after *Brown*. Even minor interracial courtesies and interactions were often suspended in the post-*Brown* racial hysteria. In 1959 John Patterson, the newly elected governor of Alabama, barred black marching bands from his inaugural parade, even though they had been warmly received in prior inaugural ceremonies. Koinonia Farm, an interracial religious cooperative in Americus, Georgia, had experienced little harassment since its founding in 1942, but after *Brown* it found its products boycotted and its roadside produce stands shot at.[15]

In the mid-1950s southern political contests assumed a common pattern. Candidates tried to show that they were the most "blatantly and uncompromisingly prepared to cling to segregation at all costs." "Moderation" became "a term of derision," as the political center collapsed, leaving only "those who want to maintain the Southern way of life or those who want to mix the races." Moderate critics of massive resistance were labeled "double crossers," "sugar-coated integrationists," "cowards," and "traitors." Most moderates either joined the segregationist bandwagon or else were retired from service. A politician in Virginia observed that it "would be suicide to run on any other platform [than segregation]."[16] *Brown* may also have directly fostered white vigilante violence against blacks. Polls revealed that 15 to 25 percent of southern whites favored violence, if necessary, to resist desegregation. A Klan leader reported that *Brown* created "a situation loaded with dynamite" and "really gave us a push." Now that the justices "have abolished the Mason-Dixon line," Klansmen vowed "to establish the Smith and Wesson line."[17]

In the late 1940s whites in Mississippi had threatened and beaten blacks for suffrage activities, but in 1955 the Reverend George Lee in Belzoni and Lamar Smith in Brookhaven were killed for voting or for encouraging other blacks to do so. The annual number of reported lynchings in Mississippi had dropped to zero before *Brown*, but in 1955, in addition to the murders of Lee and Smith, a fourteen-year-old named Emmett Till was killed for allegedly whistling at a white woman in Money, Mississippi. The NAACP published a pamphlet that year entitled "M is for Mississippi and Murder." To draw a link between these killings and *Brown* is speculative, but the timing suggests one, and it is precisely this link that some contemporaries drew. The Yazoo City (Mississippi) *Herald* declared that the blood of Till was on the hands of the justices. The unwillingness of white jurors to indict or to convict clearly guilty murderers is even more plausibly attributed to the impact of *Brown* on southern white opinion. One white in Mississippi declared that "[t]here's open season on the Negroes now. They've got no protection, and any peckerwood who wants can go out and shoot himself one, and we'll free him." Till's funeral in Chicago attracted thousands of mourners, and a photograph of his mutilated body in *Jet* seared the nation's conscience. Segregating black schoolchildren was one thing, lynching them quite another. Roy Wilkins of the NAACP condemned Mississippi's "political murders" and the "system that permits the shooting down of little boys," and he demanded federal civil rights legislation. Representative Hugh Scott, Republican of Pennsylvania, itemized the brutalities in Mississippi and called for legislation to "eliminate this kind of horror from American life."[18]

The lynching of Mack Parker in 1959 also shaped national opinion on race. Whites in Mississippi seized Parker, scheduled to stand trial for raping a white woman, from the Poplarville jail and killed him—the state's first old-style lynching since the Second World War. Whether the radicalizing effect on southern whites of *Brown* contributed to the lynching is impossible to say, though a newspaper in Mississippi blamed the Court and drew the lesson that "force must not be used in pushing revolutionary changes in social custom. Every such action produces equal and opposite reaction." Governor James Coleman condemned the murder and hoped that Mississippians would not "be punished by civil rights legislation for what a handful have done." The leading guru of the white citizens' councils, Judge Tom Brady, predicted that the NAACP would "rejoice in this highly regrettable incident" and "urge passage of vicious civil rights measures." On the latter point he was right. Parker's murder, Wilkins declared, proved that "mob violence is not dead in the South" and demonstrated "the necessity of further and stronger protection of civil rights . . . by the federal government." Constituents wrote to their congressional representatives to express horror and to demand federal legislation to curb such atrocities.[19]

Even though attributing vigilante violence to *Brown* is speculative, diehard segregationists did so. Citizens' councils in Mississippi, which claimed to repudiate violence, conceded that "there is a point beyond which even the most judicious restraint becomes cowardice." A minister in Dallas told a large citizens' council rally that if public officials would not block integration, plenty of people were prepared "to shed blood if necessary to stop this work of Satan." A handbill circulated at a huge citizens' council rally in Montgomery declared that "[w]hen in the course of human events it becomes necessary to abolish the Negro race, proper methods should be used," including guns and knives.[20] White Southerners could hardly be collectively blamed for random acts of private violence against innocent blacks. However, when public officials incited such violence, which they did both directly and indirectly, Northerners responded by demanding civil rights legislation.

Most southern politicians avoided explicit exhortations to violence, and many affirmatively discouraged it, either to immunize themselves from criticism when violence occurred or because they rightly understood that violence would "do irreparable harm" to their cause and "turn public opinion" against them. Still, a few politicians could not restrain themselves. A legislator in Alabama declared that whites must leave the state, "stay here and be humiliated, or take up our shotguns." Others promoted violence more discreetly. Senator Eastland told an enormous citizens' council rally a few days after a mob had ended Autherine Lucy's effort to desegregate the University of Alabama that he knew "you good people of Alabama don't intend to let the NAACP run your schools." On other occasions, Eastland told audiences that they were "obligated to defy [*Brown*]" and that "Southern people have been tested in the past, and have not been found wanting."[21]

Some public officials repudiated violence while using extremist rhetoric that probably encouraged it. Governor Marvin Griffin of Georgia condemned violence but insisted, referring to *Brown*, that "no true Southerner feels morally obliged to recognize the legality of this act of tyranny," and he proclaimed that the South "stands ready to battle side-by-side for its sacred rights, . . . but not with guns." Senator Eastland cautioned that "[a]cts of violence and lawlessless have no place" and insisted that "[t]he fight we wage must be a just and legal fight," after he had incited his audience with reminders that "[t]here is no law that a free people must submit to a flagrant invasion of their personal liberty" and that "[n]o people in all the history of Government have been forced to integrate against their will." Representative James Davis of Georgia insisted that "[t]here is no place for violence or lawless acts," after calling *Brown* "a monumental fraud which is shocking, outrageous and reprehensible," warning against "meekly accept[ing] this brazen usurpation of power," and denying any obligation on "the people to bow the neck to this new form of tyranny." These politicians either knew, or were criminally negligent for failing to appreciate, that their rhetoric was likely to incite violence.[22]

Whether political demagoguery actually produced violence was less im-

portant than the perception that it did. The NAACP constantly asserted
such a linkage—for example, blaming southern politicians for fostering a
climate conducive to Mack Parker's lynching. James Meredith, the first
black man to attend Ole Miss, blamed the assassination of the NAACP's
Mississippi field secretary, Medgar Evers, on "governors of the Southern
states and their defiant and provocative actions." One lawyer in Tennessee
blamed violence over school desegregation on congressmen who signed
the Southern Manifesto, which assailed *Brown* as a "clear abuse of judicial
power" and pledged all "lawful means" of resistance: "What the hell do
you expect these people to do when they have 90 some odd congressmen
from the South signing a piece of paper that says you're a southern hero
if you defy the Supreme Court." After the bombing of a temple in Atlanta
in 1958, Mayor William Hartsfield declared that "[w]hether they like it or
not, every rabble-rousing politician is the godfather of the cross-burners
and the dynamiters who are giving the South a bad name."[23]

The general connection between extremist politicians and violence is
plausible, but the linkage between particular public officials and the brutality that inspired civil rights legislation is compelling. For present purposes, I shall consider only the two most prominent exemplars of this
phenomenon, T. Eugene ("Bull") Connor, the police commissioner of Birmingham, and George Wallace, the governor of Alabama. The violence
that these men cultivated, condoned, or unintentionally fomented proved
critical to transforming national opinion on race. Connor had been first
elected to the Birmingham City Commission in 1937 on a pledge to crush
the communist and integrationist threat posed by the unionizing efforts of
the Congress of Industrial Organizations. By 1950, however, civic leaders
had come to regard Connor as an embarrassment because of his extrem-
ism and his frequent brutality toward blacks, and they orchestrated his
public humiliation through an illicit sexual encounter. In 1953 Connor retired from politics, and racial progress was achieved in Birmingham as a
result, including the establishment of the first hospital for blacks, desegregation of elevators in downtown office buildings, and serious efforts to
desegregate the police force.[24]

After *Brown*, racial progress in Birmingham ground to a halt. An interracial committee disbanded in 1956, consultation between the races ceased,
and Connor resurrected his political career. In 1957 he regained his seat on
the city commission by defeating an incumbent whom he attacked as weak
on segregation. In the late 1950s a powerful Klan element wreaked havoc
in Birmingham by launching a wave of unsolved bombings and other bru-

tality. The police, under Connor's control, declined to interfere. Standing for reelection in 1961, Connor cultivated extremists by offering the Klan fifteen minutes of "open season" on the Freedom Riders as they rolled into town. After horrific beatings inflicted upon representatives of the news media as well as demonstrators, the *Birmingham News* wondered, "Where were the police?" Voters may have been less curious, having handed a landslide victory just two weeks earlier to Connor, who had invited the violence.[25]

In 1963 the Southern Christian Leadership Conference (SCLC), after the failed demonstrations of Albany, Georgia, was searching for a city with a police chief unlikely to duplicate Sheriff Laurie Pritchett's restraint. They selected Birmingham, perhaps the South's most violent city, where Connor already had achieved notoriety by allowing the Klan to beat Freedom Riders. Martin Luther King was criticized for refusing to defer demonstrations in the city until after attempting negotiations with the new mayor, Albert Boutwell, who had recently defeated Connor. But King wanted to act quickly, while Connor remained police commissioner, a position that was to be eliminated once the mayoralty results survived a legal challenge. King's lieutenant, Wyatt Walker, later explained: "We knew that when we came to Birmingham that if Bull Connor was still in control, he would do something to benefit our movement. We didn't want to march after Bull was gone." The strategy worked brilliantly. After some initially uncharacteristic restraint, Connor unleashed police dogs and fire hoses against demonstrators, many of whom were children. Television and newspapers featured images of police dogs attacking unresisting demonstrators, including one that President Kennedy reported made him "sick." Editorials condemned the violence as "a national disgrace." Citizens voiced their "sense of unutterable outrage and shame" and demanded that politicians take "action to immediately put to an end the barbarism and savagery in Birmingham." Within ten weeks, spin-off demonstrations spread to over one hundred cities.[26]

Televised brutality against peaceful civil rights demonstrators in Birmingham dramatically altered northern opinion on race and enabled passage of the Civil Rights Act of 1964. Opinion polls revealed that the proportion of Americans who deemed civil rights the nation's most urgent issue rose from 4 percent before Birmingham to 52 percent after. Substantial majorities now favored expansive civil rights legislation. Members of Congress denounced the violence in Birmingham and introduced measures to end federal aid to segregated schools. Kennedy overhauled earlier civil

rights proposals to include broader voting rights protections, the desegregation of public accommodations, authority in the attorney general to
bring school desegregation suits, and the termination of federal funding to
programs that engaged in race discrimination. Only after the nation saw
the police dogs and fire hoses of Birmingham did Kennedy announce on
national television that civil rights was a "moral issue as old as the scrip-
tures and as clear as the American Constitution."[27]

The governor of Alabama, George Wallace, had played a minor role in
suppressing the demonstrations in Birmingham and would play a more
substantial role in the violence that lay ahead. Perhaps more than anyone, Wallace personified the post-*Brown* racial fanaticism of southern politics. Early in his political career, Wallace had been criticized as "soft" on
segregation. Unlike Connor, he was in the half of the Alabama delegation that did not walk out of the Democratic national convention in 1948
over the civil rights plank, and he had been a campaign manager for the
racially moderate governor Big Jim Folsom in 1954. Soon after *Brown*,
however, Wallace felt the changing political winds, broke with Folsom,
and cultivated conflict with federal authorities over race issues in his position as circuit judge in Barbour County. In 1958 Wallace's principal opponent in the Alabama governor's race was the state attorney general, John
Patterson, who bragged of shutting down NAACP operations in Alabama.
The Klan endorsed Patterson, whom Wallace criticized for not repudiating
the endorsement. Patterson was so extreme that Wallace unwittingly became the candidate of moderation and won heavy black support. Patterson
easily won the runoff primary, leaving Wallace to ruminate that "they out-
niggered me that time, but they will never do it again." Wallace made good
on that promise in 1962, winning the governorship on a campaign promise
of defying federal integration orders, "even to the point of standing at the
school house door in person." In his inaugural address he declared, "In the
name of the greatest people that have ever trod this earth, I draw the line
in the dust and toss the gauntlet before the feet of tyranny and I say segregation now, segregation tomorrow, segregation forever." Like most southern politicians, Wallace publicly condemned violence. Yet his actions from
1963 to 1965 directly and indirectly caused brutality that helped transform
national racial opinion.[28]

During the demonstrations in Birmingham, Wallace dispatched several
hundred state troopers, who supplemented Connor's brutality with some
of their own. He also publicly praised Connor for forcefully suppressing
the demonstrations. That summer, Wallace fulfilled his pledge to stand in

the schoolhouse door at Tuscaloosa, physically blocking the university's entrance before, in a carefully planned charade, stepping aside in the face of superior federal force. Learning from the debacle at Ole Miss the preceding fall, Wallace had warned he would not "tolerate mob action," and massive security measures kept Tuscaloosa "peaceful and serene."[29]

Yet Wallace had grown overconfident in his ability to spout defiant rhetoric without provoking violence. After Tuscaloosa he continued to promise a "forceful stand" against grade school desegregation, which federal courts had ordered in Alabama for the fall. In September Wallace used state troops to block desegregation in Birmingham, Mobile, and Tuskegee. In Birmingham white mobs demonstrated outside the schools that were scheduled to desegregate, and a minor race riot erupted, in which the police killed a black man and sixteen others were injured. Wallace had encouraged extremist groups to wage "a boisterous campaign" against desegregation, and now he defended the rioters, who he insisted were "not thugs—they are good working people who get mad when they see something like this happen." Threatened with contempt citations by all five Alabama district judges, Wallace relented. The schools desegregated, but within a week tragedy had struck. Klansmen in Birmingham, possibly inspired by the governor's protestations that he could not "fight federal bayonets" with his "bare hands," dynamited the Sixteenth Street Baptist Church, killing four black schoolgirls. Within hours of the bombing, two other black teenagers were killed, one by white hoodlums and the other by police. It was the largest death toll of the civil rights era, and Wallace received much of the blame. King publicly blamed him for "creat[ing] the climate that made it possible for someone to plant that bomb." Richmond Flowers, the attorney general of Alabama, linked the carnage to Wallace's defiance: "The individuals who bombed the Sixteenth Avenue [sic] Church in their way were standing in the schoolhouse door." President Kennedy, expressing "a deep sense of outrage and grief," thought it "regrettable that public disparagement of law and order has encouraged violence which has fallen on the innocent." Wallace may not have sought the violence, but his provocative rhetoric probably contributed to it, and he certainly took no measures to prevent it.[30]

Most of the nation was appalled by the murder of innocent schoolchildren. One week after the bombing, tens of thousands across America participated in memorial services and marches. Northern whites wrote to the NAACP to join, condemn, and apologize. A white lawyer from Los Angeles wrote: "Today I am joining the NAACP; partly, I think, as a kind of apology for being caucasian, and for not being in Birmingham to lend my physical support." A northern white woman condemned whites in Birmingham who had been involved in the bombing or condoned it as "the worst barbarians," and said she was "ashamed to think" that she bore "their color skin." She also declared that the bombing had "certainly changed" her attitude on civil rights, which previously had been "somewhat lukewarm." A white man from New Rochelle, New York, wrote: "How shall I start? Perhaps to say that I am white, sorry, ashamed, and guilty. . . . Those who have said that all whites who, through hatred, intolerance, or just inaction are guilty are right." The NAACP urged members to "flood Congress with letters in support of necessary civil rights legislation to curb such outrages," and Wilkins demanded that the federal government "cut off every nickel" going to Alabama. Northern congressmen, reflecting their constituents' outrage, introduced amendments to strengthen the administration's pending civil rights bill.[31]

Wallace's critics in Alabama attacked his schoolhouse-door routine at Tuscaloosa as "the greatest production since Cleopatra," and they accused him of making Alabama "a mockery before the nation." But most voters apparently disagreed. Wallace remained enormously popular, and in January 1964 he won a resounding victory when the state Democratic executive committee instructed the Alabama delegation to the party's national convention to support Wallace as a favorite-son candidate for president. Meanwhile, he continued to rail against "shocking" pronouncements of federal "judicial tyrant[s]" and to urge local authorities to resist desegregation, though he refrained from any more schoolhouse-door stands. But the linkage between Wallace and violence had not ended, with Selma still in the future.[32]

Early in 1965 the SCLC brought its voter registration campaign to Selma, in search of another victory like that achieved in Birmingham. There King and his colleagues refined the tactics they had successfully deployed in Birmingham, having chosen Selma partly because of the presence of a law enforcement officer with proclivities much like those of Bull Connor. The sheriff of Dallas County, Jim Clark, had a temper which "could be counted on to provide vivid proof of the violent sentiments that formed white supremacy's core." The result was another resounding success. Clark, after initial restraint which disappointed SCLC workers, finally brutalized nonresisting demonstrators. The violence culminated in Bloody Sunday, 7 March 1965, when county and state law enforcement officers viciously assaulted marchers as they crossed the Edmund Pettus Bridge on the way to Montgomery. Governor Wallace had promised that the march would be broken up by "whatever measures are necessary," and Colonel Al Lingo, Wallace's chief law enforcement lieutenant, insisted that the governor himself had given the order to attack. That evening, ABC television interrupted its broadcast of *Judgment at Nuremberg* for a lengthy film report of peaceful demonstrators being assailed by stampeding horses, flailing clubs, and tear gas. Most of the nation was repulsed. Two white northern volunteers were killed in the events surrounding Selma, a Unitarian minister from Boston and a mother of five from Detroit.[33]

Over the following week, sympathy demonstrations took place across the United States. Citizens demanded remedial action from their congressional representatives, scores of whom condemned the violence and endorsed voting rights legislation. On 15 March 1965 President Johnson proposed such legislation before a joint session of Congress, as seventy million Americans watched on television. Before Selma the administration had not contemplated voting rights legislation in the near term, but national revulsion at the brutalization of peaceful protestors prompted a change in plans.[34]

The beating of peaceful black demonstrators by southern white law enforcement officers reshaped national opinion and led directly to the passage of landmark civil rights legislation. *Brown* was less directly responsible than is commonly supposed for putting those demonstrators on the street but more directly responsible for the violent reception that they encountered. The post-*Brown* fanaticism of southern politics created a situation ripe for violence. Some of the ensuing violence was purely private, but much of it was encouraged, directly or indirectly, by extremist politicians, whom voters rewarded for irresponsible rhetoric that fomented brutality. Before the violent outbreaks of the 1960s, most white northerners had agreed with *Brown* in the abstract, but they were disinclined to push for its enforcement; many of them agreed with President Dwight David Eisenhower that the NAACP should rein in its demands for immediate desegregation. Televised scenes of officially sanctioned brutality against peaceful black demonstrators transformed northern opinion. By helping to lay bare the violence at the core of white supremacy, *Brown* accelerated its demise. President Eisenhower, Justice Hugo Black, and many southern moderates foresaw that *Brown* would temporarily retard southern racial progress and destroy southern political liberalism. They rightly anticipated the backlash to *Brown*, but not the counter-backlash.[35]

Would the same violence have confronted civil rights demonstrators without *Brown*? One cannot know for certain. But without *Brown*, school desegregation would probably not have been a pressing issue in the 1950s. Southern blacks generally had other priorities—ending police brutality, securing voting rights, gaining access to decent jobs, and equalizing public funding of black schools. Moreover, before *Brown* southern whites had proved willing to make small concessions on racial issues that were less important to them than school segregation was. In the absence of *Brown*, negotiation might have continued to produce gradual change without inciting white violence. How whites in this counterfactual universe would have responded if black street demonstrations had erupted is impossible to tell. But in the absence of post-*Brown* political fanaticism, one can imagine Freedom Riders arriving in Birmingham and Montgomery without police commissioners inviting Klansmen to beat them, and blacks demonstrating for voting rights in Selma without law enforcement officers brutalizing them. By the early 1960s most southern whites could probably have tolerated desegregated transportation and black suffrage, had *Brown* not converted all racial challenges, in their minds, into fundamental assaults on Jim Crow. Whether and how southern schools would have desegregated in this counterfactual scenario is anybody's guess, but it almost certainly would not have happened as quickly as it did under the Civil Rights Act of 1964. Only the violence resulting from the radicalization of southern politics brought about by *Brown* enabled transformative change to occur as rapidly as it did.

NOTES

Many of the ideas in this chapter are explored at greater length and more fully documented in my book *From Jim Crow to Civil Rights: The Supreme Court and the Struggle for Racial Equality* (New York: Oxford University Press, 2004).

1   Martin Luther King Jr., *Stride toward Freedom: The Montgomery Story* (New York: Harper, 1958), 198.

2   Civil Rights Cases, 109 U.S. 3 (1883); United States v. Harris, 106 U.S. 629 (1883).

3   See generally Klarman, *From Jim Crow to Civil Rights*, chap. 1.

4   See generally *id.*, chap. 2.

5   "The Right to Vote," *Washington Post*, 23 June 1915, 6.

6   See generally Klarman, *From Jim Crow to Civil Rights*, chap. 3.

7   On Scottsboro see generally Dan T. Carter, *Scottsboro: A Tragedy of the American South*, rev. ed. (Baton Rouge: Louisiana State University Press,

1979); James Goodman, *Stories of Scottsboro* (New York: Pantheon, 1994). On the criminal procedure developments see Michael J. Klarman, "The Racial Origins of Modern Criminal Procedure," 99 *Michigan Law Review* 48 (2000).

8   See generally Klarman, *From Jim Crow to Civil Rights*, chaps. 4–5.

9   On the antimajoritarian features of the Senate see Robert A. Caro, *The Years of Lyndon Johnson*, vol. 3, *Master of the Senate* (New York: Alfred A. Knopf, 2002). On Truman's civil rights policies see William C. Berman, *The Politics of Civil Rights in the Truman Administration* (Columbus: Ohio State University Press, 1970); Donald R. McCoy and Richard T. Ruetten, *Quest and Response: Minority Rights and the Truman Administration* (Lawrence: University Press of Kansas, 1973).

10 See Klarman, *From Jim Crow to Civil Rights*, chap. 6.

11 *Id.*

12 See, e.g., Robert J. Glennon, "The Jurisdictional Legacy of the Civil Rights Movement," 61 *Tennessee Law Review* 869 (1994); Michael Klarman, "An Interpretive History of Modern Equal Protection," 90 *Michigan Law Review* 213, 272–76 (1991).

13 Chambers v. Florida, 309 U.S. 227, 241 (1940). See generally Michael J. Klarman, "Rethinking the Civil Rights and Civil Liberties Revolutions," 82 *Virginia Law Review* 1 (1996).

14 On the various consequences of *Brown* see Klarman, *From Jim Crow to Civil Rights*, chap. 7.

15 Arnold Rice, *The Ku Klux Klan in American Politics* (Washington: Public Affairs, 1962), 118–20; Wilkins to W. Lester Banks, 20 August 1957, *Papers of the National Association for the Advancement of Colored People*, ed. August Meier (microfilm, 28 parts, University Publications of America, 1982), part 20, reel 12, frame 982; Benjamin Muse, *Ten Years of Prelude: The Story of Integration Since the Supreme Court's 1954 Decision* (New York: Viking, 1964), 39; *Southern School News* (SSN), February 1959, 16; Margaret Price, "Joint Interagency Fact Finding Project on Violence and Intimidation" (draft), 51–52, *NAACP Papers*, part 20, reel 11, frames 388–89.

16 Muse, *Ten Years of Prelude*, 161, 168; SSN, February 1959, 11; SSN, November 1954, 15; SSN, July 1956, 3; SSN, July 1957, 3; Weldon James, "The South's Own Civil War: Battle for the Schools," *With All Deliberate Speed: Segregation-Desegregation in Southern Schools*, ed. Don Shoemaker (New York: Harper, 1957), 23; Numan V. Bartley, *The Rise of Massive Resistance: Race and Politics in the South during the 1950s* (Baton Rouge: Louisiana State University Press, 1969), 68, 192, 247.

17 N. K. Perlow, "KKK Leader Warns: 'We Mean Business,'" *Police Gazette*, August 1956, 7, *NAACP Papers*, part 20, reel 13, frame 444; Stan Opotowsky, "Dixie Dynamite: The Inside Story of the White Citizens Councils"

(reprinted from *New York Post*, 6–20 January 1957), 15, *id.*, frame 682; Melvin M. Tumin, "Readiness and Resistance to Desegregation: A Social Portrait of the Hard Core," *Social Forces* 36 (March 1958): 258, table 1.

18   NAACP, "M is for Mississippi and Murder," *NAACP Papers*, part 20, reel 2, frames 656–58; John Dittmer, *Local People: The Struggle for Civil Rights in Mississippi* (Urbana: University of Illinois Press, 1994), 53–58; James C. Cobb, *The Most Southern Place on Earth: The Mississippi Delta and the Roots of Regional Identity* (New York: Oxford University Press, 1992), 214–22; Roy Wilkins, Keynote Address to National Delegate Assembly for Civil Rights, 4 March 1956, 6, *NAACP Papers*, part 21, reel 12, frame 193; Rep. Hugh Scott, speech before the National Assembly on Civil Rights, 5 March 1956, 3, *id.*, frame 203; Charles M. Payne, *I've Got the Light of Freedom: The Organizing Tradition and the Mississippi Freedom Struggle* (Berkeley: University of California Press, 1995), 36–40, 53–54, 138–39; Stephen J. Whitfield, *A Death in the Delta: The Story of Emmett Till* (New York: Free Press, 1988), 15–42.

19   Howard Smead, *Blood Justice: The Lynching of Mack Charles Parker* (New York: Oxford University Press, 1986), 68–70, 74–75, 95–96, 101, 105, 163–68, 175, 180–81; *SSN*, May 1959, 4, 8; *SSN*, June 1959, 8, 15; Wilkins to Ross L. Malone, telegram, 29 April 1959, *NAACP Papers*, part 20, reel 1, frames 149–50; I. J. Jilbert to Rep. John J. McFall, 7 May 1959, *id.*, frame 176.

20   *SSN*, February 1963, 17; *SSN*, August 1957, 7; handbill circulated at Montgomery citizens' council meeting, 10 February 1956, *NAACP Papers*, part 20, reel 5, frame 126.

21   Speech of Rep. James C. Davis of Georgia, 31 March 1956, Extension of Remarks of Rep. John Bell Williams, *Congressional Record*, 23 April 1956, *NAACP Papers*, part 20, reel 13, frame 351; NAACP press release, 1 March 1956, *id.*, reel 5, frame 168; *SSN*, March 1956, 7; "Are You Curious about Mississippi?," 2, *NAACP Papers*, part 20, reel 2, frame 173; Sen. James Eastland, "The South Will Fight!," *Arkansas Faith*, December 1955, 27, *id.*, reel 13, frame 322.

22   *SSN*, November 1954, 10; *SSN*, June 1956, 3; Eastland, "The South Will Fight!," 8–9 (frames 303–4); speech of Rep. James C. Davis of Georgia, 31 March 1956, frames 346, 347, 351.

23   *SSN*, August 1963, 20; J. W. Peltason, *Fifty-eight Lonely Men: Southern Federal Judges and School Desegregation* (New York: Harcourt, Brace and World, 1961), 138; Robert E. Bundy to executives of voluntary affiliate organizations, circular re recent bombing incidents, 20 October 1958, *NAACP Papers*, part 20, reel 6, frame 723.

24   Glenn T. Eskew, *But for Birmingham: The Local and National Movements in the Civil Rights Struggle* (Chapel Hill: University of North Carolina Press,

1997), 91–92, 104–5; William A. Nunnelley, *Bull Connor* (Tuscaloosa: University of Alabama Press, 1991), 4, 30, 34, 36–37, 40–44, 67.

25 Nunnelley, *Bull Connor*, 4, 51–60, 67, 74–75, 78, 98–101, 107–9; Andrew Michael Manis, *A Fire You Can't Put Out: The Civil Rights Life of Birmingham's Reverend Fred Shuttlesworth* (Tuscaloosa: University of Alabama Press, 1999), 84, 86, 137, 161, 170–73, 265, 267; Eskew, *But for Birmingham*, 118, 153, 157, 160, 165–66, 175–76; J. Mills Thornton, "Municipal Politics and the Course of the Movement," *New Directions in Civil Rights Studies*, ed. Armstead L. Robinson and Patricia Sullivan (Charlottesville: University Press of Virginia, 1991), 48–49.

26 David J. Garrow, *Bearing the Cross: Martin Luther King, Jr., and the Southern Christian Leadership Conference* (New York: William Morrow, 1986), 227–28, 231–64; David J. Garrow, *Protest at Selma: Martin Luther King, Jr., and the Voting Rights Act of 1965* (New Haven: Yale University Press, 1978), 138–41, 166–68; Martin Luther King Jr., *Why We Can't Wait* (New York: Harper and Row, 1964), 65–66, 69, 79, 114; Rose V. Russell to Pres. Kennedy, 8 May 1963, NAACP *Papers*, part 20, reel 4, frame 307; Nubar Esaian to Pres. Kennedy, 8 May 1963, *id.*, frames 313–15; Manis, *Fred Shuttlesworth*, 331–32, 345, 348–49, 365–66, 369–72; Eskew, *But for Birmingham*, 3–7, 17, 217–99.

27 George H. Gallup, *The Gallup Poll: Public Opinion 1935–1971*, vol. 3 (New York: Random House, 1972), 1769.

28 SSN, June 1962, 8; SSN, February 1963, 10–11; SSN, June 1963, 5; Dan T. Carter, *The Politics of Rage: George Wallace, The Origins of the New Conservatism, and the Transformation of American Politics* (New York: Simon and Schuster, 1995), 76, 82, 84–87, 90–96; Marshall Frady, *Wallace* (New York: World, 1968), 97–98, 106–8, 116, 121–31; SSN, March 1958, 12; SSN, June 1958, 8.

29 SSN, June 1963, 1, 5, 6; SSN, April 1963, 8; SSN, July 1963, 1, 5; Carter, *The Politics of Rage*, 110–14, 116–17, 119, 126–27, 133–51.

30 SSN, July 1963, 5; SSN, September 1963, 1–3, 17, 22; Carter, *The Politics of Rage*, 162–83; "Wallace's Defeat in 'Victory,'" *New York Times*, 11 September 1963, 42; *New York Times*, 16 September 1963, 26; SSN, October 1963, 1, 8, 10–11; SSN, November 1963, 2.

31 Donald B. Brown to Wilkins, 18 September 1963, NAACP *Papers*, part 20, reel 3, frame 941; Elouise May to NAACP, 16 September 1963, *id.*, frame 947; Robert E. Feir to Wilkins, 23 September 1963, *id.*, frame 959; NAACP press release, 21 September 1963, *id.*, frame 986; SSN, October 1963, 11; *New York Times*, 17 September 1963, 26.

32 *New York Times*, 9 September 1963, 16; SSN, November 1963, 2; SSN, January 1964, 1, 12; SSN, February 1964, 1, 12–13; SSN, March 1964, 13; Samuel

Lubell, *White and Black: Test of a Nation* (New York: Harper and Row, 1964), 112–13.

33 Thornton, "Municipal Politics," 60; Garrow, *Protest at Selma*, 2–3, 32–34, 42–45, 60–61, 73–80, 135, 146–49, 159 table 4-1, 223, 230–31; Stephen L. Longenecker, *Selma's Peacemaker: Ralph Smeltzer's Civil Rights Mediation* (Philadelphia: Temple University Press, 1987), 23–24, 36, 112–13, 123–24, 127, 129–30, 139–42, 162–64, 174–77; Adam Fairclough, *To Redeem the Soul of America: The Southern Christian Leadership Conference and Martin Luther King, Jr.* (Athens: University of Georgia Press, 1987), 229–43; Carter, *The Politics of Rage*, 246–49.

34 *Time*, 19 March 1965, 23–28; *Time*, 26 March 1965, 19–23; "Special Message to the Congress: The American Promise," 15 March 1965, *Public Papers of the Presidents of the United States: Lyndon B. Johnson, 1965*, book 1 (Washington, 1966), 281, 284; 111 *Congressional Record* 4984–89, 5014–15 (15 March 1964); Carter, *The Politics of Rage*, 250, 254–55; Garrow, *Protest at Selma*, 78–108; Gallup, *The Gallup Poll*, vol. 3, 1933.

35 Robert Fredrick Burk, *The Eisenhower Administration and Black Civil Rights* (Knoxville: University of Tennessee Press, 1984), 192; Mark Tushnet, "What Really Happened in *Brown v. Board of Education*," 91 *Columbia Law Review* 1867, 1928 (1991).

Quasi-Constitutional Law

The Rise of Super-Statutes

WILLIAM N. ESKRIDGE JR. AND JOHN FEREJOHN

Not all statutes are created equal. Appropriations laws perform important public functions, but they are usually shortsighted and have little effect on the law beyond the years for which they apportion public moneys.[1] Most substantive statutes adopted by Congress and state legislatures reveal little more ambition: they cover narrow subjects or represent legislative compromises that are short-term fixes to bigger problems and cannot easily be defended as the best policy result that can be achieved.[2] Some statutes reveal greater ambition but do not penetrate deeply into American norms or institutional practice. Even fewer statutes successfully penetrate public normative and institutional culture in a deep way. These last are what we call *super-statutes*.

A super-statute is a law that (1) seeks to establish a new normative or institutional framework for state policy and (2) over time does "stick" in the public culture and generates popular support and confirmation, such that (3) the super-statute and its institutional or normative principles have a broad effect on the law—including an effect beyond the four corners of the statute. Super-statutes are typically enacted only after lengthy normative debate about a vexing social or economic problem, but a lengthy struggle does not assure that a law will become a super-statute. The law must also prove robust as a solution, a standard, or a norm over time, such that its earlier critics are discredited and its policy and principles become axiomatic for the public culture. Sometimes a law just gets lucky, catching a wave that makes it a super-statute. At other times, a thoughtful law is unlucky, appearing at the time to be a bright solution but losing its luster because of circumstances beyond the foresight of its drafters.

Super-statutes are applied in accord with a pragmatic methodology that is a hybrid of standard precepts of statutory, common law, and constitutional interpretation. Courts will often consider the super-statute beyond the four corners of its plain meaning because the super-statute is one of the baselines against which other sources of law—sometimes including the Constitution itself—are read. Super-statutes tend to trump ordinary legislation when there are clashes or inconsistencies, even if principles of construction would suggest the opposite. Occasionally super-statutes can reshape constitutional understandings. Because super-statutes exhibit this kind of normative gravity, they have sufficient attraction to bend and reshape the surrounding landscape.

This chapter will explain how super-statutes occupy the legal terrain once called "fundamental law," foundational principles against which people presume their obligations and rights to be set, and through which interpreters apply ordinary law. Today this kind of law might be considered "quasi-constitutional"—fundamental and trumping like constitutional law, but more tentative and susceptible to override or alteration by the legislature or determined judges and administrators. This chapter will also explore the implications of this idea for modern public law. For example, super-statutes bear an interesting resemblance to, and can be contrasted with, theories by which the Constitution itself evolves outside of the formal amendment process of Article V.

A HISTORICAL INTRODUCTION TO SUPER-STATUTES AND HOW THEY FIT WITHIN AMERICAN CONSTITUTIONAL HISTORY

Although we are deploying the term "super-statute" in a novel way,[3] the core idea is a familiar one in the history of Anglo-American law. The concept that certain statutes become axiomatic to a state's fundamental law can be traced back at least as far as early modern English legal theory and was implicit in some statutory schemes throughout American history. It was not until the New Deal, however, that the super-statute phenomenon became a big feature of American public law. The power of this idea continues even, and one might even say especially, in the post–New Deal era of the Rehnquist Court.

As a historical matter, writers have sometimes contrasted common law (English) systems with civil law (Roman) systems in the following way.[4]

The baseline in civil law has traditionally been the *code*, which judges treat as a comprehensive body of rules, policies, and principles. Gaps in the code are filled by a process that civilians call the equity of the statute: judges reason by analogy from the most pertinent provision and its policy to supply the answer in the *casus omissus*, the unprovided-for case. New laws are integrated into the code either by the legislature and its drafters or by judges who reconcile their rules and policies with those of the code. The baseline in English systems has traditionally been the *common law*, a comprehensive body of rules, policies, and principles. Gaps in the common law are filled by a process of reasoning by analogy, figuring out how a new problem is akin to, or different from, prior judicial determinations. New laws are integrated into the common law through two simple canons: ordinary statutes will be construed in a manner consistent with the common law and not in derogation of it, but remedial statutes might supersede the common law and be construed to trump it. Consider, for example, Blackstone's observation that the "most universal and effectual way of discovering the true meaning of the law, when its words are dubious, is by considering the reason and spirit of it . . . for when this reason ceases, the law itself ought likewise to cease with it."[5]

The founding period of American history saw thoughtful Americans struggle with dueling notions of popular sovereignty and judicial independence protecting established liberties.[6] State constitutions emphasizing the former yielded chaotic and frequently unjust legislation, and the Framers and defenders of the Constitution emphasized the role of the "judicial power" to contain legislatures and assure the rule of law.[7] Three general principles embodied in the Constitution and discussed during the ratification debates lend some support to the proposition that the new government was one in which statutes should sometimes be considered sources of fundamental law.

First, the Constitution committed the federal government to popular sovereignty—"We the People" are the governors as well as the governed.[8] Popular sovereignty is hostile to a judge-created common law as the only basis for the rule of law, and the principle suggests that popular feedback should figure in the process by which certain legal notions become fundamental law. Second, the Constitution committed the national government to lawmaking by elected representatives deliberating for the public good. Article I's vesting legislative authority in Congress and Article III's vesting the courts with jurisdiction to interpret federal statutes suggest the principle that the primary source of law at the federal level would be statutes.

It is straightforward to deduce from these first two constitutional principles the proposition that statutes aspiring to create broader norms and structures for governance and showing robustness over time ought to be applied liberally (so long as they do not bump up against other sources of fundamental law, such as the Constitution). Within its listed spheres of unique national competence—such as interstate commerce, bankruptcy, and foreign affairs (all listed in Article I, Section 8)—the Framers wanted Congress to be able to act decisively and shift the terrain away from common law baselines if required for energetic governance in the public interest.

The first Congresses adopted few super-statutes.[9] One was the law creating the Bank of the United States, which was adopted only after a great normative debate. Hamilton and his allies maintained that a federal bank was necessary to operate the government in an orderly manner and to foster commerce and industry in the new Republic, while Jefferson and his allies maintained that the Bank was *ultra vires* for the national government and contrary to the Arcadian republic of small farmers and shopkeepers that they envisioned.[10] The law met the first criterion for super-statutes in setting an important national policy, and the second for enduring (albeit not for as long as most of the other super-statutes discussed in this chapter). The national bank policy stuck in public culture in ways that other Hamiltonian policies did not. When the first act expired in 1815, Congress voted to renew the institution, but President Madison vetoed the law for practical reasons. Even though he had vigorously opposed the bank for constitutional reasons in 1791, Madison in 1815 accepted its legitimacy but not its necessity. He reconsidered the latter conclusion in the next year, and the Second Bank of the United States, which lasted until the Jackson administration, was created in 1816.

Whereas Madison and Jefferson had maintained that the bank must give way to the Constitution, it was ultimately the Constitution that gave way to the bank. By the time the issue finally reached the Supreme Court in *McCulloch v. Maryland*,[11] Chief Justice John Marshall was able to begin his opinion with the observation that decades of experience with and acquiescence in the Bank of the United States had given it a heightened presumption of constitutionality. Not only did Marshall then proceed to sustain the bank against constitutional objections, but he set forth the most expansive theory for interpreting the Constitution ever penned by a U.S. Supreme Court justice. Although the Second Bank expired in 1836, its animating principles—that the federal government could charter corporations and create institutions to regularize and manage the nation's finances—stuck in the public culture.

The Civil War produced some putative super-statutes, namely the Civil Rights Acts of 1866 and 1871. These statutes announced great anti-discrimination principles but were narrowly construed by a post-Reconstruction judiciary afraid to disturb the political consensus in favor of racial segregation.[12] Hence these were failed super-statutes—until the civil rights movement revived interest in those laws after the Second World War and the Warren Court breathed new life into them in the 1960s with liberal interpretations.[13] The same post-Reconstruction judiciary that construed the early civil rights acts stingily protected common law baselines in a range of other cases, especially labor cases. Surly judicial reception, however, hardly deterred legislatures from creating myriad new laws. Progressive supporters of the new legislation—critics of this common law formalism—argued not only that the judiciary was wrong in resisting humane and efficient employment policies but also that the common law itself should no longer be the reflexive baseline in the modern state.[14] Thus Roscoe Pound maintained that "legislative innovation" should afford courts "not only a rule to be applied but a principle from which to reason, and hold it, as a later and more direct expression of the general will, of superior authority to judge-made rules on the same general subject."[15] Justice Harlan Stone agreed that "there is no adequate reason for our failure to treat a statute much more as we treat a judicial precedent, as both a declaration and a source of law, and as a premise for legal reasoning."[16]

These twentieth-century rationalists maintained that a pattern of statutory enactments reflecting a particular normative stance could shift fundamental law, which in turn could affect common law and constitutional law. A majority of the Supreme Court was resistant to this body of thought for several decades, but it became highly influential during the New Deal, which created a wave of super-statutes—such as the Norris-LaGuardia Act of 1932 (a precursor of the New Deal), the Securities Act of 1933 and the Securities Exchange Act of 1934, the National Labor Relations Act of 1935, the Fair Labor Standards Act of 1938, and others.

WHAT IS A SUPER-STATUTE? EXAMPLES OF
SUPER-STATUTES IN ACTION

Our first criterion for super-statutes is that they must substantially alter the existing regulatory baselines with a new principle or policy. Our second criterion can be judged only over a period of time: the new principle or policy "sticks" in the public culture in a deep way, becoming foundational or axiomatic to our thinking. In addition to these two substantive ones, there is a procedural marker for super-statutes, for they are generated in a reflective and deliberative manner over a long period. Typically, a super-statute is not just a snap response to a fleeting crisis; instead, it emerges after a lengthy period of public discussion and official deliberation. More important, the super-statute that emerges from Congress is not a completed product. It requires elaboration from administrators and judges, whose work is then subject to meaningful scrutiny and correction by the legislature or even the citizenry. Consider a couple of examples.

The Sherman Act of 1890, prohibiting combinations and conspiracies "in restraint of trade," as well as monopolies, is a classic super-statute. Scholars are divided as regards the goals of its framers, but most agree that the law was broadly enabling, as it implicitly authorized the judiciary and the Department of Justice to learn how markets work and to formulate rules and standards that would facilitate their operation and discourage anticompetitive practices.[17] That the law was enabling did not mean that it would work, and the early history of the Sherman Act is filled with false steps and odd decisions. Nonetheless, it is now widely accepted that the Sherman Act does represent a great principle—competition in a free market—and that its principle has penetrated American law and society in a pervasive way.

At the risk of abusing a metaphor, we believe that there was a kind of invisible hand guiding the evolution of the Sherman Act toward a robust, economics-driven set of rules. Even though the statutory language invoked a common law concept (restraint of trade) and a jurisdictional requirement imposed by the Constitution (in or affecting commerce), the statute's provision of both public and private causes of action (and a treble damages incentive for private actions) created an ongoing economics-focused dialogue among judges, executive branch officials, private attorneys, academics (especially economists), and legislators and their staffs. The feedback loop facilitated by that dialogue corrected ill-advised paths and pressed the statutory scheme toward robust rules that have become deeply rooted in American public law because they make sense. Consider some examples of different feedback scenarios.

On the one hand, the Supreme Court's early decisions refusing to give the law a proper breadth were criticized in presidential elections between 1896 and 1912 and were essentially reversed during the first Roosevelt and Wilson administrations.[18] Since 1912 the Court has frequently reversed itself, overruling or narrowing prior decisions that have been subject to persuasive economic as well as popular critique.[19] On the other hand, ill-advised congressional amendments, adopted without much attention by the press or the popular political process, have been narrowly interpreted by the Court and sometimes abandoned by Congress. Most of the ill-advised amendments have been of the rent-seeking variety, by which an industry group procures an exemption from the public benefit law. For example, the Miller-Tydings Act of 1937 authorized the states to permit resale price maintenance contracts, a congressional authorization of practices that are usually anticompetitive. The Supreme Court in 1952 gave the rent-seeking amendment a narrowing construction, invalidating a Louisiana law requiring all liquor retailers to charge the price set by the distributor, once any retailer agreed to the set price.[20] Congress itself repealed the law in 1975. Other statutory exemptions have survived, but as the Supreme Court has repeatedly said, "[r]epeals of the antitrust laws by implication from a regulatory statute are strongly disfavored, and have been found only in cases of plain repugnancy between the antitrust and regulatory provisions."[21] The Court has allowed narrowly crafted exemptions only where "necessary to make the [subsequent regulatory scheme] work."[22]

Finally, the Sherman Act has exercised a gravitational pull on constitutional law itself. One of the earliest Supreme Court applications ruled that the act could not be applied to the sugar trust because the commerce clause authorized congressional regulation of "commerce" but not intrastate manufacturing.[23] The Court's stingy opinion was a political sensation and an issue in the presidential campaign of 1896.[24] The post-1896 Court soon adopted the commerce clause approach of the prior dissenting opinion, which permitted congressional regulation of intrastate activities with an "effect" on interstate commerce.[25] In 1906 the Court adopted another expansive theory of the commerce clause when it upheld application of the Sherman Act to intrastate price-fixing that entailed transactions in the "current of commerce."[26] Although the Sherman Act cases by no means rescued the Court from two generations of painful struggle with the commerce clause, they were a standing exception to stingy readings of that congressional power and also a foundation upon which the New Deal Court built an expanded version of the commerce clause. Specifically, the "effect on commerce" and "current of commerce" theories in the Sherman Act cases were foundational ideas in the New Deal Court's liberalization of the commerce clause to permit expansive federal regulation of the economy.[27]

Another super-statute is the Civil Rights Act of 1964. It prohibited, or strengthened earlier measures against, race discrimination in voting (title I), public accommodations (title II), public facilities (title III), public education (title IV), programs or activities receiving federal financial assistance (title VI), and most workplaces (title VII). Sex discrimination is also illegal in the workplaces covered by title VII of the law. Like the Sherman Act, the Civil Rights Act is a proven super-statute, because it embodies a great principle (anti-discrimination), was adopted after an intense political struggle and normative debate and has over the years entrenched its norm into American public life, and has pervasively affected federal statutory and even constitutional law.[28] Again like the Sherman Act, Title VII has seen its principle debated, honed, and strengthened through an ongoing give and take among the legislative, executive, and judicial processes.

Of course the statute has been the situs of normative conflict, some of it still unresolved, as well as consensus. (Given the requirements that a super-statute be committed to a great principle and be the product of deliberation, it is hard to imagine a super-statute that did not generate intense disagreements as to the application of its principle to particular cases.) The 1964 statute did not on its face make clear its application to employment policies having a disparate racial impact or seeking to remedy the underrepresentation of minorities. Resolution of those issues required a refinement of the anti-discrimination principle: Does it entail actual integration, or just equality of opportunity? The agency charged with enforcing the statute (the Equal Employment Opportunity Commission) initially saw the statute's mission as integration, and the Supreme Court accepted that as the basis for its early interpretations in *Griggs v. Duke Power Co.*,[29] which established a cause of action for disparate-impact claims, and *United Steelworkers v. Weber*,[30] which permitted some voluntary affirmative action programs. Scholars were generally supportive of these interpretations, and the early Rehnquist Court reaffirmed *Weber* and extended its reasoning to allow at least some affirmative action programs benefiting women.[31]

In 1989, however, the Rehnquist Court bared its strict constructionist teeth in several employment discrimination cases.[32] For the particular justices on that Court, there was nothing greatly remarkable about their narrow construction in those cases. Majority opinions made it harder to prevail in *Griggs* and Title VII lawsuits. The Court's methodology was emblematic of ordinary statutory construction: hew closely to statutory plain meaning without undue intrusion into common law rights and obligations. What the majority justices did not sufficiently appreciate was that the political process did not regard these as ordinary cases. The decisions triggered a public normative alarm that a bedrock statute was being undermined, and large majorities in Congress approved the Civil Rights Act of 1991,[33] which reaffirmed *Griggs* (explicitly) and *Weber* (implicitly). This normative feedback had some effect on the Rehnquist Court, even though its membership became more conservative. The continuing and indeed strengthened popular support for a strong anti-discrimination — and pro-integration — principle has swept the field. Even onetime segregationists such as Senator Trent Lott have recently pledged allegiance to the principles of nondiscrimination and racial integration throughout American life.

Like the Sherman Act, the Civil Rights Act has pervasively affected the evolution of public law. Unlike the Sherman Act, however, it explicitly affects other statutory regimes. Title VI prohibits federally funded programs from discriminating on the basis of race, ethnicity, or religion. Title VII, as amended in 1972, prohibits state and federal agencies from discriminating in their personnel policies. These provisions contemplate that the anti-discrimination principle must animate most federal and state policies. Judges and administrators have internalized the idea well beyond the explicit commands of the statute. The most expansive example of the principle in operation is evident in the Supreme Court's decision in *Bob Jones University v. United States*.[34] Section 501(c)(3) of the Internal Revenue Code provides that "educational" institutions are entitled to an exemption from federal income taxation. The Internal Revenue Service disallowed Bob Jones University's exemption because its racially discriminatory policies were inconsistent with the overall "charitable" policy of the exemption. Although the statutory text was broad enough to include schools like Bob Jones and the exemption was originally adopted during the apartheid era in our history, the Court ruled that current federal policy required disallowance of the exemption. Of course, the main evidence of that current policy was the Civil Rights Act of 1964. In particular, the Court emphasized, Titles IV and VI were evidence of the important public principle that "racial discrimination in education violates a fundamental public policy."

Just as the Sherman Act provided occasions for the *Lochner* Court to offer ways of getting beyond earlier, stingy readings of Congress's commerce clause power, so the public accommodations provisions of the Civil Rights Act prodded the Court to render its most expansive reading of the commerce clause to date.[35] The great normative principle of the 1964 act pushed the Court to read the Constitution more broadly than it had done before, or has done since. A less-noted chain of events was in some ways more remarkable. The Supreme Court in 1973 indicated that state policies classifying on the basis of pregnancy do not necessarily amount to sex discrimination, because they divide people into pregnant women and nonpregnant men and women.[36] When the Court extended this idea to Title VII, feminist groups engaged in a campaign to educate Congress about the many bars that various kinds of pregnancy-based discrimination posed to women's workplace advancement; Congress swiftly overrode the Court with the Pregnancy Discrimination Act of 1978 (PDA).[37] The Court has not only followed the letter of the statutory response but liberally internalized its principle, that pregnancy-based discrimination is a major engine for disadvantaging women in the workplace. Hence, the Court has sweepingly applied the PDA to strike down even reasonably grounded pregnancy-based discriminations,[38] and has refused to invoke the statute against state policies which seek to remedy employment disadvantages resulting from pregnancy.[39] Because the new statutory policy applies to state and federal agencies, thanks to the 1972 amendments to Title VII, the PDA has essentially replaced the equal protection clause as the foundational protection for women against pregnancy-based discrimination.

ELABORATION AND RAMIFICATIONS OF THE SUPER-STATUTE IDEA

Our idea that a subcategory of statutes is special not only adds a new dimension to this country's statutory history but also helps to explain most of the paradoxically liberal and purposive decisions by the conservative and textualist Rehnquist Court. If we are right that at least some laws are super-statutes, what implications should that insight have for legal doctrine and theory? It should be no surprise that we think there are many implications.

General Theory and Doctrines of Statutory Interpretation

To start, our theory provides a principled and useful way to draw the vexing line between strict and liberal construction. The theory of super-statutes suggests this typology:

Super-statutes should be construed liberally and in a common law way, but in light of the statutory purpose and principle as well as compromises suggested by statutory texts.

Ordinary statutes should be construed with greater focus on the statutory text, but with attention to statutory purpose and legislative history when the statutory terms are ambiguous.

Penal statutes should be applied strictly, reading statutory text no more broadly than the prototypical, core signification of its terms permits.

The liberal approach to super-statutes is of course suggested by the Court's decisions interpreting the Sherman Act, but it is particularly well illustrated by *Burlington Industries, Inc. v. Ellerth* (1998),[40] a sexual harassment case. The issue in *Ellerth* was what responsibility an employer had under Title VII for a supervisor's unwelcome sexual advances and threats of retaliation. If Title VII were a criminal statute, the employer would not be liable for such advances absent a more specific showing of scienter. If Title VII were an ordinary statute, it is not clear that courts should fashion detailed rules for figuring out when advances by a supervisor (unknown to the employer) constitute "discrimination . . . because of . . . sex." It would be well within our legal process tradition for the Court to insist that any such rules must be fashioned by Congress. It is notable that no Justice in *Ellerth* took this position; all nine Justices—none of whom is an open activist—were willing to fashion specific rules, along common law lines, to guide the agency, courts, and attorneys in determining when the employer should be liable. The debate within the Court was entirely about what detailed set of rules the judiciary should read into the open-textured statutory text. These kinds of tradeoffs and judgments have been the life of the common law. Thus, our super-statute rule of construction requires that interpreters develop the statute along common law lines, to carry out its robust principle and purposes, but remain cognizant of countervailing costs and policies. *Ellerth* is a classic case for this kind of reasoning.

Consider how other doctrines of statutory interpretation apply to super-statutes. In part because Congress is deemed the most appropriate forum for correction, most statutory precedents are entitled to a super-strong presumption of correctness, exceeding even that which stare decisis normally accords to common law precedents. We have been critical of that super-strong presumption for ordinary statutes, because there are many barriers (including inertia) to Congress's correction of ordinary precedents, but we find the traditional rule more appropriate for super-statutes, because Supreme Court constructions are likely to attract the attention of Congress and to be overridden if they misread the statute in light of its principle—as the Court's constructions did in the pregnancy discrimination cases of the early 1970s (immediate and decisive override) and the Title VII cases of the late 1980s (immediate and angry override), but not in the sexual harassment cases of the late 1990s (Congress happily kept quiet).

The deference-to-agency canon is completely applicable to super-statutes, but with some twists. The development of a super-statute and its principle are often going to be accomplished most productively at the agency level, and so deference is appropriate, as it was in *Griggs*, *Weber*, and *Ellerth*. And the limit to deference, when the agency's position is at odds with the law, applies to super-statutes as well. Also, deference is not appropriate for an agency's litigating positions, such as the Department of Justice's positions in Sherman Act prosecutions. One twist arises because super-statutory principles become part of the fundamental law—which the judiciary is uniquely charged with developing and applying. Thus the EEOC's views, intelligent and well formed as they are, have not been a great situs for deference, because the Supreme Court is just as much involved in articulating and deliberating about the anti-discrimination principle as the agency officials are. Another twist is that super-statutes are constantly at risk of rent-seeking exceptions and loopholes. Agencies are supposed to guard against this, but they are themselves susceptible to interest-group capture on at least some issues. To the extent that courts are less susceptible to such capture, they stand as an important monitor of an agency's weakness in this regard.

Quasi-Constitutional Law: Super-Statutes as a Mediation
between the Difficulty of Amending the U.S. Constitution and
the Legitimizing Concept of Popular Sovereignty

There is a potentially deeper relationship between super-statutes and constitutional law in our country, and it has to do with the way the Constitution changes. Compared with the constitutions of other nations and of our own states, the U.S. Constitution is relatively—and exceedingly—short, old, and difficult to change through the formal Article V process.[41] These three facts about the Constitution have supported its updating through dynamic judicial interpretation of its provisions.

For any constitution to be enduring, it must be dynamic. Given the particular characteristics of our Constitution—its reliance on standards rather than rules and the difficulty of amending it through the formal process—the dynamism seems, at first blush, to have operated formally through judicial updating. This perception of judicial updating has called forth thousands of articles and books justifying or indicting or seeking to define the limits of judicial review. One criticism of judicial review is that it supplants or drains energy from popular ("We the People") participation in governance.[42] Many theorists have tackled the problem of reconciling the Constitution's meta-principle of popular sovereignty with the apparent reality of extensive and hard-to-check constitutional lawmaking by unelected judges. Consider one important author.

Bruce Ackerman maintains that Article V's rule of recognition is not necessary to change the Constitution even in a formal sense. Really fundamental constitutional enactments can occur outside the Article V procedures in special periods—*constitutional moments*—when the whole people are engaged in and attentive to the establishment of a new constitutional ordering.[43] For Ackerman, what is crucial is not a detailed set of institutional requirements, but the purpose served by such requirements: that the people, responding to a crisis pitting one institution against others, are engaged actively and purposively in reshaping the constitutional order. Whether or not they meet the Article V requirements, fundamental constitutional enactments, according to Ackerman's theory, ought to attract great deference from courts because they effect a change in the constitutional text, guided by deeply held principles of political morality, and because they are put in place deliberately by an aroused and serious public.

An extension of Ackerman's theory would be to view super-statutes as *statutory moments*. Thus the Civil Rights Act of 1964 can be read as a showdown between a normatively engaged political coalition in Congress and the determined southern Democrats in the Senate, who had repeatedly blocked anti-discrimination laws during the Eisenhower years. The election of 1960 offered proponents an opportunity to break this impasse, as it brought to power John Kennedy and Lyndon Johnson, who pushed hard for civil rights legislation. In 1962–63 the debate over the civil rights bill engaged the entire country, with religious, business, and union groups joining civil rights groups in pressing for its adoption. The determined southern opposition was decisively defeated by a coalition assembled by President Johnson and the Senate majority whip, Hubert Humphrey. In the election that immediately followed in 1964, Johnson (with Humphrey as his running mate) won a great landslide over a Republican who had voted against the act for reasons of "states' rights." This scenario roughly follows Ackerman's formula for *higher lawmaking*, whereby the people are engaged in constitutional moments.[44] "We the People" have arguably endorsed civil rights over states' rights—a principle that has altered policy as well as constitutional discourse ever since. The year 1964 might be regarded as a statutory moment permanently altering the normative foundations of public discourse.

The idea of statutory moments along Ackermanian lines is a neat project, but our super-statutes idea is broader still. Descriptively, the main difference between a concept of statutory moments and our notion of super-statutes is that the latter acquire their normative force through a series of public confrontations and debates over time and not through a single, stylized, dramatic confrontation. Thus the Civil Rights Act of 1964, which was enacted in a particularly dramatic and publicly absorbing way, acquired only some of its normative force in 1964. The act immediately transformed public culture in some ways but not in others. To take the most obvious example of an area that it left largely untouched, the law did little to transform the workplace for women, but a series of public debates and confrontations in the 1970s and 1980s yielded consensus that the anti-discrimination principle ought to have bite for women in the workplace—and that the bite entailed protections against discrimination on the basis of pregnancy and sexual harassment in the workplace. The super-statute evolved through a series of debates and confrontations. One can call each of them a statutory moment, but few of such moments meet the Ackermanian model as well as the Civil Rights Act does, and none engaged the public at the high level that it was engaged in 1963–64.

Consider the following diagram as a rough model of how super-statutes evolve:

Responding to an important problem and after careful
deliberation, Congress enacts a statute
↕
Statute is implemented by judges and/or agencies,
with feedback from Congress
↕
Normative conflict, where one institution seeks to
narrow the statute, in a major way

Court narrowly construes the statute

Agency is captured by the regulated group or a special interest
↕
Public debate about the attempted narrowing

Critical outrage, seeking to engage the public

Institutional opposition

Statutory narrowing may become an election issue
↕
Responsive to the normative debate, the government reaffirms
or modifies the core principle of the statute
↕
More crises, especially as statute is adapted to ever
newer circumstances

Like Ackerman, we understand lasting public norms to grow out of conflict. Unlike Ackerman, we also understand lasting public norms to form under conditions of consensus. Also unlike his theory, ours emphasizes evolution rather than revolution. A super-statute is not a moment, nor even a series of moments. Rather, it is a continuing process of deliberation, consensus building as to some issues, conflict as to other issues.

Quasi-Constitutional Super-Statutes as a Normatively Attractive Way for Public Norms to Evolve

The structure of our short, old, and hard-to-amend Constitution makes its dynamic interpretation inevitable—but does not assure a jurocracy. We think a jurocracy would be terrible. Furthermore, it is super-statutes instead of constitutional moments that not only save us from a gerontocracy of judges but also replicate the legitimacy-enhancing features of Article V. Recall that Article V does not entail a popular vote on constitutional amendments, and so the legitimacy of changes to the Constitution is not directly popular. Because amendments must normally be adopted by supermajorities in Congress and then ratified by three-quarters of the states, they entail a lengthy deliberative process, and their animating principles must be broadly acceptable on their merits. That lengthy deliberative process and the requirement of a robust principle give constitutional amendments a legitimacy that both augments and transcends the rule of recognition available under Article V.

The genius of Ackerman's constitutional moments theory is that it exploits the legitimacy-enhancing features of Article V (deliberation about an important principle) and makes it operate without the now unworkable Article V apparatus. Notwithstanding its genius, the theory may in fact sacrifice popular sovereignty for the sake of constitutional updating. For example, if Ackerman is read as requiring that a constitutional moment must be a precondition for real constitutional change, then his theory entails a narrow reading of some constitutional changes. Moreover, in Ackerman's world it is not clear how judges are constrained, or guided, during the long stretches between constitutional moments. The primary constraint seems to be the moral obligation of judges to engage in a process of "synthesis," reconciling earlier versions of the Constitution (the Founding, Reconstruction) with the changes wrought by the most recent constitutional moment (the New Deal). This methodology does not strike us as very constraining. If that is what prevails, Ackermanian judges can govern relatively unchecked for long periods, with no reason to fear popular intervention.

The tension between the desirability of normative updating and the need for it to be legitimate along lines of popular sovereignty is a pervasive problem for modern representative democracies. The United States is unusual in requiring constitutional change to traverse so many potential roadblocks. In many other countries, constitutional lawmaking does not require either supermajorities or the assent of other governmental institutions or the people through referenda, but only the repeated agreement of successive parliaments.[45] The normative advantage of such lawmaking is that it is not so difficult as to be unfeasible in the face of strong objection, yet the procedures (long deliberative history, repeated endorsement by differently constituted legislatures, multiple opportunities for critique and public feedback) vest its results with a great deal of legitimacy. This notion deemphasizes the "momentary" aspect of constitutional or quasi-constitutional lawmaking. One reason for such a stance is that critical moments are as likely to be temporary and governed by passions as to be lasting and ruled by reason. Fundamental principles requiring constitutional protection are more likely to be discovered when the political process takes a more sober and reflective cast. The point is that constitutional legislation is both principled and deliberative, even if it is not produced in a defined historical moment involving a normative showdown.

Super-statutes have a claim to expression of the considered judgment of the nation as a whole. Although according quasi-constitutional status to expressions of the will of the majority does risk injury to disadvantaged minorities, the fact that Congress, the Court, and agencies repeatedly revisit and revise the super-statutes in light of constitutional protections ensures that minority rights will not be lightly overridden in a super-statutory regime. In the end, if a super-statutory regime regularly violates constitutionally protected minority rights, it can be overturned by Congress or the courts.

The judicial role is indeed critical to how things go, but not because of who judges are or because the people cannot be trusted to govern themselves. Rather, the value that judges bring is that they get to see how it is that law (super-statutes) intersects with the lives of ordinary people and, from that perspective, to develop and refine the super-statute in light of that experience. Judges can make policy more precise, more intelligent, and more just, but they do not do these things by themselves. We also need the enthusiasm of interest groups, the policy expertise of agencies, and the moral concern (and sometimes outrage) of the people and their representatives.

CONCLUSION: SUPER-STATUTES, LAW'S HIERARCHY OF SOURCES, AND SOCIAL NORMS

Our project has been to identify a relatively novel way to think about the hierarchy of sources in law. The traditional distinction between ordinary law and higher lawmaking is not sufficiently fine-grained for the modern state. There is, and long has been, an intermediate category of *fundamental* or *quasi-constitutional* law. For most of American history, the common law played that intermediate role: even as it evolved in response to new phenomena and learning, the common law filled statutory gaps, affected the application of statutes, and influenced the evolution of constitutional law itself. The twentieth century inaugurated an age of statutes or, as we prefer, an age of super-statutes. It is no coincidence that the phenomena explored in our paper were coming into focus at the point in history when the common law fell from favor as the basis for fundamental law, even as judges were updating the Constitution in default of its amendment through the formal Article V channels.

Prescriptively, super-statutes mediate the tension between democracy or popular accountability and the evolution of higher law at the hands of unelected judges. Our view is that super-statutes mediate this tension more effectively than either the formal mechanisms contained in the Constitution or leading academic theories such as Ackerman's. The constitutional processes would leave higher law stagnant, and the academic theories would leave it illegitimate. Super-statutes contribute to a complex process by which fundamental law evolves with a strong connection to the people and popular needs. They also contribute to a complex process by which law coheres — if not in a wholly consistent plan, at least in a roughly consistent collection of interrelated policies and principles.

NOTES

Michael Shumsky, Yale Law Class of 2003, provided needed and excellent research assistance as well as useful comments on an earlier draft of this chapter.

1 Indeed, the Supreme Court has created a presumption against construing appropriations laws to effect any change in substantive federal law. Tennessee Valley Authority v. Hill, 437 U.S. 153, 190 (1978).

2 For two very different examples, compare the Alcohol and Drug Abuse Amendments, Pub. L. No. 98-24, 97 Stat. 175 (1983) (requiring the secretary of health and human services to report every three years on the "addictive property of tobacco" — a pallid response to the deadly effects of the drug nicotine), with the Hawaii Reciprocal Beneficiaries Act, 1997 Haw. Sess. Laws 2786, Act 383 (H.B. 118) (creating a new institution of "reciprocal beneficiaries" open to couples who cannot marry — namely, same-sex couples and couples related to one another — as part of a compromise that overrode constitutional arguments for same-sex marriage but did not satisfy the long-term demand for state recognition of same-sex relationships). For an example of an aspiring super-statute, see the Prison Litigation Reform Act of 1995, Pub. L. No. 104-134, 110 Stat. 1321-66.

3 The term "super-statute" has been used by legal commentators before, but

not in the precise way in which we deploy the term here. Earlier writers have used the term to describe a constitution, e.g., A. E. Dick Howard, *The Road From Runnymede: Magna Carta and Constitutionalism In America* (Charlottesville: University of Virginia Press, 1968), 122 (stating that American lawyers in the eighteenth century viewed the Magna Carta and the common law it was thought to embody "as a kind of superstatute, a constitution placing fundamental liberties beyond the reach of Parliament"), or, simply, a big statute with no force outside its four corners, e.g., Bruce A. Ackerman, "Constitutional Politics/Constitutional Law," 99 *Yale Law Journal* 453, 522 (1989) ("Superstatutes do not seek to revise any of the deeper principles organizing our higher law; instead, they content themselves with changing one or more rules without challenging basic premises."). We owe these references to David Fontana, Yale Law School Class of 2002.

4   The rough contrast in text is drawn from John Henry Merryman, *The Civil Law Tradition*, 2d ed. (Stanford: Stanford University Press, 1985); D. Neil MacCormick and Robert S. Summers, eds., *Interpreting Statutes: A Comparative Study* (Aldershot, Hants, England: Dartmouth, 1991).

5   William Blackstone, *Commentaries on the Laws of England*, vol. 1 (1760), *60.

6   See generally Jack N. Rakove, *Original Meanings: Politics and Ideas in the Making of the Constitution* (New York: Alfred A. Knopf, 1996); Gordon S. Wood, *The Creation of the American Republic, 1776–1787* (Chapel Hill: University of North Carolina Press, 1969).

7   William N. Eskridge Jr., "All about Words: Original Understandings of the 'Judicial Power' in Statutory Interpretation, 1776–1806," 101 *Columbia Law Review* 990 (2001).

8   Rakove, *Original Meanings*, 97–101. This was in striking contrast to England, where Parliament asserted itself as sovereign; the revolting colonists rejected this model. Martin Flaherty, Note, "The Empire Strikes Back: *Annesly v. Sherlock* and the Triumph of Imperial Parliamentary Supremacy," 87 *Columbia Law Review* 593, 619 (1987).

9   Most of the laws adopted in the first Washington administration were short measures addressing particular issues of maritime regulation, taxation and licensing, federal-state relations, and the mechanics of the new federal government. Some of these laws could be characterized as super-statutes. The Federal Judiciary Act of 1789, chap. 20, 1 Stat. 73, for example, set forth the structure and jurisdiction of the federal courts. It was a foundational statute and established a number of enduring policies. Most notable was the policy of § 34, the Rules of Decision Act, now 28 U.S.C. § 1652 (1994), which required federal courts to apply state law in diversity cases. In this respect, the 1789 law was a super-statute, because it was more than structural; from its beginning, it represented a great principle of federalism. Cf. Erie R.R.

Co. v. Tompkins, 304 U.S. 64, 71–73 (1938) (interpreting the Rules Decision Act to require federal courts to apply state common law in diversity cases).

10   The debate about the bank is told in Paul Finkelman, "The Constitution and the Intentions of the Framers: The Limits of Historical Analysis," 50 *University of Pittsburgh Law Review* 349, 358–71 (1989) (explaining the Framers' intentions and views concerning the bank's constitutionality).

11   17 U.S. (4 Wheat.) 316 (1819).

12   Blyew v. United States, 80 U.S. 581, 595 (1871) (holding that the federal Civil Rights Act of 1866 did not supply jurisdiction to a criminal case, thereby allowing application of the Kentucky statute prohibiting blacks from testifying against whites).

13   E.g., Monell v. Department of Social Services, 436 U.S. 658, 702 (1978) (extending the 1871 act to allow suits against municipalities engaged in policies or customs that violate the Constitution); Jones v. Alfred H. Mayer Co., 392 U.S. 409, 422–44 (1968) (interpreting the 1866 act to reach private discrimination); Monroe v. Pape, 365 U.S. 167, 192 (1961) (interpreting the 1871 act to allow suits against police officers).

14   Roscoe Pound, "Mechanical Jurisprudence," 8 *Columbia Law Review* 605, 614 (1908) ("That our case law at its maturity has acquired the sterility of a fully developed system, may be shown by abundant examples of its failure to respond to vital needs of present-day life.").

15   Roscoe Pound, "Common Law and Legislation," 21 *Harvard Law Review* 383, 385–86 (1908).

16   Harlan F. Stone, "The Common Law in the United States," 50 *Harvard Law Review* 4, 12–13 (1936); see also James McCauley Landis, "Statutes and the Sources of Law," *Harvard Legal Essays* 213, 214 (Cambridge: Harvard University Press, 1934) ("[T]o admit the existence of wide areas for legal administration beyond the direct governance of statutes is not to assume that statutes have no part in the solution of problems impossible to bring within the reach of their terms."). For an excellent analysis of the legal "rationalists" of the 1920s and 1930s, see generally Neil Duxbury, "Faith in Reason: The Process Tradition in American Jurisprudence," 15 *Cardozo Law Review* 601 (1993).

17   E.g., Herbert Hovenkamp, *Federal Antitrust Policy* (St. Paul: West, 1994), 53.

18   See, e.g., Henry v. A.B. Dick Co., 224 U.S. 1 (1912), construing the law not to prohibit tying arrangements, overridden in the Clayton Act of 1914, 15 U.S.C. § 14; United States v. E. C. Knight Co., 156 U.S. 1 (1895), which construed the law to be inapplicable to the sugar trust, a decision that became a campaign issue in the election of 1896, and one rendered irrelevant by Sherman Act decisions written by judges subsequently appointed, e.g., Swift & Co. v. United States, 196 U.S. 375 (1906) (Holmes, J.).

19 See, e.g., Continental T.V., Inc. v. GTE Sylvania, Inc., 433 U.S. 36, 58 (1977); William N. Eskridge Jr., "Overruling Statutory Precedents," 76 *Georgetown Law Journal* 1361 (1988) (listing cases, including Sherman Act ones).

20 Schwegmann Bros. v. Calvert Distillers Corp., 341 U.S. 384 (1952), rejecting the dissenting justices' argument that Congress clearly intended to reach these "nonsigner" statutes.

21 United States v. Philadelphia National Bank, 374 U.S. 321, 350-51 (1962), quoted in Otter Tail Power Co. v. United States, 410 U.S. 366, 372 (1973) (following the *Philadelphia National Bank* holding); see also Silver v. N.Y. Stock Exchange, 373 U.S. 341, 357 (1963) (reiterating that repeal by implication is not favored).

22 Silver, 373 U.S. at 357; see also United States v. National Association of Securities Dealers, Inc., 422 U.S. 694, 729-30 (1975) (crafting an exemption to permit the SEC regulatory scheme to work).

23 United States v. E. C. Knight Co., 156 U.S. 1, 12 (1895).

24 Gilbert Fite, "Election of 1896," *History of American Presidential Elections, 1789-1968*, ed. Arthur M. Schlesinger Jr. and Fred L. Israel, vol. 2 (New York: Chelsea House, 1971); Allan Westin, "The Supreme Court, the Populist Movement, and the Campaign of 1896," 15 *Journal of Politics* 3, 25-27 (1953).

25 Addyston Pipe & Steel Co. v. United States, 175 U.S. 211, 229-31 (1899) (holding that the commerce clause extends even to private contracts that directly affect interstate trade, thus adopting something like the approach propounded by Justice Harlan's dissent in *E. C. Knight*).

26 Swift & Co. v. United States, 196 U.S. 375, 398-99 (1906).

27 See Wickard v. Filburn, 317 U.S. 111, 127-29 (1942) (accepting a broad version of "stream of commerce" theory); NLRB v. Jones & Laughlin Steel Corp., 301 U.S. 1, 31-32 (1937) (accepting a broad version of the "affecting commerce" theory).

28 See Charles Whalen and Barbara Whalen, *The Longest Debate* (Cabin John, Md.: Seven Locks, 1985), for an excellent account of the political struggle.

29 401 U.S. 424 (1971).

30 449 U.S. 186 (1979).

31 Johnson v. Transportation Agency, 480 U.S. 616 (1987).

32 The main cases were Wards Cove Packing Co. v. Atonio, 490 U.S. 642 (1989); Patterson v. McLean Credit Union, 491 U.S. 164 (1989); and Price Waterhouse v. Hopkins, 490 U.S. 228 (1989).

33 Pub. L. No. 102-166, 105 Stat. 1071 (1991). For background see William N. Eskridge Jr., "Reneging on History? The Court/Congress/President Civil Rights Game," 79 *California Law Review* 613 (1992).

34 461 U.S. 574 (1983).

35 Katzenbach v. McClung, 379 U.S. 294 (1964). See also Heart of Atlanta

Hotel v. United States, 379 U.S. 241 (1964). Although United States v. Lopez, 514 U.S. 549 (1995), called a halt to this expansion of the commerce clause, the Court was careful not to question the authority of the Civil Rights Act precedents.

36 Geduldig v. Aiello, 417 U.S. 484 (1974).

37 42 U.S.C. § 2000e(k) (expanding the definition of "sex" to include pregnancy as a basis for unlawful discrimination), overriding General Electric v. Gilbert, 429 U.S. 125 (1976).

38 See United Auto Workers v. Johnson Controls, 499 U.S. 187 (1991) (invalidating a rule prohibiting pregnant women from working in hazardous part of the plant).

39 See California Federal Savings & Loan Association v. Guerra, 479 U.S. 272 (1987) (upholding California law requiring employers to give mothers but not fathers parental leave).

40 524 U.S. 742 (1998).

41 This proposition is documented in Donald S. Lutz, "Toward a Theory of Constitutional Amendment," *Responding to Imperfection: The Theory and Practice of Constitutional Amendment*, ed. Sanford Levinson (Princeton: Princeton University Press, 1995), 237, 248–49, 254–67.

42 E.g., James Bradley Thayer, *John Marshall* (1901; New York: Da Capo, 1974), 103–7.

43 Bruce Ackerman, *We the People*, vol. 1, *Foundations* (Cambridge: Belknap Press of Harvard University Press, 1991), 10 [hereinafter *Foundations*]; Bruce Ackerman, *We the People*, vol. 2, *Transformations* (Cambridge: Belknap Press of Harvard University Press, 1998), 72. The theory is wonderfully digested in Bruce Ackerman, "Higher Lawmaking," *Responding to Imperfection*, ed. Levinson, 63–88.

44 Ackerman's formula is this:
Interbranch impasse → decisive election → reformist challenge to conservative branch → switch in time
Ackerman, *Foundations*, 49–50. Thus the Civil Rights Act as a statutory moment might look something like this:

> Interbranch impasse on civil rights legislation during the Eisenhower administration, with the Senate blocking it → decisive election of Kennedy and Johnson in 1960 → Kennedy-Johnson reformist challenge to conservative branch (Senate), with 1963–64 civil rights bill → switch in time, when the Senate finally breaks the southern filibuster in 1964

45 Lutz, "Toward a Theory of Constitutional Amendment," 263.

Congressional Fact Finding
and the Scope of Judicial Review

∽

NEAL DEVINS

Supreme Court decision making treats the line separating law from fact as consequential, often outcome-determinative. Court decisions do not even hint at the possibility that the Court's choice of whether it should create fact-dependent standards of review or, alternatively, fact-insensitive rules is a byproduct of exogenous variables, including the justices' views on congressional fact finding. Rather, the Court speaks in platitudes about how "saying what the law is" is at the core of Article III. By contrast, the power to find facts, while not irrelevant to the exercise of judicial authority, is not considered central to the judicial function. Indeed, pointing to Congress's "role of weighing conflicting evidence in the legislative process,"[1] the Court treats the separation of powers as demanding a de minimis judicial role in questioning the accuracy of such congressional findings.

The first part of this chapter challenges this long-standing assumption, arguing that the divide between law and fact is a shibboleth, something that the Court invokes to justify a conclusion about whether it or Congress should settle an issue. As such, when employing fact-dependent reasoning, the Court is speaking more of its agreement with Congress on the merits than anything else. The second part of the chapter casts doubt on a related assumption, namely that legislators are better equipped than judges to get the facts right. In particular, while Congress has superior fact-finding capacities, it often lacks the institutional incentives to take fact finding seriously.

The rest of this chapter tackles the question of how the Supreme Court ought to sort out Congress's interest in getting the facts right. Through the use of case studies, it argues that Congress's interest in fact finding varies from issue to issue. Sometimes congressional fact finding seems little more than a recitation of special-interest preferences; on other occasions, Congress has strong incentives to take fact finding seriously. The last part of the chapter offers a preliminary assessment of how the Court can ascertain lawmakers' incentives.

THE ILLUSORY FACT-LAW DISTINCTION

In choosing between open-ended, fact-dependent standards and fact-insensitive rules, the Court is also deciding whether it or Congress should control an issue. Take the case of affirmative action: if the Court were to conclude that *all* race-based decision making were unconstitutional, the only relevant fact would be whether race is being taken into account. All other facts would be—as a matter of law—irrelevant. But if the Court embraced an open-ended standard (for example, race preferences must be substantially related to an important governmental interest), any and all facts about the social desirability of affirmative action would be legally relevant.

Supreme Court opinions suggest that the line separating law from facts is, if not artificial, indeterminate. Consider, for example, the Court's recent decisions in *Dickerson v. United States* (rejecting Congress's efforts to undo the Miranda warning) and *United States v. Morrison* (invalidating the Violence Against Women Act). In both cases the Court sidestepped the question of whether the factual premises underlying Congress's handiwork were correct; instead, the Court concluded that as a matter of law, Congress's factual inquiry was beside the point.[2] The dissenting opinions in both *Morrison* and *Dickerson* made use of quite different legal standards, however—standards by which congressional fact finding was anything but irrelevant. Indeed, the *Morrison* dissent is replete both with approving references to "the mountain of data assembled by Congress" and paeans to "Congress, whose institutional capacity for gathering evidence and taking testimony far exceeds" that of the Court.[3]

Another example of this phenomenon is the distinction between rights and remedy that the Court now utilizes in assessing Congress's power to enforce the Fourteenth Amendment. When overturning the Religious Freedom Restoration Act (RFRA), the Court in *City of Boerne v. Flores* drew a sharp line between Congress's power to "remedy constitutional violations" and the Court's power to set forth the meaning of a constitutional right and thereby "say what the law is."[4] This standard is indeterminate, however; when applying it, the justices often disagree about whether Congress's action speaks to rights (so that fact finding is not particularly relevant) or remedies (where fact finding is often dispositive). For instance, in rulings that Congress could not extend either age discrimination or disability rights protections to state workers, the Court divided 5–4 on whether these cases were about rights (law) or remedies (facts).

Morrison, Dickerson, and *Flores* are hardly unusual. The justices frequently squabble over the appropriate standard of review to apply and, with it, the types of facts (if any) that are relevant to their decision making. Whether characterizing a matter as one of law or fact is simply "a conclusion . . . that one branch of government rather than another should make the decision in question,"[5] it is undoubtedly true that a justice's views on the merits and his or her views on whether the case turns on law or facts are often one and the same. Justices sympathetic to the goals of a particular statute, if not Congress itself, typically see the issue before them as one of fact; justices skeptical of Congress, by contrast, are more apt to see the issue as one of law.

For this very reason, the justices should act cautiously before embracing fact-dependent standards of review. These standards, by constraining the Court's power to second-guess legislative decision making, give Congress the upper hand. But should the Court sort out the quality of congressional fact finding? Any attempt at answering this question must begin with an analysis of the comparative strengths and weaknesses of judicial and congressional fact finding.

FACT FINDING IN CONGRESS AND THE COURTS

Before sorting through whether lawmakers or courts are more apt to engage in accurate fact finding, it is worth making a quick tour of the comparative strengths and weaknesses of the two branches, considering both institutional capacity and institutional incentives. The concern here is not so much resolving the question of which branch does a better job; rather, it is to suggest that the answer to this question is highly contextual—Congress does a better job when it has the incentive to get the facts right, while the courts may do a better job when the litigants skillfully present conflicting social science data.

The Traditionalist's Argument:
Congress Can Do It; Courts Cannot

Congress has numerous advantages over the courts in pursuing information. Legislatures, as compared to courts, "have substantial staff, funds, time and procedures to devote to effective information gathering and sorting."[6] These assets are perhaps best employed in the committee system, which allows lawmaker experts to acquire extensive knowledge on questions of interest to them. Armed with the power to subpoena witnesses and otherwise do what is "necessary and proper" to allow Congress to effectively act on its legislative powers, committees operate both as legislative "gatekeepers" and "policy incubators."[7] Unconstrained by the need to decide a particular case at a particular moment in time, moreover, legislative committees may conduct hearings over a number of months, even years, before acting. Furthermore, rather than rely on party arguments and amicus filings, committees may act affirmatively—using their subpoena power to call any and all witnesses who may assist Congress in sorting out the facts. If that is not enough, committees can also seek expert advice from any one of a number of legislative support services, including the Congressional Research Service and the General Accounting Office.

More generally, Congress is not limited by rules against ex parte communications or other prohibitions on information gathering. Also, unlike the judiciary, "the greater number of members [of Congress] and their varied backgrounds and experience make it virtually certain that the typical legislature will command wider knowledge and keener appreciation of current social and economic conditions than will the typical court."[8] Correspondingly, the geographic diversity among lawmakers ensures that Congress will take regional differences into account when assessing the costs and benefits of proposed legislation. In these ways Congress, a truly representative body, is better positioned to find facts than the federal judiciary, whose judges and advocates are trained in a single discipline and, for the most part, are otherwise stratified by class, ambition, and the like.

Courts, as compared to lawmakers, are also shackled by the temporal and reactive nature of litigation. Specifically, with judges and advocates relying on precedent-based legal arguments, courts simply cannot engage in thorough cost-benefit analysis. Courts, moreover, are hamstrung in that they decide cases at a moment in time, so that a changed understanding of the underlying facts can only be corrected through a reversal. Correspondingly, judges must operate around "real time" constraints; rather than risk a backlog of cases, judges must do the best they can with the information they have. For the Supreme Court, real-world limits on the number of cases it can review necessarily leave broad decision-making authority in the federal courts of appeal, courts that are not national in their scope and that may disagree over standards of review, the relevance of certain facts, and much more.

Furthermore, notwithstanding amicus curiae filings, courts, including the Supreme Court, often rely on the arguments made by the parties before them. Thus the Court, unlike Congress, is constrained by the parties' framing of the issues. Correspondingly, the Court may "anchor" its decision making on its perception of whether the parties before it are sympathetic or not. Problems may arise, however, when different parties raising identical legal issues may appear more or less sympathetic and, as such, the Court's decision may well be tied to the accident of which plaintiff presents its case to the Court. Making matters worse, the justices may engage in "motivated reasoning," that is, a desire to understand the facts through the lens of prevailing social norms. Finally, the justices may be animated in part by political ideology. As such, rather than try to get the facts right, the justices may spin the facts to support a desired result. And even if political ideology is not explicitly at play, courts are susceptible to capture by interest groups.

Rethinking the Congressional Advantage

Congress undoubtedly has the capacity to find social facts, while the courts face important obstacles in attempting to engage in accurate fact finding. Nevertheless, it is far from clear that Congress will indeed do a better job than the courts in this respect. Most critically, there is good reason to doubt whether Congress has the incentives to make serious attempts at fact finding.

Lawmakers are partisans, and congressional decision making, including fact finding, is often about the pursuit of desired outcomes. One simple measure of this phenomenon is the role that party control plays in committee agenda-setting and fact finding. In particular, committee chairs can determine what the committee investigates and when, and can arrange hearings in ways that frustrate the search for the truth. For example, committee staff may screen potential witnesses to ensure that they will say what the committee wants to hear. Assuming that committee members actually attend the hearing, the questioning format typically does not lend itself to "extended exchanges between members and witnesses, analysis of different points of view, or in-depth probing of one witness's views by another."[9] Moreover, even though party leaders often choose committee members whose views reflect the median legislator of their party, some committee chairs have succeeded in packing their committees with like-minded thinkers.

The quality of the legislative record may be compromised in yet another important way. When a factual record is assembled, "information from a variety of formal and informal sources—including lobbyists supporting or opposing legislation—can make its way into the record."[10] In part, lobbyists (as well as senior staffers) understand that courts sometimes look toward legislative history, and consequently that it is useful to pad the legislative history in ways likely to support their objectives. And while the conflicting agendas of interest groups can result in an adversarial process in which interest groups are successful to the extent that they supply good information to legislators, it is sometimes the case that interest groups provide only one side of an issue to the committee. Ultimately, with fundraising, constituent service, and other demands, members of Congress cannot pursue knowledge for knowledge's sake. Instead, congressional fact finding is necessarily goal oriented and politically charged.

This does not mean that Congress inevitably sees legislation as a mere commodity that lawmakers provide to interest groups. Instead, lawmakers (at least sometimes) may seek to serve the public interest.[11] Just because special interests push for and benefit from legislation does not foreclose the possibility that Congress is also acting on behalf of the public interest. The question instead is whether Congress is interested in getting the facts right—if not initially, then over time.

What then of Congress's power to modify its handiwork? Specifically, is Congress likely to find out if the factual premises of its enactments are wrong and, if so, is Congress likely to correct fact-finding mistakes? Perhaps, but probably not. To start, Congress is a reactive institution and, as such, it is doubtful that members keep track of legislation, even legislation that they sponsor. Rather, when assessing the implementation of legislative programs, lawmakers often make use of the "fire alarm" approach, in which their attention is triggered by constituencies through "a system of rules, procedures, and informal practices that enable individual citizens and organized interest groups to examine . . . decisions . . . and to seek remedies from [Congress]." [12] Consequently, absent pressure from interest groups, there is little chance that Congress will revisit the factual predicates of one of its enactments.

Even if interest groups do trigger a "fire alarm," pressure from them or the lawmaker's commitment to the issue must be sufficiently strong to overcome the burden of inertia. In particular, if party leaders think that "other measures have a stronger claim on the limited time and energy of the [legislative] body," Congress will leave (not so) well enough alone.[13] Moreover, the "fire alarm" may well fall on deaf ears. After all, the interest group triggering the alarm is likely to have opposed the measure's enactment. And, even if the agenda setter is willing to act, a significant minority within Congress or the president may well be able to block the legislation.

Congress's reputation as an omniscient fact finder thus appears overstated. Indeed, notwithstanding the very real constraints on judicial fact finding, it may be that the courts do a better job of finding social facts than Congress does. To start, while the "adjudicative process hears and considers less" than the legislative process, there may be a greater risk of bias in the legislative process.[14] In particular, by allowing the opposing parties to put into contention the major social science issues, the adversarial process sometimes yields a fairly complete presentation of the evidence. Correspondingly, although courts lack the staff and expertise to master social science evidence, they may well make as much use of this information as lawmakers and staffers pursuing a predetermined agenda. Furthermore, just as stare decisis limits the Court's ability to reconsider fact-finding mistakes, numerous disincentives discourage Congress from reconsidering errant fact finding.

That the courts on occasion may do a better job of fact finding than Congress is certainly suggestive but hardly conclusive evidence of how the Supreme Court should look at Congress when deciding whether to craft fact-dependent standards of review. In particular, that Congress has the tools but may lack the incentives to take fact finding seriously does not necessarily mean that the Court should discount congressional fact finding. Rather, the foregoing comparative institutional analysis of judicial and legislative fact finding underscores how difficult and problematic it is for the Supreme Court to take fact finding into account when crafting standards of review. Nevertheless, real-world limits on congressional fact finding cast doubt on the presumption that Congress is an expert at finding facts, and that the Court—when sorting out whether to embrace fact-dependent standards of review—can count on Congress to take the relevant facts into account.

CASE STUDIES: TOWARD AN INCENTIVE MODEL

In assessing whether the Supreme Court can determine when Congress is likely to take fact finding seriously, it is useful to look at case studies on the separation of powers, federalism, and affirmative action. This case study approach offers several advantages over the generalist approach employed above. It avoids the problem of reading too much into an overly broad data set (Congress's general interest in fact finding). More important, Congress's institutional incentives to get the facts right may be defined by subject. For example, Congress may have different incentives on, say, the separation of powers than it does on affirmative action. In this way, justices who see the judicial role first and foremost as checking special-interest rent-seeking may well want to look to such case studies in sorting out whether to embrace fact-dependent standards or fact-insensitive rules.

Separation of Powers

The Line Item Veto Act of 1996 (struck down by the Court)[15] and the independent counsel statute (upheld by the Court but killed by the Congress)[16] call attention to the circumstances in which Congress, over time, is likely to get the facts right. In both cases, the institutional self-interest of Congress and the president resulted in strong incentives to keep these issues before Congress. Moreover, these incentives did not favor a particular political party or interest group. Finally, Congress was not seeking to expand its own power through the enactment of either measure and, consequently, had little reason to stand behind these measures if they proved unworkable.[17]

The Line Item Veto Act—granting to the president the power to rescind discretionary appropriations—was premised on the belief that omnibus appropriations had thrown off the balance of powers between Congress and the president. When enacting the measure, however, Congress did not know how the president would use the line-item veto. What it did know was that after the Republican takeover of Congress in 1994, the anti-incumbency sentiment then prevailing made it impossible for members to put their chances for reelection on the line by ignoring charges that Congress's fiscal irresponsibility jeopardized our nation's economic well-being. In other words, self-interest, not a detached look at the pertinent facts, helps to explain why both Democrats and Republicans rallied behind the measure.

That self-interest figured prominently in the measure's approval, however, does not mean that Congress was poorly positioned to monitor presidential implementation of the statute and, if need be, correct its mistake. Most significantly, the act was set to "sunset" in 2005, and consequently the act's durability was tied to its continuing appeal to Congress. Furthermore, the act was sure to trigger numerous "fire alarms," for any time a special interest saw its favored project rescinded, it would almost certainly complain to its allies in Congress. The individual interests of members of Congress and Congress's institutional interest in preserving its budget priorities were therefore likely to converge if the president made aggressive use of the line-item veto. Because the Court struck down President Clinton's first exercise of the line-item veto, Congress's claim that the veto would restore, not disrupt, the balance of powers was never put to the test. In light of the incentives identified above for Congress to monitor the president's use of the line-item veto, an empirically minded Court might have deferred a definitive ruling, allowing the line-item veto experiment to continue by making use of a flexible, fact-dependent standard of review.

The Court's decision in *Morrison v. Olson* (1988), upholding the independent counsel statute, is cut from an entirely different cloth. In *Morrison* the Court did employ a fact-dependent standard of review, thus embracing a standard of review consistent with the incentives model. The story of the independent counsel statute is tied to Richard Nixon's decision to fire Archibald Cox during the Watergate scandal. In 1974 and again in 1976, voters retaliated against Nixon loyalists, signaling that "support for post-Watergate reform was an electorally significant position to take."[18] Congress enacted just such a reform, creating a court-appointed independent counsel who could not, absent "extraordinary impropriety," be removed by the attorney general.

When enacting the statute, Congress could not have anticipated how independent counsel investigations would affect the Justice Department's control of criminal investigations. Through a five-year sunset provision, however, Congress preserved its ability to bargain with future presidents over the terms of the statute (including the retention or elimination of the special prosecutor itself). For example, responding to complaints from the Reagan administration, Congress in 1983 increased the attorney general's discretion in requesting a court-appointed independent counsel, lowered the standard for removal to "good cause," and urged the independent counsel to follow Justice Department guidelines "except where not possible."

The Supreme Court was no doubt aware of this give-and-take process when deciding the constitutional fate of the independent counsel statute. What the justices could not have anticipated was Lawrence Walsh's six-year investigation of the Iran-contra affair or Kenneth Starr's investigation of President Clinton, but these two investigations, and with them the apparent death of the independent counsel statute, point to the correctness of the result reached in *Morrison*. As with the Line Item Veto Act, there was every reason to think that bargaining between the branches would result over time in an equilibrium of sorts—in this case, an independent counsel statute that did not undermine control by the attorney general or, alternatively, no independent counsel statute at all. More to the point, presidents (and their allies in Congress) were well positioned to defend the interests of the Department of Justice. The act's sunset provision, for example, allowed the president to bargain with Congress over the statute (and, if need be, veto its reauthorization). Furthermore, because Democratic and Republican administrations would each be the target of independent counsel investigations, the possibility that the statute would harm the political fortunes of one party but not the other seemed doubtful.[19]

The president and Congress, as the above discussion suggests, have little choice but to react to and make accommodations with each other. For an empirically minded Court, there is little reason to cut off this ongoing give-and-take process by issuing rigid, rules-based decisions. In particular, when Congress and the president have both the incentives and the opportunity to defend their institutional self-interest, it may well be that bargaining between the branches will take into account the lessons of experience. Put another way: Why should an empirically minded Court eschew facts (by imposing a fact-insensitive rule) when there is ample reason to think that over time Congress and the president will take the facts into account by moderating their handiwork? This, after all, is what happened with the independent counsel statute, and there is ample reason to think that had the Court not intervened, the branches would have made accommodations to each other in implementing the Line Item Veto Act.

Federalism

Congress's fact-finding record on federalism is mixed. On the one hand, Congress often has a strong incentive to expand the size of the federal government and, accordingly, to steer clear of federalism-related fact finding. On the other hand, states and municipalities have political power. The result: Congress typically values federalism on issues in which states and local officials both disapprove of federal initiatives and work hard to make their voice heard.[20]

Congress's expansionist tendencies are easily understood. First, constituents increasingly see national legislation as preferable to state and local measures. National legislation is harder for regulated parties to avoid and has fewer transaction costs associated with it than a patchwork of laws enacted by fifty state legislatures. Second, thanks to both changes in media coverage and modern political advertising, the political culture has become increasingly nationalized. Third (and relatedly), voters expect lawmakers to support politically popular legislation, not block it for a principle as abstract as Congress's failure to show—through fact finding—that the measure addresses a national problem. "A lawmaker who voted against the national Megan's Law or the national car-jacking law, for example, would almost certainly be characterized as being soft on crime in her opponent's next thirty-second sound bite."[21]

Two examples, the Gun-Free School Zones Act (GFSZA)[22] and the Religious Freedom Restoration Act (RFRA),[23] will illustrate why Congress cannot be counted on to take fact finding seriously on federalism questions. When enacting the GFSZA, Congress did not find that gun possession affected interstate commerce, nor did any member of Congress (or, for that matter, any witness at a House hearing on the bill) suggest that interstate commerce was at issue. And why should they? The tragedy of guns in schools was very real and doing something to stop it was politically popular. Also, when enacting the bill legislators knew that the Supreme Court's commerce clause jurisprudence did not require findings of fact and was otherwise extremely deferential. With no powerful constituent interest resisting the measure, there was much to lose and nothing to gain by opposing it in order to sort out the facts. Ironically, after the Supreme Court decided to review a constitutional challenge to the statute, Congress—recognizing that its handiwork was on the line—quickly added an amendment to the bill, finding (without hearings) that gun possession affected interstate commerce.

The RFRA, an exercise of Congress's enforcement powers under Section 5 of the Fourteenth Amendment, is an even more egregious example of Congress's willingness to short-change fact finding. To place the statute within the ambit of Court precedent, Congress was advised to make specific findings of fact "that formally neutral, generally applicable laws have historically been instruments of religious persecution, that enacting separate religious exemptions in every statute is not a workable means of protecting religious liberty, and that litigation about governmental motives is not a workable means of protecting religious liberty."[24] Instead, Congress's consideration of the RFRA focused exclusively on protesting the wrongness of *Employment Division, Department of Human Resources of Oregon v. Smith* (1990),[25] a Supreme Court interpretation of the free exercise clause. Congressional hearings showcased witnesses from religious and other interest groups, nearly all of whom attacked *Smith*. Lawmakers read from a nearly identical script, routinely condemning *Smith* and calling upon the justices to reverse it. In the end, with virtually no interest-group opposition to the measure, Congress gave short shrift to fact finding in order to do precisely what the RFRA's interest-group sponsors asked for: that is, repudiate *Smith*.

The lesson of the GFSZA and the RFRA is simple. Congress finds facts when there is a reason to do so. If the Court were to precondition approval of legislation on formalized fact finding, Congress almost certainly would comply. Such fact finding might well be boilerplate, however, for interest groups and congressional sponsors would see formalized findings as essential to the enterprise. On occasion, however, the converging preferences of interest groups and party leaders demand that Congress engage in fact finding in earnest. In particular, when states and local interests resist Congress's expansionist tendencies, lawmakers will pay close attention to the costs and benefits of proposed legislation. The Civil Rights Act of 1964 is an example of this phenomenon. To overcome resistance to the legislation from southern states, sponsors of the act needed to convince fence-sitting lawmakers both that the legislation served the public interest and that private discrimination did implicate interstate commerce.[26]

Another example of the power of states and local interests is legislation designed to limit the impact of *Garcia v. San Antonio Metropolitan Transit Authority* (1985), a Supreme Court decision upholding the application of federal wage-and-hour provisions to state employees.[27] Recognizing that states and municipalities would have to pay several billion dollars in overtime pay, Congress—in response to lobbying by state and local governments—postponed the effective date of *Garcia* (decided 19 February 1985) to 15 April 1986.[28] For the most part, however, Congress has little reason to revisit its handiwork after judicial approval of a statute. On issues as diverse as guns in schools, religious liberty, and civil rights, it is doubtful (once the coalition supporting the bill is sufficiently strong to push it through Congress) that an interest group will be able to persuade both lawmakers and the president to disrupt the expectation interests of the coalition supporting the original bill.

How then should an empirically minded Court approach federalism? To start with, there is a great cost in embracing fact-dependent standards. Congress has little incentive to consistently engage in meaningful fact finding; states and local interests will only resist Congress's expansionist tendencies when something they value is on the line. For this very reason, the Supreme Court should never have ruled that Congress's power to regulate commerce extends to anything and everything "affecting commerce." At the same time, once the New Deal Court let the "affecting commerce" genie out of the bottle, it was inevitable that an empirically minded Court might well make use of boundary control standards that would deem some federalism-related issues to be questions of law, not fact.[29]

What then of the RFRA? Here Congress was acting on its Section 5 enforcement powers, but there is reason to think that special-interest politics, not fact finding in the public interest, dominated congressional decision making. For this reason, an empirically minded Court might well embrace standards, such as the one utilized in *City of Boerne v. Flores*,[30] that allow the justices to toss aside legislative action taken under the enforcement powers of the Fourteenth Amendment that is perceived to be about rights (law), rather than remedies (facts).

Affirmative Action

Congress has invested little energy in fact finding when considering affirmative action legislation. Instead the power of committees, the intensity of preferences among constituents (and, correspondingly, the members who represent them), and Congress's reactive nature are on full display. As when they legislate on federalism-related issues, moreover, there are few incentives for members of Congress to reconsider existing affirmative action programs. Congress's long-standing approval of both set-asides for minority business enterprises and diversity preferences for minority broadcasters illustrates these points.

Set-aside provisions of the Public Works Employment Act of 1977 (approved by the Supreme Court in *Fullilove v. Klutznick*)[31] and the Surface Transportation Assistance Act of 1982[32] highlight the pivotal role that interest-group preferences, not fact finding, play in affirmative action legislation. In enacting these measures Congress made no formal findings of fact, nor did it hold hearings. Instead Congress approved these set-aside programs by way of floor amendments added to larger public works bills, with virtually no debate. The simple explanation for this expedited consideration is logrolling; in particular, members of the Congressional Black Caucus, quite understandably, wanted to "get a fair share of the action" from these public works measures.[33]

Diversity preferences in broadcasting, upheld by the Supreme Court in *Metro Broadcasting, Inc. v.* FCC,[34] is another example to which an empirically minded justice could look in sorting out the politics underlying preference programs. Here, as with set-asides in 1977, power politics and not fact finding explains Congress's role in defending the FCC's diversity preferences. Unlike with set-asides, however, Congress played a largely reactive role. Rather than allow an FCC whose membership had become markedly more conservative in the 1980s to reexamine the constitutionality of race preferences, Congress passed legislation prohibiting the FCC from engaging in fact finding to see if there was a nexus between race preferences and the diversity of broadcast programming. That Congress did what it did was entirely predictable and, considering the circumstances, quite defensible. At that time, the FCC and the House Energy and Commerce Committee were locked in a bitter fight over the propriety of government regulation of broadcasting. The commission embraced market-driven solutions, suggesting to Congress that fact finding by the FCC would simply put into place a preordained conclusion. In other words, Congress was not simply defending civil rights interests; it was defending its own turf.

The question of whether Congress, over time, has the institutional incentives to examine the factual premises of affirmative action still remains. After all, it is to be expected that a Democratic Congress would simultaneously defend its turf and respond to a "fire alarm" triggered by a loyal, powerful constituent. Moreover, big business has resisted efforts to dismantle affirmative action (because the costs of these programs fall hardest on small business, because affirmative action programs shield business from employment discrimination lawsuits, and because of concerns of adverse publicity).

On the other hand, social conservatives oppose affirmative action. But this opposition has produced much smoke and relatively little fire—at least on Capitol Hill. Over the past decade, it has become clear that Republicans in Congress are unprepared to take a hard look at the factual premises of various affirmative action programs. When the Supreme Court addressed the constitutionality of affirmative action programs at the University of Michigan, for example, no Republican lawmaker filed a brief opposing affirmative action. Instead, a coalition of moderate Republicans wrote to President George W. Bush, urging the administration to "support the position that diversity is a compelling government interest." [35] The divergence between the Republican Party platform and the behavior of congressional Republicans is easily explained. Worried about "the danger[] that our [party's] aspirations and intentions will be misperceived, dividing our country and harming our party," [36] Republican leaders have made the winning of elections and the forging of coalitions their first priority. Today the costs of affirmative action are spread throughout the nonminority population, so that there is little incentive for voters (or other powerful interests) to rally behind candidates who oppose affirmative action.

It is for this very reason that the Supreme Court erred in both *Fullilove* and *Metro Broadcasting*. *Fullilove* is a paean to Congress. Deeming the Public Works Act of 1977 "a considered decision of the Congress" and on occasion employing the analytical rigor of rational basis review,[37] the Supreme Court embraced traditionalist notions of Congress's superior fact finding skills when upholding the set-aside. *Metro Broadcasting* likewise paved the way for Congress to see race preferences as a type of spoils system, something that could be used to respond to interest-group pressures rather than something that serves the public interest. By employing intermediate scrutiny, a highly malleable, fact-dependent standard of review, the justices placed great emphasis on "Congress' institutional competence as the National Legislature" and with it the "appropriate deference [owed] to Congress." [38]

An empirically minded Court, by contrast, would have wanted to signal to Congress that it would look skeptically at legislative fact finding intended to prop up the policy preferences of special interests. For example, by employing strict scrutiny review, the Court could declare—as a matter of law—that certain governmental purposes are insufficient to support race preferences,[39] thus allowing the Court to police race preferences without absorbing the legitimacy costs of second-guessing legislative fact finding. This is precisely what the Court did in 1995 in *Adarand Constructors, Inc. v Pena*.[40] Concluding that the intermediate review standard of *Metro Broadcasting* was too permissive, the Court determined that federal affirmative action programs should be subject to strict scrutiny review.

CONCLUSION: AN EMPIRICALLY INFORMED CONSTITUTIONAL JURISPRUDENCE?

The question of whether courts or lawmakers will do a better job of uncovering social facts is highly contextual. Congress is better positioned to find social facts, but it is far from clear that Congress has the incentives to make full use of its superior fact-finding resources. By calling attention to significant roadblocks to both congressional and judicial fact finding, this chapter underscores how problematic and difficult it is for the Court to craft standards of review that take into account the comparative strengths and weaknesses of congressional and judicial fact finding. In sorting out how the Supreme Court should navigate its way around these roadblocks, I have suggested that the justices should take fact finding seriously and adopt fact-dependent standards only when Congress has the institutional incentives to accurately perform the fact-finding function. Beyond identifying whether Congress or the Court is likely to do a better job at sorting out the underlying social facts, this incentives model also embraces a normative theory of constitutional interpretation—namely, that one of the principal purposes of judicial review is to guard against special-interest legislation. Specifically, in advancing the public interest, the justices should craft standards of review that take into account Congress's interest in getting the facts right, at least over time.

In this concluding part, additional details about the workings of this incentives model will be revealed. Before turning to some of the things that an empirically minded Court can do, let me dismiss some untenable possibilities, namely: a prophylactic rule favoring either Congress or the Court, due process in lawmaking, and judicial minimalism. For quite obvious reasons, there is nothing to commend a rule whereby the Court assumes that Congress takes fact finding seriously and, consequently, any and all legislative enactments are empirically grounded (whether or not Congress held hearings, made findings, and so on). Unless and until Congress has reason to make good use of its superior fact-finding skills, it is hard to see how such a rule would accomplish anything—other than to further diminish Congress's interest in fact finding.

A prophylactic rule favoring the Court is at least as untenable. Inherent limits in judicial fact finding, the tendency for justices to follow the lead of the political party that appoints them, and the need for the Court to secure support for its rulings from elected officials stand in the way of such a radical departure from the traditionalist view that—consistent with the separation of powers—deference is owed Congress's fact finding.[41]

Due process in lawmaking stands on much firmer footing, for it is largely grounded in the real world. Recognizing Congress's disinclination to explore the empirical foundations of its handiwork, due process in lawmaking is seen as a way of encouraging Congress to take fact finding seriously. Courts could, for example, make use of a constitutional interpretive canon that would condition judicial approval of legislation on the procedures that Congress employed when enacting the bill. By encouraging Congress to find facts, hold hearings, and formally tie its fact finding to the evidence that it gathers, due process in lawmaking stands as a means of ensuring that Congress lives up to its fact-finding responsibilities.

Two insurmountable hurdles to this approach remain, however. First, if Congress is acting at the behest of special interests, any fact finding is likely to be boilerplate. Committee chairs can ask members of their staffs or the bill's interest-group sponsors to sort out the measure's factual underpinnings. Second, courts cannot set manageable standards to overcome the problem of boilerplate fact finding. How, for example, can a court tell if a witness list at a hearing is skewed, or whether a bill is fairly debated? How can it tell whether members of Congress are reasonable in their assessment of social science research, the credibility of witnesses, and so on and so forth? The answers to these questions are value-laden, requiring the court to substitute its judgment for that of Congress. In other words, due process applied to lawmaking cannot be penetrating without undermining its principal virtue, that is, avoiding the pitfalls of judge-made lawmaking.

Judicial minimalism offers a way around these problems but creates problems of its own. By issuing minimalist opinions that would allow the justices to revisit an issue without overruling themselves, the Court need not reach a definitive judgment on the quality of congressional fact finding. Over time, however, a minimalist Court will never get around to settling on a standard of review either validating or devaluing congressional fact finding.

What then can the Supreme Court do both in assessing the quality of legislative fact finding and in encouraging Congress to take fact finding more seriously? To start with, rather than speculate on Congress's interest in fact finding (and, more generally, on whether Congress is acting in the public interest, not simply promoting special interests), the justices can make use of the "passive virtues," that is, procedural and jurisdictional delays that provide "a time lag between legislation and adjudication."[42] In so doing, the Court (as well as the litigants and amici who inform the justices through their filings) can gain a better appreciation of the relevant social facts. By looking to Congress's interest in overseeing the implementation of the law, its decision making on related issues, and the decision making of several lower courts, the Court can better sort out the trustworthiness of Congress's fact finding. By improving its understanding of Congress and, more generally, the social facts of the dispute before it, the Court is less apt to issue a premature, ill-informed decision.[43] Moreover, by giving Congress breathing room in the first instance, the Court creates incentives for Congress to demonstrate its bona fides by paying attention to the law's implementation.

Over time, the justices must sort out whether to embrace standards of review that either defer to, or are skeptical of, congressional fact finding. On some issues, like those implicating separation-of-powers concerns, Congress (at least sometimes) may well have the institutional incentives to moderate its handiwork to preserve the balance of powers. On other issues, like those dealing with Congress's federalism-implicated powers, this investigation may reveal that state and local interest groups do little to check Congress's desire to do that which is politically popular. By observing Congress in this way, the Court can sort out whether Congress has the institutional incentives to engage in serious fact finding. Among other things, the Court can see how Congress makes use of sunset provisions and other mechanisms to ensure that lawmakers do not lose sight of the relevant issue or shift the burden of inertia to constituents and other interests that support reenactment of a law.

Operating within the Washington beltway, moreover, the Court can take into account the circumstances surrounding the enactment of legislation. In particular, as was true with the Civil Rights Act of 1964, the Court can see whether competing interests within Congress put pressure on the institution to take seriously its fact-finding responsibilities. Alternatively, it may be that logrolling or the absence of disagreement within Congress produces legislation, like the public works set-asides, the RFRA, and the GFSZA, for which fact finding is simply beside the point.

But is it possible to have an empirically informed constitutional jurisprudence? After all, the question of whether Congress has the incentives to serve the public interest, not special interests, is value-laden and indeterminate. With that said, failings in my model call attention to how difficult it is for the Court to navigate the divide between law and fact. More to the point, by calling attention to how difficult it is for courts to check Congress when employing fact-dependent standards, this chapter offers an insight for justices who contemplate adopting standards of review that would give Congress the upper hand: they should have confidence in congressional fact finding, or should want Congress to control the issue.

NOTES

Significant portions of this chapter were first published in Neal Devins, "Congressional Factfinding and the Scope of Judicial Review: A Preliminary Analysis," 50 *Duke Law Journal* 1169 (2001). Thanks to Keith Whittington for helpful comments and much more.

1   Turner Broadcasting System, Inc. v. FCC, 520 U.S. 180, 199 (1997).

2   Dickerson v. United States, 530 U.S. 428, 431–33 (2000); United States v. Morrison, 529 U.S. 598, 684 (2000).

3   Morrison, 529 U.S. at 683 (Souter, J., dissenting); see also *id*. at 684–85 (Souter, J., dissenting). See also Dickerson, 530 U.S. at 431 (Scalia, J., dissenting).

4   521 U.S. 507, 518–19 (1997).

5   Saul M. Pilchen, "Politics v. the Cloister: Deciding When the Supreme Court Should Defer to Congressional Factfinding under the Post-Civil War Amendments," 59 *Notre Dame Law Review* 337, 396–97 (1984).

6   Robin Charlow, "Judicial Review, Equal Protection and the Problem with Plebiscites," 79 *Cornell Law Review* 527, 578 (1994).

7   Archibald Cox, "The Role of Congress in Constitutional Determinations," 40 *University of Cincinnati Law Review* 199, 249–50 (1971).

8   *Id*. at 209; see also Mark Tushnet, *Taking the Constitution Away from the Courts* (Princeton: Princeton University Press, 1999), 68 (asserting that "legislators in ordinary politics are [more] deeply embedded in the realities of public life" than judges are).

9 Walter J. Oleszek, *Congressional Procedures and the Policy Process* (Washington: Congressional Quarterly, 1978), 67.

10 Note, "Deference to Legislative Fact Determinations in First Amendment Cases after *Turner Broadcasting*," 111 *Harvard Law Review* 2312, 2322 (1998).

11 In this volume see Elizabeth Garrett and Adrian Vermeule, "Institutional Design of a Thayerian Congress."

12 Matthew D. McCubbins and Thomas Schwartz, "Congressional Oversight Overlooked: Policy Patrols Versus Fire Alarms," 28 *American Journal of Political Science* 165, 166 (1984); see also William N. Eskridge Jr., "Overriding Supreme Court Statutory Interpretation Decisions," 101 *Yale Law Journal* 331, 359–66 (1991).

13 Lawrence C. Marshall, " 'Let Congress Do It': The Case for an Absolute Rule of Statutory Stare Decisis," 88 *Michigan Law Review* 177, 190–91 (1989).

14 Neil K. Komesar, *Imperfect Alternatives* (Chicago: University of Chicago Press, 1994), 141.

15 Clinton v. City of New York, 524 U.S. 417, 421 (1998).

16 Morrison v. Olson, 487 U.S. 654, 696–97 (1988). Congress allowed the statute to expire on 30 June 1999.

17 Contrast, for example, the legislative veto struck down in *INS v. Chadha*, 462 U.S. 919, 959 (1983). Congress may have sometimes seen the legislative veto as a low-cost way of micromanaging implementation of the law by the executive branch and thus aggrandizing its own power.

18 Katy J. Harriger, *Independent Justice: The Federal Special Prosecutor in American Politics* (Lawrence: University Press of Kansas, 1992), 51.

19 Much the same can be said of the line-item veto. Democratic presidents would disappoint Republicans by protecting Democratic-sponsored initiatives, and vice versa.

20 Elizabeth Garrett, "Enhancing the Political Safeguards of Federalism? The Unfinished Mandate Reform Act of 1995," 45 *University of Kansas Law Review* 1113, 1118–31 (1997).

21 William Marshall, "American Political Culture and the Failures of Process Federalism," 22 *Harvard Journal of Law and Public Policy* 139, 145 (1998).

22 The GFSZA was invalidated in *United States v. Lopez*, 514 U.S. 549 (1995).

23 The RFRA was invalidated in *City of Boerne v. Flores*, 521 U.S. 507 (1997).

24 House Committee on the Judiciary, *Religious Freedom Restoration Act of 1991: Hearings on H.R. 2797 before the Subcomm. on Civil and Constitutional Rights of the House Comm. on the Judiciary*, 102d Cong., 2d sess., 1992, 331 (statement of Professor Douglas Laycock).

25 494 U.S. 872 (1990). For a review of the RFRA's legislative history see Neal

Devins, "How Not to Challenge the Court," 39 *William & Mary Law Review* 645, 651–56 (1998).

26 See Hugh Davis Graham, *The Civil Rights Era* (New York: Oxford University Press, 1990), 87–95.

27 469 U.S. 528 (1985).

28 99 Stat. 787 (1985).

29 This is precisely what happened in both the Gun-Free School Zones Act and Violence Against Women Act cases. Declaring that Congress's commerce clause authority is limited to "the instrumentalities, channels, or goods involved in interstate commerce," the Court concluded that congressional fact finding was irrelevant. United States v. Morrison, 529 U.S. 598, 617 (2000); United States v. Lopez, 514 U.S. 549, 551, 560, 567 (1995).

30 521 U.S. 507 (1997).

31 Pub. L. No. 95-28, 91 Stat. 116 (codified at 42 U.S.C. 6701-10 (1994)) (upheld in Fullilove v. Klutznick, 448 U.S. 448 (1980)).

32 The provision first appeared in 1983, Pub. L. No. 97-424, 96 Stat. 2097 (1983) (codified at 23 U.S.C. 101 (1994), 49 U.S.C. 1602 (1994)), and has been reenacted several times, most recently in 1998.

33 Congressional Record, 95th Cong., 1st sess., 1977, 123, part 5:5327 (statement of Rep. Mitchell). For an accounting of the legislative history see Drew S. Days III, "Fullilove," 96 *Yale Law Journal* 453, 465–66, 471–73 (1987).

34 497 U.S. 547 (1990), rev'd, Adarand Constructors, Inc. v. Pena, 515 U.S. 200 (1995).

35 Letter from Senator Arlen Specter et al. to President Bush (14 January 2003).

36 Congressional Record, 105th Cong., 2d sess., 1998, 144, no. 22:S1481, 1490 (daily ed. 6 March 1998) (statement of Sen. John McCain).

37 448 U.S. at 473. See also *id.* at 485 (noting "the well-established concept that a legislature may take one step at a time to remedy only part of a broader problem").

38 Metro Broadcasting, Inc. v. FCC, 497 U.S. 547, 563 (1990).

39 In *Wygant v. Jackson Board of Education*, 476 U.S. 267 (1986), for example, the Court concluded that as a matter of law, a school board did not have a compelling interest either in remedying societal discrimination or in providing minority role models for its minority students. *Id.* at 276.

40 515 U.S. 200 (1995).

41 Let me now make explicit something that is implicit in my argument: If the Court were captured by special interests or simply voted its policy preferences, the analysis championed in this chapter would fall on deaf ears. In particular, a Court that did not care about getting the facts right would not care about Congress's interest in fact finding.

42 Alexander M. Bickel, *The Least Dangerous Branch: The Supreme Court at the Bar of Politics* (Indianapolis: Bobbs-Merrill, 1962), 116.

43 Sometimes, however, the Court cannot make use of agenda control to delay a decision. In the independent counsel case, for example, a lower court finding that the statute was unconstitutional made it impractical for the Court to refuse to hear the case. At the same time, rather than speak definitively about the statute's constitutionality, the justices could have decided the case narrowly, upholding the statute while leaving open the possibility that they would revisit the issue in another case.

Institutional Design
of a Thayerian Congress

⌒∾

ELIZABETH GARRETT AND ADRIAN VERMEULE

The U.S. Congress frequently deliberates upon and decides questions of constitutional interpretation, and many of its decisions are immune from subsequent judicial review. To mention only the recently prominent examples, consider Congress's exclusive responsibility under Articles I and II to define and apply the impeachment clauses, and its authority under the Twelfth Amendment to certify and count electoral votes in presidential elections. In such cases, legal scholars typically draw upon controversial normative theories of constitutional interpretation to assess Congress's performance. We join the discussion by asking whether and how Congress's interpretive capacity can be improved. But we depart from the usual approach by crafting our proposals in a manner that is resolutely agnostic as among the standard normative theories of constitutional interpretation. Our aim is to propose incremental reforms to which proponents of all the standard theories might subscribe.

Our focus is thus different from that of most of the constitutional law literature exploring congressional interpretation of the Constitution. That literature addresses itself almost exclusively to a large-scale question of institutional choice: as between Congress and other institutions, particularly the Supreme Court, how should authority to render initial or conclusive interpretations of the Constitution be allocated?[1] We will pursue a different strategy by focusing not upon questions of institutional choice but upon questions of institutional design. Given some allocation of constitutional authority between Congress and the judiciary, how can the rules that structure congressional operations be arranged to produce the right quantity and quality of congressional deliberation on constitutional questions?

The first part of this chapter explains the institutional-design strategy and defines criteria for assessing competing design proposals. The second part describes and justifies our substantive proposals.

INSTITUTIONAL CHOICE, INSTITUTIONAL DESIGN, AND THE THAYERIAN CONGRESS

We first detail our assumptions, define our aims, and situate our project against the background of the relevant literatures in constitutional law, public choice, and empirical political science.

Toward a Structured Thayerian Congress

James Bradley Thayer's address on "The Origin and Scope of the American Doctrine of Constitutional Law" (1892) provides the starting point for most subsequent discussion of Congress's capacities as a constitutional interpreter.[2] Thayer argued that judges should employ a rational-basis standard for reviewing congressional determinations of constitutional questions and gave two principal reasons for his position. First, many constitutional questions encompass not merely technical legal issues but also large questions of constitutional policy and politics that legislators are better suited to decide than judges. Second, aggressive judicial review of congressional determinations would encourage Congress to slough its constitutional responsibilities onto the courts, weakening the culture of representative democracy. A "Thayerian" Congress, accordingly, is a Congress that has a great deal of responsibility for deciding constitutional questions.

For present purposes, the most important feature of Thayer's analysis is that it is solely devoted to institutional choice, including dynamic analysis of the consequences of constitutional interaction between branches, but it says very little about institutional design. Our project is to provide the internal structure for Thayer's Congress—to evaluate institutions and procedures with a view to improving Congress's constitutional performance. For two reasons, this appears a more promising avenue than continued pursuit of the institutional-choice question.

First, the institutional-choice literature has progressed far enough that a switch to institutional-design questions should now produce greater intellectual returns. Modern constitutional law literature has barely begun to explore design issues. The work on the constitutional responsibility of legislators[3] shows little awareness that legislators work within a collective institutional structure, and that this structure determines their performance as constitutional interpreters and decision makers. The design of that institutional structure more powerfully determines Congress's interpretive capacities than does any individual legislator's conscience.

Second, despite the continuing academic controversy, the institutional-choice question has largely been settled by force of economic, social, and institutional developments. And it has been settled in favor of extensive congressional authority to decide constitutional questions. Although the judiciary can and does review federal statutes for constitutionality, in many domains the realities of modern government ensure that Congress's authority to decide constitutional questions is effectively paramount.

In the twentieth century nonjudicial institutions of government grew much faster than the judiciary; consider that in 1999 the total federal judicial budget was $3.79 billion, while the administrative budget of the political branches alone ran to some $80 billion—twenty-one times larger. Congress, the White House, and the federal administrative agencies form an institutional system whose current scale and scope dwarfs the scale on which courts operate. The Supreme Court's peak capacity runs to about 150 cases per year, most of which concern statutory interpretation rather than constitutional adjudication and involve state and local actions as well as federal policy, whereas in the past decade Congress has produced an average of about 585 new public laws per year, and administrative agencies have produced thousands of new regulations

The Court still reviews federal statutes on constitutional grounds, of course. But by and large, the Court has retreated to policing a restricted domain of highly salient individual-rights issues, such as free speech and abortion rights; to occasionally invalidating novel interbranch encroachments in the name of the separation of powers; and to occasionally striking down novel exercises of congressional power in the name of federalism. In other domains, which is to say in a great deal of what government does, Congress is the ultimate arbiter of constitutionality. All the more reason to think with greater seriousness than the literature has shown to date about how Congress's internal design can be structured to improve Congress's constitutional performance.

Some Assumptions about Legislators' Behavior

Our concern to improve Congress's constitutional performance assumes that at least some legislators, some of the time, give some decisional weight to reasoned constitutional argument. That premise has been challenged by professedly "realist" strands of political science and public choice, but the challenge rests on empirical presuppositions about legislative behavior that turn out to be untenable. The starting point is the question of which ends legislators pursue. The literature contains three distinct answers to this question. After describing one answer that is excessively optimistic and another that is excessively jaundiced, we stake out a third, intermediate position.

1. *Legislators act in the public interest.* Early discussion of Congress's constitutional performance assumed an optimistic picture of legislator-statesmen who act strictly to promote their understanding of the common good. The public interest view is the positive counterpart to Burke's trustee model of representation, a normative stance that sees a good representative as one who exercises independent judgment for the common weal, rather than simply acting so as to satisfy constituents' preferences. However, naïve forms of optimism about legislators have today been displaced, in most sectors of the constitutional law academy, by a far more skeptical account of legislative behavior.

2. *Legislators maximize their chances of reelection, or personal gain more broadly defined.* Public choice literature generally models legislative behavior on the explicit assumption that legislators' sole goal is to maximize their chances of reelection. This is largely a methodological assumption, one dictated by the positivist aspiration of public choice to render testable predictions, which are unattainable without a precise maximand. As explained below, we think the assumption that legislators act solely to maximize their chances of reelection is clearly mistaken if it is treated as an empirical claim, but we have no quarrel with it as a methodological premise within its proper domain.[4]

But there is also a broader, and looser, strand in the nonformalized political science literature with which we do quarrel. This strand is harder to define; these works, sometimes called "realist," principally share an atmospheric that describes legislators as maximizing personal gain in a crudely venal sense. All legislative behavior, on this view, is rooted in relatively tangible forms of self-interest, such as the quest for money, fame, and power; realists typically ignore broader motives, such as personal satisfaction from justified accomplishment or the promotion of ideological goals. Some of this work even suggests that all constitutional discourse within legislatures (and maybe generally) is a sham, a cover for self-regarding motives and tactics.

Despite its hardheaded appeal, the "realist" view either represents a pre-empirical methodological commitment or else turns out to be indefensible. To the extent that it makes an empirical claim, it has been falsified outright by empirical work in mainstream political science. That work advances a third, intermediate view.

3. *Legislators pursue a complex set of public and personal goals.* The optimistic public interest view and the skeptical realist view both represent implausible extremes. The mainstream view in political science takes a more nuanced view of legislators' motivations. Richard Fenno's classic study found that most legislators pursue a variety of ends simultaneously, trading off goals against one another and giving no goal an overriding priority.[5] Although ensuring reelection is one goal, along with gaining colleagues' respect, another prominent goal is legislators' desire to promote their vision of the public interest. Reelection is, for most legislators, a necessary means to their preferred goals of influencing public policy for the better and accumulating prestige with colleagues; and it is not the case that legislators will trade everything else to secure reelection. In general, empirical work in mainstream political science describes legislators' diffuse ideology—their beliefs about morals, justice, good public policy, and other intangibles—as a far more powerful determinant of legislative behavior than the realist tradition acknowledges.[6]

In the subsequent discussion, we follow this consensus by assuming that some legislators sometimes treat constitutional argument as one indicator of the "public interest" or "good public policy," which in turn has some weight as against legislators' other interests, goals, and aims. This empirical starting point is not necessarily inconsistent with the methodological assumption in the public choice literature that legislators maximize their chances of reelection in preference to all other aims. It is crucial to understand that even if legislators are solely oriented to reelection, several mechanisms might cause them to give some weight to constitutional argument.

First, some constituents might desire a representative who takes constitutional argument seriously, and might punish a representative who appears wholly opportunistic about the Constitution.[7] Second, there are many legislators who enjoy slack in their agency relationship with constituents, usually because they are from safe districts and reelection is not a serious concern. Even on the public choice premise, these legislators will shift to pursuing other aims, and one of those aims will be to implement the legislators' conceptions of good public policy, including good constitutional law. Third, constitutional argument is given weight by the "civilizing force of hypocrisy."[8] Even a wholly self-interested legislator cannot afford to take positions in constitutional argument that are too transparently favorable to his or her own interests. So legislators who want to invest in credibility will have to adjust their positions to disfavor or disguise their own interests to some degree. Likewise, the pressure to maintain a reputation for consistency will, to some degree, cause even self-interested legislators to adhere to a previously established constitutional position when, in changed circumstances, that position works to the legislator's disadvantage.

But in any event, our project is normative, not (as in the public choice literature) predictive. For our purposes, the question is not how legislators' behavior should best be modeled, but rather whether legislative discourse about the Constitution is always strategic rather than sincere. We think the realist account of legislators' behavior is itself unrealistic. The claim that public-regarding discourse within legislatures, including constitutional discourse, is invariably a mask for narrowly defined self-interest verges on incoherence. That view finds it difficult to explain why legislators engage in constitutional discourse in the first place. After all, if everyone mouths constitutional formulae out of self-interest, it is unclear why anyone takes constitutional argument seriously, and thus unclear why there is any audience demand for the empty discourse. The realist account can only be salvaged either by assuming widespread myopia in the audience for constitutional discourse—assuming, in other words, that self-interested constitutional discourse successfully dupes other participants over the long term, the sort of assumption that realists usually reject in other contexts—or else by recourse to recondite theoretical epicycles. In what follows, we will not concern ourselves unduly with the skeptical position.

Defining "Improvements" in Congress's Constitutional Performance

Our aim is to propose incremental reforms in the internal design of Congress that will improve its constitutional performance, while remaining agnostic among contentious theories of constitutional interpretation and among controversial views of substantive policy and politics. To that end, we define an "improvement" as a design proposal that produces a net gain when assessed along three dimensions: (1) changes in the cost of constitutional deliberation and decision making by Congress; (2) changes in the cost of constitutional errors by Congress, defining error relative to an overlapping consensus of background interpretive theories; and (3) the costs of transition from the current design to the proposed design.

1. *Decision costs and deliberative benefits.* The most striking fact about Congress is its severely constricted agenda. The paramount legal status of the Constitution does not entail that deliberation over constitutional questions is the most important good to be supplied by Congress; constitutional decision making is one activity among many. So proposals for improvement must account for the opportunity costs of constitutional deliberation.

Deliberation also provides institutional and process benefits, however. It exploits the collective character of legislatures in ways that can in principle improve Congress's constitutional performance. Among the concrete benefits of deliberation are its tendencies to encourage the revelation of private information, to expose extreme, polarized viewpoints to the moderating effect of diverse arguments, to make outcomes more legitimate by providing reasons to defeated parties, and to require the articulation of public-spirited justifications for votes.[9]

To be sure, deliberation also suffers pathologies, quite apart from opportunity costs: it can reduce candor, encourage posturing, trigger herd behavior, and silence dissenters. Yet the alternative to deliberation is simply voting without discussion, a procedure that no modern legislature, and few if any collective bodies generally, would ever adopt. It seems indisputable that on balance, some congressional deliberation on constitutional questions is better than none at all. In what follows, we attempt to mold our proposals with a view to maximizing the benefits and minimizing the opportunity costs of congressional deliberation on constitutional questions.

2. *Error costs.* Any reference to constitutional "error" presupposes substantive criteria of right and wrong, or good and bad, in constitutional interpretation. Two such criteria dominate the legal literature on Congress's constitutional performance. The first is that the Congress commits error whenever it deviates from the Supreme Court's interpretation of the Constitution. The second is that Congress commits error when it deviates from

the outcomes dictated by whatever particular constitutional theory the interpreter holds.

Both of these criteria are unattractive. The first applies to an excessively narrow range of constitutional questions and privileges judicial analysis over other modes of reasoning about constitutional questions. The second overlooks that the aim of an institutional-design project is not to entrench some highly contentious, substantive theory, but rather to suggest consensual improvements—structural proposals that would improve Congress's constitutional performance as judged by any of the leading constitutional approaches. So the best criterion identifies "error" by reference to Congress's skill at using the wide range of sources admissible under all (plausible) interpretive theories, and by reference to Congress's ability to achieve outcomes that all (plausible) theories deem reasonable.

The first criterion holds that Congress should take the Constitution to mean whatever the Supreme Court says it means. As defended by Larry Alexander and Frederick Schauer,[10] this view does not assert the implausible interpretive view that the Constitution actually means whatever the Court says. Instead, the primary criterion for good constitutional law, the argument runs, is that it should be clear and stable. Clarity and stability in turn require a single, paramount constitutional interpreter, and that interpreter should be the Court.

Alexander and Schauer do not claim that their judicial supremacy view applies to questions exempt from judicial review. That restriction on the scope of their theory is sensible. Limitations on the judiciary's political reach and logistical capacity create a broad domain of constitutional determinations by the Congress that go unreviewed. What, for example, is the Senate to do when it must decide whether some presidential malfeasance amounts to a high crime or misdemeanor? The United States Reports do not speak to that question. So the critical objection to the view of Alexander and Schauer is not that it is wrong, although it may be, but that it is fatally incomplete.

The rest of the literature tends to posit that Congress errs whenever it arrives at outcomes that deviate from those indicated by some particular substantive account of constitutional interpretation. A list of the current contenders includes, in no particular order, original intention interpretation, original meaning interpretation, common law constitutionalism, process theory, law as integrity, minimalism, and pragmatism. Substantive approaches intended to improve congressional deliberation must be addressed to a Congress whose members do not all subscribe to that account, and who would deliberate about the proposals themselves under the diverse standards of constitutional evaluation that the members hold. Congress is not an institution noted for facing and resolving fundamental disagreements, let alone abstract fundamental disagreements about constitutional theory. But Congress is an institution skilled at reaching specific agreements that allow all parties to preserve their abstract commitments. Our approach exploits this institutional strength. We will assess institutional design proposals in part by their ability to improve Congress's constitutional performance relative to an "overlapping consensus"[11] or "incompletely theorized agreement"[12] about the criteria for successful constitutional argument. Admissible proposals, in other words, should identify improvements that are attractive to proponents of all views.

Such consensual improvements should in principle be available (however difficult they are to identify), because competing accounts of constitutional interpretation display broad overlap along two dimensions: sources and outcomes. All the major approaches to constitutional interpretation agree, for example, that constitutional text is relevant and admissible, that a broad range of potential techniques for interpreting text is barred (interpreters must assume that the text is written in English, that it has public rather than private or coded meaning, and so forth), and that certain other techniques are useful, such as the cautious use of canons of construction. The same is true for precedent, even more so. As for outcomes, every interpretive theory professes to subscribe to the small set of precedents that have, like *Brown v. Board of Education*,[13] achieved canonical status. But there are also more subtle examples of overlapping consensus on outcomes. Consider the Senate's decision not to censure President Clinton for the behavior for which he was impeached but acquitted. That decision is justified by a wide range of approaches to constitutional interpretation.[14]

If all the major interpretive approaches agree upon a core set of interpretive sources, skills, and even outcomes, then one can define deliberative "error" relative to that overlapping consensus without taking sides on fundamental questions. Proposals can be evaluated by their tendency to improve Congress's use of those sources and skills and its ability to deliberate over hard cases, while avoiding outcomes that are condemned by all approaches.

3. *Transition costs.* The Constitution fixes some features of the design of congressional institutions: bicameralism, the length of terms in each house, and the impermissibility of state-imposed term limits are examples.

It also leaves many institutional features unspecified, such as the committee structure, rules governing debate that might allow or restrict the ability to filibuster or amend proposals, the role of political parties in legislative organization, and the size and organization of staff. We confine our proposals to small-scale, feasible improvements that Congress can make without the consent of any external actor, under the expansive constitutional power of each house to "determine the Rules of its Proceedings."

One justification for this restriction is that controversial distributive implications will almost inevitably doom any proposed improvement; minor restructurings, on the other hand, are less likely to inflict large losses on any interested parties, and are thus more likely to gain widespread support. Another justification is that large-scale restructurings carry a greater risk of harmful unintended consequences, and even if all goes as planned, the increased costs of a large-scale transition from one institutional arrangement to another will usually outweigh any reduced decision costs or error costs.

Is Congress's Constitutional Performance Optimal?

Even if the institutional design question is the right one to ask, and even if our three criteria for assessing Congress's constitutional performance are sensible, there remains the possibility that Congress's performance is already optimal. The view would not hold that Congress never commits constitutional errors, but rather that no cost-justified improvements in congressional performance are possible. This view follows from a simple account of the political incentives that affect congressional deliberation. On this account, opposing legislative coalitions will ventilate opposing constitutional arguments, thereby ensuring fully adequate deliberation. Members who care to do so may raise constitutional concerns during committee deliberations or floor consideration without adopting a special procedure to force such activity.

The view that Congress is optimally designed for constitutional deliberation is surely counterintuitive, and we will argue that it is also false. The final test of whether our proposals represent cost-justified improvements in Congress's procedures for constitutional deliberation is the content of the proposals themselves, described later. But it is worth noting here that the simple account suffers from numerous conceptual and empirical difficulties.

First, the simple account assumes an implicit "fire alarm" model[15] of constitutional argument in Congress: coalitions and interest groups monitor proposed bills and sound the alarm when they detect constitutionally troublesome provisions or policies. But there is no particular reason to believe, a priori, that legislators and interest groups engage in just the right amount of monitoring if they rely on post hoc fire alarms to trigger attention and discussion. To the contrary, the empirical record suggests that Congress, as a collective body that continually adjusts its own rules and procedures over time, often rejects the fire alarm model in favor of ex ante framework legislation that structures congressional deliberation on constitutional and policy questions.

For a recent example of framework legislation addressed specifically to constitutional questions, consider the Unfunded Mandates Reform Act of 1995 (UMRA),[16] which requires congressional committees to specify, quantify, and describe any federal mandates that a proposed bill would place on state, local, and tribal governments and to identify those mandates that are unfunded by the federal government. The UMRA also allows legislators to raise a point of order during floor deliberation for the purpose of focusing debate on any unfunded mandate, and to require a recorded vote to waive the objection. The UMRA is best understood as a species of collective precommitment. It represents a judgment by legislators in their collective capacity, outside the divisive context of specific proposals, that fire alarm monitoring of the federalism questions implicated by unfunded mandates had provided insufficient consideration of constitutional values.

It should not be surprising that legislators sometimes turn to framework legislation to improve congressional performance in constitutional settings. Fire alarm monitoring will be most successful in an arena dominated by organized and sophisticated interest groups on all sides of an issue with clear and established lines of communication to lawmakers with jurisdiction. As with unfunded mandates, however, constitutional issues arise throughout the legislative arena, and affected groups will often lack the expertise to discover, analyze, and alert legislators about substantial questions of constitutionality. Furthermore, even when some members are aware of a serious constitutional objection, the chamber's rules, particularly in the House of Representatives, may bar public deliberation on the issue.

Individual legislators could address these deficiencies in the fire alarm system by monitoring, but deliberation within the Congress constitutes a collective good. All legislators benefit when a particular legislator spends time developing information, analyzing constitutional questions, and working with specialized personal staff on constitutional issues. Yet if an individual member provides those benefits, that takes time away from the tasks that contribute directly to getting reelected. There will be less time for fundraising, casework, media appearances, and obtaining particularized spending projects in the member's district; the legislator will thus be at a disadvantage and receive less of the pie of limited federal resources unless all members of Congress spend a similar amount of their time on constitutional issues. If constitutional deliberation is an individually supplied good, individual legislators do not internalize all the benefits of constitutional deliberation but do shoulder the costs. In such a system, constitutional deliberation will be underproduced.

In the face of the public-good character of constitutional deliberation, all members would benefit from a collective solution that requires lawmakers to allocate some of their scarce time to constitutional deliberation, that provides collective funding for the staff required for this deliberation, and that enforces collective commitments that support deliberation. The constitutional framework that we propose seeks to solve the collective-action problem and enforce the institutional commitment to spend some time and resources on constitutional matters.

LEGISLATIVE RULES OF ADMINISTRATION: DESIGN FEATURES OF A THAYERIAN CONGRESS

Principles of Design

As we describe the design features of a Congress able to discharge its constitutional responsibilities more effectively, we have been guided by four design principles that implement the necessary tradeoffs between decision costs, error costs, and transition costs. First, members of Congress must have adequate information about the constitutional issues raised by legislation. Second, members must be afforded an opportunity to raise constitutional questions and deliberate about them fully. Third, the institutional design should encourage very broad involvement from experts and interested parties. Fourth, the congressional structure should reflect a balance between improving congressional capacity to deliberate on constitutional questions and the need to enact legislation without undue delay or extreme difficulty, and it should do so without providing opportunities for strategic action by coalitions seeking to derail bills that they oppose on other grounds. Taken as an integrated package, our recommendations produce a set of legislative rules that serve as a Congressional Framework for Constitutional Issues.

The Congressional Framework for Constitutional Issues

1. *Production and Dissemination of Information.* In some cases Congress may neglect its responsibility to consider the constitutional ramifications of proposed legislation, either because members are not aware that they are present or because information about constitutional questions and analysis of them are collective goods that individual legislators will underproduce. Fortunately, models for more regularized collective treatment of such issues exist. The most influential and ubiquitous procedural framework designed to produce and structure information is the congressional budget process.[17] A recent addition to the budget rules, the UMRA, requires that the Congressional Budget Office (CBO) provide authorizing committees with written statements identifying and describing federal mandates in reported bills.

A modern committee report contains a great deal of mandatory information designed to address systematic gaps in information or to provide information to lawmakers who do not serve on the specialized committee. In the House, for example, each committee report contains relevant oversight findings and recommendations made by the Committee on Government Reform, cost estimates (including any new budget authority, spending authority, or changes in tax laws), a statement of the constitutional authority supporting enactment of the bill, an estimate of the costs of any federal mandate on subnational governments, a description and explanation of any such mandate, and a preemption statement.

With respect to a framework for considering constitutional issues, identifying bills that implicate constitutional questions must occur early, so that committees with jurisdiction can gather further information about the issue. The parliamentarian, typically a distinguished lawyer with a reputation for nonpartisanship, can determine at the time of referral to committee whether a proposal appears to raise a significant constitutional issue. The referral decision, which is published in the *Congressional Record*, can also contain the parliamentarian's description of any constitutional issue. In some cases, constitutional questions will arise as the proposal is considered and amended; thus, the trigger for special procedures should not only occur at the time of initial referral but remain available throughout the committee process.

The parliamentarian will specify if any constitutional issues implicated by the proposal are ones that the judiciary typically declines to review or reviews only under a deferential rational-basis standard. This will alert members of Congress to their special responsibility with respect to these bills. Initially, the parliamentarian may want to rely on a nonpartisan group of constitutional experts to provide guidelines for this process and to update the list of issues that receive very little or no judicial scrutiny.[18]

To provide members with the data required for them to make informed decisions when the bill reaches the floor, every bill will be accompanied by a constitutional impact statement. The constitutional impact statement will provide a summary of the committee's findings on the proposal's constitutional implications. If there is no significant constitutional issue raised by the bill, the statement will include that information. The constitutional impact statement will refer to any more comprehensive analyses (perhaps records of public hearings or analyses prepared by expert staff), and it will contain any dissenting views. The constitutional impact statement will be written so that nonlawyers can understand the arguments, not only because many members and most constituents are not lawyers, but also because the institutional strength of Congress is not its attention to legalisms but its expertise in the policy aspects of constitutional decisions. These statements will either be included in the committee report itself or provided to Congress as soon as practicable after the report is filed. Because conference reports can raise new constitutional issues, staff members will also analyze conference reports and include or update constitutional impact statements before floor consideration.

Constitutional impact statements will be more detailed than the parliamentarian's initial framing of the issue. Except where there is a finding that the legislation does not implicate a significant constitutional issue, the statement will be a brief summary of the constitutional issue, together with the committee's views and any dissenting views. If the constitutional issues raised by the proposal are ones that the judiciary typically declines to review, the statement will identify them as such, to signal to legislators that their deliberation and decision on these constitutional questions are likely to be the final ones. To respond to judicial requirements for clear statements in a number of quasi-constitutional areas, the statements will also declare whether provisions in the bill are severable, identify any retroactive provisions, and provide other clear statements required by the judiciary,[19] a category that may evolve over time as the jurisprudence of interpretive rules of clear statement changes. Finally, there will be explicit statements declaring whether the legislation allows a pre-implementation challenge to its constitutionality and whether any constitutional challenge receives special or expedited judicial consideration.[20]

To ensure that a constitutional impact statement is produced for all legislation, any bill that comes to the floor without such a statement will be subject to a point of order, waivable only by a majority vote. Enforcement is vital. Requiring information without also providing a sanction will result in little information, as members and staff target limited resources on higher-priority issues. We will return to the point-of-order enforcement procedures below when we focus on the rules governing floor consideration.

2. *Expert Congressional Staff on Constitutional Issues.* The modern Congress increasingly relies on others to provide information and analysis necessary for decision making, and it will do so in this context as well. Some of the information will be produced by interest groups, but outside production of information does not eliminate the need for internal production. Expert staff can analyze information from third parties with a stake in the legislative outcome and use credible information and good arguments in their own work, thereby externalizing some of the information costs. In addition, experts can study issues neglected by outside groups, provide balanced perspective in areas where there are not well-matched competing interest groups, and respond to individual requests by members of Congress.

The idea of creating a body of trained professionals to review constitutional matters is consistent with larger institutional trends in the legislative branch. Over the last century, as Congress has become more professional and the issues it faces more complex, the number of staff has increased substantially. Moreover, Congress occasionally establishes an internal body of experts to counterbalance expertise in the other branches of government. The president often has significant influence on constitutional and other legal matters because he is assisted by the attorney general, the solicitor general, and their staffs, as well as the staff of the Office of Legal Counsel. If Congress wants to step out of the shadows of the judicial and executive branches with regard to constitutional determinations, it must establish an equivalent set of experts.

Although members of Congress could hire a constitutional expert for their staffs (and many members already hire lawyers as policy aides), that strategy is a more costly route than setting up an entity analogous to the CBO or the Joint Tax Committee (JTC), which would be funded collectively and might be able to attract and retain more highly skilled and better-trained professionals. There are several options for a collective structure to provide constitutional information and analysis to all members of Congress. First, Congress could expand the duties of existing entities and provide additional staff. Congress could rely on committee staff for expertise, such as the staff of the Judiciary Committees if they were given jurisdiction over all bills with important constitutional implications. Individual members might resist this proposal because the staff of the Judiciary Committees is seen as closely tied to the chairs and ranking members of the committees, rather than as a resource for the entire Congress. Furthermore, when Congress begins to play a larger role in areas that are viewed by the public as relatively nonpartisan, members sometimes adopt an institutional framework that allows them to rely on technical experts who are somewhat insulated from the vagaries of politics to produce information that will shape the partisan debate. Such a framework permits lawmakers to gain credibility with constituents because they appear to be basing policy on relatively neutral information. For example, Congress often uses an institutional arrangement such as the CBO's, whereby the head of the organization is appointed by congressional leaders for a discrete term of office but the staff consists mainly of career professionals.

If Congress wished to use an existing staff organized to accommodate both the desire to have politics affect the information generated and the need to appear to rely on balanced and relatively nonpartisan data in policymaking, there are existing staffs that could be used.[21] Each house has an Office of Legal Counsel or General Counsel. The duties of the counsel revolve around representing the House and Senate in court and defending the constitutionality and legality of congressional enactments, subpoenas, and other legislative actions. The Offices of Legislative Counsel assist members in drafting legislation, but currently the counsel limit their advice to drafting issues. To place this new task within the jurisdiction of either of these offices would work a fundamental change in their jobs and require additional staff.

The duties of the American Law Division of the Congressional Research Service (CRS) could be expanded so that the staff would consult more extensively and regularly with Congress on constitutional issues. The option of relying on CRS staff is unlikely to appeal to lawmakers in the context of the new constitutional framework, however. The CRS is perceived as an extremely neutral entity with few if any partisan connections. Although non-partisanship is sometimes perceived as an asset, in this context members are apt to want some closer connection between political considerations and legal ones. Moreover, if it remains separate from any new staff organization, the CRS could provide a check on the new staff, which is likely to be more partisan, much as the Government and Finance Division of CRS now provides a check on the economic analyses of the CBO, the JTC, and other congressional committees.

We propose, therefore, that a new congressional office be formed, along the lines of the CBO or the JTC. The Office for Constitutional Issues (OCI) would be headed by a chief of staff appointed by some bipartisan group of party leaders. The chief of staff would appoint the office's staff, including any deputies, and all appointments would be based solely on professional competence, without regard to political affiliation. Much as in the CBO and the JTC, the staff would be a mix of lawyers and other professionals and scholars, in this case political scientists, historians, and public policy professionals with interests in constitutional law. Congress's institutional advantage with regard to constitutional matters is its ability to blend policy considerations with technical legal arguments. Thus, it is important that members hear not only legalistic arguments but also the broader policy implications of a particular constitutional interpretation relative to others. The analyses and reports produced by the staff would be publicly available so that citizens would have access to the information that shapes the constitutional deliberation and decision making of their representatives.

The OCI would consult with its counterparts in the executive branch, as CBO staff does with the Office of Management and Budget (OMB) and other agency officials, and as JTC staff does with Treasury and the Internal Revenue Service. Such consultations would often be largely informal, although it might make sense to formalize some interactions so that they occurred as a matter of course and so that the opinions of executive branch experts were available to all members of Congress. Congress would have to balance the advantage of widely disseminated views with the inevitable chilling effect that public disclosure would have. The OCI should also determine whether its staff or lawmakers consulted formally with members of the judiciary. It seems very unlikely that sitting judges would be comfortable giving their opinions about constitutional issues likely to come before them,[22] but retired judges might well serve as a source of expertise. Finally, the OCI would no doubt also rely on input and analysis by academics, many of whom would be eager to participate in the process.

3. *Committee Structure to Consider Constitutional Issues.* Most congressional deliberation does not occur on the floor; it is done in committees. So the relevant—and perhaps most important—consideration is the committee framework through which such issues are analyzed. There are at least three alternatives for the committee structure of the Congressional Framework for Constitutional Issues.

First, the jurisdiction of the current Judiciary Committees could be expanded so that they would also have responsibility for considering bills identified as having significant constitutional implications. The Judiciary Committees would have jurisdiction to consider the constitutional implications of the bill, to work with the OCI to prepare the constitutional impact statement, and to make amendments to the language designed to reflect the constitutional findings. In the House, multiple referral techniques would provide the framework for the shared jurisdiction between the substantive committee and the Judiciary Committee. The substantive committee would serve as the primary committee, so that when it discharged a bill, Judiciary would have only a limited time in which to perform its role.[23] The Judiciary Committee could also hold hearings and consider the bill concurrently with the substantive committee's deliberations. Multiple referral occurs less often in the Senate, but it is not unheard of, and it could be structured much like current House procedures.

The advantages of using the Judiciary Committees are obvious. These committees already have some constitutional expertise, and they have reputations for relatively serious and careful consideration of legal and constitutional questions.[24] The disadvantages, however, are substantial, although somewhat less apparent. First, because the committees are composed almost entirely of lawyers, their analyses tend to be legalistic and to replicate what they think judges would say on an issue. Some studies suggest that members of the Judiciary Committees are among the most deferential of lawmakers to courts and traditional legal reasoning.[25] Second, committee assignments are largely a matter of self-selection, and the lawmakers who want to serve on the Judiciary Committees tend to be at the extremes of the ideological spectrum. Thus the Judiciary Committees are often more polarized than other committees and less representative of the body as a whole.[26] Adding a constitutional dimension to the committees' portfolios with regard to pending legislation would only exacerbate this tendency, attracting more lawyers with intense preferences on matters of constitutional interpretation. The polarization might affect the committees' deliberations, making compromise less possible and potentially holding up legislation.

It is likely that the substantive committees with primary jurisdiction over legislation subject to our new Framework would vehemently object to sharing power with the Judiciary Committees. In the budget context, Congress discovered that standing committees resisted reallocations of jurisdiction to other existing committees because of turf jealousies. The solution in the budget arena—creating entirely new committees with little substantive responsibility but with significant power to coordinate the actions of other committees—may well be the best framework for considering constitutional issues and provides the second model of committee organization of the constitutional framework.

Congress has more flexibility in designing new committees and thus could avoid some of the weaknesses of the Judiciary Committees. For example, the rules setting up the new Committees on Constitutional Matters could limit the number of committee members who are lawyers. It might make some sense to appoint a few members of the Judiciary Committees to the new committees, at least in the early years, to gain from their expertise. Because the committees would be new, and thus lack a strong tradition of seniority in committee assignments, and because they would have far-ranging jurisdiction affecting many pieces of major legislation, it is likely that party leaders would rely heavily on party loyalty in making appointments and would generally exert more control over committee decisions.

Referrals to these new committees would work in the same way as the first option of using the existing Judiciary Committees. In both cases, committee members would rely on their own committee staff as well as the technical staff of the OCI. If lawmakers decide to establish new committees, they should also consider giving these new committees a role in the selection of the chief of staff of the OCI, with the ultimate decision vested in party leaders.

This second option for committee organization has problems, many shared with the first option of giving jurisdiction to the Judiciary Committees. To begin with, members willing to serve on the committees would likely have intense and outlying preferences, just as the current members of the Judiciary Committees do. Moreover, situating the constitutional analysis in specialized committees, rather than in the substantive committees that have primary jurisdiction over legislation, would artificially separate constitutional issues from the larger policy issues. Determinations about constitutional rights guaranteed are often abstract, and perhaps even meaningless, without simultaneous decisions about how resources will be directed toward vindicating those rights. Pragmatically, it is very difficult to clearly separate the two kinds of issues. Thus a bifurcated committee structure could cause confusion, duplication, or conflicting messages from the various committees to the full Congress and the public.

The third organizational option, consistent with the design of the UMRA, addresses this problem of separation. Under this model, the substantive committees would perform the constitutional analysis as they considered any bill with serious constitutional implications. Although members would develop less constitutional expertise than they would under the other two models, they could rely on the OCI's technical staff, on their own committee counsel, and on lawyers on their personal staff. In addition, individual members might well become more involved in constitutional matters because of personal preferences, although this development might be unwelcome if the specialists were lawyers whose overly legalistic approaches received too much deference.

The dynamics of committee consideration would be different if the constitutional assessment were left in the substantive committees rather than placed in specialized committees. First, the substantive committees would likely be less polarized on constitutional questions than the Judiciary or similar committees. Members would have selected the substantive committees because of their interest in the policies that fall within their jurisdiction, and only secondarily (if at all) because of their constitutional views. In other words, members of the Agriculture Committees may have firm positions on farm policy, but they have less intense views on constitutional issues that their bills implicate, such as federalism, the delegation doctrine, or the federal spending power. This characteristic of the substantive committees' membership might allow for more moderated, and perhaps more thoughtful, deliberation. On the other hand, it might mean that the constitutional element would be slighted, because members would not care much about it.[27] In such a case, the attention that constitutional issues received would depend on the salience provided by the new Framework and interest-group agitation, the latter a sort of improved fire alarm mechanism enhanced by the Framework and the information that it produced.

Second, the interest-group dynamics would be very different in the substantive committees. Substantive committees attract the attention of groups that have stakes in the policies within their jurisdiction. So the members of the Agriculture Committees interact mainly with farm groups, environmental groups, consumer groups, state and local officials with responsibility for farm policy, and others with particular interests in agriculture. The committees are monitored primarily by trade publications concerned with farmers, food production, and rural policies. Although they would not initially possess much constitutional expertise, these groups, and their lobbyists, would invest resources in studying constitutional issues and producing useful information, because the new Framework would be another strategic opportunity to affect a bill's fate. Their information might be particularly helpful because they could infuse their legal analysis with their knowledge of the underlying policies.

In contrast, using multiple referrals and specialized committees would mean that the groups having the most sustained interaction with lawmakers in the constitutional realm would be those interested in legal issues and constitutional law. Groups like the American Bar Association, the American Civil Liberties Union, the Institute for Justice, and legal academics would exert the primary influence on the deliberations of the Judiciary Committees or the Committees on Constitutional Matters. These groups would have less influence if the constitutional inquiry were done by dozens of substantive committees, because their attention would be fragmented and their resources deployed widely.

The structure of interest-group activity and conflict is a crucial element in committee design. All three options present strengths and weaknesses in this respect. We believe that it would be easier for substantive committees, working with the expert OCI and getting advice from the executive branch and other outside experts, to include the law-oriented interest groups when appropriate than it would be for specialized committees to appropriately blend policy and constitutional law in their deliberations. The OCI's formal and informal consultation with expert groups and lawyers in the executive branch would help these interest groups to overcome the problems of fragmentation and to learn of significant constitutional issues in time to weigh in on the outcome. In a sense, the contact entity for the interest groups with a constitutional law orientation would be the OCI, which would also be a conduit for informing the groups about decisions that they want to influence.

4. *Floor Consideration and Points of Order.* Procedures structuring floor deliberation seek to balance a number of competing concerns. First, cer-

tain structures, notably points of order, reduce the chances that Congress will inadvertently or intentionally ignore difficult or controversial issues. Even though most members may want to avoid such issues, and the party leaders may work to structure a bill or floor consideration to spare their members difficult votes, the availability of a point of order can allow one lawmaker (or a few) to halt proceedings, highlight the issue, and force a roll call vote. Especially in the House, where the floor is tightly controlled by the Rules Committee, a point of order that cannot be waived in a special rule empowers individual members and reduces the chance that avoidance techniques will succeed. Furthermore, the point-of-order process focuses legislative attention on the constitutional issue at hand and provides the opportunity for sustained debate for which members can be held accountable. Occasionally, constitutional issues identified by a handful of members have been brushed aside during the rush of floor debate and activity. Points of order make that more difficult.

On the other hand, points of order can be used to stall or derail legislation by lawmakers who oppose the proposal but do not care about the constitutional issue. Strategic use of the point-of-order procedure can nonetheless force sincere debate and deliberation about important issues, so the motivation behind the objection may not be relevant in all cases.[28] But as Congress adopts new procedural frameworks, it must be aware that all additional process makes enacting laws more difficult. Floor procedures must balance the need to allow lawmakers to focus on constitutional issues and the need to enact some legislation.

Currently, the Senate allows members to raise constitutional points of order;[29] the House Rules do not, although representatives have objected to legislation on the ground that it violated the prerogatives of the House under the origination clause of the Constitution.[30] The practice in both houses is that the presiding officer does not rule on the question but instead refers it to the full chamber for a vote. The Framework institutionalizes these points of order, drawing on the experience with other congressional procedural frameworks that are enforced in this way. First, under the Framework a point of order can be raised by any lawmaker to object to considering a bill that is not accompanied by a constitutional impact statement. Such enforcement is required to ensure that the statements are systematically produced in a timely fashion. Second, a point of order can be raised against any bill with provisions designed to require early judicial determination of constitutional questions. If these provisions encourage

Congress to shirk its responsibility to think carefully about constitutional matters, they should be more difficult to include in legislation. Third, a member can raise a point of order against any bill that the legislator believes raises a significant constitutional issue. The information provided in the constitutional impact statements will help alert members to objectionable or worrisome proposals, although members may also discover issues on their own. A legislator will not be limited to raising constitutional issues identified initially by the parliamentarian or discussed in the constitutional impact statement.

To reduce the strategic use of the third kind of point of order, a member objecting to consideration of the bill must present to the presiding office a petition signed by twenty members in the House and ten members in the Senate indicating their support for the objection. This innovation is not a feature of any similar congressional framework. The closest analogue arises in cloture, where a petition to vote to cut off debate in the Senate must be signed by sixteen senators. Related but less similar is the rule in the House of Representatives that a majority of the membership can force the discharge of a bill from a committee of jurisdiction.

The requirement that several members join in raising a constitutional point of order makes the strategy more costly to those trying to use it to derail or force changes in the bill, but it still allows a small group of intensely concerned lawmakers to bring a constitutional question to the attention of the full body. We favor this design feature because we anticipate that constitutional points of order will arise more frequently than, for example, budget points of order. The latter concern fairly discrete issues (for example, Is an amendment revenue-neutral?) that can be avoided by bill drafters. Constitutional issues, on the other hand, can be raised in more contexts—either sincerely or strategically—and thus pose a more far-reaching procedural threat to legislation.

Finally, we recommend that only a majority vote be required to waive any of the three types of point of order. In contrast, some budget points of order can be waived in the Senate only by a vote of sixty members. The voting rule may not matter very much in the Senate, because most of the legislation will also be subject to filibusters that can be broken only by a supermajority vote of sixty senators. But lawmakers may be more willing to vote to cut off lengthy debate than to vote against a serious constitutional objection, so it is not clear that the two votes are interchangeable. A supermajority requirement in the House would be a significant new hurdle; no budget point of order in the House requires more than a majority to waive, and only a rule applying to a narrow subset of tax increases is formally enforced through a supermajority voting requirement. Unlike with most other points of order, however, the Rules Committee cannot waive constitutional points of order in a special rule and therefore cannot circumvent the objection and recorded vote.

Our choice of majority voting rule here is driven by our principle of balance—the Framework should allow opportunities for deliberation and modification but not halt a great deal of legislative activity. We think that a separate vote is sufficient protection: it disaggregates the lawmaker's stand on the constitutional issue from his or her final vote and eliminates or reduces the lawmaker's ability to explain away a troublesome position on the constitutional matter as a necessary evil to passing, say, an omnibus bill with numerous provisions that appeal to the constituents back home. But rules can be changed, and enforcement procedures calibrated over time to account for experience. For example, the Framework could require supermajority votes in the context of constitutional issues of the sort usually left unreviewed by the judiciary and require only a majority for other constitutional points of order. Furthermore, there may be an advantage to supermajority requirements peculiar to the constitutional realm. Building consensus and demonstrating wide margins of support for constitutional positions may be important for their legitimacy. Congress already has a number of formal and informal structures that result in wide margins of victory for most major legislation.[31] The question is whether an additional supermajority vote would be beneficial: it may be that a constitutional determination even by a bare majority of each house of Congress, already a supermajority requirement, has more legitimacy in the eyes of the public than, for example, a 5–4 decision by the Supreme Court.

Our objective has been to introduce more sustained consideration of institutional design questions into a discussion that has almost exclusively focused on questions of institutional choice. Whether Congress's current role in constitutional interpretation is retained or expanded, procedural and institutional devices like those we have described here promise to enhance congressional performance in this arena. A well-functioning Thayerian Congress is one that takes advantage of the lessons learned from modern procedural frameworks to allow it to structure constitutional deliberation and decision making so as to improve outcomes.

NOTES

1   For a recent example see Mark Tushnet, *Taking the Constitution Away from the Courts* (Princeton: Princeton University Press, 1999).

2   James Bradley Thayer, "The Origin and Scope of the American Doctrine of Constitutional Law," 7 *Harvard Law Review* 129 (1893).

3   See, e.g., Paul Brest, "The Conscientious Legislator's Guide to Constitutional Interpretation," 27 *Stanford Law Review* 585 (1975).

4   Thus, David Mayhew carefully explains that certain features of legislative behavior may best be explained as if legislators cared only about getting re-elected. That the premise is methodological, not empirical, has not always been remembered by subsequent public choice scholars. David R. Mayhew, *Congress: The Electoral Connection* (New Haven: Yale University Press, 1974), 45–49.

5   Richard F. Fenno, *Congressmen in Committees* (Boston: Little, Brown, 1973). Subsequent political science work has confirmed this account. E.g., John W. Kingdon, "Models of Legislative Voting," 39 *Journal of Politics* 563, 569–70 (1977). See generally John W. Kingdon, *Congressmen's Voting Decisions*, 3d ed. (Ann Arbor: University of Michigan Press, 1989).

6   James B. Kau and Paul H. Rubin, "Economic and Ideological Factors in Congressional Voting: The 1980 Election," 44 *Public Choice* 385, 385 (1984). See generally Keith T. Poole and Howard Rosenthal, *Congress: A Political-Economic History of Roll Call Voting* (New York: Oxford University Press, 1997); Jerrold E. Schneider, *Ideological Coalitions in Congress* (Westport, Conn.: Greenwood, 1979).

7   See Mark V. Tushnet, "Clarence Thomas: The Constitutional Problems," 63 *George Washington Law Review* 466, 469 (1995). Cf. Edward L. Rubin, "Beyond Public Choice: Comprehensive Rationality in the Writing and Reading of Statutes," 66 *New York University Law Review* 1, 21 (1991).

8   Jon Elster, "Alchemies of the Mind: Transmutation and Misrepresentation," 3 *Legal Theory* 133, 176 (1997).

9   James D. Fearon, "Deliberation as Discussion," *Deliberative Democracy*, ed. Jon Elster (New York: Cambridge University Press, 1998), 44, 53–56, 63–64.

10   Larry Alexander and Frederick Schauer, "On Extrajudicial Constitutional Interpretation," 110 *Harvard Law Review* 1359, 1387 (1997).

11   John Rawls, *Political Liberalism* (New York: Columbia University Press, 1993), 133–68.

12   Cass R. Sunstein, "Incompletely Theorized Agreements," 108 *Harvard Law Review* 1733, 1735–36 (1995).

13   347 U.S. 483 (1954).

14 See Jack Chaney, "The Constitutionality of Censuring the President," 61 *Ohio State Law Journal* 979, 1004–12 (2000).

15 Cf. Mathew D. McCubbins and Thomas Schwartz, "Congressional Oversight Overlooked: Police Patrols versus Fire Alarms," 28 *American Journal of Political Science* 165, 166 (1984) (using model in context of congressional oversight of executive branch).

16 Pub. L. No. 104-4, 109 Stat. 48 (1995). For analysis of the act see Elizabeth Garrett, "Enhancing the Political Safeguards of Federalism? The Unfunded Mandates Reform Act of 1995," 45 *University of Kansas Law Review* 1113 (1997).

17 For one of the clearest explanations of the congressional budget process, see Allen Schick, *The Federal Budget: Politics, Policy, Process*, rev. ed. (Washington: Brookings Institution Press, 2000).

18 Donald G. Morgan, *Congress and the Constitution: A Study of Responsibility* (Cambridge: Belknap Press of Harvard University Press, 1966), 349.

19 William Eskridge Jr. and Philip Frickey, "Quasi-Constitutional Law: Clear Statement Rules as Constitutional Lawmaking," 45 *Vanderbilt Law Review* 593, 598–611 (1992).

20 See Neal Devins and Michael A. Fitts, "The Triumph of Timing: Raines v. Byrd and the Modern Supreme Court's Attempt to Control Constitutional Confrontations," 86 *Georgetown Law Journal* 351 (1997).

21 See Louis Fisher, "Constitutional Analysis by Congressional Staff Agencies," in this volume.

22 Robert A. Katzmann, *Courts and Congress* (Washington: Brookings Institution Press, 1997), 85.

23 Of course in some cases the Judiciary Committee would also be the substantive committee, and thus its deliberations would include discussions of the substance of the proposal as well as the constitutional issues raised.

24 Mark C. Miller, "Congressional Committees and the Federal Courts: A Neo-Institutional Perspective," 45 *Western Political Quarterly* 949, 959–61 (1992).

25 Mark C. Miller, "Congress and the Constitution: A Tale of Two Committees," 3 *Seton Hall Constitutional Law Journal* 317, 339–40 (1993). See also Bruce Peabody, "Congressional Attitudes toward Constitutional Interpretation," in this volume (finding little difference between lawyers and nonlawyers, but finding differences between Judiciary Committee members and other lawmakers).

26 E.g., Miller, "Congressional Committees," 959–60; Stephen F. Ross, "Legislative Enforcement of Equal Protection," 72 *Minnesota Law Review* 311, 358 n.190 (1987).

27 Morgan, *Congress and the Constitution*, 352–53; Miller, "Congress and the Constitution," 341–43.

28   Bruce Peabody's contribution demonstrates that lawmakers believe most questions currently raised in Congress to be bona fide and not merely strategic, suggesting that pretextual points of order may not be as significant a problem as some have feared. See Peabody, "Congressional Attitudes toward Constitutional Interpretation," table 1, question 3, in this volume.

29   Floyd M. Riddick and Alan S. Frumin, *Riddick's Senate Procedure* (Washington: Government Printing Office, 1992), 52–54.

30   Ross, "Legislative Enforcement of Equal Protection," 359 n.193.

31   Tushnet, *Taking the Constitution Away from the Courts*, 52.

Evaluating Congressional Constitutional Interpretation

Some Criteria and Two Informal Case Studies

∽

MARK TUSHNET

Many scholars have recently expressed interest in examining—and defending—the role of Congress in interpreting the Constitution. Sometimes skeptics about Congress's ability to do so will invoke historical experience and recent episodes in which members of Congress disclaimed interest in assessing the constitutionality of a proposal before them. To that extent, the question is empirical: Do members of Congress engage in constitutional interpretation, and when they do, how well do they perform? This chapter is an informal empirical inquiry, which may illuminate broader questions and, perhaps, motivate more systematic inquiries.

Conducting an empirical inquiry into Congress's performance in constitutional matters is not simple, though. In particular, cases need to be selected with some care if the goal is to evaluate Congress's performance. In the first part of this chapter I argue that there is actually only a small set of issues where we have a reasonably clean record to evaluate, and set out some criteria for selecting cases to examine. Using those criteria, I then examine some aspects of Congress's performance in the impeachment of President William J. Clinton and, more briefly, some aspects of its response to presidential military initiatives taken without formal prior endorsement by Congress. I conclude that Congress's performance in the impeachment, while not unflawed, was reasonably good, and that its performance in the war powers context may have larger flaws but may be reasonably good even so.[1]

HOW TO EVALUATE CONGRESS'S PERFORMANCE IN INTERPRETING THE CONSTITUTION

Discussions of Congress's performance in interpreting the Constitution can easily get off the track unless we take great care in ensuring that we examine only cases that offer a fair chance for sensible evaluation. A necessary first step is to define some criteria for selecting such cases.

Examine Institutional Performance, Not Individual Behavior

It is trivially easy to compile a list of constitutionally irresponsible or thoughtless *proposals* made by members of Congress. A member will shoot out a press release responding to some local outrage, or put a bill in the hopper without taking any time to consider its constitutionality. Often these proposals result from the member's desire to grandstand, to do something that gets his or her name in the nightly news in the district.[2] They are not serious proposals for legislation, and the member has no real expectation that they will be enacted.

Noting grandstanding actions of this sort provides no basis for evaluating *Congress's* behavior. What we need to examine are institutional actions, those that represent the outcome of a completed congressional process. Institutional actions can of course be *in*action as well. Grandstanding proposals may count against assertions that members of Congress act in a constitutionally responsible manner, but the failure of such proposals to move through the legislative process should count in favor of such assertions. Institutional actions have proceeded through a complex set of organizational structures. Those structures, designed for other purposes, may sometimes serve (imperfectly and as a byproduct) to screen out constitutionally irresponsible actions.

Examining institutional actions raises its own difficulties, however. Judges write opinions when they decide what the Constitution means. Congress does not. Enacted statutes typically become effective without an accompanying statement of the constitutional rationale on which Congress relied. Determining the constitutional basis for a completed action by Congress requires us to examine a range of materials, such as committee reports, floor debate, and even newspaper stories, from which we can infer the constitutional basis on which Congress acted. Inferences of this sort will inevitably be open to question. The evaluation of Congress's performance that results from such inferences will therefore often rest on a shaky foundation. Still, one should do the best one can.

In addition, often members of Congress may have varying constitutional rationales for their belief that a proposal is constitutional. Unlike judges, they need not sign an opinion giving a majority's position on the constitutional question. Members of Congress must do no more than vote for the bill. But sometimes one constitutional rationale might be a good one and another bad. Imagine a statute adopted by a vote of 80–20. Sixty members of the majority thought about the constitutional questions raised by the statute, and thought the statute justified by a rationale that one concludes, on detached reflection, was mistaken. But twenty members of the majority had a constitutionally good rationale for their vote. Without taking a position on the question, I simply observe that one could reasonably either challenge or defend the institutional action under these circumstances.

Examine Institutional Actions outside the Shadow Cast by the Courts

The existence of judicial review itself poses a problem for those who would evaluate congressional constitutional performance. Most analysts think that anticipatory obedience to the courts is desirable.[3] A legislature engages in anticipatory obedience when it predicts what a court would say about the constitutionality of a proposal were it to be enacted, and adapts the proposal to ensure that it will survive judicial scrutiny.

I have argued elsewhere that anticipatory obedience may sometimes distort enacted statutes.[4] Judicial review presents another problem for those who would evaluate Congress's constitutional performance, however. I have called this the problem of the judicial overhang.[5] Judicial review provides an opportunity for Congress as a body, not just individual legislators, to engage in grandstanding by enacting statutes that members of Congress can be confident will be held unconstitutional. Consider a situation in which members of Congress have a choice: They can enact a splashy statute that directly attacks a problem, albeit in a way that the courts will find unconstitutional, or they can enact a boring one, full of obscure details, that might be a bit less effective in achieving Congress's policy goals but that would be unquestionably constitutional. Presumably enacting a statute that advances policy goals is politically attractive, but sometimes enacting the splashy but unconstitutional statute may be even more politically attractive. Members then can take credit for trying to do something and blame the courts for their failure even though the other statute might have been both constitutional and nearly as effective in achieving Congress's policy goals.[6]

This behavior, which we might call anticipatory *dis*obedience, is pretty clearly undesirable. Even if rather common, though, anticipatory disobedience might shed little light on the question of congressional constitutional capacity. People will overeat if someone gives them free candy, but that fact says little about their actual desires regarding nutrition. To determine those desires, one would have to take people away from the setting in which they have access to free candy. Analogously, we can get a better sense of Congress's actual constitutional capacity if we examine only cases in which Congress cannot engage in anticipatory disobedience. That members of Congress behave badly when they know someone is around to bail them out tells us little about how they would behave were they to have full responsibility for their actions.

The type of anticipatory disobedience I have discussed is undesirable. Yet there is another type that is less clearly so, although critics of Congress regularly treat it as undesirable. This is anticipatory disobedience designed as a signal to the courts of Congress's disapproval of what it knows the Court is going to do with its statute. Senator Daniel Patrick Moynihan once suggested that sometimes Congress should enact statutes that were, under current doctrine, plainly unconstitutional to demonstrate to the Court that it might do well to reconsider the doctrine. Distinguishing between the undesirable grandstanding form of anticipatory disobedience and the more defensible, principled disobedience is undoubtedly difficult, which supports the argument that in evaluating congressional performance we should look at actions not closely connected to existing judicial doctrine.

Our constitutional traditions make the prospect of judicial review realistic in a wide range of cases. In addition, the tradition of judicial review may induce members to *believe* that review might be possible when in fact it is not. The problem of war powers is an example. Since the enactment of the War Powers Resolution, members of Congress have regularly sought judicial review of presidential decisions regarding the deployment of military force overseas. The Supreme Court has never ruled directly on the standing issue raised in these cases. The Court of Appeals for the District of Columbia Circuit, where nearly all these lawsuits have been brought, has developed a law of standing seemingly at odds with itself: it first holds out the hope that someday some legislator will be found to have standing, and then routinely denies standing in the court's exercise of equitable discretion. The ambiguities generated by this law mean that members of Congress may think that they have judicial review available to them, which may distort the way in which they consider war powers questions. The judicial overhang, that is, may be quite large indeed. Notably, the members who bring the lawsuits may themselves be exercising their own independent constitutional judgments, but find themselves defeated because *other* members expect the courts to correct any gross errors that Congress makes.

Even so, cases where no reasonable member of Congress could anticipate judicial review do exist, as do cases where most members correctly anticipate that courts will not intervene. In these cases members of Congress know that they have full and exclusive responsibility for arriving at a conclusion that must, according to their oath of office, be consistent with the Constitution.

Avoid Examining Problems Where People Can Reasonably Disagree about the Constitution's Meaning

One of the most serious pitfalls in evaluating congressional constitutional performance occurs when an analyst sets up a standard and asks whether Congress's action conforms to the standard, while others might reasonably set up a quite different standard. The posited standard may be the analyst's own conclusion about the Constitution's proper meaning, or it may be a standard drawn from Supreme Court decisions. Divergence from the standard may nonetheless tell us almost nothing about Congress's constitutional performance.

Take for example the problem of campaign finance and the First Amendment. Suppose we take the Supreme Court's decision in *Buckley v. Valeo*[7] as the standard by which we measure Congress's constitutional performance. Undoubtedly many existing proposals for campaign finance reform are inconsistent with the doctrine laid out in *Buckley*. Assume that supporters of such proposals do not really expect the Supreme Court to overrule *Buckley* anytime soon. It seems to me quite wrong to say that these supporters are behaving in a constitutionally irresponsible manner. After all, many respected constitutional scholars, and even some Supreme Court justices, believe that *Buckley* was wrongly decided. Congress can act responsibly, in constitutional terms, even when it enacts statutes that the Court actually holds unconstitutional, as long as the constitutional position asserted by Congress is a reasonable one.[8] So simply listing the statutes that the Supreme Court has held unconstitutional does not give us any real measure of Congress's constitutional performance.

This problem arises even outside the context of judicial review. Consider here the furious debate over whether President Clinton had committed an impeachable offense. The constitutional language was clear, but its meaning was not. Relying on their interpretation of the original understanding of the term "high Crimes and Misdemeanors," some argued that a president could be impeached only for actions taken in his official capacity that posed a serious threat to the nation's political integrity. Relying on a different interpretation of the original understanding and on some obvious functional considerations, others gave the example of a president who committed a murder for nonpolitical reasons and insisted that presidents could be impeached for actions taken in their personal capacity, where such actions cast grave doubt on the president's personal integrity and on his ability to continue to represent the nation's people.

The House voted to impeach the president, adopting a theory more like the second than the first. The second theory may be wrong, but it is clearly a reasonable one: the standard is consistent with the Constitution's language, it makes functional sense, and it is consistent with at least some aspects of Congress's past practices in impeachment. It seems clear to me that impeachment's opponents have no real ground for saying that the House acted in a constitutionally irresponsible manner in adopting the second theory, even if they believe that the first theory is the better understanding of the Constitution.[9]

The more general point is that many constitutional questions admit of reasonable disagreement, and that all sides in a dispute can take different positions while all remain faithful to the Constitution. Consider this version of the problem. Congress acts in a way inconsistent with some stipulated standard, whether it be the critic's or the Supreme Court's. The mere fact of Congress's disagreement with the Supreme Court or with the critic does not establish that Congress has shown itself to be demonstrably unable to arrive at reasonable conclusions about the Constitution. My impression is that people find it psychologically difficult to hold the following two views at the same time: first, a firm belief that the constitutional interpretation they have arrived at by sound legal reasoning is correct, and second, an acknowledgment that reasonable people using the same methods of legal reasoning could arrive at a different conclusion. Yet the persistence of real and good-faith disagreement about what the Constitution means implies that both of these views, or something like them, must be correct.

Thus Congress may be wrong, from my point of view or from the Supreme Court's. Its "errors" do not, however, show that Congress is performing badly as a constitutional decision maker. At most these "errors" show that Congress disagrees with me, or the Supreme Court, about what the Constitution means. Evaluating congressional constitutional performance must therefore take account of the fact of reasonable disagreement about the Constitution's meaning. The criterion that an evaluator must apply is, Did Congress do something that is outside the range of reasonable interpretations of the Constitution?[10] Obviously this criterion tilts the field of evaluation in Congress's favor, setting a baseline that is truly a line rather than a point, because of the fairly wide range of reasonable positions available on nearly every constitutional question. But to me, it is the only criterion that makes sense. Applying any other criterion leads to the empty conclusion that Congress acted reasonably but in a manner with which the critic disagrees—or, put more sharply, to the conclusion that the critic simply was outvoted on a matter about which reasonable people can disagree.

Examine Only Cases Where the Constitution Provides Answers

Broadly described, the Constitution creates a political structure and prescribes some particular outcomes. Across a wide range, the Constitution says nothing about which outcomes people operating within its structures must reach. To make the point obvious, the Constitution says nothing about whether the highest marginal rate in the income tax system should be 26 percent or 39 percent or 54 percent, even if there is a constitutional requirement that tax rates not be confiscatory; or whether there should be a time limit on eligibility for federally provided public assistance even if there is some constitutional requirement that legislatures provide minimum subsistence for the needy. Clearly one cannot evaluate the degree to which congressional action conforms to the Constitution when the Constitution gives Congress unfettered discretion to act.[11]

The income tax and welfare reform examples raise what we usually think of as ordinary policy questions. According to several respectable constitutional theories, some *constitutional* issues have the same analytic structure.

According to these theories, the Constitution establishes a structure giving participants incentives to respond to constitutional questions in position-specific ways, and treats as constitutionally valid the outcome of the political process operating according to those incentives. Herbert Wechsler's account of federalism is one example of such a theory.[12] According to Wechsler, the Constitution's structures gave political actors incentives to assert varying positions about the proper distribution of power between the national government and state governments. Whatever accommodation the political actors reached *was* what the Constitution meant. Jesse Choper has offered a similar theory of separation of powers.[13] The Constitution gave members of Congress and the president political interests that would be served by preserving the power of their respective institutions, setting the institutions and their members at political odds over the distribution of power within the national government. The president would seek to maximize his or her power over officials within the national government, for example, while members of Congress would try to maximize their power over the very same officials. Political combat between Congress and the president will produce some outcome, and according to Choper that outcome *is* what the separation of powers means.

The implication of such theories for evaluating congressional constitutional responsibility is clear: the concept of congressional constitutional responsibility is inapt with respect to provisions by means of which the Constitution does no more than create a political structure and incentives for the occupants of different positions. The Constitution, according to theories of this sort, provides no standard whatever against which to assess congressional action. The Constitution creates incentives, and how people respond to them is irrelevant from a constitutional point of view because the Constitution imposes no duties other than to respond to the incentives that it creates.

Of course, the Constitution *does* specify standards for many of its provisions. Further, theories like Wechsler's and Choper's are quite controversial, rejected by the Supreme Court[14] and by many constitutional scholars. The criterion that would allow us to select only cases outside the range of reasonable disagreement for evaluation suggests, however, that mere controversy is insufficient to disqualify a theory from the terrain. So, for example, a member of Congress who says openly that as far as he or she is concerned the Constitution places no limits on Congress's power to regulate state governments—a member, that is, who accepts Wechsler's theory—is acting in a constitutionally responsible manner. Or at least, to advance the discussion of whether Congress is a responsible constitutional interpreter, we have to put aside cases in which there is already substantial disagreement on the very foundation of the inquiry—that is, cases in which some people reasonably think that the Constitution does not constrain at all and others reasonably disagree.

One limitation on the scope of this fourth criterion deserves special note. Few members of Congress will in fact assert that the Constitution places no substantive limits on what they may do. As a representative, Gerald Ford notoriously asserted that an impeachable offense was whatever a majority of the House determined it to be at any particular time.[15] As far as I can tell, this position had no purchase whatever during Clinton's impeachment. Proponents and opponents of impeachment alike produced standards for determining whether what the president had done constituted an impeachable offense; no one said, at least in public, that Ford had been correct, and that the House could impeach the president simply because a majority wanted to do so. The reason for this restraint, I suspect, is an awareness among members of Congress of their constituents' belief that the Constitution—in all its provisions—means something, and an understanding by these same members that openly declaring a constitutional provision (or arrangement, like federalism and the separation of powers) to have no substantive content would demonstrate constitutional irresponsibility *to the constituents*, even if there is some theory of constitutional responsibility under which such a declaration is reasonable.

This example indicates that the criteria developed here may not restrict the range of cases we can consider quite as dramatically as it might seem. Most of the time, when Congress does something fairly described as interpreting the Constitution, Congress's interpretation will be a substantive one, not one asserting that the Constitution, properly interpreted, does no more than give members of Congress political incentives.

THREE EXAMPLES FROM CLINTON'S IMPEACHMENT

Congress's actions during Clinton's impeachment offer good opportunities to assess Congress's constitutional performance. There was a completed congressional process. The Supreme Court's decision in *Walter Nixon v. United States*, holding that challenges to the procedures used by the Senate to try Judge Nixon presented political questions,[16] made it reasonably clear that no court would review any decision taken in the course of a presidential impeachment. As noted earlier, some important legal questions in connection with impeachment have a wide range of reasonable answers, and there may be no legal standards available with respect to others. Still, some interesting legal questions about impeachment have answers within a narrow enough range that we can assess how well Congress did in answering them: We can imagine Congress doing something that would have been constitutionally unreasonable, such as resting an impeachment on evidence not disclosed to the public. The next section of this chapter considers three such questions: whether a president could be impeached and convicted but not removed from office, whether the Senate can properly proceed when presented with an impeachment completed by the House of Representatives during one session but not renewed in the next session, and whether the House of Representatives can impeach a president simply by concluding that a standard of probable cause similar to that used by grand juries has been satisfied. The response of Congress to the first question is an example of its rejection of a position that has some surface plausibility but is actually an unreasonable interpretation of the Constitution; its responses to the second and third are examples of its rejection of reasonable positions in favor of others that while perhaps a bit less reasonable, nonetheless cross the threshold of reasonableness.

Impeachment and Conviction without Removal

The prospects for President Clinton's conviction and removal from office, never large, diminished as the impeachment process went on. One law professor, Joseph Isenbergh, suggested that the House and Senate could express their disapproval of the president's conduct by impeaching and convicting him but not removing him from office.[17] It might appear that politicians unconcerned with constitutional interpretation would have found this course attractive: They could express their disapproval of the president's conduct and still conform to the apparent preference among the public that Clinton remain in office.

Looking to the text of the Constitution, Isenbergh argued that the president could be impeached for and convicted of something other than a high crime or misdemeanor, in which case removal from office was not mandatory but rather discretionary. In addition, Isenbergh noted that the Framers (probably) anticipated that an official might commit misconduct, like murder, unconnected to office and yet deserving of public sanction. Impeachment for and conviction of such an offense, coupled with a sanction other than removal, is an appropriate response. Finally, Isenbergh suggested, the scenario that he imagined made some functional sense, as the Clinton episode itself indicated. Presidents might engage in misconduct that was not severe enough to justify removal from office but sufficiently severe to deserve the high degree of formal condemnation that impeachment and conviction would represent.

Isenbergh's proposal received some endorsement in the press but got nowhere in Congress. The reasons are clear. First, and in my judgment less important, proponents of impeachment really did believe that the president should be removed from office, and that any step short of that was tantamount to approval of the president's conduct. Second, and more important, Isenbergh's proposal, while not entirely insupportable, was wildly at odds with well-settled understandings about impeachment. As far as I know, no serious consideration had ever been given before to the possibility that civil officers could be impeached for and convicted of something less than a high crime or misdemeanor. Isenbergh accurately noted that the Constitution's text made this possibility available. But text—and even modest functional sense—is not all that matters in constitutional interpretation. Practice and settled understandings matter as well. Here practice and settled understandings were so firmly established that Isenbergh's proposal lay outside the bounds of reasonable interpretation. Nor did Isenbergh suggest why those settled understandings should be displaced in favor of an interpretation that on his view had *always* been available. Congress's inattention to the proposal demonstrated its ability to reject unreasonable constitutional interpretations.

"Lame Duck" Impeachments

Another law professor weighed in with a similarly innovative proposal. According to Bruce Ackerman, a "lame duck" impeachment was constitutionally questionable.[18] Again, accepting Ackerman's view would have given the Senate a graceful way out of a difficult political situation. A "lame duck" impeachment, in Ackerman's terms, was one in which the impeachment was voted by a House of Representatives that had convened for a session after an election, but was tried by the newly elected Senate. Ackerman noted some functional concerns about lame-duck impeachments, particularly that some House members who voted in favor of impeachment might have been rejected by their constituents, perhaps precisely because the constituents found unacceptable a vote by their representative in favor of impeachment. He also acknowledged that impeachments in the past had continued from one legislative session to another, and that practice before the New Deal included several examples of impeachments that carried over from one congressional session to another.

But, Ackerman argued, everything changed with the adoption of the Twentieth Amendment in 1933. According to Ackerman, the campaign for that amendment's adoption centered on charges that actions taken by lame-duck Congresses lacked democratic legitimacy. The amendment compressed the time between an election and the convening of a new Congress, to eliminate or at least reduce the possibility that a Congress repudiated by the voters would take significant action. On Ackerman's view, therefore, the House of Representatives could indeed *impeach* the president in a lame-duck session, because impeachment was an act that could be completed by the House alone. Ackerman argued, however, that the newly convened Senate should not proceed to a trial "unless and until [the new House of Representatives] . . . soberly and self-consciously reaffirm[ed]" that the president should be impeached.

I believe that Ackerman's proposal received less serious consideration than it should have, in contrast to the appropriate lack of consideration given to Isenbergh's proposal. Ackerman's argument had several large analytic problems, however. First, he agreed that lame-duck Congresses could *enact* quite significant laws, even by majorities that had been repudiated in the election. The distinction that Ackerman sought to draw between completed acts, including legislation and impeachments, and continuing ones, such as the trial of an impeachment charge already made, was quite thin. Second, the Twentieth Amendment shortened the time in which a lame-duck Congress could sit, but it did not eliminate the possibility of lame-duck sessions entirely. Ackerman therefore had to rely on the amendment's general policy to cast doubt on the legitimacy of a trial based on an impeachment voted by a lame-duck House of Representatives. One might reasonably ask for more than this as the basis for repudiating clear pre-1933 precedent.

These problems are perhaps sufficient to make Ackerman's argument unacceptable, but the Senate should have done more work in thinking through Ackerman's proposal before rejecting it.[19] Why did it not? Again, politics played a role. Even on Ackerman's view, the question was whether the Senate should proceed with a trial. By the time the Senate had to act, however, it was clear to most observers that a trial would not result in a conviction. Terminating the proceedings in the ordinary way probably seemed cleaner to senators than doing so by adopting a novel theory of the law of impeachment. Further, Ackerman's argument resembled Isenbergh's in that it was simply too fancy. Here part of the difficulty arose from Ackerman's position in the legal academy and his rhetoric. He is well known, and sometimes disparaged, as clever and thought-provoking, but also as a scholar whose views, on reflection, seem unacceptable to many others. The Senate gave Ackerman's proposal less attention than it should have, but its failure in this instance is understandable and, to some degree, excusable.

The Standard of Proof in Impeachment

House members had to decide not only what constituted an impeachable offense but what standard of proof they should require once they had settled on a definition. As the issue came to be framed in the House, two standards of proof (roughly speaking) were available. The first focused on facts alone and was referred to as the "grand jury" standard: Did the factual evidence provide a reasonable basis (probable cause) for concluding that the president had committed an impeachable offense? Some House members were attracted to the grand jury standard because they drew an analogy between the House, which in impeaching acted like a grand jury preferring charges, and the Senate, which in trying an impeachment acted like a trial jury. The second standard of proof incorporated a normative conclusion: Given what a House member concluded the president did, was the president's action such as would justify removing him from office? This second standard would build into the House action some of the judgments that senators charged with the ultimate decision would have to make. Applying the second standard, a House member would ask, "Should a senator convinced to the degree that I am that the president committed the acts charged vote to convict and thereby remove the president from office?"

The grand jury analogy supported the grand jury standard, but in my judgment that standard was probably outside the range of reasonable interpretations because the stakes were so large—larger for the public than the stakes of a criminal prosecution are for an individual defendant as a general matter. One may criticize the House as an institution for failing to conduct a focused debate on the standard of proof even if the grand jury standard was a reasonable one. Of course each House member could decide independently what standard of proof should be required. But a process that allowed members to think clearly about the question was clearly desirable, and did not take place.

The issue of standard of proof was obscured because it was easy to frame the issue as dealing solely with the standard of proof *of facts*, rather than as one implicating a political judgment about the ultimate decision on whether the president should be removed from office. The House had a massive submission of facts from the independent counsel. It would have been ridiculous to plow the same ground again. Nor, on analysis, was a factual inquiry likely to alter the conclusions that a reasonable person could draw from the independent counsel's submission. The facts supporting the central charges could not reasonably be challenged. It was reasonable for those House members who thought that the standard of proof involved only the application of a standard to factual matters to conclude that the grand jury standard was satisfied—and, indeed, that many higher standards than probable cause were satisfied—given the factual record before the House. The problem, in other words, was not that the grand jury standard was the correct or incorrect one. Rather, the question was badly framed to the extent that it focused on facts alone and ignored the issue of the president's removal. Impeachment was designed to be a political process. It seems unreasonable to structure the impeachment process so as to make the House of Representatives, the body closest to the people, merely the processor of facts. The impeachment process should have clearly induced House members to exercise a political, not simply a factual, judgment about whether the president had committed acts that justified removing him from office.

Here I think Congress can be faulted for failing to frame the issue clearly. The independent counsel's factual presentation made it too easy for the House to focus on facts and (ordinary) law rather than political judgment. And of course politics played a role here, as in other aspects of the impeachment. Some House members found it politically desirable to obscure the question of removal. The interaction of politics and the independent counsel's factual submission led the House to act in a less than adequately responsible manner.

An Overall Assessment

Clinton's impeachment satisfies most of the criteria for evaluating congressional constitutional interpretation. There was no chance that judicial review would distort Congress's actions, and of course the impeachment and acquittal were completed actions. The episodes examined here involved matters about which the range of reasonable disagreement was small. Yet of course, "[g]reat cases, like hard cases, make bad law."[20] At the time the impeachment seemed like a great case, and Congress's performance under the heightened political tensions that it faced may have been worse than it would have been under more usual circumstances.[21] The perception that the impeachment was a great case may well have adversely affected the performance of members of Congress. Overall, though, Congress did not do badly during the impeachment. Isenbergh's proposal was correctly rejected. The Senate did not perform as well as it might have, to the extent that it failed to grapple with Ackerman's argument. And the House should have come to a clearer conclusion about the validity of using the grand jury standard as the basis for impeaching a president. Against the backdrop of the specific politics of the late 1990s and the emotions surrounding the impeachment, however, Congress's underperformance is understandable, and does not, in my view, seriously undermine the claim that Congress can do a decent job of constitutional interpretation. Recall in addition that *decency* is necessarily a comparative standard, and that according to academics, the Supreme Court routinely underperforms as well.

THE WAR POWERS PROBLEM

Why the War Powers Problem May Be a Good Case Study

Controversies over the Constitution's allocation between Congress and the president of the power to make war come close to satisfying the criteria for evaluating congressional constitutional interpretation. In addition, war powers controversies have been common enough that they are almost routine. While military commitments that put U.S. soldiers' lives at risk are clearly matters of great moment to members of Congress, I believe that such commitments are probably not perceived by members of Congress as the kinds of great cases that might make bad law.

One major qualification complicates the picture. There is clearly a wide range of reasonable interpretations of the Constitution's allocation of power in this area. Some scholars defend the view that Congress has the primary role in committing U.S. armed forces in relatively large-scale operations where they might meet armed resistance.[22] Others contend that the president has the primary power to initiate such operations, subject only to subsequent congressional control through the appropriations process.[23] It may be difficult to locate any completed congressional action inconsistent with some position within the reasonable range. A further complication is that according to one position, probably also a reasonable one, the Constitution does not specify an allocation of power between Congress and the president, but makes that allocation depend solely on the outcome of political interactions between the branches.

It is important, I believe, to distinguish this position from another position that finds, in the accumulated weight of practice, criteria for determining the proper allocation of power between Congress and the president.[24] The latter position holds that at any given time, the accumulated weight of practice determines the proper allocation of authority. It acknowledges that practice can change incrementally and sometimes convulsively as a result of deep deliberation, leading to the conclusion that different allocations may be constitutionally commanded at different times. The former position, by contrast, is that there is never a constitutionally mandated allocation of authority, except in the sense that the Constitution creates a framework within which president and Congress contend for power; not one determined by text, nor one determined by practice, but only by the outcome of political struggles over that allocation at particular moments in time. Not surprisingly, lawyers are uncomfortable with a position that finds nothing in the Constitution other than politics to determine so important a matter, and it is accordingly difficult to find lawyers or legal academics making strong statements of this position.

Perhaps we can avoid or work around the difficulty arising from the fact that the Constitution's implications for Congress's role in constitutional interpretation are reasonably contested in the war powers context. Sometimes critics charge Congress with irresponsibility in exercising whatever power it has. In the most general terms, the charge is that Congress fails to take *any* position on the allocation of authority between it and the president. By doing so, critics assert, Congress puts itself in a position to criticize the president if the military operation fails and to claim credit if it succeeds. We can evaluate the accuracy of this charge without taking a position on the difficult question of constitutional interpretation that I have described.

The Kosovo Episode

Congress's action in connection with the military operation in Kosovo in 1999 provides an opportunity to evaluate the charge of irresponsibility, and thereby to see how well Congress did as a constitutional interpreter. The military operation began on 24 March. On the previous day the Senate had adopted, by a vote of 58–41, a concurrent resolution authorizing the president "to conduct military air operations and missile strikes" against Yugoslavia. Almost a month later, the House rejected the concurrent resolution by a tie vote of 213–213. On the same day the House rejected a declaration of war against Yugoslavia by the overwhelming margin of 2 in favor, 427 against. It also rejected a concurrent resolution to direct the president to remove troops from Yugoslavia, by a vote of 139 in favor and 290 against. The House did adopt a bill prohibiting the use of ground forces in Yugoslavia, but the bill did not come up for a vote in the Senate. Finally, Congress approved an emergency supplemental appropriations bill to cover the costs of the Kosovo operation.

Congress's failure to take a clear position on the Kosovo operation might seem to exemplify irresponsibility. As Louis Fisher puts it, the House took "multiple and supposedly conflicting votes," and "the Senate decided to duck the issue."[25] And yet, the example is not as clear as one might hope. First, one must remember, as the title of a classic political science article puts it, "Congress is a 'They,' not an 'It.'"[26] That is, every single member of Congress might have a fully formed and defensible position on the allocation of war power between president and Congress, and even so the aggregation of those positions in a majority voting system might produce an outcome in which Congress as an institution took no clear position on that allocation. Such an outcome might seem to support the criticism of Congress as an interpreter: individually defensible action results in indefensible institutional inaction. The requirement that one must evaluate only completed actions makes it difficult to assess the actions of Congress: each completed action, in each house, might be constitutionally responsible, but the series of actions supports the charge of irresponsibility.

There is, though, a bit more to be said. Perhaps institutional inaction is not constitutionally irresponsible even if every member of Congress thinks that the Constitution requires Congress to do *something*. As noted above, one of the contending options about the allocation of the war power is that once military action has been undertaken without a declaration of war, Congress's only role comes when it exercises its power to appropriate funds. Congress, as an institution, played that role—and perhaps only that role—in connection with the Kosovo operation. To that extent, Congress did adopt a position within the range of reasonable options available on the question of allocating the war power. Second, and again as noted earlier, perhaps the Constitution says nothing about the allocation of war power between president and Congress, leaving the branches to work out their differences through the political process. If so, the notion of congressional irresponsibility is inapt: Congress will do what it does, and the president will respond, in part perhaps by charging Congress with irresponsibility. As the controversy proceeds, some accommodation will be worked out, or one or the other side will prevail entirely. And that, according to the "political process" option, is all that the Constitution requires.

Further, I am unsure about the cogency of the charge of irresponsibility. War powers decisions can be highly contested, and people can reasonably differ about the wisdom of any particular operation. What to one observer seems irresponsible might be characterized by another as an appropriate ambivalence about the proper course to pursue in a situation of ambiguity. Making war is serious business, and though a single executive might be decisive, perhaps the Constitution gives Congress the role, should Congress choose to play it, of expressing an appropriate ambivalence about making war.

Finally, precisely to the extent that the critical observer can charge Congress with irresponsibility, so can constituents. Recall that according to the charge, members of Congress may be trying to have their cake and eat it too, by taking positions that allow them to criticize an unsuccessful military operation and claim credit for a successful one. Irresponsibility, that is, is said to be politically beneficial. But constituents can notice a member of Congress's course of conduct just as readily as a critic can. Constituents can punish their representatives for the perceived irresponsibility of Congress as an institution, thereby eliminating the purported political benefits to individual members of irresponsibility. To the extent that Congress behaves irresponsibly, then, each member may lose the electoral benefits thought to flow from irresponsibility. That, in turn, increases the likelihood that Congress acts responsibly. One might think, for example, that the accretion of presidential power in war making results in part from this sort of dynamic, and that members of Congress with a political interest in sustaining their power will eventually try to recapture public respect by acting decisively. Here the recent example of members of Congress who insisted on a role in authorizing substantial military action against Iraq, and the president's accession to their insistence, seems to me to support the proposition that members of Congress do respond when constituents want them to take a position on matters so serious.

Perhaps, however, irresponsibility is structural. Political scientists have noted how many veto points there are in the legislative process. That is, for Congress to take what I have called a completed action, many individual members of Congress, acting on their own rather than through some version of majority rule, must refuse to exercise a power to halt the action's advance. Consider the meaning of a failure to exercise an effective veto by a member situated at a veto point and empowered by his or her constituents to act according to the member's sense of constitutional responsibility. When the action proceeds through the veto point, it receives real constitutional consideration and thereby gains some constitutional respectability. With many veto points and some members of Congress free to act on their sense of constitutional responsibility, completed actions may frequently be constitutionally responsible as well.

When members exercise their vetoes sequentially, though, a problem of irresponsibility may arise. The difficulty is that the completed *action* we are looking for turns out to be *inaction* as soon as a veto is exercised, even by a member who is personally acting in a constitutionally responsible manner. Were the Constitution to require action on some matter, inaction as an outcome would be irresponsible. Yet the occasions on which the Constitution uncontroversially requires action are rare indeed—although exercising the power to declare war may be one of them. And yet, of course, precisely *when* the Constitution requires a declaration of war as a predicate for military action is itself a matter of substantial constitutional controversy.

More problematically, the presence of many veto points at which individual members can act according to their own views of the Constitution may skew outcomes *against* action. As a general matter that may satisfy a person for whom the government is best that governs least, but not others. More particularly, in the context of separation of powers, coordination difficulties may lead systematically to outcomes that favor presidential over congressional power. I emphasize that as a matter of substantive constitutional interpretation, both the libertarian and presidentialist interpretations of the Constitution are entirely reasonable ones. The difficulty here is that the complexity of Congress—the existence of multiple veto points—may build a bias into the outcome, thereby producing constitutionally reasonable outcomes by a process that reduces the role of reasoned deliberation in generating outcomes.

I believe that the pattern exhibited by Congress's response to the military operation in Kosovo is typical: Charges of congressional irresponsibility or abdication are made, but on analysis they turn out to be less cogent than one's initial reaction to Congress's actions suggests. On the whole, we can understand what individual members of Congress did as clear commitments on contested constitutional questions, within the range of reasonable answers, and we can understand what Congress did in its institutional capacity as consistent with at least two (and perhaps more) reasonable interpretations of the Constitution's allocation of power between the president and Congress.

CONCLUSION: ACCOUNTING FOR CONGRESSIONAL CONSTITUTIONAL RESPONSIBILITY

The informal case studies I have presented suggest that Congress can be, and frequently has been, a responsible interpreter of the Constitution. I suspect that the sense of congressional irresponsibility prevalent among many commentators arises from a failure to examine cases selected on the basis of suitable criteria. Specifically, I believe, the judicial overhang in cases involving individual liberties may reduce the incentives that members of Congress have to act responsibly.

Just as courts operate under structures and with incentives particular to them, which commentators believe incline courts to provide reasonable constitutional interpretations, so too may Congress. Members of Congress usually want to be reelected. To do so they must satisfy their constituents' desires. Those desires have two components. There are the usual interests that we typically label "special interests": the desires of constituents who make a living as farmers regarding agriculture policy, the desires of constituents who are union members regarding labor policy, and the like. A member of Congress who satisfies enough constituent interests of this sort has some freedom to pursue other goals, including advancing the member's vision of the Constitution to the extent that that vision does not conflict with constituents' other interests. In addition, constituents themselves may have constitutional visions and, more important, may think it valuable for their representatives to be *independent* constitutional thinkers— independent, that is, of the constituents' special interests and constitutional visions. Taken together, these components of constituent interests make it possible for *some* members of Congress to vote their constitutional consciences without endangering their electoral prospects, and sometimes even enhancing those prospects.[27]

How then should we understand Congress as a constitutional interpreter? The problem of the judicial overhang and the possible structural bias in favor of presidential authority in the war powers context suggest that Congress will do best when it operates as what we might call a free-standing interpreter, not interacting with the courts or the president on matters important to the courts and the presidency as institutions. As I have mentioned, our traditions make the domain within which Congress can act in such a free-standing manner quite small. One might have thought that this domain would expand to include areas of substantive constitutional interpretation in which the courts do act, such as the First Amendment, because the courts need not have a strong institutional commitment to defending the decisions that they reach on matters not implicating their ability to operate. Some political scientists have identified departmentalist approaches to constitutional interpretation. One version of departmentalism accords to each branch final authority over the interpretation of provisions dealing with its own operation, but no special authority over anything else. That version of departmentalism might expand the domain in which Congress could act in a free-standing manner. Yet recent Supreme Court decisions emphasizing the Court's supremacy in interpreting substantive constitutional provisions like the free exercise clause and the Fifth Amendment suggest that in the Court's eyes, we do not now have a departmentalist system of this sort. And the lack of a strong public response to those decisions suggests that the Court may be right.

Congress will not always act in a constitutionally reasonable manner, no matter how wide the range of reasonableness is, nor how narrow the domain within which it operates as a constitutional interpreter. But then, neither will the courts. Taking everything into account, we have little reason to think that Congress will be systematically worse than the courts, at least when Congress acts free of the judicial overhang.

NOTES

A different version of this essay appears in 50 *Duke Law Journal* 1395 (2001).

1 Of course in the end one needs to evaluate congressional performance—and judicial performance—across the entire range of action. My informal case studies are designed to give some credibility to the claim that Congress does *generally* act in a constitutionally responsible manner, but they cannot establish that claim.

2 The behavior is related to what political scientists have called *position-taking* actions by members of Congress. See, e.g., David Mayhew, *Congress: The Electoral Connection* (New Haven: Yale University Press, 1974), 61.

3 I draw the term *anticipatory obedience* from Jutta Limbach, "The Role of the Federal Constitutional Court," 53 *Southern Methodist University Law Review* 429, 433 (2000).

4 See Mark Tushnet, *Taking the Constitution Away from the Courts* (Princeton: Princeton University Press, 1999), 58–60.

5 *Id.* at 57–58.

6 I believe that the Communications Decency Act, held unconstitutional in *Reno v. ACLU*, 521 U.S. 844 (1997), is an example of congressional grandstanding through enactment of a statute certain to be held unconstitutional.

7 424 U.S. 1 (1976).

8 Larry Alexander and Frederick Schauer have argued that such action is irresponsible because it undermines the finality of judgment that is necessary in any system of law. I have argued elsewhere that Alexander and Schauer overestimate the finality produced by insisting that the Court's decisions are indeed final, and underestimate the finality produced by a complex system of interacting institutions. See Tushnet, *Taking the Constitution Away from the Courts*, 27–30.

9 At this point I am making no observation about whether President Clinton's behavior actually was inconsistent with the standard defined by this second theory. My concern is only with the adoption of the theory as the basis upon which to evaluate his behavior.

10 The evaluator must therefore be careful to ensure that he or she not label as unreasonable a constitutional position with which he or she disagrees. So, for example, while I believe that impeachment's opponents had the better case on what the standard for impeachment is, I believe as well that impeachment's supporters offered a reasonable, albeit erroneous, standard.

11 Although of course there can be disagreement over the question, Is this a matter in which the Constitution gives Congress unfettered discretion? Here I am assuming that Congress does have such discretion in setting tax rates (within the limits of confiscation).

12 Herbert Wechsler, "The Political Safeguards of Federalism: The Role of the States in the Composition and Selection of the National Government," 54 *Columbia Law Review* 543 (1954).

13 Jesse H. Choper, *Judicial Review and the National Political Process: A Functional Reconsideration of the Role of the Supreme Court* (Chicago: University of Chicago Press, 1980).

14 See, e.g., INS v. Chadha, 462 U.S. 919 (1983) (rejecting Choper's theory); United States v. Lopez, 514 U.S. 549 (1995) (rejecting Wechsler's theory).

15 Quoted in Michael J. Gerhardt, *The Federal Impeachment Process: A Constitutional and Historical Analysis* (Princeton: Princeton University Press, 1996), 103.

16 506 U.S. 224 (1993).

17 The argument is set out in Joseph Isenbergh, "Impeachment and Presidential Immunity from Judicial Process," Occasional Papers from the University of Chicago Law School, no. 39 (31 December 1998), published in revised form as Joseph Isenbergh, "Impeachment and Presidential Immunity from Judicial Process," 18 *Yale Law and Policy Review* 53 (1999).

18 Bruce Ackerman, *The Case against Lameduck Impeachment* (New York: Seven Stories, 1999).

19 Perhaps some of the work was done informally, in discussions with staff members. According to the criterion that asks us to examine only completed actions, the public record matters more in evaluating Congress's performance, but to the extent that the concern is the seriousness with which members of Congress take constitutional questions, however they resolve them, examination of what happens outside the public record might be important.

20 Northern Securities Co. v. United States, 193 U.S. 197, 400 (1904) (Holmes, J., dissenting).

21 The election of 2000 shows that the heightened political tensions associated with the impeachment may not be as extraordinary as they seemed at the time.

22 See, e.g., John Hart Ely, *War and Responsibility: Constitutional Lessons of Vietnam and its Aftermath* (Princeton: Princeton University Press, 1993); Louis Fisher, *Congressional Abdication on War and Spending* (College Station: Texas A&M University Press, 2000).

23 See, e.g., John C. Yoo, "The Continuation of Politics by Other Means: The Original Understanding of War Powers," 84 *California Law Review* 167 (1996).

24 See, e.g., Peter J. Spiro, "War Powers and the Sirens of Formalism," 68 *New York University Law Review* 1338 (1993).

25 Fisher, *Congressional Abdication on War And Spending*, 102.

26 Kenneth A. Shepsle, "Congress Is a 'They,' Not an 'It': Legislative Intent

as Oxymoron," 12 *International Review of Law and Economics* 239 (1992). Shepsle's article deals with a different topic, but his title accurately describes the difficulty I discuss here.

27   This does not ensure that these members will advance constitutionally reasonable positions. My argument is only that under some conditions some members of Congress are in a position to think about constitutional matters independently of the "special interest" pressures asserted by their constituencies.

Can Congress Be Trusted

with the Constitution?

The Effects of Incentives

and Procedures

ᗯ

BARBARA SINCLAIR

"The worst argument to use with a member when you're trying to persuade him to vote against a proposal is that 'It's unconstitutional,'" explained a senior Democratic leader to a group of staffers as they were sitting around late one evening waiting for the House to finish its business. "Oh, thank God," the leader quoted the member's response as he pantomimed, vigorously fanning himself. "I can vote for this monstrosity and the Supreme Court will take care of it."

This story—a true one—reflects critics' worst suspicions about Congress and the Constitution; legal scholars especially fear that members of Congress pay little attention to questions of constitutionality and, worse, when faced with a popular but unconstitutional proposal, they pusillanimously pass the buck—to the other chamber, the president, or the Court. Others argue that Congress "often lacks the institutional incentives to take fact finding seriously;"[1] purported congressional fact finding, contaminated by the impact of special interests, may really be just a "recitation of special-interest preferences."[2] Public choice scholars go as far as to depict "Congress as a greater auction house, in which legislation is sold to those narrowly focused, rent-seeking interest groups that channel the most money into legislators' campaign coffers."[3]

In this chapter I examine members' incentives and the congressional process to determine their likely effect on congressional consideration of the

Constitution and adherence to it. My objective is to provide a congressional scholar's perspective on whether Congress can indeed be trusted with the Constitution.

Briefly summarized, my argument is that so long as members pursue good public policy and not solely reelection, they must, for purely instrumental reasons, take into account the constitutionality of the legislation they pass. Furthermore, to the extent that the congressional legislative process promotes fact finding and deliberation and thereby the making of good public policy, Congress has as good a claim as the Court to determine constitutionality in domains where its policy and political expertise are key. This is the more so since the legislative process and the broader governmental structure force compromise and encourage consensus building; the notion that the Court needs to keep an eagle eye on Congress to prevent it from regularly trampling minority interests is premised on a lack of understanding of how the legislative process actually works.

MEMBERS' GOALS AND THEIR IMPACT

If members of Congress are in fact "single-minded seekers of reelection," as some scholars argue, then they can be trusted with the Constitution only if constituents use conformity with the Constitution as a key criterion of electoral choice, certainly a heroic assumption.[4] Some voters probably do—law professors, for example—but that there are enough such voters to make the difference seems unlikely. If we buy the assumption that members care about nothing except reelection, then it follows that members will "trash" the Constitution without compunction if doing so is popular with their voting constituents; they will choose to do what's popular, even if it is clearly not constitutional.

Although there probably are members who care only about reelection, I contend that according to both theory and data most members are motivated by multiple goals. All scholars are familiar with David Mayhew's elegant little book *Congress: The Electoral Connection*, which makes the case that much of how Congress operates can be explained by the reelection motive; yet it is often overlooked that Mayhew himself could not make his model consistent with that assumption only. When Mayhew sought to explain how tasks essential for the maintenance of the institution got performed, he was forced to smuggle in another goal—prestige or power in the chamber.

Mayhew argues that as single-minded seekers of reelection, members do not care whether legislation is enacted; that they see legislative battles as only an opportunity for electorally productive position taking. Again this conclusion is not completely consistent with other elements of his model. If, in order to assure reelection, members "service the organized," then surely actually producing laws is important. Ordinary voters may not know if the member talks a good game but does nothing else, but interest groups do, and they want not just a good try but results. The end-of-the-session rush during which members often make increasingly significant compromises to get legislation enacted also suggests that members are not indifferent to the fate of legislation. And if members, for whatever reason, actually want to see legislation enacted, they should care about the constitutional status of the bills they pass. Furthermore, many policy battles—over foreign aid or over obscenity-related restrictions on grants from the National Endowment for the Arts, for example—are either totally inexplicable or require bizarre contortions to explain within the reelection-only model. After a public outcry over federal funding of photographs depicting sado-masochistic homosexual acts and artworks consisting of crucifixes submerged in urine, it is implausible to suggest that members who nevertheless voted for artistic freedom were motivated solely by reelection concerns.

Explaining the time-and-effort allocation of many members of Congress is even more difficult. Why would a white Democrat representing a predominantly white, GOP-leaning district in south central Michigan concentrate his legislative efforts on Africa policy, working strenuously over a number of years on passing sanctions against white-ruled South Africa and providing food relief for Ethiopia? How to explain a Republican from Nebraska focusing on foreign policy and advocating a moderate internationalist line? Why would one member make the promotion of gay rights a central part of his legislative agenda, or another make anti-abortion legislation his crusade? For some of these members, their choices about where to focus their legislative efforts have created no constituency problems. Others have had to explain and to compensate with effective constituency service. "Opponents have tried to convince voters that the congressman is so obsessed with abortion that he does not adequately represent other interests. But [he] has secured his position with diligent constituency work and careful attention to the interests of blue-collar workers and organized labor," Congressional Quarterly's *Politics in America* reports.[5] The same publication said of the Africa specialist, "The key to [his] survival is constituency service."[6] None of these members ignored locally important issues. And none chose issues that were, given his district, tantamount to committing political suicide. Yet is it plausible to argue that the time-and-effort allocation decisions of Howard Wolpe, Doug Bereuter, Barney Frank, and Christopher H. Smith can best be explained by the reelection motive?

To argue that many members of Congress do care about making good public policy (where, for each member, "good" is defined by his or her own ideology and other relevant views) is not to argue that members do not care about reelection. "You have to be reelected to be a statesman" is a well-known maxim on Capitol Hill. The key question, then, is how members balance their multiple and potentially conflicting goals. Individual political circumstances and perhaps individual proclivities influence that balance for any particular member, making a general answer impossible. What is possible—and a good deal more interesting and important—is examining the impact of the legislative process on the character of the trade-offs and on the likely result. Does the process make it easy or hard for members to pursue the making of good public policy? Does the process encourage or discourage the sorts of activities and decisions that are likely to result in good public policy? And to what extent does the process promote the Madisonian constitutional values of compromise and consensus building?[7]

I emphasize here the making of good public policy, not concerns about constitutionality directly, because that is, I believe, the key issue. As I argued above, if members sincerely want to make policy and not just create an election issue, they must take constitutionality into account. To be sure, constitutionality is only one criterion for members of Congress; members must concern themselves with whether the legislation can pass their own and the other chamber; whether the president will accept it; whether, if enacted, it is likely to accomplish its aim. Given the multitude of criteria that members must attempt to satisfy, they may well sometimes, as Justice Scalia complained, "push the constitutional envelope."[8] Often when that is so, Congress is attempting to come up with a politically and substantively sensible policy solution to a complex problem, as, for example, with the legislative veto. And Congress, as an elected and representative body, is in a much better position to judge what makes political and substantive sense than the Court is.

Thus if members attempt to make good public policy and if the congressional process encourages the sorts of activities and decisions that are likely to result in good public policy, Congress deserves deference from the Court. If there are constitutional traps around every corner, it is the current Court and not the Constitution that has laid them.

THE LEGISLATIVE PROCESS AND ITS IMPACT

To promote the making of good public policy, the legislative process should encourage fact finding and deliberation. Presumably it should also encourage members to "do what's right, not just what's popular."

There is broad consensus on fact finding and deliberation as desirable criteria for the lawmaking process; most of us would agree that public policy is more likely to be effective at achieving its aim, whatever that may be, if it is based on careful fact finding and serious deliberation than if it is slapped together hastily and without much thought.[9] Encouraging members "to do what's right, not what's popular" when thus phrased would also seem to be an unexceptionable criterion. Yet do we really want Congress to regularly thwart popular majorities? Furthermore and critically, uncertainty about the link between a specific policy choice and the societal outcome means that in most major policy areas, legitimate differences of opinion as to what constitutes good public policy can and do exist. Too often those who tell members to "do what's right, not what's popular" are essentially saying "do what I want, not what your constituents want." Nevertheless, members are sometimes faced with choosing between doing what they themselves strongly believe is right and what their constituents want them to do. Given members' powerful incentives to do what their constituents want and that members will usually have a great deal more information about the issue than their constituents do, a process that allows them to do what they think is right without paying too great a political cost might be justified.

According to these criteria, how does the legislative process in Congress measure up?

Most educated people are familiar with the hoary "bill becomes a law" story of American government textbooks. Once introduced in one chamber of Congress, a bill is sent to a committee (or subcommittee) where most of the serious legislative work takes place. Assuming it is major legislation, hearings are held at which a wide range of interested parties and disinterested experts testify. The members of the committee or subcommittee then meet to mark up the bill—that is, to amend and rewrite it—

and to report it out. Assuming that the first chamber is the House, the bill comes to the House floor as drafted and approved by the committee. It is considered there under an open rule allowing all germane amendments. If passed the bill goes to the Senate, where the process is similar: the bill is considered by a committee and, once reported out, is debated and amended on the floor. After each chamber has passed a bill, a small group of senior members of the two committees get together as a conference committee and work out a compromise between the House and Senate versions. The compromise must be approved by the membership of both chambers.

Scholars who pay attention to Congress know that in recent decades the legislative process has changed significantly.[10] Rather than being sent to one committee in each chamber, many measures are considered by several committees, especially in the House, while some measures bypass committee altogether. Not infrequently, after a bill has been reported but before it reaches the floor, major substantive changes are worked out informally. Omnibus measures of great scope are a regular part of the legislative scene, and formal summits between the executive and legislative branches to work out deals on legislation are no longer considered extraordinary. On the House floor most major measures are considered under complex and usually restrictive rules, often tailored to deal with problems specific to that bill. In the Senate bills are regularly subject to large numbers of not-necessarily-germane floor amendments; filibuster threats are an everyday fact of life, affecting all aspects of the legislative process and making cloture votes a routine part of the process.

Congress's claim to competence at fact finding and deliberation is generally thought to rest on its standing committee system. The issues and problems with which the federal government deals are too numerous, diverse, and complex for any one person to master. For a relatively small body such as Congress to hold its own vis-à-vis the executive branch and outside interests, it must divide labor and rely on its members' expertise in their areas of specialization. Some scholars, Devins for example, question the adequacy and consistency of members' incentives to engage in real fact finding, and argue that agenda setters such as committee chairs may well have both the incentive and the means to bias the process so that it "frustrate[s] the search for the truth."[11] Of course hearings are not a search for knowledge for its own sake, nor do members come to policy questions without preconceptions; yet that hardly makes the committee process as useless as Devins seems to think. First, thoroughly biasing committee processes by, for example, slating only witnesses expressing one point of view is not so easy when the membership of the committee holds diverse views, as most though not all do. A complex mix of criteria operates in the committee assignment process, including members' preferences and, especially for the more important and desirable committees, party loyalty and geographical representativeness. Committee chairs cannot pick their own members—even those on the majority side. And of course, every committee includes members of the minority party, in numbers usually roughly in proportion to its presence in the chamber. Furthermore, grossly stacked hearings do not command respect later in the legislative process and seldom result in legislation that gets very far. Finally, congressional fact finding and deliberation neither are nor should be only about "objective" facts or "scientific" truths; political facts are highly relevant. Whether a proposed policy approach will "work" often depends as much on the political support of various groups and interests as on its technical feasibility.

Have the changes in the legislative process in the post-reform period reduced Congress's competence at fact finding and deliberation? Have procedures and practices such as multiple referral, post-committee adjustments, and the bypassing of committees eroded Congress's ability or incentive to engage in these crucial prerequisites to sound lawmaking? Multiple referral, whatever its other effects, especially delay, should enhance rather than impair fact finding and deliberation. By bringing several committees and a diversity of members into the bill-drafting process, multiple referral can increase the breadth of perspectives brought to the process and dilute the influence of special interests. As for post-committee adjustments, when committee-drafted legislation is altered after being reported by the committee but before it goes to the floor, the aim is usually to enhance its chances of floor passage. Most frequently, the majority leadership determines that the bill produced by the committee is in danger of failing on the floor. The committee may be unrepresentative in its membership and not sufficiently sensitive to sentiment in the chamber as a whole, or the political context may have changed, or, if several committees are involved, they may not have been able to work out their differences. The process of making such post-committee adjustments usually involves committee leaders from the majority party, who have a big stake in seeing the legislation pass and who bring substantive expertise to the task. When interested members who do not serve on the drafting committee are involved they diversify the perspectives brought to bear. Party leaders bring a broader, less parochial, and longer-range perspective to the endeavor; they have to concern themselves with the impact on their membership as a whole and on the party's reputation.

Some argue that the involvement of party leadership hardens party lines and enforces an ideological purity that hinders productive compromise. True, party leaders have been known to replace a bipartisan committee bill with legislation that the party majority and the president consider more acceptable, as Speaker Hastert did with the Judiciary Committee's PATRIOT bill in 2001. Yet the involvement of leadership can have the opposite effect. Because leaders do need to concern themselves with the party's reputation and because that reputation rests in part on legislative results, leaders may be forces for moderation and compromise. For example, when the chairman of the House Ways and Means Committee, Bill Archer, drafted an ideologically pure tax bill with huge benefits for big business, the equally conservative members of the House Republican leadership pressured him into moderating the bill so that they could defend it publicly. When they were in the majority, Democratic leaders regularly leaned on especially liberal committees such as Education and Labor to tone down their legislation to make it passable in the chamber and defendable in the public arena.

It is when committees are bypassed altogether that it is most likely for fact finding to be lacking and deliberation truncated. Yet in many cases when a committee seems to have been bypassed, the legislation was in fact reported by the committee in a previous Congress. For example, the Civil Rights Restoration Act, which became law after bypassing committee in the House, had gone through the full committee process in the previous congress. The same is true of the Congressional Compliance Act that the House passed on the first day of the 104th Congress (1995–96). In those instances when Democratic House leaders used task forces rather than committees to draft legislation, they chose as the leaders of the task forces members who had great substantive as well as political expertise, and since the 104th Congress Republicans have generally followed suit.[12] Thus even when committees are bypassed, committee experts are not necessarily cut out of the process and others involved do not necessarily lack substantive expertise. Furthermore, the involvement of party leaders may again broaden the perspective and lessen the parochialism of the process. For example, when in 2002 the Senate majority leader, Tom Daschle, took the energy bill away from the Energy and Natural Resources Committee, he removed it from a body made up almost completely of western and southern senators (twenty of twenty-three members), many with a strong bias toward the interests of users.

I am not arguing that post-committee adjustments and the bypassing of committees are unproblematic; the process that results is not always one that meets minimally acceptable standards of fact finding and deliberation. The 104th Congress presents the most egregious example. Especially during 1995, House Republican leaders put extraordinary pressure on committees to report legislation quickly. Hearings, if they were held at all, were perfunctory; markups, often held before most members had had an opportunity to study the legislative language at issue, were so hurried that they were in effect pro forma. Party leaders, and task forces on which inexperienced freshmen predominated, exercised considerable influence on the substance of legislation in committee and through post-committee adjustments, and committees were frequently bypassed both to move legislation more quickly and for substantive reasons. Deliberation and the quality of legislation did suffer. Many Republicans, members and staff alike, concede privately that the legislation brought to the floor was sloppy at best; the careful substantive work had not been done.

Furthermore, substantive sloppiness was not the only problem. When committees do not hold meaningful hearings, as was common during the "Contract with America" period in early 1995, an important forum for expressing a diversity of views is unavailable. To an unprecedented extent in the mid-1990s, the minority party was excluded from decision making at the pre-floor stage; committee procedures made meaningful participation impossible, and often the real decisions were made elsewhere, within Republican-only task forces or by the Republican leadership itself. Interest groups that the Republican Party considered hostile—environmental groups, for example—were not given access to make their case, while the party's business allies participated in drafting legislation in which they had a direct interest.

With the benefit of hindsight, we can now conclude that those modes of decision making arose out of highly unusual circumstances—a new House majority and the attendant sense of mandate—and were a temporary response to them.[13] Understandably, the first Republican House majority in forty years had a lot that it wanted to accomplish; these extraordinary circumstances led to a truncated process. Furthermore, Republicans paid a price for their exclusionary procedures. Because neither the committees nor the leadership did the hard and often ideologically painful work of building a coalition broad enough to survive the entire process, much of the legislation passed by the House did not become law; excluded interests blocked it elsewhere.

So long as the parties remain as ideologically polarized—and as closely balanced in seats—as they have been since the mid-1990s, House decision making is likely to be characterized by somewhat greater involvement of the leadership than in the pre-1995 period and much greater involvement than in the pre-reform period. The difficulties of legislating under these circumstances force the majority party leadership to involve itself in all phases of the legislative process. Even a leader such as the current speaker, Dennis Hastert, who on his election committed himself to a return to regular order, has found himself drawn into what would otherwise be committee business over and over again. Nevertheless committees have regained influence, and in the foreseeable future they are unlikely to be again relegated to the subordinate role that they played in the House in 1995.

Because the parties are polarized, committee decision making is often along party lines, especially in the House, and in the House the compromises on much of the major legislation are made within the majority party. Yet even when partisan polarization is unusually high by American standards, as it is at present, Senate committees seldom operate in a similar fashion. Senate committee leaders know that to pass their legislation on the floor, they require the support of a supermajority and, given the narrow margins, that means a bipartisan majority.[14]

If changes in the process decreased the incentives for members to specialize and gain expertise, they would be detrimental to Congress's power in the system and to its capacity to make good public policy. Expertise is essential for the making of good public policy; representatives of special interests with expertise can too easily bamboozle a legislature that has none. Too much of a diminution in the influence of committees would decrease members' incentives to develop expertise. In fact, while committees are not autonomous as they were before the reforms of the 1970s, they are still the primary locus of substantive decision making, and even when decisions are made elsewhere committee experts are usually involved. Thus the incentives for members of the House to develop committee expertise, although weaker than in the committee government days before the mid-1970s, are still strong. Becoming a committee specialist is not the only route to influence, but it remains a major one. Senators do specialize less than they used to, but notable specialists still exist. The effective senator must develop some expertise; a senator must know what he or she is talking about to be taken seriously. To some extent, senators can substitute staff expertise for personal expertise, and in both chambers the increase in staff has made it possible for members to involve themselves effectively in more issues than was once possible.

The upgrading of the Congressional Research Service and the Government Accounting Office and the establishment of the Congressional Budget Office greatly enhanced the Congress's in-house expertise; because these entities provide information generated independently of the executive and interest groups, they aid Congress in playing an independent role in policy making to the extent that members want to do so. Furthermore, they are accessible to the members of the minority as well as the majority party and so, like the substantial minority committee staffs, provide the minority party in both chambers with the information they need to make their case to the public. In a period of high partisan polarization, this is especially important to the minority party in the House, where majoritarian rules make it possible for the majority party to limit the role of the minority.

Both Republican and Democratic minorities have claimed that the especially tailored and usually restrictive special rules under which the House now considers most major legislation degrade floor deliberation, and a good many commentators have bought that argument. This contention is, I argue, based on a false premise; it is unrealistic to expect deliberation, as a great many people use the term, to take place on the floor of either chamber, and certainly not in the House. If deliberation is defined as the process by which a group of people get together and talk through a complex problem, mapping the problem's contours, defining the alternatives, and figuring out where they stand, it is unrealistic to expect all of that to occur on the chamber floors. Deliberation in this sense is a nonlinear, free-form process that depends on strictly limiting the size of the group; subcommittees, other small groups, and possibly committees are the forums where this sort of deliberation might be fostered. Deliberation so defined certainly did not occur on the House floor before restrictive rules became prevalent.

What we can and should expect on the chamber floors is informed and informative debate and sound decision making. Restrictive rules can in fact contribute toward those goals. Rules can provide order and predictability to the consideration on the floor of complex and controversial legislation; they can be used to ensure that floor time is apportioned in a reasonable and sensible way for each bill, and that debate focuses on the major alternatives, not on minor or side issues. In addition, through the use of restrictive rules, committee compromises can be protected from being picked apart on the floor.[15]

One's conclusions about the appropriate form of special rules depend on what sorts of decisions one believes can and cannot be made effectively on the House floor. The membership as a whole can and should make the big decisions; it can and should choose among the major alternatives that have been proposed. A body of 435 should not, I believe, get involved in a detailed rewriting of legislation on the floor through a multitude of individual amendments; the institution is too large and unwieldy, the necessary expertise is often lacking, and the time is almost always too short for a full consideration of the impact of proposed changes. One could very well argue that the Senate's permissive amendment rules are a greater problem than restrictive rules in the House. Senators can offer a large number of amendments on the floor, amendments that have not necessarily undergone any sort of serious scrutiny, and those amendments need not even be germane to the bill at issue.

Restrictive rules, in and of themselves, have not damaged the quality of consideration on the House floor. Admittedly, both Democrats and Republicans, when in the majority, have sometimes used rules that were unnecessarily restrictive. Nevertheless, despite the rhetoric implying otherwise, the House seldom considers legislation under closed rules barring all amendments. Most rules, by ensuring that one or more major substitutes are in order, do allow the membership as a whole to make at least the biggest decisions.

While House floor consideration has become more predictable and more firmly under the control of the majority party leadership, the Senate has moved in the opposite direction. The greatly increased frequency of "holds" and other filibuster threats has reduced predictability and the control of party leadership, neither of which was high even before these changes in practice.[16] "Holds," which are notifications by senators to their party leaders that they will object to the consideration of a particular bill, are an everyday fact of life in the Senate, so much so that the notification process has been routinized. Since Senate rules require sixty votes to cut off debate over any senator's objections, the party leaders who do the floor scheduling and do not want to expend floor time unproductively will usually not schedule low-priority legislation until "holds" have been removed. Must-pass and other high-priority legislation will be brought to the floor, but assuming that the opposition is reasonably intense, passing that legislation will first require winning a cloture vote.

In the contemporary Senate, passing legislation is therefore harder and blocking action easier than it used to be; minorities command enormous bargaining leverage, especially when time is tight, and intensity counts for more in the legislative process. If one puts a high premium on the responsiveness of the national legislature to public sentiments, the Senate's nonmajoritarian character can certainly be deplored. It can also, however, serve as a barrier to and a safeguard against "bad" legislation; certainly much of the "Contract with America" legislation so hastily passed in the House died in the Senate, often because it could not amass the necessary sixty votes.

Informed decision making on the floor requires that members not directly involved in the crafting of legislation nevertheless have available sufficient information to make a considered choice. When Congress legislates through large omnibus measures, the likelihood that members will not know about or understand all the measures' provisions increases. Such measures offer their drafters the opportunity to insert provisions that may well slip unnoticed by most members and all of the press. Omnibus measures are thus the perfect vehicle for special-interest provisions that no member would be willing to defend publicly. When high-level summits between party leaders and the president make legislative decisions, members are also likely to face information problems. This is not a problem unique to such unorthodox processes of lawmaking; it also occurs with much other complex legislation. In all these cases the problem can be ameliorated—but not solved—by strictly adhering to layover rules requiring that language be available for a minimum time before a vote can be taken.

The problems that such legislative processes create and the possibilities for abuse that they present must be weighted against the advantages they offer. They may allow peak-level deals, including hard tradeoffs which are not attainable in other ways. The big budget deals of the 1990s that eventually balanced the budget were mostly reached at executive-legislative summits, and all were passed as omnibus measures. Omnibus bills can be used for nefarious purposes, but they can also provide the cover and the "grease" necessary for the Congress to make hard decisions. The involvement of party leaders is probably the best protection—though certainly no guarantee—that the side payments necessary to get the bill through are not excessive. Leaders have to worry about the impact of possible disclosure on the party's reputation.

Legislative leaders have always used the tools at their command to make it easier for their members to "do what's right, not just what's popular." With the increase in leadership resources in the post-reform period, leaders' capacity to do so has increased considerably. The packaging of unpopular measures with popular ones in omnibus bills can make it politically possible for members to vote for legislation that they believe necessary but hard to explain to their constituents. In the House, leaders can craft rules so as to make tough votes easier to cast—by, for example, packaging, excluding certain alternatives, crafting and offering amendments that provide political cover, and reducing the visibility of decisions by transforming substantive votes into procedural ones.[17] Of course, long-established components of the legislative process can serve the same purposes. Thus rules that require an up-or-down vote on conference reports also provide members with cover; they can argue that they had to take the bitter with the sweet or get no bill at all.

In the last few years, the majority Republicans have increasingly responded to the problems that the Senate's supermajority requirement creates for them by using conferences to recoup losses that they have suffered in the Senate. During the latter years of Democratic control of Congress, when the party had become more ideologically homogeneous, the actual compromises between House and Senate, just as those within the chambers, were most often made within the Democratic Party. Recently, Republicans with much narrower margins of control have taken to excluding most Democrats from conference negotiations altogether. In 2003 no Democrats were allowed to participate in the energy bill conference, and only two, who were considered accommodating, were admitted to the negotiations on the Medicare prescription drugs bill; Republican leaders took a highly active role in working out a final deal on the prescription drugs bill, with Speaker Hastert and the Senate majority leader, Bill Frist, conducting the final negotiations personally; and the conference reports on both the energy bill and the prescription drugs bill tilted strongly toward the more conservative House versions. Republicans gambled that Senate moderates in both parties would be loath to vote against bills on such important issues even if the specifics of the bills were considerably further to the right than they preferred. On the prescription drugs legislation the wager paid off, and the bill passed the Senate easily. The energy bill, by contrast, was blocked by a filibuster. A priority-legislation success rate of 50 percent when one party controls both chambers and the presidency suggests that exclusion of the minority party does not pay off. The lukewarm public reception that the prescription drugs legislation has received since being enacted suggests that the strategy also brings with it major political risks in the long run, even if successful in the short run.

CAN CONGRESS BE TRUSTED WITH THE CONSTITUTION?

In sum, the legislative process in Congress does encourage fact finding and deliberation. And it does so not just in the narrow sense of fact finding (gathering technical information) and deliberation (seriously thinking about that information), but even more in the broad sense of including a wide range of views and interests. The process can even encourage "doing the right thing." And the changes in the process in the post-reform era have on balance increased the inclusiveness of the process without much diminishing the extent to which it encourages the development of expertise.

The basic character of the process—two-chambered and within each chamber sequential—makes it likely that a variety of perspectives and interests will be brought to bear and a variety of arguments heard. It is true that this character can also encourage buck passing; faced with a choice between what the member considers right and what he or she knows is popular, the member may choose the latter, relying on others at some later stage in the process to rectify the outcome. Yet given the diversity of the membership of Congress, some members are almost always willing to swim against the tide. The constituencies that they represent usually allow some members to speak out against decisions that the member thinks are popular but wrong. Certainly the legislative process internal to Congress as well as the broader governmental structure make the enactment of bold policy departures extremely difficult; compromise and consensus building are usually required for positive action even of a more modest sort. With a multitude of stages and diversity of actors, the American legislative process is not one in which narrow majoritarianism is often a problem.

The standing committee system encourages members to specialize and gain expertise, and to put that expertise to use in the legislative process. Public committee hearings may not be a dispassionate search for truth, but they are often an important part of making the case and building the coalition for a particular policy approach. Making a convincing case requires allowing opposition views to be heard. And making the case and building the coalition often require high levels of both substantive and political expertise. The powerful committee chairmen of the last several decades—the John Dingells, Bud Shusters, and Bobby Byrds—were powerful because they commanded both. It is important to remember, however, that not all fact finding goes on in committee or through a formal process at all. In the course of doing their jobs—meeting with lobbyists, traveling around their districts, communicating with their constituents face-to-face and by mail and phone, and yes, going on junkets—members are engaged in fact finding. In addition, the experiences that members bring to the Congress— whether those of a corporate lawyer, farmer, or welfare mother—inform their decision making. This is, of course, why a more inclusive process as well as a more diverse membership makes for better policy making.

On balance, the changes in the legislative process in the post-reform period have increased the inclusiveness of the process. More members have the opportunity to participate on a wider range of issues and the process is more open to a diversity of outside groups. In addition to innovations such as multiple referral and the use of task forces, sometimes to draft legislation and more often to engineer its passage, sunshine rules and the increased availability of staff have enhanced effective participation. In comparison to the contemporary legislative process, the pre-reform legislative process could often be quite exclusionary. One committee had a monopoly on legislative action in a given area and was not necessarily responsive to the wishes of the chamber or of the majority party. Decisions were made behind closed doors. And the membership of many committees was biased in a way that favored some interests and excluded others. Diffuse interests—consumer and environmental interests in particular, which are seldom represented by wealthy and well-connected organizations— had little access. Furthermore, the contemporary legislative process, while more open and inclusive, also provides congressional leaders with tools that they can use to make it easier for their members to do "what's right, not what's popular," at least some of the time. Thus special rules in the House and various forms of packaging, sometimes under the auspices of the Budget Act, can provide "cover" to members faced with tough legislative choices.

Do the changes in the legislative process guarantee thorough fact finding, serious deliberation, and members' putting their sense of the national interest above their own political survival in every instance? Of course not. Like the old standard process, the contemporary process can work very well or very badly; sometimes we can agree on which is which and sometimes that judgment is inextricably intertwined with our substantive, ideological views. When Congress oversteps constitutional boundaries in the area of individual rights, where the temptation may be greatest and the justification least, there is clearly a role for the Court. My point is that members do care about making policy—they are not simply engaged in posturing—and the process does allow for fact finding, deliberation, and even "doing what's right, not what's popular." Therefore the Court owes Congress deference, particularly on issues where the political and policy expertise that Congress possesses and the Court lacks is key. The issues raised in the division of powers and federalism cases are of exactly that sort.

Scholars concerned with how Congress considers and adheres to the Constitution have proposed a number of reforms. Approaching the issue from a congressional scholar's perspective, I contend that remedies should take into account that Congress confronts real constitutional quandaries relatively rarely; they are not an everyday problem. Reforms that foster better fact finding and deliberation even if they have no impact on how Congress treats the Constitution should produce better policy and thus are worthwhile—so long as the costs are not too high. In institutional design there are always tradeoffs, and because of the multiple and not completely compatible objectives that we expect a democratic legislature to further, the tradeoffs are especially problematic. In the American context, the constitutional structure, the institutional rules and procedures, and often the political context make successful lawmaking difficult. New rules or procedures that would make it still harder to enact legislation should be regarded cautiously. If we agree that we want to focus on relatively egregious violations of the Constitution, then we do not need an instrument so sensitive that it can identify any whiff of a possible constitutional problem. And that greatly alleviates some of the tradeoff difficulties.

Take, for example, the special processes that Elizabeth Garrett and Adrian Vermeule propose in their careful and thoughtful chapter.[18] Proposals that in effect enhance the working of a "fire alarm" sort of scrutiny are worth serious consideration. Thus giving the parliamentarian the authority to flag possible constitutional problems when he refers legislation to committee would alert both members and interested outsiders cheaply. Perhaps more important, it would impose some cost on those members who introduce such bills. That the parliamentarians are already quite overburdened and could not devote great amounts of time to the enterprise is, on balance, an advantage and not a disadvantage if what we want them to do is flag egregious cases. Perhaps these cases would be more difficult to justify if committees were required to produce constitutional impact statements to accompany every reported bill, a requirement which might encourage the committee to give a bit more attention to constitutional questions. And the statements would of course lower information costs for committee outsiders. Still, the proposal needs to be thought through carefully, so that the required statements do not become mere boilerplate or, on the other hand, a significant burden on the committee staff.

The proposal to create a special professional staff—an Office of Constitutional Issues—to provide expert constitutional analysis of legislation is, in my view, enormously problematic. Simply by virtue of its charge, such a staff would acquire a vested interest in finding constitutional problems, and highly technical and complex ones at that. Giving to the Judiciary Committee or a new committee jurisdiction to review legislation for constitutional flaws would create the same problem and also add another step in a legislative process that has plenty of steps already. I also have doubts about adding points of order; these could too easily be used for purposes of delay, no matter what sorts of purported safeguards were attempted. And under no circumstances should supermajorities be required to waive such points of order.

I began by asking whether Congress could be trusted with the Constitution. My answer is that Congress can be trusted as much as the Supreme Court can. Members are not single-minded seekers of reelection, and the legislative process does not thwart attempts by members to make good public policy; in fact it provides some encouragement and some tools for doing so. Of course incentives to pander and pass the buck also exist. After all, we expect Congress to be responsive to public sentiments; we do not want it to be too easy for Congress to make unpopular decisions! Congress does not always make good public policy, no matter how one might define that, but then the Court does not always make good decisions either. Whatever one's assessment of the legislative process, it is hard to argue that the problem is a thin but rampaging majority regularly disregarding all interests other than its own and forcing major policy change on a large and intense minority.

NOTES

1 Neal Devins, "Congressional Fact Finding and the Scope of Judicial Review," 220, in this volume.

2 *Id.* at 221.

3　This is Yoo's characterization of the public choice scholar's depiction. Quoted from John C. Yoo, "Lawyers in Congress," 132, in this volume.

4　The phrase is of course Mayhew's. David Mayhew, *Congress: The Electoral Connection* (New Haven: Yale University Press, 1974).

5　Brian Nutting and Amy Stern, eds., *Politics in America 2002: The 107th Congress* (Washington: CQ Press, 2001), 635.

6　Alan Ehrenhalt, ed., *Politics in America: The 100th Congress* (Washington: CQ Press, 1987), 727.

7　Keith E. Whittington, "Constitutional Theory and the Faces of Power," *Alexander Bickel and Contemporary Constitutional Theory*, ed. Kenneth Ward (Albany: SUNY Press, forthcoming).

8　Quoted in *Los Angeles Times*, 19 April 2000.

9　See Devins, "Congressional Fact Finding"; see also Elizabeth Garrett and Adrian Vermeule, "Institutional Design of a Thayerian Congress," 242, in this volume.

10　For an elaboration of this argument see Barbara Sinclair, *Unorthodox Lawmaking*, 2d ed. (Washington: CQ Press, 2000).

11　Devins, "Congressional Fact Finding," 224.

12　Barbara Sinclair, *Legislators, Leaders, and Lawmaking: The U.S. House of Representatives in the Postreform Era* (Baltimore: Johns Hopkins University Press, 1995), 188–92.

13　Barbara Sinclair, "Transformational Leader or Faithful Agent? Principal Agent Theory and House Majority Party Leadership in the 104th and 105th Congresses," 24 *Legislative Studies Quarterly* 421 (August 1999).

14　The budget process is the big exception; budget resolutions and reconciliation bills are protected from filibusters in the Senate, and this does affect the Senate process on those measures.

15　Sinclair, *Legislators, Leaders, and Lawmaking*, 136–62.

16　See Barbara Sinclair, "The New World of U.S. Senators," *Congress Reconsidered*, 7th ed., ed. Lawrence C. Dodd and Bruce I. Oppenheimer (Washington: CQ Press, 2001).

17　R. Douglas Arnold, *The Logic of Congressional Action* (New Haven: Yale University Press, 1990); Barbara Sinclair, "Do Parties Matter?," *Party, Process, and Political Change in Congress*, ed. David Brady and Mathew McCubbins (Stanford: Stanford University Press, 2002).

18　Garrett and Vermeule, "Institutional Design of a Thayerian Congress."

About the Contributors

∽

DAVID P. CURRIE is the Edward H. Levi Distinguished Service Professor and Arnold and Frieda Shure Scholar at the University of Chicago Law School. He is the author, most recently, of *The Constitution in Congress: The Federalist Period, 1789–1801* and *The Constitution in Congress: The Jeffersonians, 1801–1829*.

NEAL DEVINS is the Goodrich Professor of Law and a professor of government at the College of William & Mary. He is the author of *Shaping Constitutional Values* and a coauthor of *Political Dynamics of Constitutional Law*, among other works.

WILLIAM N. ESKRIDGE JR. is the John A. Garver Professor of Jurisprudence at Yale Law School. He is the author of *Dynamic Statutory Interpretation* and a coauthor of *Legislation*, among other works.

JOHN FEREJOHN is the Carolyn S. G. Munro Professor of Political Science at Stanford University, where he is also a senior fellow of the Hoover Institution, and a visiting professor at the New York University Law School. He is a coeditor of *Constitutional Culture and Democratic Rule*, among other works.

LOUIS FISHER is a senior specialist in separation of powers at the Congressional Research Service of the Library of Congress. He is the author of *Constitutional Conflicts between Congress and the President* and a coauthor of *Political Dynamics of Constitutional Law*, among other works.

ELIZABETH GARRETT is a professor of law at the University of Southern California and Director of the USC-Caltech Center for the Study of Law and Politics. She is a coauthor of *Legislation and Statutory Interpretation*, among other works.

MICHAEL J. GERHARDT is the Arthur B. Hanson Professor of Law at the College of William & Mary. He is the author of *The Federal Appointments Process*, among other works.

MICHAEL J. KLARMAN is the James Monroe Professor of Law and Professor of History at the University of Virginia. He is the author of *From Jim Crow to Civil Rights* and numerous articles on constitutional law and history.

BRUCE G. PEABODY is an assistant professor of political science at Fairleigh Dickinson University. He has written widely on American constitutional law and politics.

J. MITCHELL PICKERILL is an assistant professor of political science at Washington State University. He is the author of *Constitutional Deliberation in Congress* and a number of articles on American politics and law.

BARBARA SINCLAIR is the Marvin Hoffenberg Professor of American Politics at the University of California, Los Angeles. She is the author of *Legislators, Leaders, and Lawmaking*, among other works.

MARK TUSHNET is the Carmack Waterhouse Professor of Constitutional Law at the Georgetown University Law Center. He is the author, among other works, of *The New Constitutional Order*.

ADRIAN VERMEULE is a professor of law at the University of Chicago. He is the author of numerous articles on constitutional and administrative law.

KEITH E. WHITTINGTON is an associate professor of politics at Princeton University. He is the author of *Constitutional Construction*, among other works.

JOHN C. YOO is a professor of law at the University of California, Berkeley. He is the author of numerous articles on constitutional and international law.

Index

∽

LIBRARY OF CONGRESS CATALOGING-IN-PUBLICATION DATA

Congress and the Constitution / Neal Devins and
Keith Whittington, eds.
p. cm. — (Constitutional conflicts)
Includes bibliographical references and index.
ISBN 0-8223-3586-7 (cloth : alk. paper)
ISBN 0-8223-3612-X (pbk. : alk. paper)
1. Constitutional law—United States 2. Law—United States—
Interpretation and construction. 3. United States. Congress—Powers and
duties. 4. United States. Constitution. I. Devins, Neal. II. Whittington,
Keith E. III. Title. IV. Series.
KF4550.C568 2005
342.7302—dc22   2005006505